Calvin, the Bible, and History

Calvin, the Bible, and History

Exegesis and Historical Reflection in the Era of Reform

BARBARA PITKIN

OXFORD
UNIVERSITY PRESS

OXFORD
UNIVERSITY PRESS

Oxford University Press is a department of the University of Oxford. It furthers
the University's objective of excellence in research, scholarship, and education
by publishing worldwide. Oxford is a registered trade mark of Oxford University
Press in the UK and certain other countries.

Published in the United States of America by Oxford University Press
198 Madison Avenue, New York, NY 10016, United States of America.

Library of Congress Control Number: 2019053142
ISBN 978–0–19–009327–3

1 3 5 7 9 8 6 4 2

Printed by Integrated Books International, United States of America

Dedicated to my teachers
Susan E. Schreiner and B. A. Gerrish
and to the memory of
David C. Steinmetz and Robert M. Kingdon

Contents

Acknowledgments

The German inscription above the original woodcut image that appears on the cover of this book reads "John Calvin, Teacher of Holy Scripture." In presenting this investigation into how Calvin's historical consciousness shaped his engagement with scripture, I acknowledge with gratitude the many people who have shaped this study, serving, as it were, as my teachers in Calvin.

The book is dedicated to four scholars who have particularly influenced my work, in two cases through their actual instruction, and in all cases through their pioneering scholarship on Calvin's theology, biblical exegesis, and contexts, as well as through their mentorship and friendship: Susan E. Schreiner, B. A. Gerrish, and, *in memoriam*, David C. Steinmetz and Robert M. Kingdon.

I am also indebted to a vast network of scholars working on Calvin, the history of exegesis, Reformation thought, the history of Geneva, and early modern intellectual and social history more broadly, so many of whom have generously shared their time and expertise with me. If I were to list all of these colleagues and friends here, I would go well beyond the press's word limit for the book, and so I hope instead that their impact and guidance will be evident in the chapter discussions and in the citations in the notes and bibliography. To all of you, and also to those whose important work did not get cited in the book, I am profoundly grateful for years of academic exchange and friendship. What a blessing!

I also wish to thank those directly involved in shepherding this project into print: Cynthia Read and the editorial team at Oxford University Press, and two anonymous peer reviewers for Oxford who offered encouragement and important suggestions. One reader, in particular, deserves credit for suggesting the order of the chapters, which vastly improved the book's coherence and argument. My longtime friend and fellow Reformation scholar, Beth Kreitzer, stepped up to help me cross the finish line; the book is much better for her wisdom and meticulous attention to detail. Of course, I take full responsibility for any errors and infelicities.

Finally, this book draws upon previously published material, and I am grateful both to the peer reviewers and editors who read and responded to earlier versions of the studies found in this book, as well as to the original publishers for granting me permission to reuse part or all of the articles listed below. In every case, the presentation has been significantly revised and updated.

"Imitation of David: David as a Paradigm for Faith in Calvin's Exegesis of the Psalms," *Sixteenth Century Journal* 24, no. 4 (1993): 843–63.

"Calvin as Commentator on the Gospel of John," in *Calvin and the Bible*, ed. Donald K. McKim (Cambridge, UK: Cambridge University Press, 2006), 164–98.

"Prophecy and History in Calvin's Lectures on Daniel (1561)," in *Die Geschichte der Daniel-Auslegung in Judentum, Christentum und Islam: Studien zur Kommentierung des Danielbuches in Literatur und Kunst*, ed. Katharina Bracht and David du Toit (Berlin: de Gruyter, 2007), 323–47.

"Calvin's Reception of Paul," in *A Companion to Paul in the Reformation*, ed. R. Ward Holder (Leiden: Brill, 2009), 267–96.

"John Calvin and the Interpretation of the Bible," in *A History of Biblical Interpretation*, vol. 2, ed. Alan J. Hauser and Duane F. Watson (Grand Rapids, MI: Eerdmans, 2009), 341–71.

"Calvin's Mosaic Harmony: Biblical Exegesis and Early Modern Legal History," *Sixteenth Century Journal* 41, no. 2 (2010): 441–66.

"Exil im Spiegel der Geschichte: Calvins Jesajakommentar (1559)," in *Calvin und Calvinismus: Europäische Perspektiven*, ed. Irene Dingel and Herman Selderhuis (Göttingen: Vandenhoeck & Ruprecht, 2011), 215–28.

"John Calvin, François Hotman, and the Living Lessons of Sacred History," in *Politics, Gender, and Belief: The Long-Term Impact of the Reformation*, ed. Amy Nelson Burnett, Kathleen Comerford, and Karin Maag (Geneva: Droz, 2014), 19–44.

Barbara Pitkin
Stanford, California
August 1, 2019

Abbreviations

BC	*Bibliotheca Calviniana: Les oeuvres de Jean Calvin publiées au XVIe siècle,* 3 vols. Edited by Rodolphe Peter and Jean-François Gilmont. Vol. 1, *Écrits théologiques, littéraires et juridiques 1532–1554.* Geneva: Droz, 1991. Vol. 2, *Écrits théologiques, littéraires et juridiques 1555–1564.* Geneva: Droz, 1994. Vol 3, *Écrits théologiques, littéraires et juridiques 1565–1600.* Geneva: Droz, 2000. Cited by item's year of publication and catalogue number.
CO	John Calvin, *Ioannis Calvini opera quae supersunt omnia,* 59 vols. Edited by G. Baum, E. Cunitz, and E. Reuss. Vols. 29–87 of *Corpus Reformatorum.* Brunswick: C. A. Schwetschke and Son [M. Bruhn], 1863–1900. Cited according to volume (CO 1 = CR 29) and column number.
CR	Philip Melanchthon, *Philippi Melanchthonis opera quae supersunt omnia,* 28 vols. Edited by C. G. Bretschneider and H. Bindseil. Vols. 1–28 of *Corpus Reformatorum.* Halle: C. A. Schwetschke and Son, 1834–1860. Cited according to volume and column number.
Institutes (1559)	John Calvin, *Calvin: Institutes of the Christian Religion,* 2 vols. Edited by John T. McNeill and translated by Ford Lewis Battles. Library of Christian Classics, vols. 20–21. Philadelphia: Westminster Press, 1960. Cited according to book, chapter, and section.
LW	Martin Luther, *Luther's Works,* 55 vols. American Edition. Edited by Jaroslav Pelikan and Helmut T. Lehman. St. Louis: Concordia; Philadelphia: Fortress, 1955–1986.
MBW	Philip Melanchthon, *Melanchthons Briefwechsel: Kritische und kommentierte Gesamtausgabe.* Edited by Heinz Scheible. Stuttgart-Bad Cannstatt: frommann-holzboog, 1977–. Cited by letter number.
OE	John Calvin, *Opera exegetica veteris et novi testamenti.* Series 2 of *Ioannis Calvini opera omnia denuo recognita et adnotatione, critica instructa, notisque illustrata.* Geneva: Droz, 1992–. Cited according to volume number within series 2 and page number.

OS   John Calvin, *Ioannis Calvini opera selecta*, 5 vols. Edited by Peter
              Barth, Wilhelm Niesel, and Dora Scheuner. Munich: Chr. Kaiser,
              1926–1952.
SC   John Calvin, *Supplementa Calviniana: Sermons inédits*. Edited
              by H. Rückert, E. Mülhaupt, G. Barrois, et al. Neukirchener-
              Vluyn: Neukirchener Verlag, 1936–2012.
WA   Martin Luther, *D. Martin Luthers Werke: Kritische
              Gesamtausgabe*. Weimar: H. Böhlau, 1883–2009.
WADB   Martin Luther, *D. Martin Luthers Werke: Deutsche Bibel*.
              Weimar: H. Böhlau, 1906–1961.

1

John Calvin's Historicizing Interpretation of the Bible

Introduction

The contributions of John Calvin (1509–1564), the French Protestant reformer in Geneva, to the history of Christian biblical interpretation have long been recognized, frequently extolled, and occasionally contested. In many respects, Calvin's achievements represent the fruit of developments in biblical scholarship and new attitudes toward scriptural authority that were planted and cultivated in the medieval era and took firm root in the sixteenth century. Of course, there were many noteworthy contemporary exegetes, both Roman Catholic and Protestant, who sought to combine humanist learning with renewed appreciation for the authority of scripture and who decisively shaped the practice of interpretation. Few, however, attained the widespread recognition that was accorded to Calvin; even fewer found their exegetical virtues so enduringly lauded, or, alternatively, their shortcomings so heavily criticized by later generations.

In part, Calvin's reputation is due to the sheer volume of his work and the number and dissemination of his publications. Though popularly remembered as the defender of double predestination and the author of an important theological summary entitled *Institutes of the Christian Religion*, he was not a man of one doctrine or even of one book. He was a busy pastor, preacher, teacher, and exegete, not to mention correspondent and polemicist. He lectured and preached on the Bible throughout his career, published commentaries on nearly every book of the Old and New Testaments, and agreed to have his sermons, which were delivered extemporaneously, preserved by a team of scribes.[1] His academic training was in law, not theology,

---

[1] A comprehensive but concise overview of Calvin's work on the Bible can be found in Wulfert de Greef, *The Writings of John Calvin, Expanded Edition: An Introductory Guide*, trans. Lyle D. Bierma (Louisville, KY: Westminster John Knox, 2008), 69–133. For broad but accessible discussions of Calvin as an interpreter of the Bible, see John L. Thompson, "Calvin as a Biblical Interpreter," in

Calvin, the Bible, and History. Barbara Pitkin, Oxford University Press (2020). © Oxford University Press.
DOI: 10.1093/oso/9780190093273.001.0001

but he was knowledgeable about biblical teaching and had formed opinions about interpretation prior to embarking on his career as a minister. Before being appointed to his position as a lecturer in sacred scripture in Geneva in 1536, he had tried his hand already at the commentary genre in his first publication, a commentary on Seneca's treatise *De Clementia* (1532), was involved in the production of a French translation of the Bible (1535), and had begun to express his ideas on how the Bible should be interpreted in the first edition of the *Institutes* (1536).

Calvin's interest in proper interpretation of the Bible is not surprising, given the fact that he shared with most other sixteenth-century evangelicals an insistence on "scripture alone" as the ultimate authority in matters of faith, as well as the conviction that the central meaning of scripture was fundamentally clear and intelligible. Recent scholarship has expanded earlier understandings of Calvin as an exegete by supplementing ongoing discussions of his hermeneutical theory and understanding of biblical authority with careful attention to the range of his exegetical activity and more detailed attention to his working hermeneutic through analysis of his actual exposition. In addition, studies of the history of biblical interpretation have filled out a rich picture of the exegesis of Calvin's contemporaries and predecessors. Together, these have revised earlier judgments that seemed to imply that his exegetical achievements were virtually without precedent and their quality beyond comparison.[2] While establishing Calvin's position well within the traditions of previous and contemporary exegesis, these new approaches have also shed light on what is truly distinctive in his use of the Bible.

This book investigates Calvin's interpretation of the Bible through the lens of one of its most distinctive and distinguishing features: his historicizing approach to scripture. Each of the subsequent chapters explores the varied ways that Calvin's sense of history past and present permeates and shapes his engagement with the biblical text. The roots of Calvin's historicizing approach are complex. They can be traced to a growing appreciation for the

---

The Cambridge Companion to John Calvin, ed. Donald K. McKim (Cambridge, UK: Cambridge University Press, 2004), 58–73; Dawn DeVries, "Calvin's Preaching," in *The Cambridge Companion to John Calvin*, ed. McKim, 106–24.

[2] Philip Schaff, "Calvin as a Commentator," *Presbyterian and Reformed Review* 3 (1892): 462. For a summary of some other modern evaluations of Calvin's exegesis and its historicizing character, see David L. Puckett, *John Calvin's Exegesis of the Old Testament* (Louisville, KY: Westminster John Knox, 1995), 7–12.

grammatical, literal, or historical sense of scripture in medieval and late medieval Christian exegesis, to new interpretive practices that emerged with the Renaissance, and to the theological priorities of contemporary evangelical reforming movements. Calvin's strategies for recovering meaning for his contemporary readers and auditors in his biblical commentaries, lectures, and sermons also resonate with broader cultural trends in his day for appropriating the past.

One of the most pressing intellectual and, ultimately, practical issues of the age in which Calvin lived concerned the nature of history and, in particular, the proper way to read and interpret the past. While interest in these matters was clearly not new, questions surrounding the meaning of history and the best way to view events gone by were especially urgent in Calvin's day—not least because of the rival readings of the Christian past that were being fueled by the raging religious controversies. Yet even prior to and apart from the contentious religious climate, attitudes toward and approaches to the past were being transformed, and history in the middle of the sixteenth century was being composed, in the words of Anthony Grafton, in a "new key."[3] As Irena Backus has shown, even sixteenth-century theologians were interested in history for its own sake, beyond using it simply as a polemical weapon.[4] The Bible and Christian salvation history had long been central to Western conceptions of the history of the world, but, as Euan Cameron demonstrates, over the course of the early modern era, attitudes toward the Bible as a historical source shifted dramatically.[5] Heightened scrutiny of sources, debates over university curricula and religious institutions, and an explosion of new information all contributed to a climate of interpretive chaos that absorbed the attention of many of Calvin's contemporaries—and of Calvin himself.[6] Rising enthusiasm for defining adequate and more formalized approaches

[3] Anthony Grafton, *What Was History? The Art of History in Early Modern Europe* (Cambridge, UK: Cambridge University Press, 2007), 21.

[4] Irena Backus, *Historical Method and Confessional Identity in the Era of the Reformation (1378–1615)* (Leiden: Brill, 2003).

[5] Euan Cameron, "The Bible and the Early Modern Sense of History," in *The New Cambridge History of the Bible*, vol. 3, *From 1450 to 1750*, ed. Euan Cameron (Cambridge, UK: Cambridge University Press, 2016), 657–85.

[6] For more general discussions of Calvin's sense of history, see Danièle Fischer, "Jean Calvin, historien de l'église: Sources et aspects de la pensée historique, et de l'historiographie du Réformateur" (Ph.D. diss., University of Strasbourg, 1980); Danielle Fischer, "L'histoire de l'église dans la pensée de Calvin," *Archiv für Reformationsgeschichte* 77 (1986): 79–125; Barbara Pitkin, "Calvin, Theology, and History," *Seminary Ridge Review* 12 (2010): 1–16; Barbara Pitkin, "John Calvin's Vision of Reform, Historical Thinking, and the Modern World," in *The Oxford Handbook of Calvin and Calvinism*, ed. Bruce Gordon and Carl R. Trueman (New York: Oxford University Press, forthcoming).

to the past manifested itself across the spectrum of European humanists and yielded a number of creative and experimental proposals for reading, interpreting, evaluating, and transmitting historical knowledge.

Calvin's relationship to these new ideas and methods and to their proponents and their impact on his interpretation of the Bible invites closer attention. Through his legal and humanistic training and throughout his career as a church leader, theologian, and polemicist, Calvin had personal or literary contact with a number of scholars of the French school (*mos gallicus*) whose writings decisively shaped the discipline of history by laying (in the words of Donald Kelley) the "foundations of modern historical scholarship." These contacts included his law professor Andrea Alciato (1492–1550); his fellow student François de Connan (1508–1551); his former secretaries François Baudouin (1520–1573) and François Hotman (1524–1590), and their former mentor Charles Du Moulin (1500–1566).[7] Though he wrote no treatise on history per se, Calvin himself had to deal with the role of the past not only in his early humanistic commentary on Seneca's *De Clementia* (1532) but also in his work of a more religious nature as well—defining and defending Protestant doctrine in the *Institutes* and in his polemical writings and also implementing ecclesiastical and educational reforms in Geneva.

Virtually all Christian interpreters prior to and contemporary with Calvin valued the letter of scripture, but few if any were as consistent as Calvin was in seeking to preserve the integrity and unity of that history—as Christian salvation history, to be sure, but as history nonetheless. In his works of biblical exposition, Calvin preserves and perpetuates traditional Christian images of biblical figures such as Moses, David, Isaiah, Daniel, John, and Paul; they are prophets, evangelists, or apostles who teach true doctrine and provide examples for godly behavior. At the same time, he resists and sometimes explicitly rejects many of the common views of the teachings propounded by these biblical figures, insisting instead that they speak to later generations of the faithful principally out of and through their own historical experience. Calvin's historical consciousness is so marked that his rejection on historical grounds of certain traditional dogmatic interpretations of passages as christological and trinitarian prooftexts led to later accusations of "judaizing" from a Lutheran polemicist.[8] In perhaps the strongest expression of this, he

---

[7] Donald R. Kelley, *Foundations of Modern Historical Scholarship: Language, Law, and History in the French Renaissance* (New York: Columbia University Press, 1970).

[8] See G. Sujin Pak, *The Judaizing Calvin: Sixteenth-Century Debates over the Messianic Psalms* (New York: Oxford University Press, 2010); David C. Steinmetz, *Calvin in Context*, 2nd edition (New York: Oxford University Press, 2010), 207–16.

took a distinctive historicizing approach to the book of Daniel in his lectures published in 1561, in which he, in contrast to nearly all prior and contemporary Christian interpreters, viewed the four monarchies of Nebuchadnezzar's dream (Daniel 2) and the four beasts (Daniel 7) as representing kingdoms and situations that were long past.[9]

This historicizing approach has at times given rise in earlier generations of scholars to an image of Calvin as a forerunner of modern historical biblical criticism. Yet the emergence in the late seventeenth century of critical approaches to the study of the Bible were part of a much broader and complicated reevaluation of history that accelerated over the sixteenth century.[10] Calvin occupies a mediating position in this larger transformation of worldview. As the following chapters demonstrate, Calvin's historical sensibility extended beyond the original contexts of scripture to an equally deep appreciation of the needs and demands of his own age. For Calvin, it was a question not merely of the proper recovery of the past but also of the appropriate application of the past to the present. Different genres of biblical writing—narrative, prophecy, poetry, legal material, doctrinal teaching— and canonical location (in Old or New Testament) might configure this relationship differently, so that in some cases (as in the case of his interpretation of Daniel) Calvin's sense of historical anachronism might be quite sharp, whereas in others (for example, his engagements with some aspects of Paul's or John's theology) the gap between past and present might be nearly imperceptible. But even in the latter instances, Calvin's historical consciousness clearly shapes his interpretation.

Each chapter to follow explores ways in which historical consciousness manifests itself in Calvin's treatment of distinct books of the Bible, biblical figures, or themes. As connected case studies, they examine this subject from various angles, focusing, for example, on Calvin's historicizing treatment of Old Testament prophecy, or his engagement with contemporary historiographical trends, or his efforts to relate the biblical past to an aspect of the present historical situation, such as the reform of the church, the experience of religious exile, or the crisis of religious-political civil war. Collectively they illustrate as no one of them can do alone the multifaceted character and

---

[9] Barbara Pitkin, "Prophecy and History in Calvin's Lectures on Daniel (1561)," in *Die Geschichte der Daniel-Auslegung in Judentum, Christentum und Islam: Studien zur Kommentierung des Danielbuches in Literatur und Kunst*, ed. Katharina Bracht und David S. du Toit (Berlin: De Gruyter, 2007), 323–47, revised as chapter 6 in this book.

[10] Admirably traced in Cameron, "The Bible and the Early Modern Sense of History," which notes Calvin's mediating stance (663, 682).

expansive impact of Calvin's sense of history on his reading of the Bible. They demonstrate, moreover, *how* Calvin engages particular biblical books or figures as past authorities who speak beyond their original contexts. This task was by no means new: Christian exegetes had developed a wide range of tools and strategies for reconciling the letter of scripture with a spiritual meaning for later believers. But Calvin's deep historical sensibilities, combining a strong sense of historical anachronism with an equally profound sense of the unity and utility of sacred history, rendered this recovery of the past all the more challenging and led him to unusual, unprecedented, and occasionally deeply controversial exegetical conclusions.

In order to set the stage for exploring some of Calvin's distinctive resolutions of this traditional issue in his engagement with scripture, this chapter provides some important background. First, it outlines the contexts of Calvin's exegetical program, including previous and contemporary understandings of the historical sense of scripture and the authority of tradition more broadly and also the broader intellectual and social contexts that shaped his work. Second, it delineates four central aspects of Calvin's exegetical method that ground and permeate his historicizing approach: his commitment to continuous exposition and lucid brevity; his focus on the mind of the biblical author and prioritizing of the literal sense; his views on the authority of Paul and the role of exegetical tradition; and his theological assumptions about the *scopus* and unity of scripture. Finally, it provides an overview of the remaining chapters of this book.

Contexts for Calvin's Exegesis

Years ago, Hans-Joachim Kraus cautioned against speaking monolithically about "*the* biblical exegesis of the Reformation" and urged scholars to remember the importance of exegetical tradition for Calvin, who "was unwilling to give up the consensus of interpretation."[11] Since then, many studies have vastly enriched understanding of this exegetical context by exploring it from various angles: Calvin's immediate and broader intellectual and theological contexts; the exegetical, philological, and other sources he may have used; the different venues and media in which he engaged and expounded scripture; and, less fully, the actual impact or reception of his exegetical work.

---

[11] Hans-Joachim Kraus, "Calvin's Exegetical Principles," *Interpretation* 31 (1977): 8, 11.

Attention to context requires that Calvin not be read in isolation from prior and contemporary interpreters, both those whose commentary he may have consulted as well as those who reflect the dominant interpretive climate of his day. More broadly, context also includes consideration of Calvin's intellectual milieu and the social, cultural, and political contexts in which he worked.

Exegetical Traditions

Reassessments of the relationship between medieval and sixteenth-century exegesis have yielded a view of Calvin's place in an interpretive tradition that contrasts sharply with the image of him as the father or even founder of modern historical-critical method, as found in some of the older literature.[12] Calvin embodied tendencies common to his age that also had deep roots in the Christian exegetical tradition. For example, he shared with earlier and contemporary exegetes a concern for reconciling the letter of scripture— what is variously called the literal, grammatical, historical, or plain sense— with its spiritual meaning, respect for the exegesis of the ancient Christian writers, and an interest in grammar and philology. Consequently, Calvin's interest in the literal sense and his alleged repudiation of all allegory, his wide reading in patristic exegetes such as Chrysostom and Augustine, and his employment of philological tools such as the knowledge of biblical languages and classical rhetoric are no longer seen as constituting a break with the past. Rather, these elements are viewed in continuity with a medieval tradition that was itself not uniform.[13]

Like earlier exegetes, such as Hugh (ca. 1096–1141) and Andrew (ca. 1110–1175) of St. Victor, Thomas Aquinas (1225–1274), Nicholas of Lyra (ca. 1270–1349), and Lefèvre d'Étaples (ca. 1455–1536), Calvin and many of his contemporaries emphasized the dignity and even priority of the literal sense of scripture. Earlier interpreters reconciled the letter with the spirit of scripture through the idea that scripture possesses both a literal and multiple

---

[12] For example, Frederic W. Farrar, "Calvin as an Expositor," *The Expositor*, 2nd series, 7 (1884): 440; Frederic W. Farrar, *History of Interpretation: Eight Lectures Preached before the University of Oxford in the Year MDCCCLXXXV* (London: Macmillan, 1886), 346–47; Schaff, "Calvin as a Commentator," 466; see also Thomas F. Torrance, *The Hermeneutics of John Calvin* (Edinburgh: Scottish Academic Press, 1988), 61, 72.

[13] Two classic studies of this diversity are C. Spicq, *Esquisse d'une histoire de l'exégèse latine au moyen âge* (Paris: J. Vrin, 1944) and Beryl Smalley, *The Study of the Bible in the Middle Ages*, 3rd edition (Oxford: Basil Blackwell, 1983). See also Christopher Ocker, *Biblical Poetics before Humanism and Reformation* (Cambridge, UK: Cambridge University Press, 2002).

spiritual senses (later formalized as the *quadriga*, which posited four levels of meaning: a literal sense and three spiritual senses of allegory, tropology, and anagogy) or, in some cases, through the notion of a duplex literal sense. The late Middle Ages and the Renaissance saw an expansion of the literal sense in light of new theories of authorship, language, and meaning that resulted from reading Aristotle and developments in logic, rhetoric, and poetics as well as encounters with Jewish exegesis.[14] Following this trend to incorporate meanings previously ascribed to the spiritual senses into the literal sense, Calvin and those who adopted a similar program did not seek spiritual senses beyond the text, but rather spiritual meaning within the text, tending to overstuff this single, literal sense with spiritual meanings.[15] Though Calvin eschewed "bad" allegories, he embraced "good" allegories such as Paul's in Galatians 4, often preferring, however, to call these extended meanings typologies, similitudes, or anagogies.[16] Nonetheless, the desire of some sixteenth-century exegetes to find what they appeared to view as a *single*, literal sense, while it represented a culmination of medieval trends, also distinguished their efforts from previous approaches that showed a preference for or at least recognized the multivocality of the biblical text.

Also in continuity with the exegetical past, Calvin and other sixteenth-century reformers did not practice interpretation in isolation, but sought guidance, especially from the great interpreters of the ancient church. Granted, sixteenth-century interpreters, Calvin among them, were arguably better read in the church fathers than most of their predecessors, thanks to the availability of new, comprehensive editions of these works. Moreover, Calvin was part of the Reformation's overall reevaluation of the authority of the previous tradition. However, this did not mean that he rejected tradition entirely; indeed, his respect for patristic exegesis has long been recognized.[17] David Steinmetz pioneered efforts to demonstrate more precisely how

---

[14] Ocker, *Biblical Poetics*; Deeana Copeland Klepper, "Theories of Interpretation: The *quadriga* and Its Successors," in *The New Cambridge History of the Bible*, vol. 3, *From 1450 to 1750*, ed. Euan Cameron (Cambridge, UK: Cambridge University Press, 2016), 418–38.

[15] Richard A. Muller, "Biblical Interpretation in the Era of the Reformation: The View from the Middle Ages," in *Biblical Interpretation in the Era of the Reformation: Essays Presented to David C. Steinmetz in Honor of His Sixtieth Birthday*, ed. Richard A. Muller and John L. Thompson (Grand Rapids, MI: Eerdmans, 1996), 3–22; David C. Steinmetz, "Divided by a Common Past: The Reshaping of the Christian Exegetical Tradition in the Sixteenth Century," *Journal of Medieval and Early Modern Studies* 27 (1997): 245–64; Ocker, *Biblical Poetics*, 184–213.

[16] John L. Thompson, "Calvin's Exegetical Legacy: His Reception and Transmission of Text and Tradition," in *The Legacy of John Calvin*, ed. D. L. Foxgrover (Grand Rapids, MI: CRC Product Services, 2000), 35; Puckett, *John Calvin's Exegesis*, 105–24; Steinmetz, *Calvin in Context*, 273–75.

[17] Schaff, "Calvin as a Commentator," 465.

earlier interpretive patterns conditioned Calvin's reading of scripture, both in raising key questions and suggesting answers based on the texts, as well as by providing a fund of "exegetical lore," such as the customary practice of comparing Abraham's laughter to the astonishment of the Virgin Mary.[18]

Finally, Calvin and many contemporaries shared with the exegetical tradition an interest in grammar and philology. To be sure, their skill in these matters had been heightened by developments in humanistic textual scholarship, and their exegesis took into account more diversity in the texts of the Old and New Testaments. But knowledge of biblical languages and concern with textual matters, including establishing the best text, did not constitute a reversal of medieval practice but rather a shift in emphasis.[19] Taken together, these reassessments underscore how much of Calvin's method and commentary were not unprecedented.

Much of the scholarship on the traditional antecedents underlying Calvin's exposition of the Bible relies on a broad, representative portrayal of ancient, medieval, and contemporary patterns of interpretation in order to determine where Calvin is making an original point, or where he is repeating a traditional insight.[20] Complementing these efforts to locate Calvin in relation to the dominant traditions that shaped the exegetical world of his day are a few studies that seek to determine exactly which sources he actually used in the course of his commentary and preaching, and how he used them.[21] Adding precision to studies that suggested what works Calvin *might* have used, these more specific investigations have focused on his actual citations of or clear references to Bible versions or traditional interpretations. In general, they

---

[18] Steinmetz, *Calvin in Context*, 73.

[19] Muller, "Biblical Interpretation," 12–13.

[20] See, for example, Elsie Anne McKee, *Elders and the Plural Ministry: The Role of Exegetical History in Illuminating John Calvin's Theology* (Geneva: Droz, 1988); John Lee Thompson, *John Calvin and the Daughters of Sarah: Women in Regular and Exceptional Roles in the Exegesis of Calvin, His Predecessors, and His Contemporaries* (Geneva: Droz, 1992); Susan E. Schreiner, *Where Shall Wisdom Be Found? Calvin's Exegesis of Job from Medieval and Modern Perspectives* (Chicago: University of Chicago Press, 1994); Steinmetz, *Calvin in Context*; Pak, *Judaizing Calvin*; Barbara Pitkin, "Calvin's Commentary on Psalm 1 and Providential Faith: Reformed Influences on the Psalms in English," in *Crossing Traditions: Essays on the Reformation and Intellectual History in Honour of Irena Backus*, ed. Maria-Cristina Pitassi and Daniela Solfaroli Camillocci (Leiden: Brill, 2018), 164–81.

[21] See, for example, T. H. L. Parker, *Calvin's New Testament Commentaries*, 2nd edition (Louisville, KY: Westminster John Knox, 1993); T. H. L. Parker, *Calvin's Old Testament Commentaries* (Edinburgh: T. & T. Clark, 1986); Anthony N. S. Lane, *John Calvin: Student of the Church Fathers* (Edinburgh: T. & T. Clark, 1999); Johannes van Oort, "John Calvin and the Church Fathers," in *The Reception of the Church Fathers in the West: From the Carolingians to the Maurists*, 2 vols., ed. Irena Backus (Leiden: Brill, 1997), 2: 661–700; Irena Backus, "Calvin's Judgment of Eusebius of Caesarea: An Analysis," *Sixteenth Century Journal* 22, no. 3 (1991): 419–37; Irena Backus, "Calvin and the Greek Fathers," in *Continuity and Change: The Harvest of Late Medieval and Reformation History*, ed. R. J. Bast and A. C. Gow (Leiden: Brill, 2000), 253–76.

have concluded that Calvin, though widely read in a number of the patristic writers, had a relatively modest collection of writings ready to hand when preparing his commentaries and lectures. Moreover, he may have relied on medieval compendia or works of contemporaries for traditional insights, and often cited both the fathers and other biblical passages from memory. Indeed, in his biblical commentaries, and even more so in his sermons, Calvin refrains from citing others' views, mentioning them (usually anonymously) only when he has reason to disagree with them.[22]

Of course, simply identifying explicit references cannot completely explain Calvin's relationship to traditional and contemporary exegetes. The most comprehensive image of Calvin's context emerges from the combination of the extensive approach of those who study Calvin against the rich texture of Christian (and sometimes Jewish) exegesis, with the intensive approach of those who focus on which aspects of this tradition Calvin actually cites. Taking both into account, we find an interpreter who is well acquainted with the major features of patristic theology and exegesis, which he acquired through his own study of newly available sources or through a passing familiarity with the major medieval textbooks such as Gratian's *Decretum* (ca. 1140) and Peter Lombard's *Sentences* (ca. 1150) and with the exegetical works of such contemporaries as Martin Luther (1483–1546), Philip Melanchthon (1497–1560), Martin Bucer (1491–1551), Heinrich Bullinger (1504–1575), and others. Comparison with the works of others thus is fruitful and demonstrates that Calvin truly did learn from other commentators, especially the ancient ones, as he himself claimed in the dedicatory epistle to his Romans commentary. At the same time, as an exegete, Calvin was always pressed for time. When writing a commentary, preparing a lecture, or thinking about one of the eight sermons he might preach in a given week, he had little time to consult his sources, but instead relied chiefly on his memory, theological instincts, and rhetorical skill in crafting his comments. As John Thompson has suggested, sometimes Calvin's alleged independence may have stemmed simply from the fact that he worked in haste.[23] In addition, as will be discussed more fully below, Calvin's understanding of the ultimate aims of scriptural exposition led him to eschew extended engagement with others' ideas in his commentaries, sermons, and lectures.

---

[22] Van Oort, "John Calvin and the Church Fathers," 675, 677–78; see also Steinmetz, *Calvin in Context*, 98; Lane, *John Calvin*, 3–4.
[23] Thompson, "Calvin's Exegetical Legacy," 50.

Broader Intellectual Milieu

Calvin's approach to biblical interpretation and his historical sensitivities were also shaped by his broader intellectual milieu, and particularly his studies of law and exposure to humanistic scholarly trends as a student in France. When he was fourteen, Calvin went to Paris, where he first was trained in Latin and rhetoric by Mathurin Cordier (ca. 1479–1564) at the Collège de Marche and then continued his studies in the arts curriculum at the Collège de Montaigu. About 1528, after taking his arts degree, he went to Orléans, where he studied law with Pierre de l'Éstoile (1480–1537) and Greek with Melchior Wolmar (1497–1560). He then transferred to Bourges, where he continued his legal studies with the Italian jurist Andrea Alciato.[24] Finally, he returned to Paris in 1531 to further his humanistic studies in Greek, Hebrew, and the classics.

Of particular importance was Calvin's exposure to the new approaches to the study of civil law in Orléans and Bourges. Rejecting the traditional methods of scholastic jurists, who studied Roman law topically without attention to historical context or development, scholars like Guillaume Budé (1467–1540) and Alciato advocated philological criticism and pioneered the study of Roman law in its original context. They drew broadly on classical Roman literature to illuminate the conditions surrounding the formation of the various components of the *Corpus iuris civilis*—the civil law code compiled under emperor Justinian I (ca. 482–565) in the sixth century. This approach was not merely antiquarian but was motivated by practical concerns. As Christoph Strohm points out, issues of law, morality, justice, and ethics were also featured in humanistic legal theory, which aimed to address present needs and concerns on a sounder textual basis.[25] From this combination of legal and classical training, Calvin acquired the necessary linguistic and rhetorical skills for a life as a humanist scholar, an ambition that came to fruition with his first publication, the commentary on Seneca's *De Clementia* (1532).[26]

---

[24] See Christoph Strohm, "Sixteenth-Century French Legal Education and Calvin's Legal Education," trans. Barbara Pitkin, in *Calvin and the Early Reformation*, ed. Brian C. Brewer and David M. Whitford (Leiden: Brill, 2020), 44–57.

[25] Strohm, "Sixteenth-Century French Legal Education." See also Kelley, *Foundations*.

[26] John Calvin, *Calvin's Commentary on Seneca's De Clementia*, ed. and trans. Ford Lewis Battles and André Malan Hugo (Leiden: Brill, 1969).

While Calvin's legal studies and humanistic orientation toward classical languages and literature provided the initial foundation for his approach to the Bible, a further key component was his adoption of evangelical theological sensibilities. There is much debate about how and when Calvin came to join the evangelical cause, whether under the influence of the avid Lutheran Wolmar in the late 1520s or only at the point that he resigned his ecclesiastical benefices in 1534. Few details survive of Calvin's activities between the publication of *De Clementia* and the end of 1533. During most of this time, Calvin was in Orléans to complete his legal training. His studies had already brought him into contact with reform-minded teachers and friends, and it is likely that he deepened his familiarity with reformist ideas by reading the Bible and patristic writers while working toward his license in law. At the end of 1533, Calvin was back in Paris and moving in reformist circles, including that of Nicholas Cop (ca. 1501–1540), the new rector at the Sorbonne, seeking to advance evangelicalism in France.[27] The next year he composed his first theological treatise (*Psychopannychia*), possibly began work on the first edition of the *Institutes*, and ultimately fled to Basel in the wake of the arrests of Protestants following the Affair of the Placards (1534).[28]

Now openly allied with the evangelical cause, Calvin used the time in Basel to deepen his knowledge of the Bible and to publish the first edition of the *Institutes*, which he conceived of as a "summary of piety" designed both to teach the rudiments of the reformed doctrine of salvation and to offer a defense of this very teaching before the French king.[29] He aimed now to live the life of a Christian humanist, one whose scholarship would serve the church. After a failed attempt to join the reformists in Ferrara, Italy, at the court of Renée of France (1510–1574), Calvin intended to settle in Strasbourg. However, he was forced to detour through Geneva, where Guillaume Farel (1489–1565) recruited him on the spot to help build up the fledgling reformed church. Holding at first the position of lecturer in scripture, Calvin—with no formal theological training—soon gained recognition as a leading

---

[27] Barbara Pitkin, "Calvin on the Early Reformation," in *Calvin and the Early Reformation*, ed. Brian C. Brewer and David M. Whitford (Leiden: Brill, 2020), 200–24. On the Navarrian network supporting these endeavors under the patronage of Marguerite of Navarre, see the important study by Jonathan Reid, *King's Sister—Queen of Dissent: Marguerite of Navarre (1492–1549) and Her Evangelical Network*, 2 vols. (Leiden: Brill, 2009).

[28] No copies of this early edition of the *Psychopannychia* survive; a revised edition was published in 1542.

[29] CO 1:1–248; English translation as John Calvin, *Institutes of the Christian Religion: 1536 Edition*, revised edition, trans. and ann. Ford Lewis Battles (Grand Rapids, MI: Eerdmans, 1986).

theological authority, and at the end of 1536 began serving as one of the city's pastors. Fired from his post in April 1538, he left for Strasbourg, where he finalized and published his first biblical commentary and the second edition of the *Institutes* (1539) while spending three years as the pastor to the French refugee congregation. During this time he also married Idelette de Bure (1500–1549) and represented Strasbourg at religious conferences and colloquies in Germany. In 1541, he was recalled to Geneva, where he remained as pastor for the rest of his life. Thus, in addition to his humanistic education and his early evangelical sensibilities, Calvin's subsequent vocation as pastor and leader in religious reform—despite its rocky beginnings—constitutes a further, important context for his exegetical activity.

Social, Cultural, and Political Contexts

A final context for situating Calvin's historicizing interpretation of the Bible can be found in the relevant social, cultural, and political conditions of his day, both local and international, which were constantly before his eyes whenever he engaged with the biblical text. In general, he did not frequently reference these contexts in his exegesis. He was reticent to speak biographically in his commentaries, lectures, and sermons, and likewise he did not often remark on current events in his commentaries and lectures. In his sermons, Calvin more often ventured comments on present challenges at home and abroad. But just as he did not often make explicit references to the sources he used when interpreting the Bible, the contemporary historical context usually has to be inferred from other sources, such as Calvin's correspondence, his theological-polemical writings, and Geneva's consistorial and civic records. An understanding of this background opens up new perspectives on aspects of Calvin's theology—for example, as Karen Spierling has admirably shown with respect to baptism.[30] These contexts are also illuminating for Calvin's biblical interpretation.

Upon his return to Geneva from Strasbourg, Calvin was not just active in building up the church in Geneva, but was also involved in broader social reforms (such as education and marriage reforms) and civic institutions. He helped draft the republic's first constitution and served as a frequent legal

---

[30] Karen E. Spierling, *Infant Baptism in Reformation Geneva: The Shaping of a Community, 1536–1564* (2005; repr., Louisville, KY: Westminster John Knox, 2009).

advisor to the town's civic authorities, who worked to create, maintain, and enforce laws and policies for this newly independent municipality, which was governed by several levels of councils elected by the town's male citizens. This was not an easy relationship, especially for the first fourteen years after Calvin's return. In 1541, Geneva's citizenry was still split among various factions stemming from its political and religious transformation in the 1520s and 1530s from a Catholic prince-bishopric under the Duke of Savoy to an autonomous republic dependent on the military protection of the powerful Protestant city-state of Bern. William Naphy has traced the rocky evolution of relations between Calvin and his largely French refugee pastor colleagues and the native-born Genevans, identifying two special periods of intense crisis with the prominent citizens in the mid-1540s and early 1550s.[31] This contentious domestic climate clearly shaped Calvin's diagnosis of present historical conditions, even after his supporters gained control of the city's governing bodies in 1555 and embarked on a more cooperative relationship with the ecclesiastical leaders.

In Geneva, Calvin assumed primary leadership over the program of religious and moral reform, which focused on restructuring the worship life of the city, educating its inhabitants in the new faith, providing pastoral leadership, and regularizing pastoral care and ecclesiastical discipline.[32] The Bible was central to the religious life of reformed Geneva and the religious and moral reeducation program instituted by Calvin and his colleagues. As in other Protestant churches, the vernacular sermon became the ritual centerpiece of worship, and Calvin himself was a regular preacher. The subject of the sermon was nearly always a passage from scripture. Preaching usually followed a pattern of continuous exposition of a book of the Bible, with the books of the Old Testament as the subject of the weekday sermons and the books of the New Testament, and occasionally the Psalms, the subjects of the Sunday sermons. The congregation experienced the exposition of scripture in the sermon; they also sang psalms and recited the Lord's Prayer in the liturgy. Psalm-singing and -reading took place also outside of worship: in homes, in workplaces, and on the streets. By the end of Calvin's lifetime, most

---

[31] William G. Naphy, *Calvin and the Consolidation of the Genevan Reformation*, revised edition (Louisville, KY: Westminster John Knox, 2003); William G. Naphy, "Calvin and Geneva," in *The Reformation World*, ed. Andrew Pettegree (London: Routledge, 2000), 309–22.

[32] For an in-depth study of the scope of Calvin's reforms of ministry and worship, see Elsie Anne McKee, *The Pastoral Ministry and Worship in Calvin's Geneva* (Geneva: Droz, 2016). See also Thomas Austin Lambert, "Preaching, Praying, and Policing the Reform in Sixteenth-Century Geneva," Ph.D. diss., University of Wisconsin–Madison, 1998.

Genevans possessed psalters, which despite being common were still considered objects of great value.[33]

Thus, the Bible featured prominently in Genevan life beyond church services and preaching. Calvin wrote catechisms and established a program of parish catechetical services to guide the laity in their understanding of scripture; he also intended that instruction in the basic prayers and tenets of evangelical faith take place in the schools and at home. At a more advanced level, public lectures on scripture and the weekly Bible studies afforded interested and educated persons the opportunity to learn more. Such persons could also read Calvin's commentaries and sermons, as well as his *Institutes*. For ministers and theology students, Calvin intended his commentaries and *Institutes* to support their efforts to teach the faith: the *Institutes* by providing a topically ordered and detailed summary of biblical teaching, and the commentaries by providing a compendium of scriptural teaching and guide to interpretation. Ministers, too, participated in the *congrégations* and took turns leading these communal studies, which were modeled on the practice of the Zurich church. It is important to underscore the communal dimension of interpretation for Calvin. Again, this was not unique to his program, but the idea that the meaning of scripture is not puzzled out on one's own, but discerned in the context of worship and study with others, is an important feature of his approach to biblical interpretation. Another dimension of scripture's communal significance was economic. Over the course of Calvin's lifetime, Geneva became a powerful publishing center, and the printing and marketing of the Bible and psalters (along with Calvin's own writings) were key contributors to the commercial success of printers and financiers.[34] It is important to keep in mind the role of the Bible as an artifact and biblical interpretation in daily life in Geneva when thinking about the broader contexts of Calvin's engagement with scripture.

All the while in Geneva, Calvin never turned his back on his French homeland. He kept abreast of political and religious developments there and in other francophone regions (such as the territories subject to the monarchs of Navarre) through an active correspondence and, increasingly over the 1540s and 1550s, frequent personal interactions with religious exiles arriving

---

[33] Robert M. Kingdon, "Uses of the Psalter in Calvin's Geneva," in *Der Genfer Psalter und seine Rezeption in Deutschland, der Schweiz und den Niederlanden: 16.–18. Jahrhundert*, ed. E. Grunewald, H. P. Jürgens, and J. R. Luth (Tübingen: Max Niemeyer, 2004), 21–32.

[34] See Andreas Würgler, "Buchdruck und Reformation in Genf (1478–1600): Ein Überblick," *Zwinglinana* 45 (2018): 281–310; Paul Chaix, *Récherches sur l'imprimerie à Genève de 1550 à 1564: Étude bibliographique, économique et littéraire* (Geneva: Slatkine, 1978).

in Geneva from France. In the 1550s and 1560s, Calvin orchestrated what Hugues Daussy has described as a diplomatic offensive carried out by an elite corps of pastor-ambassadors sent to support and advance the French Reformed cause among Protestant magistrates in Germany and Switzerland and among the French nobility.[35] His political and diplomatic engagement was part of a coordinated but clandestine Genevan effort to support Huguenots and eventually their armies by sending, in Robert Kingdon's memorable words, "small groups of men, large sums of money, and substantial quantities of gunpowder" into the French kingdom.[36] Books—particularly psalters—also constituted part of the Calvinist arsenal.[37] The early 1560s also witnessed an explosion of pamphlets addressing the religio-political crisis in France.[38] Even Calvin's exegetical work from this period reflects the contemporary French situation. He dedicated his published lectures on Daniel to the French Reformed Christians in 1561 and his commentary on the last four books of the Pentateuch to young prince Henri of Navarre (1553–1610), the future Henri IV of France, in 1563.[39] He subtly but unmistakably imparted spiritual and political lessons to contemporary French readers in his published lectures on the Minor Prophets (1559) and in his commentary on Joshua (1564) and to Genevan worshipers in his direct references to current events in his sermons.[40] These subtle engagements with current events signal an important dimension of Calvin's historical consciousness.

[35] Hugues Daussy, "L'action diplomatique de Calvin en faveur des Églises réformées de France (1557–1564)," Bulletin de la société de l'histoire du protestantisme français (1903–) 156 (2010): 197.

[36] Robert M. Kingdon, Geneva and the Coming of the Wars of Religion in France, 1555–1563 (Geneva: Droz, 1956), 124.

[37] Kingdon, Geneva, 98–103.

[38] Francis Higman, La diffusion de la réforme en France, 1520–1565 (Geneva: Labor et Fides, 1992), 237–39.

[39] On the latter dedication to a young prince who would later become Henri VI of France, and its connection to the unusual format of Calvin's commentary, see Barbara Pitkin, "Calvin and Politics According to the Mosaic Harmony (1563 | 1564): Text, Paratext, and Context," in Calvin frater in Domino, ed. Arnold Huijgen and Karin Maag (Göttingen: Vandenhoeck & Ruprecht, 2020), 37–56.

[40] Jon Balserak, Establishing the Remnant Church in France: Calvin's Lectures on the Minor Prophets, 1556–1559 (Leiden: Brill, 2011); Raymond A. Blacketer, "The Moribund Moralist: Ethical Lessons in Calvin's Commentary on Joshua," in The Formation of Clerical and Confessional Identities in the Sixteenth Century, ed. Wim Janse and Barbara Pitkin, Dutch Review of Church History 85 (2005) (Leiden: Brill, 2006): 149–68; Barbara Pitkin, "John Calvin, François Hotman, and the Living Lessons of Sacred History," in Politics, Gender, and Belief: The Long-Term Impact of the Reformation, ed. Amy Nelson Burnett, Kathleen Comerford, and Karin Maag (Geneva: Droz, 2014), 19–44, revised as chapter 8 in this volume.

Distinctive Features of Calvin's Biblical Exposition

With this appreciation of the varied contexts shaping Calvin's engagements with scripture, we can now turn to the most distinctive aspects of the form, content, and purpose of his exegesis. By "distinctive," I do not mean to imply that these features are necessarily unique to Calvin, but rather that they are essential characteristics of his approach to interpretation. Moreover, this discussion should not be taken as an exhaustive representation of his hermeneutic, but rather as an outline of the aspects critical for understanding and appreciating its historicizing dimension. Though not always expressed explicitly, Calvin's commitment to continuous exposition and the ideal of lucid brevity; his aim to unfold the mind of the author and attend to what he considered the literal or genuine sense of the text; his embrace of Paul as a theological and exegetical lodestar and his engagement with other, sometimes unnamed, conversation partners; and his views on the *scopus* and unity of scripture permeate his scriptural exposition. At times, however, some of these commitments and orientations led him in directions or to conclusions not often or even ever pursued by his predecessors and contemporaries, even by those who shared many of his theological and hermeneutical presuppositions. One reason for this lies in the way that Calvin's historical consciousness manifests itself in each of these key features of his hermeneutical method.

Continuous Exposition and Lucid Brevity

With respect to the formal elements of scriptural exposition, Calvin drew on traditional and more recent patterns in order to develop a program for interpreting the Bible in a variety of settings and in two languages. During his time in Geneva, he explained scripture in four related but distinct venues: in academic lectures (*praelectiones*) held in Latin for students and other interested auditors; in sermons in French for the general populace; in formal commentaries for clergy and literate laity published in both Latin and French; and in weekly Bible study discussions (*congrégations*) conducted in French for ministers and interested laity. Common to nearly all of these was the fact that the Bible was explored book-by-book and verse-by-verse, rather than in a thematic fashion. The only deviations from this strict adherence to the order of the text were some of Calvin's treatments of the three Synoptic

Gospels and last four books of the Pentateuch. In his commentaries on these texts, he harmonized the events into a single narrative—and in the case of the latter, reorganized the biblical legislation into a cohesive body—and then commented according to his regular pattern of continuous exposition. Also common to all forms of exposition was the general pattern of the comments, as well as the fact that all the oral presentations were delivered extemporaneously. Calvin gave the section of text to be discussed, made a few philological, historical, or theological observations to explain its meaning, and then applied the text to the situation of his readers or audience. Technical explanatory comments, including references to the exegesis of others, were more prominent in the commentaries and lectures than in the sermons, although even here they do not figure largely. The sermons, in turn, dwelt more on the application of the text to the present situation, though this concern was not at all absent from the commentaries. Calvin clearly had a sense of the differences in genre and tailored his comments accordingly.

Of course, the practice of continuous exposition was not new to Calvin, nor were the use of philological tools or theological insights or the interest in application of the text to the present. What gives Calvin's combination of all of these its distinctive stamp is his self-professed commitment to what he calls lucid brevity in exposition. Calvin transformed a Renaissance love of brevity that itself drew on the work of the Roman rhetorician Quintilian (ca. 35–100) into a method that David Steinmetz claims constitutes one of his principal contributions to the intellectual heritage of the Reformation.[41] In the dedicatory letter accompanying his very first biblical commentary (on Romans, published in 1540), Calvin claimed that "the chief virtue of an interpreter consists in lucid brevity" and indicated his wish to conform his exposition to this idea.[42] This meant that his comments would be kept relatively brief and would not digress into related subjects, especially avoiding dogmatic excursuses and philological intricacies. This form, Calvin thought, was best suited to the purpose of biblical interpretation. It lent itself to focus on the narrative details of the text and, in Calvin's case, provided ready opportunity to explore its historical dimensions. Though detailed philological examination,

---

[41] Steinmetz, *Calvin in Context*, 13; see also Parker, *Calvin's New Testament Commentaries*, 87. For fuller analysis of the rhetorical context of Calvin's approach to scripture, see Olivier Millet, *Calvin et la dynamique de la parole: Étude de rhétorique réformée* (Paris: Honoré Champion, 1992), and Benoît Girardin, *Rhétorique et théologique: Calvin, le commentaire de l'Épître aux Romains* (Paris: Beauchesne, 1979).

[42] OE 13: 3 = CO 10/2: 402–3. The dedication to Simon Grynaeus (1493–1541) is dated October 18, 1539.

rhetorical analysis, and consideration of historical background, theological import, and the exegeses of others provided tools for understanding and were required in preparation, in the actual exposition these ought to be kept to a minimum.

Calvin's ideal of lucid brevity manifests itself differently in the various forms of exposition. In the commentaries, Calvin is most concise and balances his brief philological observations with explanations of what the text means and, occasionally, succinct suggestions about how to apply this message. In the lectures, Calvin discusses the text in somewhat more detail and freely, and, in the sermons, he spends little time on the technical aspects and speaks at much greater length about the implications for contemporary belief and behavior.[43] In fact, according to the sixteenth-century editors who published some of his sermons, Calvin was reluctant to have them appear in print precisely because he felt they did not adhere to his ideal. He is said to have found them too prolix and too concerned with the situation of his particular congregation.[44] Perhaps, however, one might suggest simply that Calvin accommodated his method of lucid brevity to the specific needs and capacities of those for whom he was expositing. T. H. L. Parker notes that lucid brevity is best understood not as a style of writing but as "the rhetorical method by which the expositor achieves his task of revealing the mind of the writer."[45] While the sermons are undoubtedly more wordy and repetitive, this strategy was best suited to render the biblical writer's message clear to those listening.

The Mind of the Author and the Literal Sense

Calvin's biblical exposition took the form it did because he thought this was the form best suited to convey the content most appropriate to a work of scriptural interpretation. In the dedicatory letter to his Romans commentary,

---

[43] See Max Engammare, "Le Paradis à Genève: Comment Calvin prêchait-il la chute aux Genevois?," *Études théologiques et religieuses* 69 (1994): 329–47; Wulfert de Greef, "Das Verhältnis von Predigt und Kommentar bei Calvin, dargestellt an dem Deuteronomium-Kommentar und den-predigten," in *Calvinus Servus Christi*, ed. Wilhelm H. Neuser (Budapest: Presseabteilung des Ráday-Kollegiums, 1988), 195–204.

[44] Jean-François Gilmont, "Les sermons de Calvin: De l'oral à l'imprimé," *Bulletin de la société de l'histoire du protestantisme français* 141 (1995): 145–62; Wilhelmus H. Th. Moehn, *God Calls Us to His Service: The Relation between God and His Audience in Calvin's Sermons on Acts* (Geneva: Droz, 2001), 191–92.

[45] Parker, *Calvin's New Testament Commentaries*, 91.

Calvin also claimed that the aim of interpretation was to determine and make intelligible the mind of the author.[46] His concern for authorial intention reflects his humanistic interests, but the idea also has roots in the ancient and medieval interpretative traditions. Traditionally, however, Christian exegetes recognized a multiplicity of meanings, all of which were intended by the divine author of scripture. Calvin, however, prioritized the mind of the *human* biblical writer, writing under the guidance of the Holy Spirit to be sure, but in a particular historical context.[47] Presupposing a firm knowledge of biblical languages and history, he attended to the biblical author's historical situation and the stylistic peculiarities of various writers, even within a single book.

A few examples here of Calvin's historicizing interests with respect to human authorship will, I hope, pique the reader's interest in the more detailed analyses in the chapters to come. In his commentary on the Psalms (1557), Calvin sought whenever possible to refer each psalm to a particular event in Israel's history or in the life of the psalmist (not always assumed to be David), often distinguishing between the psalmist's meaning and the use of a passage by a New Testament writer. For example, he explains that in Psalm 8:5 ("For you have made him a little lower than the angels"), David is speaking of human nature before the fall, but when the author of Hebrews refers this verse to Christ (Heb. 2:7), he is not explaining the original meaning of the Psalm text, but rather enriching the subject by accommodating this verse to a different meaning.[48] In his exposition of the New Testament, Calvin resolved the apparent conflict presented in the statements about faith and works by Paul and James (Rom. 3:28 and Jas. 2:26) by arguing that, out of concession to their respective opponents, each writer uses "faith" and "justify" in a different sense.[49] Even in his sermons, Calvin always attended to the intention of the author. Having explained the author's meaning, Calvin then applied this to his auditors or readers, often by drawing analogies between the original situation described in the text and contemporary circumstances. The lessons derived from the text were both doctrinal and moral, depending on the content of the scriptural passage and the circumstances in which Calvin interpreted it.

---

[46] OE 13: 3 = CO 10/2: 403

[47] Fuller discussion of Calvin's views on the dual authorship of scripture is in Puckett, *John Calvin's Exegesis*, 26–37; see also Randall C. Zachman, *John Calvin as Teacher, Pastor, and Theologian: The Shape of His Writings and Thought* (Grand Rapids, MI: Baker, 2006), 109–22, 128–30.

[48] CO 39: 93.

[49] OE 13: 76–77 = CO 49: 65–66.

In order to best unfold the mind of the biblical writer, Calvin thus focused on what is variously designated the historical, literal, plain, or genuine sense of the text—that is, the meaning conveyed by the words or the intention (*consilium*) of the author. As discussed earlier, his emphasis on the literal sense followed certain medieval trends and drew also on Renaissance humanist interest in the original setting of the text and the author's style. Proper understanding of the literal sense required attention to the original biblical languages and to literary devices and narrative context as well as historical circumstances. For Calvin, the literal sense was not a bare, grammatical sense; nor did it refer only to the history behind the text in the way it often does in modern historical criticism. Rather, it included both the history or the events that the author narrated, as well as the spiritual or moral lessons that the writer sought to inculcate. The events narrated and lessons, moreover, were instructive both to those in the author's original setting and to later generations of the faithful. For Calvin, proper identification of these lessons required not only theological acumen and philological and rhetorical skills but also historical insight.

Calvin's exegesis thus evidences a deep appreciation of the actual history of the Jewish people and the early church, an appreciation he shared with the Antiochene exegetes of the early church, Nicholas of Lyra, and contemporaries such as Martin Bucer, John Oecolampadius (1482–1531), Philip Melanchthon, and Heinrich Bullinger. Yet he often related this *historia* to his sixteenth-century present in a way that sought to preserve the integrity of the past to a greater degree than did most of his like-minded contemporaries. The most pronounced examples of this are in his treatment of Old Testament prophecies and the Psalms. For example, Calvin usually connected Old Testament passages referring to the "day of the Lord" to a time of judgment within the history of ancient Israel, and he understood the prophecies in Daniel as referring to events fulfilled around the time of Christ's coming.[50] Moreover, in his explanation of Isaiah 7:14 ("Behold, a virgin shall conceive and bear a son"), he follows Christian exegetical tradition in understanding the verse to be a prediction of the future Christ, but at the same time criticizes "all writers, both Greek and Latin," for moving too quickly to assert this prophecy. Instead, Calvin labors to show how the

---

[50] Richard A. Muller, "The Hermeneutic of Promise and Fulfillment in Calvin's Exegesis of the Old Testament Prophecies of the Kingdom," in *The Bible in the Sixteenth Century*, ed. David C. Steinmetz (Durham, NC: Duke University Press, 1990), 70–71. On Daniel, see chapter 6 in this volume.

promise of Christ has everything to do with assuring Ahaz that Jerusalem will be delivered by reminding him of the foundation of the divine covenant. While Calvin maintains the traditional Christian reference to Christ, he also tries to demonstrate how precisely this meaning is both relevant and appropriate to Ahaz's current situation.[51]

In his interpretation of New Testament passages citing from the Old Testament, Calvin notes, often critically, where a New Testament writer had applied the passages in a way that deviated from the original sense, as, for example, is the case of the citation of Psalm 8:5-6 in Hebrews 2 discussed earlier. He was not the only sixteenth-century exegete to follow these paths. Bucer, for example, also focused on the psalms in Israel's history, and most good Hebraists also raised questions about the citations of the Old Testament in the New.[52] Nevertheless, in the case of Psalm 19:4 cited in Romans 10:18, Calvin is the first to resolve an apparent discrepancy by arguing that Paul, like the psalmist, is also talking about the glory of God revealed to the Gentiles in nature.[53] Such reversals of traditional exegesis were controversial and led to the accusations of "judaizing" exegesis. Steinmetz has suggested that Calvin's rejections of traditional exegesis are best viewed as an attempt to ground the church's dogmatic claims on the best possible scriptural foundation.[54] For Calvin, this meant a reading of scripture in which the present did not eclipse the past and where dogmatic or moral concerns emerged only when the historical human author might reasonably be assumed to be giving voice to them.

The Authority of Paul and the Role of Exegetical Tradition

Calvin's commitment to the literal or genuine sense and the mind of the author did not mean he believed that an interpreter could arrive at the meaning of a biblical text simply by contemplating the words on the page, without any

---

[51] CO 36: 154–55.

[52] R. Gerald Hobbs, "Martin Bucer on Psalm 22: A Study in the Application of Rabbinic Exegesis by a Christian Hebraist," in *Histoire de l'exégèse au XVI siècle: Textes du colloque internationale tenu à Genève en 1976*, ed. Olivier Fatio and Pierre Fraenkel (Geneva: Droz, 1978), 144–63. For an overview of Calvin's treatment of these passages, see Puckett, *John Calvin's Exegesis*, 91–100. On Bucer and Calvin on the messianic psalms, see Pak, *Judaizing Calvin*, 55–102.

[53] R. Gerald Hobbs, "Hebraica Veritas *and* Traditio Apostolica: Saint Paul and the Interpretation of the Psalms in the Sixteenth Century," in *The Bible in the Sixteenth Century*, ed. David C. Steinmetz (Durham, NC: Duke University Press, 1990), 94–97.

[54] Steinmetz, *Calvin in Context*, 214.

additional guidance. Fundamentally, one needed the guidance of the Holy Spirit. One profited also from reading in community, whether literal or literary. Moreover, one needed a prior theological orientation in order to approach scripture with an appropriate understanding of what one ought to seek there. Calvin thus prepared the *Institutes* and his catechisms as such guides. This raises the question of which theological presuppositions played the most important role in shaping Calvin's own hermeneutic and interpretive practice. There are two key components to the answer, the first of which is to identify what or who constituted the principal source and guide for Calvin's theological orientation and exegesis.

In a seminal study from 1976, Alexandre Ganoczy argued that Calvin was fundamentally a "Pauline theologian" and that both his biblical theology and his hermeneutic reflected emphases found principally in the Pauline and deuteropauline writings, even if the biblical figure with whom he most explicitly identified was not Paul but rather David.[55] The importance of Paul for sixteenth-century evangelical theology and approaches to the Bible was not a new insight, but with this argument Ganoczy pressed the question of the nature of Paul's influence on Calvin in particular.

Recognizing the priority of Paul for Calvin's theology and the preeminent place of Paul's writings in Calvin's interpretive program, scholars have investigated how Calvin characteristically read Paul and in what ways his use of Paul might be distinctive.[56] Calvin began his exegetical lectures with and wrote his first commentaries on the Pauline epistles, and, as Ward Holder has demonstrated, these were where he honed his craft as an interpreter.[57] To provide just one example of how Paul's theology influenced Calvin's theology and exegesis, the understanding of the nature and function of faith that emerges in Calvin's commentaries on Paul provides and reinforces the theological point of orientation for the treatment of faith set forth in the *Institutes*.

[55] Alexandre Ganoczy, "Calvin als paulinischer Theologe: Ein Forschungsansatz zur Hermeneutik Calvins," in *Calvinus Theologus*, ed. Wilhelm H. Neuser (Neukirchen: Neukirchener Verlag, 1976), 39–69. See also the discussion of the rebirth of Paulinism in European humanism in Alexandre Ganoczy and Stefan Scheld, *Die Hermeneutik Calvins: Geistesgeschichtliche Voraussetzungen und Grundzüge* (Wiesbaden: Franz Steiner, 1983), 22–47.

[56] See, for example, Girardin, *Rhétorique et théologique*; Steinmetz, *Calvin in Context*, 23–39, 108–54, 197–206, 262–77. See also Barbara Pitkin, "Calvin's Reception of Paul," in *A Companion to Paul in the Reformation*, ed. R. Ward Holder (Leiden: Brill, 2009), 267–96, revised as chapter 2 in the present volume.

[57] R. Ward Holder, *John Calvin and the Grounding of Interpretation: Calvin's First Commentaries* (Leiden: Brill, 2006).

In addition, this "Pauline" view functions as a lens through which Calvin reads other New Testament images of faith.[58]

More precise understandings of the nature of Calvin's Paulinism are also indebted to studies of his actual exposition of Paul in light of other exegetical treatments of the apostle. Steinmetz in particular has undertaken numerous comparative investigations of Calvin's commentary on Romans and found that, consistent with his ideals of interpretation, Calvin focused his exposition of Paul on the mind of the writer. He only occasionally engaged the interpretations of others, usually only to disagree with them. This can give the mistaken impression that Calvin's reading of Paul was remarkably original or independent, as it appears, for example, in his reading of Romans 8:1–11.[59] In fact, however, his exegesis frequently shares questions, concerns, and even the substance of others' interpretations of the same passage. It is clear that he used the exegesis of others not as authorities in the medieval sense, but as what Steinmetz designates "partners in conversation."[60] Irena Backus and Anthony Lane have observed that this partnering way of engaging patristic literature is different from the way Calvin appeals to the fathers in the *Institutes* and in his polemical writings.[61]

One should not underestimate the role of these exegetical partners in shaping Calvin's reading of Paul, even when they usually go unnamed. Often Calvin would have agreed with their interpretations, as in the case of Romans 7:14–25, where he along with the majority of his Protestant and Roman Catholic contemporaries followed the reading of the older Augustine and applied Paul's description of an inner conflict to believers rather than to those outside grace.[62] Thus, in his expounding the mind of his main theological and exegetical authority, he often swims with the broad stream of Pauline interpretation, which makes his occasional struggles against the current all the more impressive. One such instance is Calvin's singular interpretation of Romans 1:18–32.[63] Most Western interpreters of this passage held, along with Paul himself, that humans perceive God in the created order and then proceed to suppress this knowledge because of sin. Calvin, however, argued that because of sin, fallen human beings misperceive God's self-revelation in

---

[58] Barbara Pitkin, *What Pure Eyes Could See: Calvin's Doctrine of Faith in Its Exegetical Context* (New York: Oxford University Press, 1999), 9–97.

[59] Steinmetz, *Calvin in Context*, 120–38.

[60] Steinmetz, *Calvin in Context*, 134.

[61] Backus, "Calvin and the Greek Fathers," 274; Lane, *John Calvin*, 3–4.

[62] Steinmetz, *Calvin in Context*, 108–19.

[63] Steinmetz, *Calvin in Context*, 23–39.

nature, and this culpable misperception in turn leads them to further suppression of the knowledge of God. Here Calvin's explanation of the mind of Paul was decisively shaped by his assumptions about the character of human fallenness. Although his dismal assessment of fallen human nature had its basis in his particular reading of other parts of the Pauline corpus, it led to an idiosyncratic and unprecedented interpretation of Paul's meaning in Romans 1.

The *Scopus* and Unity of Scripture

For Calvin, the different genres of biblical exposition combined in a broader program to proclaim the gospel and nurture Christian faith. The method of exposition (lucid brevity) and the ideal of interpretation (to explain the mind of the author) aimed at something larger, namely, the edification of the contemporary faithful.[64] Calvin's historical approach to scripture does not yield a simple history lesson about the past but engages with that past history to build up present faith. Authoritative theological guidance derives from a Pauline orientation that is shaped by subtle engagement with the exegetical tradition. Now we consider the second part of the answer to the question of the theological presuppositions that played the most important role in shaping Calvin's hermeneutic and exegetical practice toward the entire biblical canon. These assumptions relate to the overall purpose or goal (*scopus*) of scripture and its underlying unity, particularly the unity of the two testaments.

Like Wittenberg (Luther and Melanchthon), Rhineland (Bucer), and Swiss Reformed (Zwingli [1484–1531], Oecolampadius, and Bullinger) interpreters, Calvin stressed the christological focus of scripture and the ultimate goal of interpretation to build up faith in Christ.[65] A clear statement of this principle appears in an early preface to the French New Testament traditionally attributed to Calvin: "This is what we should in short seek in the whole of scripture: truly to know Jesus Christ and the infinite riches that are comprised in him and are offered to us by him from God the

---

[64] Peter Opitz, "The Exegetical and Hermeneutical Work of John Oecolampadius, Huldrych Zwingli, and John Calvin," in vol. 2 of *Hebrew Bible / Old Testament: The History of Its Interpretation*, ed. Magne Sæbø (Göttingen: Vandenhoeck & Ruprecht, 2008), 429–34, 441.

[65] Bruce Gordon, "The Bible in Reformed Thought, 1520–1750," in *The New Cambridge History of the Bible*, vol. 3, *From 1450 to 1750*, ed. Euan Cameron (Cambridge, UK: Cambridge University Press, 2016), 462, 464, 467, 473.

Father."[66] Of course, this "christoscopic" focus clearly fits well within the general Christian practice of reading the Old Testament through the New and may have been more recently inspired, as Jeff Fisher has argued, by Oecolampadius.[67] Significantly, for Calvin (as for Luther and Melanchthon), Paul functions as the lodestar for Calvin's method of Christ-focused reading. In the Argumentum prefacing his Romans commentary, Calvin echoes the Wittenberg view that this New Testament writing in particular provides the entrance to all of scripture.[68] In his comments on 2 Corinthians 3:16, Calvin writes: "Moreover, what is said of the law applies to all scripture— that where it is not directed to Christ as its one aim, it is twisted and per- verted."[69] John the evangelist also articulated for Calvin this key purpose. In his comments on John 5:39, in which Jesus urges his audience to search for him in the scriptures, Calvin notes: "we ought to read the scriptures that we might find Christ in them."[70] Yet Calvin's way of arriving at this common goal was somewhat different from both the Lutheran and—as will be discussed shortly—other Reformed patterns. For Luther and Melanchthon, the the- ological and dialectical distinction between law and gospel (derived from Paul) provided the fundamental method for finding Christ, particularly in the Old Testament. Though Calvin embraced law/gospel as a theological dis- tinction, he did not employ this as an exegetical principle in the same way. And though he often followed Melanchthon's theological and exegetical lead (as chapters 2 and 3 of this book will demonstrate), his approach to finding Christ in the scriptures used the tools of history and rhetoric differently to unlock this meaning. Moreover, as Sujin Pak has shown, Calvin uncovers in

---

[66] CO 9: 815; English in John Calvin, *Calvin: Commentaries*, ed. Joseph Hartounian (Philadelphia: Westminster, 1958), 70. The 1535 French preface to the Olivétan's New Testament has been widely attributed to Calvin, but Van Stam recently argued that it was the work of Olivétan him- self. Frans Pieter Van Stam, "Der Autor des Vorworts zur Olivetan-Bibel *A tous amateurs* aus dem Jahr 1535," *Nederlands archief voor kerkgeschiedenis / Dutch Review of Church History* 84 (2004): 248– 67. The passage quoted here, however, appears first in a revised version of the preface that appeared both as a separate treatise under Calvin's name in 1543 and in later French Bibles published in Geneva: John Calvin and Pierre Viret, *Deux epistres: L'une demonstre comment Jesus Christ est la fin de la loy; l'autre pour consoler les fideles qui souffrent persecution* [Geneva]: [J. Girard], 1543; see Irena Backus and Claire Chimelli, ed., *"La vraie piété": Divers traités de Jean Calvin et Confession de foi de Guillaume Farel* (Geneva: Labor et Fides, 1986), 18–24.

[67] Jeff Fisher, *A Christoscopic Reading of Scripture: Johannes Oecolampadius on Hebrews* (Göttingen: Vandenhoeck & Ruprecht, 2016), 68–70. B. A. Gerrish also notes this echoes Erasmus; B. A. Gerrish, "The Word of God and the Words of Scripture: Luther and Calvin on Biblical Authority," in *The Old Protestantism and the New: Essays on the Reformation Heritage* (Edinburgh: T. & T. Clark, 1982), 298n61.

[68] OE 13: 7 = CO 49: 1.

[69] OE 15: 63–64 = CO 50: 45. This sentence was added in 1556, but Calvin expresses the idea that Christ is the end of the law throughout the earlier comments that appeared in 1548.

[70] OE 11/1: 180 = CO 47: 125.

his reading of the Psalms and the prophets different christological content than that discovered by Lutheran interpreters.[71]

In addition to the goal of knowing Christ, the view that the Bible is the word of God is a further assumption pertaining to the unity of scripture that Calvin derives from Paul and that he also shares with the broader precritical Christian tradition. Even though Calvin places special emphasis on the mind of the human author, he maintains that the Holy Spirit not only inspired the biblical witnesses but also guides interpreters to grasp their intentions. In his comments on 2 Timothy 3:16 (which he naturally takes to be a Pauline text), Calvin remarks: "we are certain that the [Old Testament] prophets did not just speak from their own understanding, but as instruments of the Holy Spirit, they uttered only what they had been told to say from heaven."[72] As Bruce Gordon has argued, Calvin is not articulating here the strong doctrine of verbal inspiration that would emerge in the seventeenth century and downplay the role of the human authors.[73] Rather, for Calvin what makes the historically conditioned words of the biblical writers relevant both in and beyond their own time and place is this divine oversight and guidance. This applies not just to the Old Testament writings, which he acknowledges are the subjects of John 5:39 and 2 Timothy 3:16, but to the New Testament scriptures as well. B. A. Gerrish has argued that Calvin did not quite adopt the new element in Luther's view of biblical authority and continued to work with it as medieval interpreters did as a formal and external authority—as a deposit of heavenly doctrine. Yet he points out that for Calvin, too, what gave scripture its unity in addition to its authority was not just what it contained (Christ) but what it, through the work of the Spirit, did to edify and strengthen faith in him.[74]

What is distinctive about Calvin's understanding of the unity of scripture rests not on the goal or his assumptions about divine authorship, but on how history and historical consciousness aid him in determining and delineating what is to be grasped about Christ and his pursuit of it in his exegesis. Commenting on Paul's use of the example of Abraham in Romans 4:23, Calvin refers to an oft-cited dictum from the Roman orator Cicero

---

[71] Pak, *Judaizing Calvin*, 77–101; G. Sujin Pak, *The Reformation of Prophecy: Early Modern Interpretations of the Prophet and Old Testament Prophecy* (New York: Oxford University Press, 2018), 234–36; see also Opitz, "Exegetical and Hermeneutical Work," 448–51.

[72] CO 52: 383.

[73] Gordon, "Bible in Reformed Thought," 462, 473, 480, 485; see also Cameron, "Bible and the Early Modern Sense of History," 663.

[74] Gerrish, "Word of God," 61–68.

(106 BCE–43 CE) concerning the character and value of the past: "The pagan writers have truly said that history is the teacher of life." He adds, however, that "no one makes sound progress in [history] as it is handed down to us by them: scripture alone claims for itself this kind of teaching office."[75] For Calvin, scripture prescribes the general rules for deriving meaning from the past by testing all other history; distinguishes which actions should be followed from those to be avoided; and, uniquely, shows God's providential care of the righteous and the judgment of the wicked. The chapters to come will demonstrate how this doctrine of providence—God's active superintendence over all events—underlies Calvin's understanding of scriptural unity and decisively shapes his strategies for unearthing the lessons of the biblical past for later times.

Calvin balanced his theological embrace of the Lutheran dialectic of law and gospel with a Reformed emphasis on a single divine covenant spanning the history before and after the incarnation and both the Old and New Testaments. In this, he followed in the footsteps of interpreters like Bucer, Zwingli, Oecolampadius, and Bullinger in stressing the continuity of God's covenant of grace and one church of Christ through the ages, distinguishing between two different dispensations that accounted for the different religious practices and the shadowy versus clear proclamation of Christ.[76] Of course, the general idea of continuity between Old and New Testament was by no means novel, and even the Lutheran approach with its sharp distinction found both law and gospel in both testaments. What was new in the Reformed approach was a deeper appreciation for the historical processes and distinctive conditions—and even the remoteness—of the biblical past. Euan Cameron has argued that the Swiss Reformed in particular found that "the *covenant* or covenants made by God with the people provided frameworks for understanding the flow of time."[77]

This understanding of time and its processes led to a deeper appreciation of the historical details referenced in and underlying the biblical text, especially, as Sujin Pak has shown, with respect to the sacred history portrayed by the Old Testament prophets.[78] Pak demonstrates that in treatments of Old Testament prophecies, Luther tends to separate out and distinguish

---

[75] OE 13: 98 = CO 49: 86.
[76] Calvin's mature discussion of the issue is in *Institutes* (1559), 2.10–11. See Puckett, *John Calvin's Exegesis*, 37–45; Opitz, "Exegetical and Hermeneutical Work," 434–38.
[77] Cameron, "Bible and the Early Modern Sense of History," 672.
[78] Pak, *Reformation of Prophecy*, 214–54.

the prophets' words relevant only to the time of their own contemporaries from those that are related to the history of Christ. Oecolampadius, Zwingli, and Bullinger, however, downplayed this stark contrast and showed a willingness to identify many of the prophecies as having been fulfilled on various levels: historically in the prophets' times; in Christ's person; and in the church through the analogy of head and members. This, of course, is a prime example of how interpreters infused what they considered the literal sense with multiple layers of meaning. These Swiss Reformed interpreters were interested in drawing analogies from the prophets' time for the present church, but "they were less concerned with the intention of the original author and more concerned about what this history conveyed about the single, eternal covenant of God."[79]

Pak finds that Calvin was even more concerned than his Reformed colleagues with the original biblical prophets' intention and his times, and that he places their emphasis on the divine covenant in service of God's providence: "for Calvin the providential shape of history came immediately to the forefront: sacred history is a concrete historical account of God's providential care of the church across time, in which the saving historical events of Christ's life are the crucial centerpiece but do not constitute the whole."[80] In other words, for Calvin, the unity of scripture and the covenant in Christ to which it bears witness are grounded in God's providence. The providentially guided events themselves and their divinely inspired and intended narrations in scripture are for Calvin signs of God's guidance of human history and his unremitting care for and salvation of the covenant people through changing times.

It is this particular feature of the divine nature and activity that unifies not only the scriptural witness but all of human history and undergirds Calvin's attention to original historical context, which he pursues not simply for the sake of the past itself but in order to determine how God's actions in the past can best be related to the present. Calvin's historical sensitivities thus include also an understanding of the current historical situation, and he has several related strategies that he uses to link the past meanings to the present day. Sometimes he recognizes elements of the scriptural past as typologies, according to which the reality of the past is not diminished but rather expanded and extended when it functions also as a prophecy of some future

---

[79] Pak, *Reformation of Prophecy*, 237.
[80] Pak, *Reformation of Prophecy*, 235.

fulfillment—e.g., David's temporal kingdom as a foreshadowing of Christ's spiritual kingdom; David himself as representing Christ; ceremonial aspects of Mosaic religion that prefigure the new dispensation. Calvin also appeals to a principle of similarity between times in the past and the present situation. In such cases, the interpreter can make an application of an earlier event—such as an experience of persecution or exile—through an analogy or anagogy. In all these cases, whether the future application would have been known by the original speaker (in the case of, for example, a prophet extending his own meaning by speaking simultaneously of present and future redemption) or whether the connection between past and present is drawn by the exegete through the guidance of the Holy Spirit, Calvin often invokes the image of the mirror to talk about how his contemporary readers and auditors can find in sacred history an instructive, edifying, and consoling reflection of their own experience.

Overview of This Book

The remaining chapters in this book form a set of connected case studies, each investigating Calvin's interpretation of a single biblical book or author with an eye to one or more of the particular exegetical, intellectual, or cultural contexts outlined above. This approach builds on and complements the work of those who, like David Puckett, have treated Calvin's historicizing approach to the Old Testament synthetically, and those who, like Sujin Pak and Euan Cameron, have focused on Calvin's treatment of particular books (the Psalms) or genres (prophecy).[81] In contrast, this book analyzes Calvin's historicizing exegesis with regard to both Old and New Testament material. By combining in one volume individual studies of Calvin's treatment of particular biblical writings and figures, it illuminates the subtle and sometimes stark variations in Calvin's approach to different subjects—thus demonstrating the breadth and complexity of his historical sensitivities. Some of the chapters explore Calvin's distinctive approaches, emphases, and findings in light of traditional and contemporary exegetical traditions, and others place them in the context of broader cultural trends and current

---

[81] Puckett, *John Calvin's Exegesis*; Pak, *Judaizing Calvin*; Pak, *Reformation of Prophecy*; Euan Cameron, "Calvin the Historian: Biblical Antiquity and Scriptural Exegesis in the Quest for a Meaningful Past," in *Calvin and the Book: The Evolution of the Printed Word in Reformed Protestantism*, ed. Karen E. Spierling (Göttingen: Vandenhoeck & Ruprecht, 2015), 77–94.

historical developments. Moreover, each chapter foregrounds an especially intriguing aspect of Calvin's historicizing engagement with that particular book or figure, as in every case he aims to uncover the biblical past and its relevance for the present. In many cases, but not all, Calvin's treatment is explicitly or implicitly compared to that of traditional or contemporary figures whose work provides context to bring Calvin's historicizing approach to the fore. Tracing the multifaceted character and expansive impact of his sense of history on his reading of the Bible, these studies situate Calvin's biblical exegesis and broader engagement with scripture among the efforts to identify a meaningful past manifest in the writings of Renaissance humanists, early modern historical theorists, and religious reformers across the confessional spectrum.

The order is for the most part chronological, beginning with the sections of the Bible on which Calvin published first (Paul and the Gospel of John) and progressing to his commentaries, lectures, and sermons on parts of the Old Testament, which engaged him especially in the last decade of his life. This is in part because as a Christian exegete, Calvin reads the Old Testament in light of the New, and Paul's theology in particular functions as a lens for Calvin's reading of other biblical material. At the same time, however, Calvin understands Paul and John not only as teachers of universal doctrine but as historical human beings who laid the foundations of the church for their own age, and he subjects their messages and examples to his contextualizing treatment. Moreover, when Calvin turns to the Old Testament, he does not harmonize the Old Testament material with the New in predictable ways. Instead, Calvin shows deep appreciation for the integrity of the biblical past and recovers for his own time a message that balances the intentions of the divinely inspired human authors writing in their own contexts with the needs of believers living in the present age.

Chapter 2, "History Past and History Present in Calvin's Reception of Paul," takes up Calvin's central biblical authority, the apostle Paul. Because of Paul's significance for the entirety of Calvin's reforming program, this chapter broadens the focus from Calvin's exegesis to his wider engagement with the apostle in order to determine the character of Calvin's "Paulinism." The investigation proceeds from Calvin's reception of Paul in his biblical exegesis (with an example from his treatment of Galatians 2), to the role of Paul in his reformation agenda (viewed through the program outlined in his 1543 treatise *Supplex exhortatio*), and finally to the ways in which he can be considered a "Pauline" theologian (in the development of the *Institutes*). On the foundation of a historically informed engagement with Paul, Calvin built a distinctive program of biblical exegesis, established a reformed church in Geneva, and developed a systematic theology that constituted the only serious rival to that of his mentor in Pauline studies, Philip Melanchthon.

Chapter 3, "Salvation in History in Calvin's Commentary on the Gospel of John," examines Calvin's interpretation of the Fourth Gospel and its place in the history of Johannine interpretation through detailed comparison with previous and contemporary exegetical traditions. Calvin's commentary, written at a particularly contentious period in his Genevan career and published in 1553, represents the culmination of a novelty found in some sixteenth-century evangelical approaches to the Gospel traditionally held as the most spiritual. This new orientation, which was introduced by Luther and Melanchthon, redefined the Gospel's spiritual character and reversed traditional views that John offered advanced and more difficult teaching than Matthew, Mark, and Luke. In his commentary, as with his treatment of the Psalms and Isaiah, Calvin downplays the traditional emphasis among Christian exegetes on christological doctrine and does not view teaching Christ's divinity as the Gospel's central purpose. Instead, he emphasizes the overarching theme of human salvation in history. John, for Calvin, provides not a deeper grasp of Christ's person but rather a more complete portrayal of his historic salvific mission, emphasizing what Christ as incarnate mediator does for humans more than who he is.

Chapter 4, "David, Faith, and the Confusion of History in Calvin's Commentary on the Psalms," considers Calvin's portrayal of the psalmist David as a paradigm for the faith of sixteenth-century Christians and illuminates a development in his doctrine of faith that his commentary on the Psalms (1557) makes especially clear. In contrast to most of the earlier exegetical tradition, Calvin focuses on the historical person, David, and downplays David's prophetic status. In order to retrieve David's example for his own day, Calvin takes a restrained view of traditional messianic interpretations of the psalms and posits a similarity between David's situation and the present that acknowledges but also bridges the vast historical distance—and the two dispensations of the covenant. Questions concerning the visibility or knowability of divine providence and the possibility of faith despite the apparent confusion of history unite past and present in Calvin's treatment.

Chapter 5, "Exile in the Mirror of History in Calvin's Commentary on Isaiah," turns to one of Calvin's favorite prophetic books, Isaiah—a book which he interpreted orally at least three times. In his 1559 commentary, this refugee pastor ventures a largely ecclesiological rather than a christological reading of this book, written at a time when Geneva experienced a large influx of religious exiles (1556–1559). For Calvin, the majority of Isaiah's prophecies reference in the first instance the experience of the people of ancient Israel and their future return from Babylon. This history from the time of Isaiah then becomes a mirror for the contemporary historical experience of exile. Calvin explores the true church throughout the ages as a refugee community, literally and metaphorically. The image of the past as mirror—common in Calvin's other exegetical works—is here particularly well-developed to maintain the integrity of the people of Israel's history and allow sixteenth-century Christians to make sense of their own experience and to foster trust in divine providence for the restoration of the church.[82] The theme of exile and the fact of Calvin's own prophetic self-awareness are so powerful that Calvin in this commentary evidences less concern with historical anachronism than he does, for example, in his lectures on Daniel (discussed in chapter 6) or in his *Mosaic Harmony* (discussed in chapter 7).

Chapter 6, "Prophecy and History in Calvin's Lectures on Daniel," investigates Calvin's singular treatment of this book in lectures held in the new Genevan Academy from 1559 to 1560 and published in 1561. As with his engagement with David in his Psalms commentary and the prophet Isaiah in his Isaiah commentary, Calvin sees clear analogies between the situations facing Daniel and his companions during the Babylonian Exile and Reformed Christians in the sixteenth century; however, he relates these two situations in a surprising and unprecedented way that evidences an unusually strong sense of historical anachronism. Although he derives moral lessons from Daniel's behavior, Calvin pursues a predominantly prophetic-historical rather than a moral exegesis of this book. He limits the scope of Daniel's prophecies to Christ's first advent—that is, to historically past events. Unlike many of his contemporaries, he did not view the book of Daniel as an eschatological handbook for the end times, and he has been credited with inaugurating a critical shift in the history of Danielic interpretation. For Calvin, the proper interpretation of Danielic prophecies involves understanding and explaining their significance in their original, past context. Analogies to later times are possible not because they are inherent in the prophet's original message, but because of the connectedness of historical events under divine providence. Only in this way can people living in later periods in history

[82] For other examples of Calvin's use of mirror, see Pak, *Reformation of Prophecy*, 231–32.

recognize the similarities of their own situation to the biblical ones and find meaning in events long past.

Chapter 7, "Biblical Exegesis and Early Modern Legal History in Calvin's Mosaic Harmony," examines Calvin's commentary on Exodus through Deuteronomy (1563) through the lens of sixteenth-century historical jurisprudence, exemplified in the works of Calvin's contemporaries François de Connan and François Baudouin, whose own projects help illuminate the purpose and extraordinary form of Calvin's commentary. As discussed earlier in this chapter, recent scholarship has demonstrated how Calvin's historicizing exegesis is in continuity with broader previous and contemporary trends in Christian biblical interpretation; chapter 7 explores another, and biographically prior, context for Calvin's approach to the Bible. The intermingling of narrative and legal material in the last four books of the Pentateuch inspired Calvin to break with his customary practice of *lectio continua* and apply his historical hermeneutic more broadly and creatively to explain the Mosaic histories and legislation. Calvin's unprecedented arrangement of the material in this commentary and his attention to the relationship between law and history reveal his engagement with his generation's quest for historical method.

Chapter 8, "The Consolation of History in Calvin's Sermons on Second Samuel," shifts the venue from the scholar's study or lecture hall to the preacher's pulpit. As civil war, divided along confessional lines, erupted in France in the spring of 1562, Calvin began a series of eighty-seven sermons on Second Samuel—a biblical book that details Israel's own civil wars under David. These sermons offer an important resource for exploring the ideals, mindsets, and emotions that Calvin sought to evoke among his listeners as he sought to shape the response of ordinary Genevans to unfolding events by appealing to biblical history to illuminate the present. Calvin the preacher instructs his listeners how to learn from scripture and distinguish elements of perpetual significance from anachronisms relevant only to the history of Israel. He presents biblical history as a unique record of the past that, unlike profane history, can relate to subsequent ages through a version of typology that enables scripture to speak to the present situation through its chronicle of past events. Critically, Calvin urges his listeners to compare the events depicted in 2 Samuel to their own experience. This historical vision, in which biblical history becomes a living and lived lesson, was not only a key spiritual weapon for those in Calvin's Genevan congregation. As comparison with a small tract written by François Hotman during the third civil war in the late

1560s shows, Hotman—Calvin's colleague in reform and theorist of legal history—also sought and found the consolation of the Holy Spirit through the avenue of the sacred history of the Old Testament, viewed afresh from the experience of present wartime affliction. For both Reformed thinkers, the biblical past and the experience of war combined to forge a key spiritual weapon: a historical vision of the present tied into divine providence throughout the ages.

2

History Past and History Present
in Calvin's Reception of Paul

Introduction

In the dedication that prefaced his first work of biblical commentary, a commentary on Paul's epistle to the Romans published in 1540, John Calvin echoed a growing sentiment among certain of his contemporaries about the unique significance of this book of the Bible: "if anyone understands [Romans], he will have entrance thrown open for himself to the understanding of all of scripture."[1] Paul's letter, for Calvin, provides the key that unlocks the meaning of the Old and New Testament. However, the inhabitants of Lystra were mistaken to call Paul "Hermes" (Acts 14:12), and Romans' hermeneutical function—crucial as it is—is but one piece in the puzzle that is Calvin's reception of Paul. More than any other biblical writer or figure, Paul shaped Calvin's work not only as a biblical scholar but also as a reformer of the church and a theologian. Calvin gave priority to the Pauline epistles in his exegetical program and also viewed all of scripture through a Pauline lens; he drew upon Paul to delineate the deficiencies he perceived in the state of the church and to structure its reform; finally, themes derived from Paul provided the center and organizing principles of Calvin's theological vision. In light of this, the question is—to draw upon the title of an essay by Karlfried Froehlich—"which Paul" exercised such a pervasive influence on Calvin?[2] And how, moreover, did Calvin's historical consciousness

---

[1] John Calvin, *Commentarii in epistolam Pauli ad Romanos* (Strasbourg: W. Rihel, 1540), OE 13: 4 = CO 10/2: 403; English translation as John Calvin, *Commentary on the Epistle of Paul to the Romans*, ed. and trans. John Owen, repr. in *Calvin's Commentaries* (Grand Rapids, MI: Baker Books, 1989), xxiv; hereafter *Commentary on Romans*. Martin Bucer also attributes to Romans the function of hermeneutical key. See Alexandre Ganoczy, "Calvin als paulinischer Theologe: Ein Forschungsansatz zur Hermeneutik Calvins," in *Calvinus Theologus*, ed. Wilhelm H. Neuser (Neukirchen: Neukirchener Verlag, 1976), 46.
[2] Karlfried Froehlich, "Which Paul? Observations on the Image of the Apostle in the History of Biblical Exegesis," in *New Perspectives on Historical Theology: Essays in Memory of John Meyendorff*, ed. Bradley Nassif (Grand Rapids, MI: Eerdmans, 1996), 279–99.

Calvin, the Bible, and History. Barbara Pitkin, Oxford University Press (2020). © Oxford University Press.
DOI: 10.1093/oso/9780190093273.001.0001

shape his engagement with the apostle as a past leader of the church and a proclaimer of universal doctrine? To answer these questions and determine the character of Calvin's Paulinism, we must consider first the sources for Calvin's attraction to and approach to Paul. Afterward this chapter will examine Calvin's historically informed reception of Paul in his biblical exegesis, the role of Paul in his reformation agenda, and, finally, the ways in which Calvin can be considered a "Pauline theologian."

Calvin's Access to Paul

Of course, Calvin's esteem for Paul was not new; he stands in a long line of admirers in a debate over the interpretation and authority of Paul that goes back to Christianity's earliest days. In the sixteenth century those discussions received renewed impetus in the West through the rediscovery of the Greek Paul, easier access to his writings, and debates over the nature of salvation, in which Paul's writings played an important role. In his appropriation of Paul, Calvin trod paths first laid out by his humanist and evangelical predecessors. As noted in chapter 1, his own educational background prepared him for just this approach.[3]

Reflecting his humanist orientation, Calvin's primary access to Paul was directly through the writings of the New Testament, which he read in recent Greek editions.[4] He engaged Paul as the author of thirteen letters and as a subject in Acts in a variety of formats: in biblical commentaries, extemporaneously delivered sermons, and academic lectures.[5] He also discussed

---

[3] See also Alexandre Ganoczy, *The Young Calvin*, trans. David Foxgrover and Wade Provo (Philadelphia: Westminster John Knox, 1987).

[4] For discussions of which Greek editions and Latin translations Calvin used, see T. H. L. Parker, *Calvin's New Testament Commentaries*, 2nd edition (Louisville, KY: Westminster John Knox, 1993), 123–91; R. Ward Holder, "Calvin as Commentator on the Pauline Epistles," in *Calvin and the Bible*, ed. Donald K. McKim (Cambridge, UK: Cambridge University Press, 2006), 239–40. In his comments on Eph. 4:12, Calvin invites his readers to compare his translation with that of Erasmus and the Vulgate: [*Commentarii in epistolam Pauli ad Ephesios*], in John Calvin, *Commentarii in quatuor Pauli epistolas: ad Galatas, ad Ephesios, ad Philippenses, ad Colossenses* (Geneva: J. Girard, 1548), OE 16: 231–32 = CO 51: 198–99; English translation as John Calvin, *Commentaries on the Epistle of Paul to the Ephesians*, ed. and trans. William Pringle, repr. in *Calvin's Commentaries* (Grand Rapids, MI: Baker Books, 1989), 281; hereafter *Commentary on Ephesians*.

[5] Calvin thinks that Paul wrote other letters that are not in the biblical canon, as he maintains in his comments on Eph. 3:4 (OE 16: 202 = CO 51: 178; *Commentary on Ephesians*, 249). He is also aware of extra-canonical writings about Paul, and in the introduction to his commentary on Acts he mentions (and dismisses) the Acts of Peter and Paul: John Calvin, *Commentariorum in Acta Apostolorum liber I* (Geneva: J. Crespin, 1552), OE 12/1: 13 = CO 48: ix; English translation as John Calvin, *Commentary on the Acts of the Apostles*, 2 vols., ed. Henry Beveridge and trans. Christopher Fetherstone, repr. in

Pauline texts as a participant in the weekly Bible study discussions known in Geneva as *congrégations*. These four types of biblical exposition shared similar exegetical and hermeneutical strategies that reflected a humanist approach to interpretation. Significantly for the present topic, it was through application of these humanistic methods that Calvin judged that Hebrews was not written by Paul.[6] First, with very few exceptions, Calvin's commentaries, sermons, and lectures as well as the *congrégations* all pursued a continuous, verse-by-verse unfolding of the text. Second, all aimed at lucid and brief explanation of the mind of the biblical author, in this case, the apostle Paul, by focusing the analysis on his argument and main concerns. The expositions in the commentaries were understandably shorter than in the sermons, which were delivered orally in French. Third, all exhibited sensitivity to history, philology, and rhetoric in reconstructing the meaning of the text. In general, the commentaries and lectures—intended for pastors and future pastors—focused more on philological matters and explaining the historical circumstances of the original events described in the text; in contrast, the sermons—addressed to ordinary Genevans—spent more time relating the lessons of the passage to the present day, while still attending to the rhetorical presentation of the biblical writer.[7] Nevertheless, and finally, all sought to some degree to instruct and edify believers by applying the lessons of the passage to the church of Calvin's day.

Although the scope of their influence is frequently difficult to detect, the exegetical and theological traditions of the church and their images of Paul also shaped Calvin's appropriation of his person and message. Calvin was familiar with commentaries by the church fathers and his contemporaries and utilized other exegetical aids, but his references to others' views in the course of his own comments are infrequent and usually anonymous. The fact that Calvin did not frequently name a particular interpreter does not mean that Calvin's reading was not shaped by him; alternatively, the fact that Calvin

Calvin's Commentaries (Grand Rapids, MI: Baker Books, 1989), 1: xxix; hereafter *Commentary on Acts*, followed by volume and page number.

[6] See Parker, *Calvin's New Testament Commentaries*, 114; John Calvin, *Commentarii in epistolam ad Hebraeos* (Geneva: J. Girard, 1549), OE 19: 11–12 = CO 55: 5–6; English translation as John Calvin, *Commentaries on the Epistle of Paul* [sic] *the Apostle to the Hebrews*, ed. and trans. John Owen, repr. in *Calvin's Commentaries* (Grand Rapids, MI: Baker Books, 1989), xxvi–xxvii; hereafter *Commentary on Hebrews*.

[7] For a comparison of Calvin's commentary and sermons on Ephesians, see Randall C. Zachman, *John Calvin as Teacher, Pastor, and Theologian: The Shape of His Writings and Thought* (Grand Rapids, MI: Baker, 2006), 147–72.

does cite a particular source does not mean that he had actually consulted it in preparing his exposition.[8] Despite the complexity of this picture, several significant exegetical works shaping Calvin's appropriation of Paul can be identified: the homilies of John Chrysostom (ca. 349–407), the editions and annotations of the epistles by Erasmus (1466–1536), and the commentaries on Romans by Martin Bucer (1491–1551), Heinrich Bullinger (1504–1575), and Philip Melanchthon (1497–1560).[9] Beyond these exegetical models, Calvin's reading of Paul was shaped by decidedly Augustinian and evangelical theological sensibilities, which he frequently contrasts to ideas he attributes to Jerome (ca. 347–420), Origen (ca. 184–253), and those he identifies as present-day "papists." In regard to the shape of Calvin's evangelicalism, one should not underestimate the role of Melanchthon's *Loci communes*, which had its origins in his own interpretation of Romans and which was a text that Calvin knew in several of its editions.

Calvin and the Biblical Paul

Calvin's extended engagement with the biblical Paul in his lectures, sermons, and commentaries on scripture constitutes the point of departure for investigation into the character of his reception of Paul. This section will discuss the prominence of Paul in Calvin's exegetical program and sketch a portrait

[8] For discussion of Calvin's use of tradition, see Anthony N. S. Lane, *John Calvin: Student of the Church Fathers* (Edinburgh: T. & T. Clark, 1999); Johannes van Oort, "John Calvin and the Church Fathers," in *The Reception of the Church Fathers in the West: From the Carolingians to the Maurists*, ed. Irena Backus (Leiden: Brill, 1997), 2: 661–700.

[9] For insights into the relationship of Calvin's exegesis of Paul to that of these predecessors, see John Walchenbach, "John Calvin as Biblical Commentator: An Investigation into Calvin's Use of John Chrysostom as an Exegetical Tutor" (Ph.D. diss., University of Pittsburgh, 1974); M. de Kroon, "Bucer und Calvin: Das Obrigkeitsverständnis beider Reformatoren nach ihrer Auslegung von Römer 13," in *Calvinus servus Christi*, ed. Wilhelm H. Neuser (Budapest: Presseabteilung des Ráday Kollegiums, 1988), 209–24; David C. Steinmetz, *Calvin in Context*, 2nd edition (New York: Oxford University Press, 2010), 23–39, 108–54, 197–206, 262–77; Joel E. Kok, "The Influence of Martin Bucer on John Calvin's Interpretation of Romans: A Comparative Case Study" (Ph.D. diss., Duke University, 1993); Joel E. Kok, "Heinrich Bullinger's Exegetical Method: The Model for Calvin?" in *Biblical Interpretation in the Era of the Reformation: Essays Presented to David C. Steinmetz in Honor of His Sixtieth Birthday*, ed. Richard A. Muller and John L. Thompson (Grand Rapids, MI: Eerdmans, 1996), 241–54; Richard A. Muller, "'Scimus enim quod lex spiritualis est': Melanchthon and Calvin on the Interpretation of Romans 7.14–23," in *Philip Melanchthon (1497–1560) and the Commentary*, ed. Timothy J. Wengert and M. Patrick Graham (Sheffield, UK: Sheffield Academic Press, 1997), 216–37; on Erasmus, see Parker, *Calvin's New Testament Commentaries*, 147–50, 164–84; Kirk Essary, *Erasmus and Calvin on the Foolishness of God: Reason and Emotion in the Christian Philosophy* (Toronto: University of Toronto Press, 2017).

of the apostle drawn from Calvin's exegesis of Galatians 2, with references to other key texts.

Biblical interpretation was a central aspect of Calvin's career from start to finish, and within the broad range of his exegetical activity the figure of Paul held a singular position.[10] When Calvin arrived in Geneva, his first duties were lecturing on scripture, and his first lectures were on Paul, presumably on Romans. It is likely that he also began preaching on Paul's letters, particularly Romans, at this time.[11] After being banished from Geneva in 1538, he settled in Strasbourg, where he lectured on the Gospel of John and 1 Corinthians and was probably preaching on Paul's epistles or John.[12] Little is known about the subject of his sermons or lectures in the 1540s; a short exposition of Jude (1542) published in French is assumed to have its origin in his lectures or sermons. Elsie McKee suggests that between 1542 and 1549, Calvin preached through the Gospel of John, Hebrews, and occasionally one of the Psalms on Sundays, and on Genesis, Isaiah, and Jeremiah on the weekdays.[13] However, it is likely that Calvin continued to lecture on Paul's epistles, laying the foundation for a series of commentaries. It appears that Paul's epistles were also the subject of the *congrégations* in the 1540s.[14]

The publishing history of Calvin's commentaries reveals with exceptional clarity the precedence of Paul over all other biblical writers and figures. Calvin's very first biblical commentary, published while he was in Strasbourg, was a Latin commentary on Romans. Within a few years of returning to Geneva in 1541, Calvin resumed his program of commenting on all the Pauline epistles and published his second commentary, on 1 Corinthians (1546). This he followed in short order with commentaries on 2 Corinthians (1548); Galatians, Ephesians, Philippians, Colossians (1548); 1 and 2 Timothy (1548); Titus (1550); 1 Thessalonians (1550); 2 Thessalonians (1550); and Philemon (1551).[15] In 1551, all of these commentaries appeared

---

[10] For more details concerning Calvin's commentaries, sermons, and lectures on the Pauline epistles and Acts, see Parker, *Calvin's New Testament Commentaries*, 6–36; Wulfert de Greef, *The Writings of John Calvin, Expanded Edition: An Introductory Guide*, trans. Lyle D. Bierma (Louisville, KY: Westminster John Knox, 2008), 75–82, 98–100; Holder, "Calvin as Commentator on the Pauline Epistles," 226–32.

[11] Elsie Anne McKee, *The Pastoral Ministry and Worship in Calvin's Geneva* (Geneva: Droz, 2016), 482.

[12] McKee, *Pastoral Ministry and Worship*, 483.

[13] McKee, *Pastoral Ministry and Worship*, 483–91.

[14] See the introduction to Jean Calvin, *Deux congrégations et exposition du catéchisme*, ed. Rodolphe Peter (Paris: Presses Universitaires de France, 1964), xi–xii, xv–xvi.

[15] Dates refer to the publication of the first Latin edition, as given in BC 1. The commentaries were also published in French translation.

in a single volume along with Calvin's 1549 commentary on Hebrews—a text Calvin did not think was written by Paul. Notably, Calvin revised and expanded his comments on Romans for this collected edition and again, more briefly, for a new edition of the entire set in 1556.

About the time that Calvin was beginning to finish up commentaries on the Pauline letters, he began a preaching cycle that brought him back to the apostle. On Sundays from 1549 to 1554 Calvin preached on Acts. These sermons were the first to be recorded by a paid stenographer, Denis Raguenier, and transcribed with the help of a team of assistants.[16] Simultaneously, Calvin began writing his commentary on Acts, which appeared in two parts in 1552 and 1554.[17] Having finished Acts, Calvin apparently was not done with Paul, but rather preached on Sundays from March 1554 until the summer of 1559 on 1 and 2 Thessalonians, 1 and 2 Timothy, Titus, 1 and 2 Corinthians, Galatians, and Ephesians.[18] At the end of his life, Calvin was still dealing with Paul; he presented at least twice on Galatians in the weekly *congrégations* in late 1562 or early 1563.[19]

Thus, Paul's presence looms large in Calvin's exegetical work; however, he did not receive Calvin's exclusive attention. As mentioned earlier, Calvin published a commentary on Hebrews in 1549; around the time he was finishing his commentaries on the Pauline corpus, he also commented on most of the canonical epistles (James, 1 and 2 Peter, 1 John, and Jude), which likewise appeared in a single volume in 1551.[20] Furthermore, our knowledge of the details of Calvin's exegetical activity beyond the commentary genre is much more complete beginning in 1549, and a snapshot from 1550 indicates that the range of biblical texts simultaneously engaging Calvin's attention was broader yet. During that year, Calvin was not only finishing his commentaries on Paul and the canonical epistles and preaching and commenting on Acts, but he was also preaching on the Psalms on Sunday afternoons and on Lamentations and then on Micah during the weekday sermons every other

---

[16] Only the sermons on Acts 1–7 survive; for a reconstruction of Calvin's preaching cycle, see McKee, *Pastoral Ministry and Worship*, 464–91. On the transcription of Calvin's sermons and the loss of a number of these manuscripts, see T. H. L. Parker, *Calvin's Preaching* (Louisville, KY: Westminster John Knox, 1992), 65–75.

[17] On Calvin's interpretation of Acts, see Wilhelmus H. Th. Moehn, "Calvin as Commentator on the Acts of the Apostles," in *Calvin and the Bible*, ed. McKim, 199–223; Stefan Scheld, "Die missionarische Verkündigung des Paulus in Calvins Kommentar der Apostelgeschichte," in *Creatio ex amore: Beiträge zu einer Theologie der Liebe*, ed. Thomas Frank, Markus Knapp, and Johannes Schmid (Würzburg: Echter, 1989), 312–28.

[18] De Greef, *Writings of John Calvin*, 95–100; Parker, *Calvin's Preaching*, 51–64.

[19] These were published in 1563; modern edition in Calvin, *Deux congrégations*, 1–31.

[20] The commentary on James appeared in French as a kind of "avant-première" in 1550; BC 1: 50/2.

week; lecturing on Isaiah and then Genesis in the school and trying to write a commentary on the latter; and, finally, discussing the Gospel of John in the *congrégations*. One reason that the commentary on Acts appeared in two parts was because Calvin broke off his work in 1552 in order to write a commentary on John, which appeared in 1553.

This wide-ranging involvement with scripture does not diminish but rather heightens the prominence of Paul in Calvin's exegetical program. Among the many biblical texts upon which Calvin commented, lectured, and preached, the Pauline texts were not only the first to receive his attention, but they were also the place where he, as Ward Holder has shown, "honed his craft" as a biblical commentator.[21] Furthermore, Calvin's exegetical engagement with Paul was continuous over more than twenty years, from 1536 to 1559; indeed, he was still commenting on Pauline texts in 1563. Apparently Calvin thought that the church could never stop learning from Paul, whose writings and person constitute the red thread guiding a lifetime of scriptural interpretation.

We can now take up the question of which image of Paul emerges in the course of Calvin's exegetical work on the Pauline epistles and Acts. A case study approach will orient the investigation around one biblical episode that is key for reconstructing Paul's image: Galatians 2. Paul's refutation of Peter at Antioch shows how Calvin interprets and presents Paul's autobiographical account of the incident and his theological rationalization of his behavior. We also see how Calvin fits Paul's account into the chronology of Acts and reconciles Galatians with Acts' depiction of Paul. Focusing on this one incident provides insight into Calvin's understanding of Paul's authority, his central message, and his apostolic and pastoral activity. Moreover, Galatians 2 allows for examining Calvin's treatment of a Pauline passage in three different formats: in the 1548 commentary; in the sermons of 1558–1559; and in the two *congrégations* of 1562–1563. Although this case study approach limits the text basis, it has the advantage of providing a more extensive account of Calvin's reception of the biblical Paul than any other passage.

As would be expected from his humanistic and historicizing approach, Calvin's initial focus, whether in commentary, sermon, or *congrégation*, is on Paul's own context. For example, in the introduction to the commentary, Calvin refers to Strabo, Pliny, Ausonius, and Caesar to explain the origins of

---

[21] R. Ward Holder, *John Calvin and the Grounding of Interpretation: Calvin's First Commentaries* (Leiden: Brill, 2006), 11.

the Galatians, and he provides background on the Galatians' religious defection in order to explain the vehemence of Paul's language.[22] In his commentary on Paul's visit to Jerusalem mentioned in Galatians 2:1, he argues that
this could only be the visit referred to in Acts 12:25, for the episode would
not make sense had it occurred after the decision of the Apostolic Council
described in Acts 15.[23] In his sermon on Galatians 2:3–5, he reminds his congregation that "we know that everyone made threats against Paul; and we
know how many struggles and difficulties he had undergone because of the
resistance of the heathen and the unbelieving." Paul now indicates an even
worse trial in that certain deceivers had infiltrated the circle of believers in
Antioch.[24] These types of explanation are typical: at the outset of each of
his commentaries on Paul's letters and throughout his sermons, he signals
the circumstances that gave rise to or shaped the writing and unfolds Paul's
meaning as it pertains to the original occasion of each letter.[25] Thus, there is
a definite historical dimension to Calvin's portrait of Paul: he presents Paul as
a past leader of the church, dealing with issues peculiar to his own historical
situation.

The specific context of Galatians 2 invites reflection on Paul's authority.
Calvin wants to ensure that his readers or listeners understand that Paul was
an apostle on equal footing with Peter and the other apostles and, therefore,
that his rebuke of Peter was justified, appropriate, and, moreover, genuine.
Here Calvin engages a traditional debate over the interpretation of this incident that has significant ramifications for the image of Paul. According to
Calvin, Peter dissimulated out of too great affection for his fellow Jews, but
he allowed himself to be corrected by Paul and confessed his failing. Calvin
refers to and rejects a traditional view that Peter and Paul merely feigned
their debate. He relates this in most detail in the commentary, where he
discusses the Greek word in question and attributes this interpretation to
John Chrysostom and Jerome; moreover, he identifies Augustine (354–430)
as the one who correctly rejected it.[26] He also discusses the debate without

[22] OE 16: 5–6 = CO 50: 161; *Commentary on Galatians*, 13–15.

[23] OE 16: 30–31 = CO 50: 182; *Commentary on Galatians*, 46–48. Calvin repeats this judgment in
his comments on Gal. 2:11 in the commentary and in the *congrégation*; see OE 16: 42 = CO 50: 191–
192; *Commentary on Galatians*, 61; Calvin, *Deux congrégations*, 4.

[24] *Sermons sur l'Epistre aux Galates* (Geneva: F. Perrin, 1563), CO 50: 363; in English in John
Calvin, *Sermons on Galatians*, trans. Kathy Childress (Edinburgh: Banner of Truth, 1997), 111.
Occasionally I have altered this English translation.

[25] For example, in his comments on Rom. 1:1, 5 he observes that Paul deliberately asserts the authority of his call to those in Rome and reminds them repeatedly of his apostolic office (OE 13: 14,
17 = CO 49: 8, 10; *Commentary on Romans*, 41, 46–47).

[26] OE 16: 44–45 = CO 50: 191–92; *Commentary on Galatians*, 62–63.

naming the church fathers in the *congrégation*; finally, he even remarks in his sermon, "We must diligently remember this, for in days gone by some have thought that all this happened by prior arrangement. They have said that Peter was angry that those of his own nation were difficult to please, and that he had secretly agreed to this public rebuke by Paul. But all this is nonsense!"[27] Similarly, Calvin does not think Peter's behavior can be excused by saying that he was the apostle to the circumcised and therefore should take special consideration for the Jews.[28] Paul, according to Calvin, was right to call Peter out publicly, and in condemning his behavior was exercising his apostolic office and speaking as an organ of the Holy Spirit.[29]

At the same time, Calvin emphasizes the ultimate agreement and collegial relations between Paul and Peter, which allows for consideration of Calvin's depiction of Paul's place among the historic Christian leadership. In his commentary on Galatians, Calvin underscores that Paul and Peter were perfectly agreed about doctrine; Peter's failing was only that he yielded too much out of a desire to please others.[30] In the sermon he notes that Paul did not spare him, "despite the fact that he was his associate [*compagnon*]."[31] This assessment of the situation reflects Calvin's portrayal of Paul's missionary work in Acts, where he stresses the general harmony among the apostles. Calvin notes that Paul's opponents usually came from outside the church, and he finds only a few instances of internal discord of the type indicated in Galatians 2 or Acts 15. In his commentary on Acts, Calvin marvels at the amicable solution to the "domestic war" over ceremonies within the early church, which was resolved by Paul's appearance in Jerusalem and Peter's defense, in Calvin's view, of Paul and his doctrine, especially his understanding of the law. At the same time, he qualifies this harmonious outcome by noting that Paul did away with the minimal expectations for Gentile observance (Acts 15:28) when he judged that the need was past, declaring that nothing is unclean (Rom. 14:14) and that even meat sacrificed to idols might be eaten (1 Cor. 10:25–27).[32] Moreover, Calvin has trouble justifying Paul's falling out with Barnabas shortly thereafter (Acts 15:39); here he judges that Paul appears to have let his zeal get the best of him, when he might rather have found the

[27] CO 50: 392; *Sermons on Galatians*, 145; cf. Calvin, *Deux congrégations*, 8–9.

[28] OE 16: 46 = CO 50: 193; *Commentary on Galatians*, 64.

[29] Calvin, *Deux congrégations*, 3, 5.

[30] OE 16: 46 = CO 50: 193; *Commentary on Galatians*, 64.

[31] CO 50: 394; *Sermons on Galatians*, 147.

[32] John Calvin, *Commentariorum in Acta Apostolorum liber posterior* (Geneva: J. Crespin, 1554), OE 12/2: 59 = CO 48: 363; *Commentary on Acts*, 2: 78–79.

middle way in a dispute that threatened neither true doctrine nor human salvation.[33] In these ways Calvin presents Paul with a certain degree of independence within the movement.

Although he holds that Paul might have compromised with Barnabas over John Mark, for Calvin there could be no compromise in essential theological matters. Paul's brotherly chastisement in Galatians 2 does not signal a rift in the true church, but it is nevertheless urgent and necessary, for it is the "truth of the gospel" (Gal. 2:14) that is ultimately at stake. Calvin spends a good deal of time with each of these pieces of interpretation explaining why Paul presses a question about the ceremonies of the Mosaic law into a general discussion of justification by faith. He thus presents Paul as an apostolic leader who can see beyond the immediate issue to address the underlying challenge to what Calvin believes is Christianity's central doctrine.

Turning now to Calvin's construal of Paul's message, it is important to note that despite his sensitivity to Paul's original context, for Calvin, Paul's authority, argument, and example pertain not only to the Galatians but also to later generations of Christians. Paul's words and actions have relevance beyond their immediate context, and Calvin draws these connections for his students or congregation. This is particularly true in cases where Calvin unpacks Paul's theological claims, as is the case in his expositions of Galatians 2:14–21. Although he indicates in the commentary that Paul addresses first Peter (Gal. 2:14–16) and then the Galatians themselves (Gal. 2:17–21), his comments quickly transcend the original rhetorical setting to focus on the universal, doctrinal lessons of Paul's contentions and their ramifications for Calvin's sixteenth-century readers and auditors. This is especially true in the sermons, where phrases such as "this is what we are to take away from this text" occur frequently.[34] In the commentary, Calvin signals the historical distance between Paul's situation and the sixteenth century when he defends his use of Paul's arguments to contend with Roman Catholic views of first grace and the merit of works: because Calvin's opponents now, like Paul's back then, ascribe part of salvation to works, he claims that "in refuting them, we are at liberty to employ Paul's argument."[35]

Indeed, the central feature of Calvin's image of Paul is as a teacher of doctrine, both for the churches he founded and also for all Christians. Not

---

[33] OE 12/2: 64–66 = CO 48: 367–69; *Commentary on Acts*, 2: 87–89.
[34] CO 50: 450; *Sermons on Galatians*, 212.
[35] OE 16: 57–58 = CO 50: 201; *Commentary on Galatians*, 77–78.

surprisingly, Calvin understands Paul's main doctrine to have been justification by faith alone. In the dedicatory preface to his commentary on Romans,
Calvin identified justification by faith as the epistle's main subject and understood this theme to provide the key to understanding all of scripture.[36] This
central question also shapes the epistle to the Galatians. However, Calvin
drew more broadly from Paul as well. Ward Holder has outlined three important theological themes that characterize Calvin's commentaries on the
Pauline epistles—justification by faith, living the holy life, and building
the church.[37] To these we might add the related topics of faith, the law, and
anthropology.

All of these characteristic themes can be seen in Calvin's exegesis of
Galatians 2, from which select examples will serve to illustrate how Calvin
fleshes out Paul's meaning in order to relate history past to history present.
First, Calvin notes in his comments on Galatians 2:15 that the main question
of the controversy in Antioch was whether human righteousness is by works
or faith, and in a sermon on this passage he observes that Paul here enters
into "the chief point of contention against those who mixed ceremonial law
with the gospel."[38] In order to unpack Paul's position, Calvin explains the
concept of justification as being reckoned righteous and repeatedly defends
extending the original debate over ceremonies to works in general. Second,
he also examines in detail the meaning of the "law." For example, in the
congrégation he notes that Paul's brevity in Galatians made his teaching about
the law in verses 19–21 somewhat obscure, but that Romans 7 provides the
key to understanding this passage. In all of his expositions of the law, Calvin
appeals explicitly to Romans 7 to explain more fully how the law drives to
despair and how God's grace alone raises desperate sinners to new life. He
thus understands "works of the law" to include the moral law and sees Paul as
teaching an evangelical understanding of law and gospel. Third, underlying
this interpretation of the law is a particular anthropology. In his commentary
Calvin contrasts the sinner made dead to the law to the person who lives to
God by being engrafted into Christ, alluding to ideas about believers' union
with Christ that he finds elsewhere in Paul to explain justification by faith.
Fourth, Calvin indicates the relationship between justification and living a
holy life. Also in the commentary, he notes that Christ lives in believers by

---

[36] OE 13: 4 = CO 10/2: 403; *Commentary on Romans*, xxiv.

[37] Holder, "Calvin as Commentator on the Pauline Epistles," 253–54.

[38] OE 16: 48 = CO 50: 194; *Commentary on Galatians*, 67; CO 50: 404; *Sermons on Galatians*,
159–60.

justifying and regenerating them, using his own distinction between justification and sanctification to interpret "Christ lives in me" (Gal. 2:20).[39] Fifth, in both the commentary and sermons, he has excurses on what faith means, which further underscores his didactic use of Paul.[40] This indicates, finally, how even in a non-paranetic passage Calvin uses Paul's account of the encounter with Peter at Antioch to build up the present-day church.

For Calvin, Paul not only teaches central Christian truths but also models appropriate Christian behavior. This is especially prominent in Calvin's sermons but also features in his commentaries. For example, in his sermon on Galatians 2:11–14, Calvin draws various lessons from the passage for his Genevan congregation: they should be gentle when they rebuke those who have fallen and submit themselves when they are rebuked. He also warns against those in his own day who seek to purchase peace by compromising too much and underscores the importance of public correction of faults, points he also makes in his commentary and in the *congrégation*.[41] In the sermon, Calvin carefully points out a difference, however, between his audience's duty to resist traditional Catholic practices and Paul's criticism of his opponents:

> Indeed, of all causes for battle, ours seems more favorable than Paul's must have seemed in his day. While it is true that the cause is one and the same and proceeds from the same source, yet Paul opposed ceremonies which God had appointed with his own mouth. Why was this? Well, because the gospel had been obscure as yet to them; the grace of the Lord Jesus Chris had been overshadowed and they began to stress the doctrine of human merit instead. They had not understood the purpose for which God had given the law. Today, for the same reasons, we are fighting against the abominations that have arisen in the papal church, yet with this added reason: that their doctrine has been invented by Satan and by human beings.[42]

In order to emulate Paul's example properly, sixteenth-century believers need to grasp this key difference between their historical situation and that of Paul.

---

[39] OE 16: 55 = CO 50: 199; *Commentary on Galatians*, 74.

[40] OE 16: 55–56 = CO 50: 199; *Commentary on Galatians*, 75; CO 50: 444–48; *Sermons on Galatians*, 206–10.

[41] CO 50: 394–98; *Sermons on Galatians*, 147–51.

[42] CO 50: 398; *Sermons on Galatians*, 152.

Calvin finds Paul's exemplary character to be an important theme also in Acts, where there is less focus on Paul's teachings, since, in Calvin's view, Luke frequently condensed Paul's longer sermons and speeches. In Acts and in his other exegetical treatments of Paul beyond Galatians 2, Calvin presents Paul as the premier practical model not just for Christians but also especially for pastors. In the commentary on Acts, Paul serves as a model teacher. For example, when he disputed in the synagogue (Acts 18:4), he accommodated his teaching to the occasion.[43] Similarly, when Paul told the elders at Ephesus that he had held back nothing that might profit them (Acts 20:20), both his pattern of teaching and his desire for edification of the church were exemplary.[44] Holder has investigated further ways that Calvin's exegetical engagement with Paul yielded practical models for ministerial behavior, and, moreover, he has shown that Calvin did not think that Paul was to be imitated in every instance.[45] Even where Calvin is especially eager to hold up Paul's example, his historical consciousness and sense of anachronism still shape his reading.

From these broad strokes we can trace the outlines of Calvin's portrait of the biblical Paul. Calvin views Paul as a historical leader of the Christian church, a singularly inspired instrument of the Holy Spirit, and the first among equals. Paul's preeminence among the apostles derives largely from the fact that, in Calvin's mind, Paul is without parallel as a teacher of doctrine. As he observes in his commentary on Acts, Paul is "the principal doctor of the church, even unto the end of the world."[46] As an exegete, Calvin strives to explain the meaning and relevance of this teaching both in Paul's historical context and for Calvin's own generation. His ideal of unfolding the mind of this preeminent biblical author does not, however, prevent him from offering at times a genuinely idiosyncratic interpretation of Paul's teaching. A prominent example of this can be seen in Calvin's comments on Romans 1:18–32, in which he diagnoses a far more acute noetic impairment affecting fallen humanity's perception of God than Paul's argument and, indeed, the readings of his exegetical predecessors can sustain.[47]

---

[43] OE 12/2: 136 = CO 48: 425; *Commentary on Acts*, 2: 182.

[44] OE 12/2: 178–79 = CO 48: 461; *Commentary on Acts*, 2: 242–43.

[45] R. Ward Holder, "Calvin's Exegetical Understanding of the Office of Pastor," in *Calvin and the Company of Pastors*, ed. David Foxgrover (Grand Rapids, MI: Calvin Studies Society, 2004), 179–209; R. Ward Holder, "Paul as Calvin's (Ambivalent) Pastoral Model," *Dutch Review of Church History* 84 (2004): 284–98.

[46] OE 12/1: 281 = CO 48: 213; *Commentary on Acts*, 1: 390.

[47] Steinmetz, *Calvin in Context*, 28–32.

In addition to being a teacher of doctrine, Paul, for Calvin, is also an out-standing model of contemporary Christian and pastoral behavior: for the most part he is moderate and gentle but also firm. While respecting and instructing his readers and auditors about the historical circumstances of Paul's teaching and ministry, Calvin also finds that Paul's words and actions speak to his own day because of the essential character of his teaching and the similarities Calvin finds between the contemporary situation and that of the early church—though Calvin is also careful to point out differences be-tween these contexts. The fact that Paul's Romans provides the entrance to the understanding of all of scripture provides the theological rationale for the priority of Paul's writings and explains the prominence of Paul's epistles in Calvin's exegetical program.

Two implications of Calvin's biblical portrait of Paul deserve under-scoring. First, Calvin's reading of Paul is a polemical reading of Paul. In Calvin's interpretations of Galatians, Paul provides ammunition to counter Roman Catholic views of justification, the law, the role of works in salvation, and more. But this polemical rescue operation is not limited to Galatians. Elsewhere Calvin underscores repeatedly that Paul's example does not justify the views and practices such as veneration of the saints and relics, confirma-tion as a sacrament, making religious vows, and so on that Calvin claims his Roman opponents seek to derive from Paul. Second, Calvin's reading of Paul is a canonical reading. Calvin reads Paul in light of the corpus of his writings and Acts and, importantly, he views other parts of scripture—particularly those that address his favorite Pauline themes—through a Pauline lens. In Acts, for example, Calvin fills out Paul's construal of messianic expectation with material consistent with his teaching in his epistles.[48] His discussions of faith in his commentaries on Hebrews, James, 1 John, and the Gospel of John are shaped by his reading of Paul on this topic.[49] In this very concrete way Paul provides Calvin with a hermeneutical key for reading the rest of scripture. At the same time, Calvin is aware that Paul is still human—as Paul himself contends in Acts 14:15. He sometimes lets his zeal get the best of him, as in the dispute with Barnabas, and sometimes his use of passages from the Old Testament strays from what Calvin takes to be the genuine sense in-tended by the original author and therefore requires careful explanation.[50]

---

[48] Scheld, "Die missionarische Verkündung," 314.

[49] Barbara Pitkin, *What Pure Eyes Could See: Calvin's Doctrine of Faith in Its Exegetical Context* (New York: Oxford University Press, 1999), 70–97.

[50] See, for example, Calvin's comments on Eph. 4:8; OE 16: 223–24 = CO 51: 193; *Commentary on Ephesians*, 271–72.

Thus, though Paul is the preeminent theological and biblical authority whom Calvin endeavors to claim totally for the evangelical side, both his authority and his example have their limits.

Calvin's Pauline Program for the Reformation of the Church

While there is extensive literature examining the question of Calvin's exegesis of Paul, there is less explicit reflection on the way in which Paul might have shaped Calvin's understanding of church reform, his specific recommendations for rebuilding the church, and his implementation of ecclesiastical reforms in Geneva. Reformers who broke with Rome were faced immediately with the practical matter of reconstituting the liturgy and rituals, the personnel, pastoral care, discipline, finances, and property of the church to conform to the doctrine they claimed justified the rupture in the first place. Obviously many things and—even in Geneva—many individuals shaped this process of restructuring. Yet given Calvin's role in the reforms in Geneva, especially after his return in 1541, consideration of his hand in the process is not unwarranted. Moreover, in light of the unparalleled significance of Paul for Calvin's exegetical program and, as we shall see in the next section, for his theological orientation, it is worth asking whether his reception of Paul extends to this area as well—and, if it does, in what ways this engagement with Paul can be construed. This section opens reflection on these issues and the ways in which Calvin's historical consciousness also manifests itself in his engagement with Paul for the task of institutional reform in the sixteenth century.

Although the range of sources for Calvin's understanding of and proposals for church reform might arguably be extremely broad, the most fruitful sources include writings from the early 1540s in which Calvin justifies the reform of the church and discusses the areas in need of reform and his proposals for reforming them: the 1543 *Institutes*; the appeal to Charles V (*Supplex exhortatio*), also from 1543; and, finally, the specifically ecclesiastical documents that Calvin produced upon his return to Geneva—the *Ecclesiastical Ordinances*, the liturgy, the catechism—which illustrate the concrete reforms he sought to implement. The writings from this period are particularly important because Calvin composed them at a time in which he was both actively involved in rebuilding the church at Geneva and also engaged in imperial dialogues concerning the need and status of religious reforms. His preoccupation with the concrete details of reform is markedly evident in the additions he made to the discussions of ecclesiastical topics in the 1543 edition of the *Institutes*. This is also, not incidentally, the period in which Calvin launched his exegetical program with his commentaries on the Pauline epistles.

Thus, while the case for looking especially at the writings of an ecclesiastical nature from the early 1540s is a solid one, there is nevertheless a methodological difficulty, namely, how to determine which aspects of Calvin's writings on the reformation and nature of the church and his practical work in this area could be designated legitimately "Pauline." It is not enough to look simply for explicit appeal to Paul to justify reform of the church in general or specific practices or structures in particular. For example, just because Calvin does not cite Romans 1 when he describes the Catholic theology of the saints as idolatrous and superstitious in his *Supplex exhortatio* does not mean that Paul is not a resource for his polemic. At the other extreme, it is not particularly illuminating to identify allegedly Pauline principles and assume that these provide the main impetus for a particular agenda. Calvin's concern for idolatry in this treatise, for example, resonates not only with Paul but also with the worldview of the Hebrew prophets. Yet given that Paul is Calvin's central theological authority and also the primacy of the Pauline epistles in Calvin's exegetical program, one *is* led to wonder to what extent Calvin's justification of ecclesiastical reform in the *Supplex exhortatio* and his recent efforts to build up the church in Geneva reflect his general Pauline orientation. And, more specifically, we might wonder whether elements of Calvin's ecclesiastical reform could be construed as *unique* implementations of principles that have their foundation in engagement with Paul. To initiate reflection on this relatively unexamined aspect of Calvin's ecclesiastical reforms, I will again take a case study approach and focus primarily on the *Supplex exhortatio*, with occasional references to the other sources identified earlier.[51] My goal is to suggest ways in which a Pauline echo might be heard

[51] John Calvin, *Supplex exhortatio ad invictissimum caesarem Carolum quintum et illustrissimos principes aliosque ordines spirae nunc imperii conventum agentes. Ut restituendae ecclesiae curam serio velint suscipere. Eorum omnium nomine edita qui Christum regnare cupiunt* ([Geneva]: [J. Girard], 1543), CO 6: 453–534; the running head of the Latin edition is "De necessitate reformandae ecclesiae," and in his 1547 polemical commentary on the first session of the Council of Trent, Calvin invites his readers to first peruse "my treatise on the necessity of reforming the church" before reading his antidote to Trent (CO 7: 369–70). The English translation uses this running head as the title of the treatise: John Calvin, *The Necessity of Reforming the Church,* in *Tracts and Treatises on the Reformation of the Church,* trans. Henry Beveridge, ed. Thomas Torrance (Grand Rapids,

in Calvin's ideas about the need for reformation, how to organize the church, and the nature and duties of the pastoral office. The investigation will focus in more detail on the first area and only briefly on the last two.

Justification of church reform was obviously a major theme in Calvin's writings beginning with the dedicatory epistle to the very first edition of the *Institutes* in 1536. It was, however, in his writings in the mid-1540s that Calvin articulated the need for reform on the basis of nearly of decade of experience as a church leader and a participant in religious dialogues— experience that provided him with a closer personal acquaintance with both the concrete possibilities for change as well as the obstacles to it. Calvin's most sustained apology for church reform from this time appears in the *Supplex exhortatio*, which was written at the request of Martin Bucer for presentation at the imperially convened Diet at Speyer in February 1544. In a letter to Guillaume Farel (1489–1565), Calvin complained of the difficulty of writing this apology for the reformation of the church, but in the end the treatise circulated throughout Europe in both Latin (1543) and French translation (1544) and won the praise of his colleagues in reform.[52] Is it possible to detect a Pauline echo in Calvin's diagnosis of the problems necessitating the reform of the present-day church and in his defense of the remedies put forth by the Protestant reformers? In his treatise Calvin justifies evangelical reform by enumerating the evils besetting the church and demonstrating the salutary effects of the Reformers' remedies and the urgency of the situation. Within this framework, he identifies the "soul" of Christianity to be a proper knowledge of the worship of God and whence salvation is to be sought; the "body" is the sacraments and church order.[53] Doctrine concerning proper worship and salvation animates church order and makes it lively; reform is justified when proper doctrine is obscured. How does Paul help Calvin make his plea to the emperor?

MI: Eerdmans, 1958), 1: 123–234; hereafter *Necessity*. For details about the writing of the treatise see BC 1: 43/7; de Greef, *Writings of John Calvin*, 147–48; J. J. Steenkamp, "Calvin's Exhortation to Charles V (1543)," in *Calvinus Sincerioris Religionis Vindex: Calvin as Protector of the Purer Religion*, ed. Wilhelm H. Neuser and Brian G. Armstrong (Kirksville, MO: Sixteenth Century Journal, 1997), 309–14; Theodore W. Casteel, "Calvin and Trent: Calvin's Reaction to the Council of Trent in the Context of His Conciliar Thought," *Harvard Theological Review* 63 (1970): 91–117. A more polemical justification of the reform appears in the same year in the tract against Albert Pighius: John Calvin, *Defensio sanae et orthodoxae doctrinae de servitute & liberatione humani arbitrii, adversus calumnias Alberti Pighii Campensis* (Geneva: J. Girard, 1543), CO 6: 225–404.

[52] CO 11: 642–44.

[53] CO 6: 459–60; *Necessity*, 126–127; cf. 159, 165.

First, it is striking in this treatise how consumed Calvin is with the problem of worship that he alleges is vitiated, superstitious, fictitious, idolatrous. He identifies this as a point of doctrine on a par with—or even prior to—justification by faith alone.[54] The use of Paul is subtle but nevertheless detectable, as Calvin alludes to or cites Paul to confirm his diagnosis and, later, to outline his remedy. Worship of God that is not sanctioned by God's word includes the cult of the saints, which robs God of his glory and transfers it to creatures.[55] Moreover, it includes ceremonies that represent a "new Judaism, as a substitute for that which God has distinctly abrogated."[56] Finally, false worship extends to a false understanding of repentance that focuses on "the external exercises of the body, which, as Paul assures us, are not of the highest utility," even though they have the appearance of wisdom (Col. 2:23).[57]

Later in the treatise Calvin outlines the changes to worship in the reformed churches and defends these against the challenges of his opponents. In support of the simplified worship, he links his cause to the Old Testament prophets, but he notes an important difference in historical circumstances: while the prophets condemned false attitudes toward ceremonies instituted by God, the reformers complain about humanly devised superstitions. Paul provides the reason for this distinction between the old and new dispensations when he explains that the shadows have been withdrawn when the "body" or substance has been manifested in Christ and that God now instructs the church in a different manner.[58] Calvin also cites Paul explicitly (Rom. 10:14) to justify three changes to the practice of prayer,

[54] See also Carlos M. N. Eire, *War against the Idols: The Reformation of Worship from Erasmus to Calvin* (Cambridge, UK: Cambridge University Press, 1986), 198–200. Further evidence for this concern at this time is attested by the appearance in the same year of the French treatise against relics: John Calvin, *Advertissement du profit qui reviendroit à la Chrestienté s'il se faisoit inventaire des reliques* (Geneva: J. Girard, 1543), CO 6: 405–52; also in Jean Calvin, *"La vraie piété": Divers traités de Jean Calvin et Confession de foi de Guillaume Farel*, ed. Irena Backus and Claire Chimelli (Geneva: Labor et Fides, 1986), 153–202; English translation in John Calvin, *Three French Treatises*, ed. Francis M. Higman (London: Athlone, 1970), 12–16, 47–97. Relevant also is Calvin's ongoing concern with religious dissimulation, which resulted in the issuance of tracts against the so-called Nicodemites in 1543 and 1544 (for details, see Eire, *War against the Idols*, 240–43).

[55] CO 6: 462; *Necessity*, 130; cf. Rom. 1:25. Compare "an Dei gloriam illi ereptam transferant ad creaturas" (CO 6: 462) with Calvin's comment on Rom. 1:25: "Creaturae enim dari honor religionis causa, non potest quin a Deo derivetur et transferatur" (OE 13: 35–36 – CO 49: 28; *Commentary on Romans*, 78).

[56] CO 6: 463; *Necessity*, 131; cf. 152.

[57] CO 6: 464; *Necessity*, 132; cf. 153.

[58] CO 6: 478; *Necessity*, 151–52. There are references in the text to Gal. 4:3 ff. and Col. 2:4, 14, and 17.

namely, doing away with intercession to the saints, praying with confidence, and praying with understanding.[59]

Understandably the use of Paul becomes even more prominent in Calvin's detailing of the second area of doctrine he claims that the present church has obscured: the way of salvation.[60] Calvin's initial sketch outlines three stages of human salvation: being humbled by despair over sin, turning to Christ as sole source of salvation, and confident rest in Christ. He claims Catholic theology perverts this doctrine by underestimating the effect and power of original sin, adding the merit of works to supplement the righteousness of Christ, and insisting that believers possess at best conjectural certainty concerning their salvation. Calvin cites Romans explicitly to refute this last point: true Christian faith is confident before God (Rom. 5:2) because Christians have received the spirit of adoption (Rom 8:15); true faith is made void if salvation is through the law (Rom. 9:14).[61] Later Calvin discusses in greater detail the remedy to the corruptions of this second area of doctrine. His argument is basically a pastiche of proof texts from Paul; his main defense is that reformed teaching adds nothing to Paul's doctrine.[62]

Finally, Paul also figures into Calvin's discussion of the external form of the church—the sacraments and church order that best preserve proper doctrine. His main argument against the Catholic sacraments echoes his earlier complaints about superfluous ceremonies in worship. Humanly devised ceremonies have been added to the two sacraments instituted by Christ, and these two, moreover, have been so corrupted through "theatrical exhibitions" that their purpose is no longer evident. In his later justification of the changes made to sacramental practice by the reformers, Calvin cites Paul explicitly (1 Cor. 10:17) only once to argue against transubstantiation. However, his argument that the revival of the practice of explaining the meaning of the sacraments and their fruit in the context of the worship service reflects his view of the pastoral office as a teaching office—which, as we will see, he justified earlier in the treatise by appeal to Paul.

While Paul remains behind the scenes in the discussion of the sacraments, he emerges more clearly in Calvin's diagnosis of the problems concerning church order and government. Paul provides the rationale for the pastoral

[59] CO 6: 481–82; *Necessity*, 156–57. In discussing the second point, Calvin also refers to Matt. 21:22 and Jas 1:6.

[60] CO 6: 464–67; *Necessity*, 133–37.

[61] CO 6: 466–67; *Necessity*, 136.

[62] CO 6: 484–85; *Necessity*, 162. Calvin also refers to Is. 53:5, Augustine, and Leo to refute the notion of merit; CO 6: 486; *Necessity*, 163–64.

office: pastors are to edify the church with sound doctrine, and thus the primary job of the pastor is to teach,[63] a view that Calvin later buttresses by appeal to Peter.[64] Though there is no explicit reference to Paul, I suspect he underlies Calvin's insistence that "those who preside in the church ought to excel others, and shine by the example of holier lives."[65] Paul, in his letters to Timothy and Titus, sets the standard for the examination of clerical appointments.[66] In Calvin's later defense of the implementation of these principles in reformed churches, he also marshals the support of the canons and fathers of the ancient church.

It is here that Calvin also addresses the charges that the reformers are too hasty in making changes and, moreover, that they neglect discipline and morals. Alluding to Paul, Calvin avers that they have no problem with ecclesiastical regulations to ensure that things are done "decently and in order" (cf. 1 Cor. 14:40), and where they have abrogated practices and rules, they can provide just cause.[67] While he allows that laws concerning external policy ought to be obeyed, it is otherwise with humanly devised laws that seek to regulate the conscience. These subvert the honor of God and infringe upon the freedom of conscience, "which Paul strenuously insists, must not be subject to the will of men."[68] Calvin details three areas in which the changes were made to preserve this liberty: freedom to eat meat on any day; clerical marriage; and rejection of private confession. In defense of the first two practices, Paul is Calvin's star witness.[69] In justifying the rejection of necessary private confession, Paul retreats behind the scenes again: Calvin identifies the principle he earlier attributed to Paul—that "the conscience must not be brought into bondage"—as "the perpetual rule of Christ" and points to the relative novelty of the requirement.[70]

In Calvin's case for a biblical reformation of the church in the *Supplex exhortatio*, Paul is not his only witness, and Calvin's historical interests shape the entire vision of reform that the treatise lays out, not just its Pauline elements.[71] Nevertheless, Paul is certainly the most prominent source for

---

[63] CO 6: 469; *Necessity*, 140; cf. 170.
[64] CO 6: 471; *Necessity*, 143.
[65] CO 6: 470; *Necessity*, 141; cf. 1 Tim. 3:1–13; Titus 1:6–9.
[66] CO 6: 470; *Necessity*, 142.
[67] CO 6: 494; *Necessity*, 175.
[68] CO 6: 494; *Necessity*, 176.
[69] CO 6: 495–96; *Necessity*, 177–78.
[70] CO 6: 496, 498–99; *Necessity*, 179, 182.
[71] See Barbara Pitkin, "John Calvin's Vision of Reform, Historical Thinking, and the Modern World," in *The Oxford Handbook of Calvin and Calvinism*, ed. Bruce Gordon and Carl R. Trueman (New York: Oxford University Press, forthcoming).

Calvin's argument, even when only behind the scenes. He serves as an aid in the diagnosis of the evils in need of reform and as Calvin's primary authority for defending the proposed corrections. It should be noted even if it is not terribly surprising that in discussing the doctrine of proper worship and the understanding of salvation that constitute the "soul" of true Christianity, Calvin appeals mostly to Romans and Colossians. In treating the "body," the external elements of Christian faith, Calvin draws mostly on 1 Corinthians and the epistles to Timothy and Titus. Finally, in the third section of his apology, in which Calvin makes the case for the urgency of reform, refutes at length charges against reform, and appeals to the emperor for a council, there seems to be less direct or even indirect reference to Paul. There is, however, detailed discussion of the early church in this section. This is a clear indication that Calvin supplements the testimony of his star witness, who nevertheless provides the doctrinal foundation for building the church. Paul is most useful for setting the theological standards for reform of the church—most particularly, he provides Calvin with the key to understanding the proper role of rituals and ceremonies. Moreover, Calvin uses Paul to some degree to structure church order, offices, and devotional practice.

In concluding this piece of the investigation into Calvin's historically informed reception of Paul, I follow this latter point to make some brief observations about how Calvin uses Paul to think more practically and constructively about the organization of the church and the duties of clergy. In his more practically oriented ecclesiastical writings, such as the *Ecclesiastical Ordinances,* the Genevan liturgy, and the catechism, Calvin outlines a structure for religious life in Geneva and particularly for church governance and the duties of church ministers. It is important to remember that in Geneva, unlike many other reformed cities, the pastoral clergy was entirely replaced.[72] Thus, it is definitely worth inquiring into the many sources that Calvin used to establish the ecclesiastical offices and ecclesiastical discipline. Elsie McKee has advanced the most sustained analyses demonstrating the exegetical—and particularly Pauline—underpinnings of Calvin's views of proper church order; her studies also provide a model for articulating the way in which this understanding of church order was biblical and represented a reformed implementation of *sola scriptura*.[73] As noted earlier, Ward Holder

---

[72] Thomas Austin Lambert, "Preaching, Praying and Policing the Reform in Sixteenth-Century Geneva" (Ph.D. diss., University of Wisconsin–Madison, 1998), 199.

[73] Elsie Anne McKee, *John Calvin on the Diaconate and Liturgical Almsgiving* (Geneva: Droz, 1984); Elsie Anne McKee, "Calvin's Exegesis of Romans 12:8—Social, Accidental, or Theological?," *Calvin Theological Journal* 23 (1988): 6–18; Elsie Anne McKee, *Elders and the Plural Ministry: The Role of*

has investigated what Calvin's Pauline commentaries contribute to his understanding of the pastoral office and how Paul functions as a "veritable paradigm of pastoral practice."[74] The significance of Paul for the development of Calvin's theology of ministry has been examined also by Alexandre Ganoczy and Louis Goumaz.[75]

Pressing these rich analyses further, one can reflect on the extent to which Calvin's biblical church order and understanding of the pastoral office are specifically Pauline. Of course, it is not remarkable that Calvin used Paul to develop his views on these topics—when seeking to articulate and implement a new church order and pastoral office, he had precious little other biblical material to consider: e.g., Acts (which as we saw earlier includes "Pauline" sources as well); Matthew 18; and even perhaps the Old Testament. Yet Paul is not by any means Calvin's only source—biblical or otherwise—and, moreover, Calvin does not slavishly seek to imitate a Pauline church. He distinguishes Paul as a teacher of universal doctrine from the institutional order that Paul established best fitted to his own time and place. At the same time, there is a definite "Pauline" moment in Calvin's concrete restructuring of the church in Geneva.

In short, Calvin uses the Pauline motto "decently and in good order" to justify his adaptation of certain Pauline ideas and practices to his situation in Geneva. First, Calvin developed a clear and precise theory of a plurality of ministries with his idea of the fourfold offices. Second, Calvin's lay ecclesiastical offices represent a unique implementation of the priesthood of all believers, which he took to be a Pauline principle. The uniqueness of Calvin's adaptation of this notion is seen, in particular, in his notion of a lay ministry of discipline that was distinct from the ordained pastorate and from civil authorities, which as McKee has shown reflects an innovative reading of 1 Timothy 5:17.[76] Finally, there is Calvin's emphasis on the teaching function of the pastoral office and the implementation of a teaching role for pastors

Exegetical History in Illuminating John Calvin's Theology (Geneva: Droz, 1988); Elsie Anne McKee, "Les anciens et l'interpretation de I Tim 5, 17 chez Calvin: Une curiosité dans l'histoire de l'exegese," *Revue de théologie et de philosophie* 120 (1988): 411–17; Elsie Anne McKee, "Calvin's Teaching on the Elder Illuminated by Exegetical History," in *John Calvin and the Church: A Prism of Reform*, ed. Timothy George (Louisville, KY: Westminster John Knox, 1990), 147–55.

[74] Holder, "Paul as Calvin's Model, " 285–86; cf. Holder, "Calvin's Exegetical Understanding."

[75] Alexandre Ganoczy, *Calvin: Théologien de l'église et du ministère* (Paris: Editions du Cerf, 1964); Louis Goumaz, *Timothee, ou le ministère évangélique: D'après Calvin et ses commentaires sur le Nouveau Testament* (Lausanne: Editions la Concorde, 1948).

[76] McKee, "Calvin's Teaching on the Elder," 152–54.

in Geneva. While all of these have elements of continuity with traditional Christian and sixteenth-century Protestant views, Calvin draws some unique conclusions from Pauline texts that are reflected in his implementation of these churchly offices. In keeping with his historical sensitivities, Calvin consciously and creatively adapts rather than imitates Paul's exemplary model.

Calvin as a "Pauline Theologian"

The final stroke in this sketch of Calvin's reception of Paul traces how Paul functioned as Calvin's central theological authority. Analogous to the approach taken in the previous section, it is not sufficient to draw attention to the fact that many of Calvin's favorite theological themes—e.g., justification by faith, sanctification, faith in Christ, providence, predestination, human fallenness, and knowledge of God—found their echo in Pauline texts. Rather, I explore how Calvin used Paul theologically in order to gain insight into the type of Paulinism that shapes the biblical theology expressed in his *Institutes of the Christian Religion*. To this end, this section focuses on the Pauline roots of Calvin's theological enterprise. The investigation begins by furthering a line of inquiry posed by previous scholarship into the relationship between the 1539 *Institutes* and Calvin's 1540 Romans commentary. Afterward, the discussion turns to the role of Melanchthon's exegetical and theological work on Paul in shaping the 1539 *Institutes* and stamping it with its particular Pauline character.

In his study from 1976, Alexandre Ganoczy investigated the Pauline orientation of Calvin's hermeneutics, arguing that both Calvin's exegesis and his biblical theology have a pronounced Pauline character.[77] To illustrate this, he notes that already in the letter to the king of France that prefaces the 1536 *Institutes*, Calvin appeals to Romans 12:6 to argue that scripture itself provides the key to its own interpretation—a key Calvin holds is most clearly expressed in Paul's Romans, when this is properly understood. In 1539, Calvin envisions the revised *Institutes* as the key to this door onto the rest of scripture, as it were, and thus allies this revised edition with his commentary on Romans as hermeneutical guides. Ganoczy argues that Calvin perceives his cause as analogous to Paul's and that he develops a thorough reflection on the scripture as the word of God with support of Pauline theology

---

[77] Ganoczy, "Calvin als paulinischer Theologe," 43.

and texts; that his view of the Holy Spirit's relationship to the word and the authority of scripture is also from Paul, particularly from 1 Corinthians and Romans 8:16–26; and, finally, that Calvin takes up a Pauline view of the Old Testament, interprets and reinterprets it.[78] Ganoczy contends that in all these ways Calvin reflected but also further developed Martin Luther's fundamental exegetical principles. He concludes by indicating the crucial role of Romans for Calvin's treatment of two of his central theologomena: the knowledge of God and moral consciousness of the heathen, and divine predestination. The treatment of these topics in the 1539 *Institutes* clearly evidences Calvin's recent exegetical engagement with Romans.

The intimate connection between the second edition of Calvin's summary of Christian doctrine and his first biblical commentary has certainly not gone unnoticed, although it is usually mentioned to indicate how Calvin conceived of the relationship between the *Institutes* and his commentaries as complementary: the commentaries would aim at brief elucidation of the mind of the biblical author, whereas the *Institutes* would provide a topically arranged guide and orientation to biblical teaching.[79] Building, however, on Ganoczy's observation that Calvin describes both the *Institutes* and Paul's letter to the Romans as providing an opening to the rest of scripture, we note that the relationship between the *Institutes* and the commentary on *this* biblical book is more than complementary—it is also functionally identical. On the one hand, Calvin claims both in his dedicatory letter to Simon Grynaeus and in his Argument to his commentary that anyone who understands Romans has an entrance into the understanding of all of scripture and its treasures.[80] On the other hand, in his prefatory letter to the 1539 *Institutes* and the Argument to the 1541 French translation, he describes this work as a virtual handbook and key to their discovery.[81] He views Romans as the "theological center of the Bible," from which the student of scripture, with the aid of the *Institutes*,

---

[78] Ganoczy, "Calvin als paulinischer Theologe," 56, 58–60.

[79] Calvin expresses this in the letter to the reader prefacing the 1539 *Institutes*: "For I think that I have so embraced the sum of religion in all its parts and arranged it systematically, that if anyone grasps it aright, he will have no difficulty in determining both what he ought especially to seek in scripture, and to what end he should refer everything contained in it. And so I have, as it were, paved the way. And if I shall hereafter publish any commentaries on Scripture, I shall always condense them and keep them short, for I shall have no need to undertake lengthy digressions on doctrines, and digress into *loci communes*" (quoted in Parker, *Calvin's New Testament Commentaries*, 89).

[80] OE 13: 4, 7 = CO 10/2: 403, 49: 1; *Commentary on Romans*, xxiv, xxix.

[81] CO 1: 255–56; for French see Jean Calvin, *Institution de la religion chrestienne*, 5 vols., ed. Jean-Daniel Benoit (Paris: J. Vrin, 1957–63), 1: 12; English translation in John Calvin, *Institutes* (1559), 4–7.

takes his point of departure.[82] Calvin thus makes his summary of Christian faith and the theological task itself essentially Pauline.

Ganoczy is primarily interested in Calvin's theology of scripture and its interpretation. In this regard he argues that Calvin holds a fundamentally Lutheran hermeneutical criterion (*Deo omnia, hominibus nihil*), but that he develops this and other Lutheran principles, such as the clarity of scripture, in distinctive directions. Shifting our focus to the Pauline element in Calvin's theology as a whole, however, it is not Luther but rather Philip Melanchthon who paved the way for Calvin's mature conception of the theological task and decisively influenced its fundamentally Pauline character. Like Melanchthon's summary of Christian doctrine, his *Loci communes*, Calvin's *Institutes* was intimately connected to his engagement with Romans. But the relationship goes much deeper than this parallel working method. Indeed, both Calvin's mature understanding of the theological task as well as his exegesis of Romans were forged in response to the pathbreaking endeavors of Melanchthon, the first Protestant to publish a commentary on Romans and the author of the first systematic explanation of evangelical theology.

The first edition of Melanchthon's *Loci communes* grew out of lectures on Romans he held from 1520 to 1522. As Timothy Wengert details, Melanchthon understood *loci* to constitute "the underlying structure of a text, which the author intended to use in explicating a particular theme." Reading Paul this way, Melanchthon discovered a new way of viewing Romans, coming to believe that "the early chapters of Romans constituted the heart of the Christian gospel" and that this text thus provided a *methodus* for reading the rest of scripture.[83] To aid the students in his lectures on Romans in 1519, he drew up a list of theological topics in the letter, *Rerum theologicarum capita seu loci*. When these were published without his permission the following year, he set to work on a revised and more comprehensive exposition of the focal topics that Paul himself used to structure his letter. In the dedicatory letter prefacing the result of his labors—the *Loci communes rerum theologicarum* (1521)—he describes the text as an "index" that points out the principal topics of Christian teaching and summons students to the study of scripture itself.[84] In justifying the choice of topics, moreover, he avers that in Romans Paul

[82] Ganoczy, "Calvin als paulinischer Theologe," 48.

[83] Timothy J. Wengert, "The Rhetorical Paul: Philip Melanchthon's Interpretation of the Pauline Epistles," in *A Companion to Paul in the Reformation*, ed. R. Ward Holder (Leiden: Brill, 2009), 129.

[84] Philip Melanchthon, *Loci communes rerum theologicarum seu hypotyposes theologicae* [1521], CR 21: 82; in English in Philip Melanchthon, *Loci communes theologici*, trans. Lowell J. Satre, in *Melanchthon and Bucer*, ed. Wilhelm Pauck (Philadelphia: Westminster, 1969), 19.

"was writing a compendium of Christian doctrine."[85] Melanchthon thus uses biblical commonplaces drawn from Romans, the heart of scripture, as categories for studying theology—perceiving this method, moreover, as an evangelical alternative to the traditional categories and arrangement of the classic medieval textbook, Peter Lombard's *Sentences*.[86] With the *Loci communes*, Melanchthon thus inaugurated a new way of using Paul as a source for theology, making the author of Romans *the* Christian theologian par excellence in terms not only of doctrine but also of method. He refined this reading over a lifetime, renewing and rewriting both his expositions of Romans and his explications of the commonplaces of Christian faith. Although the latter grew to take on topics not immediately suggested by Romans, Melanchthon appears always to have reviewed his reading of Romans prior to each significant revision of the *Loci communes*.[87]

As many have noted, the first edition of Calvin's *Institutes* from 1536 follows a traditional catechetical structure for its first four chapters on the law, the Apostle's Creed, the Lord's Prayer, and the sacraments. Ganoczy has argued that Calvin took Luther's *Small Catechism* as his specific model, but points also to Calvin's "superior eclecticism" in setting forth his discussion in conversation with a variety of other sources from Luther, Zwingli, Bucer, and Melanchthon—including the 1521 *Loci*.[88] It is only, however, when Calvin revises this first edition that he seriously engages Melanchthon's new way of using Romans as a source for theology in its most recent manifestation, the revised *Loci communes* of 1535. Still exhibiting the independence

---

[85] CR 21: 85; *Loci communes theologici*, 22.

[86] Wengert points out that Melanchthon was supposed to begin lecturing on the *Sentences*, but instead he sought in his new approach to Paul an alternative route to theology ("Rhetorical Paul," 129).

[87] Melanchthon lectured on the structure and outline of Romans in 1528 and 1529 and published two versions of his rhetorical and dialectical analysis of Romans in 1529 and in 1530 (CR 15: 443–92); he lectured on Romans again in 1531 and published a new commentary on the basis of these lectures in 1532: Philipp Melanchthon, *Commentarii in epistolam Pauli ad Romanos*, in *Römerbrief-Kommentar 1532*, ed. Rolf Schäfer, vol. 5 of *Melanchthons Werke in Auswahl*, ed. Robert Stupperich (Gütersloh: Gerd Mohn, 1965). Shortly thereafter he began revising the *Loci communes*, and in 1535 he published the second of three major revisions of this text (CR 21: 331–560). Similarly, he published a reworked commentary on Romans in 1540 (CR 15: 493–796) and followed this with the third major revision to the Latin *Loci* in 1543 and its subsequent editions (CR 21: 601–1106). Melanchthon continued to lecture on Romans in the 1540s, with his last set of lectures beginning in 1552 and a new commentary appearing in 1556 (CR 15: 797–1052). In 1552 Melanchthon also undertook a massive revision of the German version of his *Loci communes*, which included numerous changes to the discussions of the cause of sin, free will, and the nature of sin, and which was published in 1553. For details, see Timothy J. Wengert, "The Biblical Commentaries of Philip Melanchthon," in *Philip Melanchthon (1497–1560) and the Commentary*, 133–39; Johannes Schilling, "Melanchthons loci communes deutsch," in *Humanismus und Wittenberger Reformation*, ed. Michael Beyer and Günther Wartenberg (Leipzig: Evangelische Verlagsanstalt, 1996), 337–52.

[88] Ganoczy, *Young Calvin*, 134, 146–51.

of mind that characterized his use of his sources in the first edition, Calvin does not slavishly adhere to either structure or the substance of the 1535 *Loci*. Nevertheless, his radical expansion of the topics and their order in the summary, not to mention his view of the new purpose of his *Institutes*, all reflect Melanchthon's innovation.

The nature of the influence of Melanchthon's 1535 *Loci* on the 1539 *Institutes* has been investigated more precisely by Richard Muller and Olivier Millet. Muller demonstrates the role of Melanchthon's 1535 version in Calvin's reconception of the theological task and argues, moreover, that Calvin's shift in genre from catechism to *loci communes* and the reorganization of the topics "bear the unmistakable marks of a Melanchthonian influence."[89] The positive element of this influence can be seen in that Calvin, like Melanchthon, believed that the theological topics must be elicited from the biblical text—especially Romans—and that there was a certain proper order for discussing the topics. True, Calvin disagreed with Melanchthon on the best form for the biblical commentary; in particular, he thought that long doctrinal discussions of the *loci* in a commentary and skipping verses not relevant to the present topic should be avoided. But this was a disagreement over exegetical, not theological, method, and Muller argues that the new topics introduced in 1539 are precisely those "identified by Melanchthon as Pauline *loci*—and they are place into the *Institutes* in the Pauline order, as defined by Melanchthon."[90] Considering in detail these new topics introduced by Calvin in the second edition, Millet similarly argues that Melanchthon's precedent formed if not a model at the least a decisive point of reference for the new order of the material and Calvin's conception of his own book.[91] In particular, Calvin's discussion of providence and predestination attests to points of contact and reveals an attentive reading and critique of the 1535 *Loci*.[92]

If Calvin crafted the Pauline shape of his theology in reference to Melanchthon's approach, did his historical consciousness inform this process, and if so, in what way? Although full consideration of this lies beyond

---

[89] Richard Muller, "*Ordo docendi*: Melanchthon and the Organization of Calvin's *Institutes*, 1536–1539," in *Melanchthon in Europe: His Work and Influence Beyond Wittenberg*, ed. Karin Maag (Grand Rapids, MI: Baker, 1999), 125.

[90] Muller, "*Ordo docendi*," 137.

[91] Olivier Millet, "Les *Loci communes* de 1535 et l'*Institution de la Religion chrétienne* de 1539–1541, ou Calvin en dialogue avec Melanchthon," in *Melanchthon und Europa*, part 2, *Westeuropa*, Melanchthon-Schriften der Stadt Bretten 6, ed. Günter Frank and Kees Meerhoff (Stuttgart: Thorbecke, 2002), 86.

[92] Millet, "Les *Loci communes*," 93.

the scope of this chapter's consideration of Calvin's reception of Paul, a few comments are in order. Melanchthon and Calvin shared a common fascination with the past and with divine providence, even though they differed in important ways in their explication of and emphasis on the latter. Both, moreover, incorporated sacred and profane history into their theological projects, though here, too, there are significant differences between their approaches. One difference can be seen in their handling of the doctrine of the church in the versions of their theological summaries that appeared in the 1540s.

Background for Melanchthon's discussion lies in his involvement in a historical project spanning nearly three decades. In 1532, he reworked and published a chronicle of world history originally compiled by the Brandenburg court astrologer, Johannes Carion (1499–1537). Near the end of his life, he revised, expanded, and republished the first half of the text, covering the period from the beginning of the world up through the time of Charlemagne. After Melanchthon's death, his son-in-law, Casper Peucer (1525–1602), completed the project and brought it up to the sixteenth century.[93] *Carion's Chronicle* (as the text was known) combined the history of the world and the history of the church in order to demonstrate God's providence and the value of studying history; it was wildly popular and, according to Wengert, was likely used as a textbook in the Genevan Academy after its establishment in 1559.[94] In his treatment of the early church, Melanchthon shows deep interest in historical events, documents, figures, and the details of theological history, but (typically for his age) his overall engagement with the ecclesiastical past is driven by an ideological purpose: namely, to show that the true church was always an embattled minority and to utilize earlier doctrinal battles to combat contemporary heresy.

These same presumptions underlie Melanchthon's doctrinal discussion of the church in the 1535 *Loci* and the revised and expanded discussions of this topic in the 1543 and 1545 editions.[95] In the latter, Melanchthon makes only limited use of historical details to illustrate his claims about the nature of the church and its members, its foundation in the gospel of Christ, and its

[93] *Chronicon Carionis*, in CR 12: 709–1094. For discussion of the view of history in this text, see Irena Backus, *Historical Method and Confessional Identity in the Era of the Reformation (1378–1615)* (Leiden: Brill, 2003), 326–38.
[94] Timothy J. Wengert, "Philip Melanchthon on Time and History in the Reformation," *Consensus: A Canadian Journal of Public Theology* 30 (2005): 17.
[95] CR 21: 505–10; CR 21: 826–43. Melanchthon rewrote this discussion for the 1543 edition, and then rewrote the first part of it again for the 1545 edition published by Seitz.

authority. He briefly mentions examples from the Old and New Testament and the early church to show that the saints are always mixed with the unregenerate in the visible church and that even some of those who held to Christ as the foundation (citing Paul, 1 Cor. 3:11) had weaknesses and allowed inappropriate human traditions to shape spiritual practice. An expanded excursus against the Donatists is intended not to instruct about the past, but rather to prepare contemporary evangelicals to understand the authority of the office of ministers and to reject Anabaptist demands for morally pure leaders. History supplements and illustrates the authoritative scriptural justifications for this teaching, most of which come from Paul.

In contrast to Melanchthon, Calvin did not write a work devoted to world or church history, but his historical consciousness manifests itself unmistakably in his summary of Christian doctrine. It is apparent already in his treatments of the church and ecclesiastical power in the 1539 edition and particularly in the vastly expanded treatment of these topics in chapter 8 of the 1543 *Institutes*.[96] This latter edition bears witness to Calvin's intensive study of the history and institution of the church—including an array of patristic writings—in Strasbourg and during the period when he returned to Geneva and was actively restructuring religious life for the city and, as discussed earlier, drawing on Paul in this process. To be clear, Calvin's aim is to present evangelical teaching on the nature of the church, its two signs or marks, and its authority, and just as in the *Supplex exhortatio*, he often appeals to Pauline texts to advance his position. Moreover, his discussions of these topics frequently echo points made by Melanchthon in the *Loci*: the visible church as containing both regenerate and unregenerate; the two marks of proper preaching and administration of the sacraments; the inability to determine who the hypocrites are; and the rejection of the moral perfectionism of the Donatists and Anabaptists (Calvin also includes the Cathars).[97] Also like Melanchthon, Calvin references past examples from church history with an eye to serving the present. Yet Calvin justifies the schism from the Roman church at greater length, and in so doing, he deepens his appeal to history to advance his case. He compares the condition of Roman Catholic religion to the idolatry of Israel under Jeroboam in order to show how God preserves

---

[96] John Calvin, *Institutio christianae religionis nunc vere demum suo titulo respondens* (Strasbourg: W. Rihel, 1543), 160–242. See Anette Zillenbiller, *Die Einheit der katholischen Kirche: Calvins Cyprianrezeption in seinen ekklesiologischen Schriften* (Mainz: van Zabern, 1993), 44–49.

[97] Calvin, *Institutio* (1543), 159–61; cf. *Institutes* (1559), 4.1.7–13.

a vestige of the church there, even though the marks of the church are no longer present and thus schism is justified.[98] To legitimate this picture further, he traces the history of the forms of church governance and power from New Testament times until the present to show the corruption of the various ecclesiastical offices, the neglect of Christ's headship, the stages of the emergence of papal primacy, the defining of nonscriptural doctrines, and the deterioration of church councils over time.[99] This is clearly a polemical use of history, but nevertheless Calvin's account provides rich historical detail to, in essence, refute his opponents' appeals to the past and claim history for the evangelical cause. Thus, analogous to his employment of Paul for reform of the church, Calvin's use of Paul as theological tutor needs to be seen in the context of Calvin's historical consciousness. As for Melanchthon, Calvin's summary of piety rests on a Pauline foundation, but, more than Melanchthon, he uses history within the text itself not only to supplement and illustrate scriptural teaching but also to defend it.

Much more needs to be done on the complex interconnections between Calvin's and Melanchthon's lifelong efforts to craft an evangelical alternative to the medieval theological textbooks and the role of their humanistic historical sensibilities in this process. Regarding their reception of Paul in this process, however, this much can be said: as a theologian, Calvin followed the spirit, if not the letter, of Melanchthon's radically new Pauline orientation. This is not to discount the important role played by other conversation partners—notably, Erasmus—in shaping Calvin's theology and his reception of Paul.[100] Nor does it diminish Calvin's characteristic independence of mind. In their articulation of key theological topics—most notably on the fallenness of human nature, the power of the human will, predestination, divine agency, and the nature of Christ's eucharistic presence—Calvin and Melanchthon not only differed from each other but they also addressed and criticized one another's positions anonymously in revisions to their respective writings.[101] Yet this can be seen as a disagreement over the conclusions each one drew from a common reading of Paul. Following Melanchthon's footsteps, Calvin at points charted a different landscape. Yet to return to the

---

[98] Calvin, *Institutio* (1543), 166–68; cf. *Institutes* (1559), 4.2.7–12.

[99] Calvin, *Institutio* (1543), 174–222; cf. *Institutes* (1559), 4.4–9. See also Charles H. Parker, "Bourges to Geneva: Methodological Links between Legal Humanists and Calvinist Reformers," *Comitatus: A Journal of Medieval and Renaissance Studies* 20, no. 1 (1989): 63–65.

[100] See, for example, Essary, *Erasmus and Calvin*.

[101] See, for example, Barbara Pitkin, "The Protestant Zeno: Calvin and the Development of Melanchthon's Anthropology," *Journal of Religion* 84 (2004): 345–78.

question posed at the beginning of this investigation—Which Paul exercised such a pervasive influence on Calvin?—there can be no doubt that as a Pauline *theologian* Calvin was in many important respects Melanchthonian. He accepted completely Melanchthon's view of Paul as *the* Christian theologian and of Romans as the generator of the primary biblical *loci* to be elucidated in a summary of Christian piety. Calvin's own reading of the Pauline sources led him often to different conclusions, which he often crafted in conscious response to Melanchthon's own views, and in his theological magnum opus he combined his Pauline theological orientation with his historical consciousness in a somewhat distinctive way.

Conclusion

Calvin's reception of Paul was wide-ranging, shaping foundationally and profoundly his activities as a biblical exegete, church reformer, and theologian over the course of his entire career. In his lifelong engagement with the one he held to be the first among the apostles and the principal doctor of the church, he took the humanist route *ad fontes*, discovering in Paul an everlasting well of truth and example that could not be drunk dry. In this and other ways, his approach to, esteem for, and reading of Paul were very much conditioned by the intellectual, religious, and political climate of his day. Distinctive to Calvin's engagement with Paul was his deep appreciation of Paul's own historical context; for Calvin, Paul spoke first and foremost to his own contemporaries in the early church. And yet Paul also addressed later generations through the universality of his message and the exemplary character of his ministry. Calvin viewed his own age as a time for spreading the true gospel and building up the church in the face of resistant forces. Because of this perceived similarity of times and because of Paul's unique apostolic authority, he saw in Paul's own efforts to do the same in his context an unparalleled theological orientation, a model for collegial leadership, and a mirror of the setbacks and challenges facing his own agenda. Paul for Calvin was not beyond criticism, but he was nevertheless the primary biblical model and authority for Calvin's own program.

The Paul who exercised such a pervasive influence on Calvin's work was largely Paul the theologian and pastor of the apostolic church, known from his thirteen letters and Acts viewed through evangelical theological convictions. Calvin assumed that the letter to the Romans laid out the central Christian truths that guided the interpretation of all of scripture. On the foundation of this common assumption he built a distinctive program of biblical exegesis, established a reformed church in Geneva, and developed a Protestant systematic theology that constituted the only serious rival to that of his mentor in Pauline studies, Melanchthon. His unique bequest to his contemporaries and successors consists in a historically informed reading of Paul combined with a heightened appreciation for the centrality and contemporary relevance of Paul's theological insights.

3

Salvation in History in Calvin's Commentary on the Gospel of John

Introduction

In his preface to his 1553 commentary on the Gospel of John, Calvin joined a long line of Christian thinkers in expressing high esteem for the Fourth Gospel's unique teaching. Although all four gospels, he claims, aim to make Christ known, the first three exhibit his "body," whereas John exhibits his "soul."[1] Despite this traditional affirmation of John's special character, Calvin's commentary occupies a singular place in the history of Johannine interpretation. It represents the culmination of certain sixteenth-century approaches to the Fourth Gospel, redefining its "spiritual" character and reversing traditional views that this gospel offered advanced and more difficult teaching than Matthew, Mark, and Luke. Calvin's understanding of John follows key contemporary trends, but is also uniquely shaped by his historical consciousness. As with his treatment of the Old Testament books of Psalms and Isaiah (discussed in chapters 4 and 5), Calvin downplays the traditional emphasis among Christian exegetes on christological doctrine. Instead, he emphasizes the overarching theme of human salvation and Christ's salvific mission within human history.

This commentary marks an important stage in Calvin's exegetical activity and his career in Geneva. This was his first gospel commentary, and it was published in the midst of what was clearly the most turbulent period in his time in the city.[2] He discusses these trials in his dedication to the syndics and town council—a cagey political move, given that the majority of the members of the council at the time were sympathetic to Calvin's opposition. Protesting

---

[1] John Calvin, *In evangelium secundum Johannem, commentarius Johannis Calvini* ([Geneva]: R. Estienne, 1553), OE 11/1: 8 = CO 47: vii; English translation as John Calvin, *Commentary on the Gospel of John*, 2 vols., ed. and trans. William Pringle, repr. in *Calvin's Commentaries* (Grand Rapids, MI: Baker Books, 1989), 1: 22; hereafter *Commentary on John*, followed by volume and page number.
[2] William G. Naphy, *Calvin and the Consolidation of the Genevan Reformation,* revised edition (Louisville, KY: Westminster John Knox, 2003), 173–78.

Calvin, the Bible, and History. Barbara Pitkin, Oxford University Press (2020). © Oxford University Press.
DOI: 10.1093/oso/9780190093273.001.0001

the charges of excessive severity and reminding these magistrates of their duty to refute the slanders against him, Calvin reasoned that it was important to have a special monument to his teaching—namely, this commentary— inscribed with their name. Echoing Jeremiah, he expressed his hope that this commentary would take a firmer hold of their memory: "I pray to God to inscribe it so deeply with his own finger on your hearts that it may never be obliterated by any stratagem of Satan."[3] Investigation of the circumstances surrounding Calvin's commentary, the general trends in the history of the interpretation of the Fourth Gospel prior to Calvin, and the important methodological and substantive aspects of Calvin's own commentary will demonstrate both its singular place in the history of Johannine interpretation and the impact of his historical sensitivities on the interpretation of the gospel that even he held to be less focused on conveying historical narrative than the other three.

Calvin's Engagement with the Fourth Gospel

Calvin had lectured on the Fourth Gospel early in his career, in 1539 at Johannes Sturm's (1507–1589) humanist academy in Strasbourg.[4] No record of these early lectures has survived. Nevertheless, that Calvin lectured on John before Matthew, Mark, or Luke and that he later made this gospel the subject of a written commentary before turning to the Synoptics fits with the conviction expressed in the Argument to the commentary that John's Gospel provides the key to understanding the other three.[5] Two years after the appearance of his commentary on John, he published a commentary on Matthew, Mark, and Luke in which he harmonized their respective accounts into a single narrative. From this point on, the two commentaries—on the Harmony and on John—were always printed together and occasionally appeared in French and Dutch along with the commentary on Acts.[6]

---

[3] OE 11/1: 5 = CO 47: vi; *Commentary on John*, 1: 18–19.
[4] Johannes Ficker, *Die Anfänge der akademischen Studien in Straßburg* (Strasbourg: Heitz, 1912), 41; François Wendel, *Calvin: Origins and Development of His Religious Thought*, trans. Philip Mairet (1963; rpt. Durham, NC: Labyrinth, 1987), 61. For broader discussion of Calvin's activities in Strasbourg, see Cornelis Augustijn, "Calvin in Strasbourg," in *Calvinus Sacrae Scripturae Professor: Calvin as Confessor of Holy Scripture*, ed. Wilhelm H. Neuser (Grand Rapids, MI: Eerdmans, 1994), 166–77.
[5] OE 11/1: 8 = CO 47: vii; *Commentary on John*, 1: 22.
[6] See BC 3: 645.

Calvin's commitment to the theological priority of the Pauline epistles, especially Romans, and their prominence in his exegetical program
(as discussed in chapter 2) suggests why he completed his commentaries
on Paul and Hebrews before turning to other New Testament writings.
Having taken over a decade to work his way through the Pauline epistles and
Hebrews, Calvin might have made the practical decision to focus in 1549–
1550 on the short, remaining epistles of the New Testament before tackling
the much longer Acts and the gospels, especially since the canonical epistles
were conveniently the current topic of the weekly communal Bible studies
(congrégations). As Erik de Boer has shown, the congrégations functioned as
an incubator for Calvin's published commentaries.[7]

Beginning in 1550, the topic of the congrégations was the Gospel of John,
and Calvin may have begun conceiving of his commentary at this time.[8] At
this point, Calvin was also lecturing on Genesis in the school and trying,
without much success, to write the commentary on it.[9] In addition, he was
working on a commentary on Acts, the book that was the current focus of
his Sunday morning sermons. His ecclesiastical duties, of course, were not
confined to lecturing, preaching, and participating in the congrégations.
Energy-consuming also was the fact that the early 1550s witnessed the
gradual increase of tension between Calvin and the city council of Geneva,
which came to a head in 1553.[10] It is no wonder then that he had no time to
write on John. This changed, however, in 1552, or perhaps even earlier, when
Calvin interrupted his work on Acts, sent the first half of that commentary to

---

[7] On the congrégations, see Erik A. de Boer, Genevan School of the Prophets: The congrégations
of the Company of Pastors and Their Influence in 16th Century Europe (Geneva: Droz, 2012); Erik
A. de Boer, "The Presence and Participation of Laypeople in the congrégations of the Company of
Pastors in Geneva," Sixteenth Century Journal 35, no. 3 (Fall 2004): 651–70; Erik A. de Boer, "The
congrégation: An In-Service Theological Training Center for Preachers to the People of Geneva,"
in Calvin and the Company of Pastors, ed. David L. Foxgrover (Grand Rapids, MI: Calvin Studies
Society, 2004), 57–87; Erik A. de Boer, "Calvin and Colleagues: Propositions and Disputations in
the Context of the congrégations in Geneva," in Calvinus Praeceptor Ecclesiae, ed. H. J. Selderhuis
(Geneva: Droz, 2004), 331–42.

[8] The introduction to John presented by Calvin in the congrégation was published in 1558 as a kind
of a preface to a collection of Calvin's sermons; see BC 2: 58/5. The text can be found in CO 47: 465–
84; in English in John Calvin, Sermons on the Deity of Christ and Other Sermons, ed. and trans. L.
Nixon (1950; rpt. Audubon, NJ: Old Paths Publications, 1997), 13–34. Unfortunately, the English
version perpetuates the misunderstanding that this is a sermon.

[9] Already in July 1542 Calvin wrote to Farel of his wish to write on Genesis, should God grant
him a long life and spare time (CO 11: 418). Eight years later, Calvin reported that he was beginning
the project, but by November 1550 he complained that he had had to put the project on the shelf for
a while (CO 13: 623, 655). See also BC 1: 54/8. The commentary on Genesis was finally published
in 1554.

[10] See Naphy, Calvin, 167–99.

the printer, and devoted himself to finishing his commentary on John, which appeared in January 1553.

Why Calvin shifted his priorities at that point in time to John is not known exactly. In the introduction to the recent critical edition of the commentary, editor Helmut Feld suggests that the immediate impetus may be sought in Michael Servetus's (1511–1553) *Christianisimi restitutio*, a work possibly conceived as an antidote to Calvin's *Institutes*. Servetus's work defended its unorthodox christological and trinitarian doctrine by appealing to passages in the Fourth Gospel. Although Servetus's book was not published until January 1553, the year in which he, in August, made his ill-fated appearance in Geneva, Calvin had a manuscript copy, obtained during a period of cor-respondence with the author in 1546 and 1547. Calvin was certainly trou-bled by Servetus's heterodoxy and refers to him in his comments on John 1. However, it is probably too much to claim that Calvin "seemed to have found it to be necessary to counter Servetus's views . . . as quickly as pos-sible with an orthodox christology and doctrine of the Trinity based on a correct exegesis of the text of the Gospel."[11] As will be argued in the rest of this chapter, Calvin does not understand the defense of orthodox doctrines of the trinity and Christ's person to be the *main* intention of the evangelist, and, moreover, he criticizes earlier interpreters who held this to be the case. Criticism of Servetus's interpretation of certain passages is evident in a lim-ited way in Calvin's commentary, but it is hard to see this as the primary moti-vation for writing it. Simply put, in 1552, there were more pressing challenges for Calvin to address.

One of these has its origins more directly in current debates in Geneva. In October 1551, Jerome Bolsec (d. ca. 1584) challenged the Genevan ministers' teaching on predestination during a *congrégation*. The text for the day was John 8, which was expounded by minister Jean de Saint-André with subse-quent comments by Guillaume Farel (1489–1565). Bolsec argued against the interpretation of John 8:47 ("He that is of God hears God's words") and was refuted by Calvin's extemporaneous defense of the Genevan doctrine. Bolsec was arrested immediately and a lengthy trial ensued, catching the attention of notables outside of Geneva, such as Philip Melanchthon (1497–1560), Heinrich Bullinger (1504–1575), and Laelius Socinus (1525–1562).[12] Even

---

[11] OE 11/1: xi.

[12] For a brief summary, see Wulfert de Greef, *The Writings of John Calvin, Expanded Edition: An Introductory Guide*, trans. Lyle D. Bierma (Louisville, KY: Westminster John Knox, 2008), 34–35; for a full account, see P. C. Holtrop, *The Bolsec Controversy on Predestination, from 1551 to 1555*, 2 vols. (Lewiston, ME: Edwin Mellen, 1993).

after Bolsec was banished at the conclusion of the trial in December, the controversy continued to agitate the city. A public debate on the topic was held in the fall of 1552 between Calvin and Jean Trolliet, who cited from the French translation of Melanchthon's *Loci communes* to support Bolsec's criticisms.[13] Although election and reprobation are major themes in Calvin's commentary on John, I think that Calvin's emphasis on these topics is likely suggested by certain passages in the biblical text. It is not sufficient to attribute his motives in writing on John to a desire to defend his teaching on predestination any more than to a wish to defend orthodox understandings of christology and the trinity. Nevertheless, the fact remains that a particular point of interpretation of John had been challenged publicly in Geneva, and it could be that Calvin found himself at a natural break in the Acts commentary and decided to shift his energies to finishing the commentary on John.

Despite the contentious climate surrounding the writing of his commentary, Calvin—as was his custom in his commentaries—rarely alludes to current ecclesiastical and political difficulties in Geneva.[14] Indeed, the main polemical target he identifies is "papal religion" in general, claiming in his dedicatory epistle that he hopes that this commentary will show it to be a satanic monstrosity. It is thus probably wise to consider Calvin's decision to write on John as a logical next step in the exegetical program he had been carrying forth since the early 1540s. And yet, the dedication cloaks the entire commentary in the aura of an apology, in which Calvin pleads the case for his teaching not for the benefit of Roman opponents but rather before the officials of Geneva. In a certain sense, therefore, this commentary can be viewed as a defense of his teaching and pastoral authority in the face of the challenges of his own historical situation. Responding to these challenges, Calvin offers a novel interpretation of the Fourth Gospel's claims about Christ that uses his historicizing approach to draw a recent shift in Johannine interpretation to some controversial conclusions.

Interpretations of John Prior to Calvin

Appreciation of what is novel in Calvin's interpretation of John is possible only against the background of traditional attitudes toward and exegesis

---

[13] CO 14: 371–83.

[14] Explicit political and polemical criticism do appear in his sermons from this time; see Naphy, *Calvin*, 154–62.

of the Fourth Gospel. This section provides a general sketch of the exegetical tradition and does not—indeed, cannot—attempt to convey all the variety and richness of the conversation concerning John prior to Calvin.[15]
Moreover, there can be no question here of identifying precisely *how* these
traditional concerns were mediated to him. Rather, the discussion will identify key questions that arose out of the biblical text itself as viewed by some
of its most influential interpreters and sketch some of their most common
responses to these issues.

A fundamental question addressed by many patristic interpreters was
the relationship of John to the other three gospels.[16] Early Christian writers
responded by reflecting on the unique character and purpose of John's account. According to the church historian Eusebius (d. ca. 340), John wrote
his gospel primarily to supplement the other three (which he had read and
approved) with an account of Jesus's earlier ministry.[17] Yet as Eusebius points
out, tradition also held that John complemented the Synoptics not only in
the scope of its coverage of Jesus's ministry but also in its teaching about
Jesus himself. The long history of viewing the Fourth Gospel as more spiritual than the other three and having as its distinct purpose the conveying
and defending of spiritual mysteries has its origins as early as Clement of
Alexandria (ca. 150–215). According to Clement, John wrote after the other
three: "Last of all, aware that the physical facts had been recorded in the gospels [according to Matthew, Luke, and Mark], encouraged by his pupils and
irresistibly moved by the Spirit, John wrote a spiritual gospel."[18] Soon thereafter Origen (ca. 184–253) wrote his commentary on John, which he viewed
as the "first fruits" of the gospels—indeed, of all scripture.[19] Judgments about
the unique visionary nature and eminence of John were echoed two centuries later by Jerome (ca. 347–420) and found their place in the homilies and

---

[15] For a sometimes rough and bibliographic catalogue of the history of the interpretation of
John that draws on secondary studies, see Sean P. Kealy, *John's Gospel and the History of Biblical
Interpretation*, 2 vols. (Lewiston, ME: Edwin Mellen, 2002). Feld discusses possible sources for
Calvin's commentary in OE 11/1: xxii–xxiv.

[16] On patristic interpretation of the Gospel of John, see Maurice Wiles, *The Spiritual Gospel: The
Interpretation of the Fourth Gospel in the Early Church* (Cambridge, UK: Cambridge University Press,
1960); Steven P. Brey, "Origen's Commentary on John: Seeing All Creation as Gospel" (Ph.D. diss.,
University of Notre Dame, 2003); Lars Koen, *The Saving Passion: Incarnational and Soteriological
Thought in Cyril of Alexandria's Commentary on the Gospel According to St. John* (Stockholm: Almqvist
& Wiksell, 1991).

[17] Eusebius, *The History of the Church from Christ to Constantine*, revised edition, trans. G. A.
Williamson (New York: Penguin, 1989), 86–88 [book 3, chapter 24].

[18] As reported by Eusebius, *History of the Church*, 192 [book 6, chapter 14].

[19] Origen, *Commentary on the Gospel According to John, Books 1–10*, trans. R. E. Heine
(Washington, DC: Catholic University of America Press, 1989), 38 [book 1, section 23].

commentaries of John Chrysostom (ca. 347–407), Augustine (354–430), and Cyril of Alexandria (ca. 376–444).

To varying degrees, patristic writers also endeavored to explain discrepancies between the Fourth Gospel and the Synoptic accounts.[20] In comparing them, many suggested or openly proclaimed the superiority of John. Their esteem reflects a popularity that is evident, moreover, in the material culture of the early church. The Fourth Gospel's representation in papyrus finds of the second and third centuries is "unusually strong," and examples of Christian art from the catacomb paintings in Rome "also testify to the popularity of the Johannine presentation of the events of Jesus' life."[21] Popular also, albeit somewhat later, were images of the evangelist himself, represented as an eagle rising above the others. The basis for this iconography was laid down by Jerome, who revised Irenaeus's (ca. 130–200) correlation of the four evangelists with the four-faced heavenly beings of Ezekiel 1:10 or the four living creatures of Revelation 4:6–8. According to Jerome, John becomes the eagle, who "soars aloft, and reaches the Father Himself, and says, 'In the beginning was the Word.'"[22] Interpreters sometimes expanded this comparison by further reflections on eagle behavior. Augustine, for example, relates that parent birds test young eaglets in the following way: "[The fledgling] is suspended, of course, on the claws of the father and held up to the rays of the sun; if it gazes steadily [into the sun], it is acknowledged as a son; if it quivers at the sight, it is dropped from the claw as a bastard."[23] Thus, John, as the eagle, is particularly and uniquely qualified to contemplate and proclaim sublime truths. Interpreters found justification for John's loftier spiritual insight in the fact that he was the disciple whom Jesus loved; that he reclined at the breast of Jesus and received Jesus's mother as his own at the foot of the cross; and, finally, that he was presumed to be the author not only of his gospel but of three epistles and, significantly, the book of Revelation.[24]

[20] Wiles, *Spiritual Gospel*, 13–21.

[21] Charles E. Hill, *The Johannine Corpus in the Early Church* (New York: Oxford University Press, 2004), 469.

[22] Jerome, *Against Jovinianus*, book 1, section 26, in *St. Jerome: Letters and Select Works*, Nicene and Post Nicene Fathers, series 2, vol. 6 (Grand Rapids, MI: Eerdmans, 1996), 366. For Ireneus, see his *Against Heresies*, in "An Exposition of the Faith: Selections from the Work *Against Heresies* by Irenaeus, Bishop of Lyon," ed. and trans. Edward Rochie Hardy, in *Early Christian Fathers*, ed. Cyril C. Richardson (Philadelphia: Westminster, 1953), 382–83.

[23] Augustine, *Tractates on the Gospel of John 28–54*, trans. J. W. Rettig (Washington, DC: Catholic University of America Press, 1993), 87.

[24] Early patristic writers were also concerned to establish the Johannine authorship of the Gospel; see Wiles, *Spiritual Gospel*, 7–10. For a recent analysis of early views of the relationship of the Gospel of John to the Johannine epistles and Revelation that challenges the position that the Gospel was considered problematic in the second and third centuries, see Hill, *Johannine Corpus*.

Early interpreters of John also identified a polemical motivation underlying the evangelist's purpose. Irenaeus argued that John wrote his spiritual gospel particularly to combat the errors planted by Cerinthus and the Nicolaitans.[25] Jerome repeated this claim and added that John wrote also to refute the Ebionite assertion that Christ did not exist before Mary.[26] Christian writers also found the Fourth Gospel relevant to their own polemical situations; for example, Irenaeus drew on John 1:1–3 to refute Valentinian Gnostics.[27] Johannine passages were particularly influential in fourth-century trinitarian debates, which had only heightened the evangelist's reputation as the proclaimer and defender of spiritual mysteries, especially concerning the nature of God and the Father's relationship to the Son. Both Chrysostom and Augustine expanded the scope of the polemic in their comments on John to criticize pagan philosophy.[28]

The idea that the Gospel of John proclaimed a deeper spiritual truth than the other three and did so in order to refute supposed perversions of heavenly mysteries invited reflection on the relationship of historical and symbolic meanings in the text. Did the deeper spiritual truth of the Fourth Gospel require a more thoroughgoing spiritual exegesis? Here interpreters' answers appear to depend more on their general hermeneutical orientations than on their perceptions of the Gospel itself. As Wiles notes, Origen, "always on the alert to find deeper meaning in the words of Scripture," believes that "many incidents are recorded for doctrinal purpose, and not as a strict historical account."[29] Theodore of Mopsuestia (ca. 350–428), in contrast, insists more consistently on the narrative's historical accuracy, and, with Cyril and Chrysostom, sees the purpose of many of the historical details to guarantee "the truly divine character of the events" recorded in the Gospel.[30] Regardless of their views on the purpose of historical details, however, all patristic interpreters pursued some deeper spiritual exegesis of many passages. For some, the focus was on uncovering doctrinal truths (a more allegorical interpretation), while others stressed the application of

---

[25] Irenaeus, *Against Heresies*, in "Exposition of Faith," 378–79.

[26] Jerome, *On Illustrious Men*, trans. T. P. Halton (Washington, DC: Catholic University of America Press, 1999), 19.

[27] Irenaeus, *Against Heresies*, in "Exposition of Faith," 379–81.

[28] John Chrysostom, *Commentary on Saint John the Apostle and Evangelist, Homilies 1–47*, trans. T. A. Goggin (New York: Fathers of the Church, 1957), 14–19; Augustine, *Tractates on the Gospel of John 1–10*, trans. J. W. Rettig (Washington, DC: Catholic University of America Press, 1988), 63–64.

[29] Wiles, *Spiritual Gospel*, 22.

[30] Wiles, *Spiritual Gospel*, 26.

the teachings or events for the Christian life (a more moral or tropological interpretation).[31]

Yet for all their differences with respect to attention to the historical sense, early Christian writers agreed on the main purpose and meaning of the Fourth Gospel. Though they approached it via different hermeneutical paths, interpreters held in common that John's central theme is Christ's divine nature.[32] The fourth evangelist supplements the other three by proclaiming this openly, and thus he refutes current *and* future heresies concerning Christ's person. It is the delineation of this particular doctrinal truth that makes the Gospel of John more spiritual than the rest and justifies for many interpreters its preeminent status. It also means that John is, for many, seen as a more difficult book to interpret. Yet an understanding of the Gospel's main purpose and the proper exegetical tools unlock the mysteries and reveal that, in the words of Chrysostom, John's "teachings are clearer than sunbeams."[33]

Medieval interpreters of John embraced the understanding of the Gospel's central purpose advanced in early Christian literature.[34] They accepted the familiar iconography of the eagle for John and the traditional reasons why it applied to him, even when they disagreed over whether Mark or Matthew should be the lion or the man.[35] Patristic opinions on these matters had been enshrined in the *Glossa ordinaria*, a continuous commentary on the Bible compiled in the early twelfth century and serving as the foundation for biblical study and scholarship for over two centuries.[36]

Given the traditional and conservative aims of most medieval biblical commentary, interpreters consciously report, seek to synthesize, and, very subtly, build on patristic ideas. For example, in the prologue to his commentary on John, Thomas Aquinas (1225–1274) repeats earlier judgments

---

[31] For a comparison of the different approaches of Cyril and Theodore, see Wiles, *Spiritual Gospel*, 32–40. Genre might also play a role in the interpretation of symbolism; for example, Chrysostom's homilies generally stress the moral ramifications of the passage for his congregation.

[32] Wiles, *Spiritual Gospel*, 11–12.

[33] Chrysostom, *Commentary on John Homilies 1–47*, 17.

[34] See, e.g., Mark Hazard, *The Literal Sense and the Gospel of John in Late Medieval Commentary and Literature* (New York: Routledge, 2002); James A. Weisheipl, "The Johannine Commentary of Friar Thomas," *Church History* 45 (1976): 185–95. On the gospels in general, see Beryl Smalley, *The Gospels in the Schools, c. 1100–c. 1280* (London: Hambledon Press, 1985). The most important medieval commentaries on John were the commentary of the Bulgarian archbishop Theophylact, the *Glossa ordinaria*, the commentary by Hugh of St. Cher, the commentary of Thomas Aquinas and his collection of authoritative opinions in his *Catena Aurea*, the *Postilla* of Nicholas of Lyra, and the commentary of Denis the Carthusian.

[35] Kevin Madigan, *Olivi and the Interpretation of Matthew in the High Middle Ages* (Notre Dame, IN: University of Notre Dame Press, 2003), 17.

[36] See Lesley Smith, *The Glossa Ordinaria: The Making of a Medieval Bible Commentary* (Leiden: Brill, 2009).

about John writing after the other three and aiming to refute the Ebionites and Cerinthus. He also claims that the special subject matter of John's Gospel is Christ's divinity and discusses in detail John's unique heavenly vision. However, he explicates John's contemplation of the eternal Word in connection with Isaiah's vision in Isaiah 6:1 and, moreover, outlines the Gospel's purpose in terms of its four Aristotelian causes.[37] He also explains that John's full, high, and perfect contemplation surpasses that of the moral and natural sciences, since it contains completely what they have only in a divided way. Similarly, Denis the Carthusian (1402–1471), referring explicitly to Augustine and Bede (ca. 672–735), affirms the preeminence of the Fourth Gospel over other scriptures on the grounds that John wrote more fully, clearly, and profoundly about many things and more sublimely about the Savior's teachings. He refers to the eagle iconography and repeats the standard view that John wrote after the others and wrote against christological heresies. He adds that because John's material is so sublime, one must be particularly humble and more earnestly appeal to the teaching of the Holy Spirit.[38]

Medieval interpreters of John continued to be sensitive to resolving discrepancies between the Fourth Gospel and Synoptic accounts and tended to be more interested than most of their patristic forebears in a more systematic delineation of the relationship between historical and symbolic meanings. In this regard they reflected and deepened the variety of hermeneutical approaches to this gospel taken in the patristic period. In general, medieval interpreters continued to assume that the text has two levels of meaning, a literal-historical and a mystical-spiritual. For example, commenting on John 1:23, where John the Baptist characterizes himself as a "voice crying in the wilderness," Thomas claims that the "wilderness" can be understood literally as the place where John the Baptist lived and says that he lived there in order to remain immune from sin and be more worthy to bear witness to Christ. The wilderness also refers symbolically to two things. On the one hand, "wilderness" or "desert" can mean paganism, so it signifies that God's word would be heard among the Gentiles. Alternatively, "wilderness" can mean Judea, or the Jews whom God has deserted.[39] It should be noted that Thomas does not

---

[37] Weisheipl, "Johannine Commentary of Friar Thomas," 191–93.

[38] Denis the Carthusian, *Enarratio in evangelium secundum Joannem*, in vol. 12 of *D. Dionysii Cartusiani opera omnia*, 42 vols. in 44 (Monstrolii: S. M. de Pratis, 1901), 267–68.

[39] Thomas Aquinas, *Commentum in Matthaeum et Joannem Evangelistas*, vol. 10 of *Sancti Thomae Aquinatis Doctoris Angelici Ordinis Praedicatorum opera omnia* (Parma: P. Fiaccadori, 1861; rpt. New York: Musurgia, 1949), 315–16. Note this is a good example of the interpretive principles that

always label the different levels of meaning, as he does in this instance, but throughout the commentary he nevertheless includes both literal and spiritual explanations similar to this one. Medieval commentators on John also reflected the variety of early interpreters in the weight or importance they assigned to these historical and symbolic meanings, but they were becoming more explicit about how they related them to one another. For Thomas, the "spiritual sense is based on the literal sense and presupposes it," and "nothing necessary to faith is contained within the spiritual sense which Scripture does not openly convey elsewhere through the literal sense."[40] Hence Thomas supports each of his interpretations of "wilderness" with cross-references to other scriptures that express literally the ideas symbolized in John 1:23.

The trend among some medieval interpreters, Thomas included, toward seeing the literal sense as foundational for spiritual meaning thus did not diminish but in a certain sense heightened the prestige of the so-called spiritual gospel.[41] There were two reasons for this. In the first place, the greater appreciation of the literal or historical sense did not necessarily mean a diminishing of the spiritual senses but rather, according to the original program of Hugh of St. Victor (ca. 1096–1141), led to a strengthening of allegory by placing it on a firmer footing.[42] Second, in some cases, this resulted in a blurring of the boundaries between the historical-literal and mystical-spiritual levels, with the literal sense being expanded to contain the meanings formerly contained in the spiritual senses. An example of this can be seen in Nicholas of Lyra's (ca. 1270–1340) interpretation of the healing pool of Bethesda (John 5). Traditional exegesis followed Chrysostom's explanation that the waters of the pool presented a typological figure of Christian baptism.[43] Thomas, for

---

Aquinas outlines in the *Summa Theologica*, Ia I, art. 9 and 10, especially his claim that the parabolic sense is contained within the literal sense: the "voice" is a figure for John, who came to make known God's word. But for Thomas that is the literal, not a mystical meaning. For an English translation, see A. J. Minnis and A. B. Scott, *Medieval Literary Theory and Criticism, c. 1100–c. 1375: The Commentary Tradition* (Oxford: Clarendon Press, 1988), 239–43.

[40] Thomas Aquinas, *Summa Theologica*, Ia I, art. 10, in Minnis and Scott, *Medieval Literary Theory*, 241–42.

[41] C. Spicq, *Esquisse d'une histoire de l'exégèse latine au moyen âge* (Paris: J. Vrin, 1944), esp. 209–15, 273–78; see also Beryl Smalley, *The Study of the Bible in the Middle Ages*, 3rd edition (Oxford: Basil Blackwell, 1983); Christopher Ocker, *Biblical Poetics before Humanism and Reformation* (Cambridge, UK: Cambridge University Press, 2002).

[42] Hazard, *Literal Sense*, 5.

[43] Chrysostom, *Commentary on John Homilies 1–47*, 352. Craig Farmer notes that Tertullian also suggested the baptismal symbolism of the passage. Craig Farmer, *The Gospel of John in the Sixteenth Century: The Johannine Exegesis of Wolfgang Musculus* (New York: Oxford University Press, 1997), 217n39.

example, cited this opinion as one of the mystical meanings of the pool and explains the reasons why the Lord chose water to prefigure the grace of baptism in the sacrament. Nicholas of Lyra made no reference to a "mystical" meaning and instead related the theme of baptism more intrinsically to the literal sense of the passage.[44] Indeed, for Nicholas, it was precisely the Gospel of John with its more spiritual character that provided the opportunity to work out more precisely an intrinsic link between the levels of meaning.[45] As Mark Hazard observes, "The Gospel of John's theme, that divine word and sign are intimately related, provided Lyra with important scriptural material and allowed him to base this connection [that the spiritual sense was included in the literal] on Gospel history."[46] Paradoxically, then, the spiritual gospel could be construed according to a certain logic as also the most literal gospel, since as the fullest, most complete, and perfect expression of the words, deed, and person of Christ it narrates the fulfillment of sacred history toward which all of the rest of scripture merely points.

Medieval commentary on John furthered the understanding of the Fourth Gospel's central purpose, its origins, and its author that were products of the early church. By blending these insights together and formalizing them as aids to the study of scripture, for example in the glosses accompanying the biblical text or in commentaries for use in the new university context, medieval exegetes crafted a rich interpretive tradition, which guided their reading of scripture. Their approaches to John thus differed from those of their patristic forebears in two fundamental ways. First, they consciously read through the lenses of tradition, interpreting the Fourth Gospel not just in relation to the other scriptures but in light of authoritative opinions of the church fathers. Second, their engagement with the richness of the exegetical past led them to seek more systematic ways to relate these various levels of meaning one to another.

Enthusiasm for the Gospel of John and appreciation for its unique qualities spilled over into the sixteenth century.[47] Martin Luther (1483–1546)

[44] Hazard, *Literal Sense*, 68–69.
[45] Hazard, *Literal Sense*, 6–7.
[46] Hazard, *Literal Sense*, 8.
[47] On the interpretation of the Gospel of John in the sixteenth century, see especially Farmer, *Gospel of John*; Albert Rabil, Jr., "Erasmus' Paraphrase of the Gospel of John," *Church History* 48 (1979): 142–55; Timothy J. Wengert, *Philip Melanchthon's Annotationes in Johannem in Relation to Its Predecessors and Contemporaries* (Geneva: Droz, 1987); Ulrich Gäbler, "Bullingers Vorlesung über das Johannesevangelium aus dem Jahre 1523," in *Heinrich Bullinger, 1504–1575: Gesammelte Aufsätze zum 400. Todestag*, ed. U. Gäbler and E. Herkenrath (Zurich: Theologischer Verlag, 1975), 13–27; Eduard Ellwein, *Summus Evangelista: Die Botschaft des Johannesevangeliums in der Auslegung Luthers* (Munich: Chr. Kaiser, 1960); Irena Backus, "Church, Communion, and Community in

famously asserted that the Gospel of John, Paul's letters (especially Romans), and 1 Peter were the best and noblest books in the New Testament, and that John was the "one, fine, true, and chief gospel . . . far, far to be preferred to the other three and placed high above them."[48] Erasmus (1466–1536), more reserved with regard to preference, nevertheless held that John's "grand theme" was even more majestic than that of Matthew.[49] These attitudes were reflected in a sudden outpouring of new commentaries on the Fourth Gospel beginning in 1522 to 1523. Up to that time, interpretations of John by four patristic authors and nine medieval commentators or compilers had become available in print. Erasmus's *Annotations* on the New Testament also appeared beginning in 1516. However from 1522 to the middle of the century, over thirty living writers published exegetical treatments of the Fourth Gospel. In the same period, the appearance of previously unpublished medieval commentaries paled in comparison and the republication of those previously printed slowed considerably.[50]

If this interest in and esteem for the Gospel of John reflected long-standing attitudes, traditional as well was the variety of hermeneutical approaches these works embodied. Craig Farmer has demonstrated the complexity of early modern interpretations of the Fourth Gospel, which cannot be classified according to simplistic confessional stereotypes. Protestant interpreters, for example, did not uniformly reject traditional exegesis, nor did they all eschew allegorical interpretations. Although Martin Bucer (1491–1551) explicitly rejected allegory in his preface to his commentary on the Synoptic Gospels, other Protestants, such as Melanchthon, embraced it or, following

Bucer's Commentary on the Gospel of John," in *Martin Bucer: Reforming Church and Community*, ed. D. F. Wright (Cambridge, UK: Cambridge University Press, 1994), 61–71; Barbara Pitkin, "Seeing and Believing in the Commentaries on John by Martin Bucer and John Calvin," *Church History* 68, no. 4 (1999): 865–85; Craig Farmer, "Wolfgang Musculus's Commentary on John: Tradition and Innovation in the Story of the Woman Taken in Adultery," in *Biblical Interpretation in the Era of the Reformation: Essays Presented to David C. Steinmetz in Honor of His Sixtieth Birthday*, ed. Richard A. Muller and John L. Thompson (Grand Rapids, MI: Eerdmans, 1996), 216–40; Craig Farmer, "Changing Images of the Samaritan Woman in Early Reformed Commentaries on John," *Church History* 65, no. 3 (1996): 365–75.

[48] This in his preface to the German New Testament of 1522; WADB 6: 10; in English in LW 35: 362.

[49] In his dedicatory letter prefacing his 1523 *Paraphrasis in Ioannem*; in English in Erasmus, *Paraphrase on John*, trans. and ann. J. E. Phillips, vol. 46 of *Collected Works of Erasmus* (Toronto: University of Toronto Press, 1991), 2.

[50] These figures are taken from Wengert, *Melanchthon's Annotationes*, 20–21; see also the appendix detailing works printed from 1470 to 1555.

the trend exemplified by Nicholas of Lyra, crammed formerly mystical-symbolic or tropological meanings into the literal sense.[51]

Despite this continuity with the antecedent traditions of interpretation, there were significant shifts in approach to the Fourth Gospel in the sixteenth century. In the first place, many interpreters embraced humanistic scholarship and employed critical philological tools to a greater and more systematic degree than medieval interpreters had done. More of them could read the Old and New Testaments in the original languages. Less concerned consciously to synthesize the inherited wisdom of the fathers, early modern exegetes frequently shifted the focus of their comments to the evangelist's own meaning, often uncovered through philological or rhetorical analysis of the text. Thus, Erasmus found *sermo* to be a more accurate translation for *logos* in John 1:1 and 1:14 than the Vulgate's *verbum*, though this substitution in his Latin translation of the New Testament and his *Annotationes* aroused heated controversy.[52] Melanchthon expressed the same humanistic spirit in the way he organized and structured his comments on John according to key "common places" or topics suggested by his reading of the text, even though he used the Vulgate as his base text and frequently ignored or distanced himself from the substantive interpretations in Erasmus's *Annotationes*.[53] It is important to note that interest in textual matters and thematic or topical organization in a commentary was not new but was in certain fundamental ways in continuity with previous commentary traditions. At the same time, the development of these methods in humanistic biblical scholarship and their self-consciously classical basis signaled a new direction in biblical interpretation, best characterized perhaps as a shift in emphasis.

This new direction was perhaps most evident in the changing role that the exegetical past played in sixteenth-century commentaries on John. The new printing technology made possible the wider dissemination of the works of ancient commentators. Sixteenth-century interpreters could more easily read the entire commentary of Augustine or the homilies of Chrysostom rather than encountering their opinions only as sound bites in biblical glosses, in the commentaries of others, or in anthologies of excerpts. To be sure, the exegetical heritage continued to appear in this excerpted fashion; in the

---

[51] On Bucer and Melanchthon, see Wengert, *Melanchthon's Annotationes*, 110–12; on Musculus, who used allegory occasionally but focused primarily on tropological exegesis, see Farmer, *Gospel of John*, 50–52.

[52] See C. A. L. Jarrott, "Erasmus' *In Principio Erat Sermo*: A Controversial Translation," *Studies in Philology* 61 (1964): 35–40.

[53] Wengert, *Melanchthon's Annotationes*, 132–34.

Annotationes, Erasmus cited traditional interpretations of passages and used these as guides for unlocking the meaning of difficult passages. Interpreters on both sides of the confessional divide expected that the church fathers had important insights into the meaning of scripture and that their wisdom served as a guide to interpretation, as evident in the popularity of editions of patristic commentary. But whereas in their commentaries most medieval biblical interpreters tended to synthesize and harmonize what were considered authoritative interpretations of the sacred text, many sixteenth-century commentators viewed the tradition with a more critical eye, rejecting some ideas as false or simply bypassing them altogether. Even Erasmus noted in his *Paraphrases* that the ancient interpreters had at times distorted the sense of the text "with some force."[54] Caution is warranted at this point, for recent scholarship has demonstrated the enormous complexity of the reception of the fathers in both the Middle Ages and in the sixteenth century.[55] Nevertheless, one clearly senses in reading the commentaries themselves a distinct difference in the way interpreters engage the inherited tradition and view its authority.

The roots of a final and crucial difference lie in the most significant religious event of the sixteenth century, namely, the schism that led to the emergence of different Christian confessional churches. As David Steinmetz has argued, Protestants and Catholics did not "disagree in predictable ways over the exegesis of biblical texts, aside, of course, from a few texts on which they had principled and irreconcilable disagreements."[56] Farmer has demonstrated this to be true for the interpretation of the Gospel of John. However, although confessional differences did not influence interpretation in ways one might expect, the issue at the root of the divide—that is, divergent soteriologies—shaped the exegesis of the Fourth Gospel in a profound way. In the first commentary on John by a Protestant writer, Melanchthon exhibited a certain reticence toward the trinitarian and christological dogmas that figured so prominently in patristic and medieval exegeses of John. Although he discussed and agreed with orthodox interpreters on these issues, he shifted the focus from christological or trinitarian problems to the more pressing soteriological questions.[57]

[54] Erasmus, *Paraphrase*, 12.

[55] Irena Backus, ed., *The Reception of the Church Fathers in the West: From the Carolingians to the Maurists*, 2 vols. (Leiden: Brill, 1997).

[56] David C. Steinmetz, "Divided by a Common Past: The Reshaping of the Christian Exegetical Tradition in the Sixteenth Century," *Journal of Medieval and Early Modern Studies* 27 (1997): 245–46.

[57] Wengert, *Melanchthon's Annotationes*, 93, 113.

He thus unwittingly inaugurated a trend that ran counter to the traditional consensus about John's central purpose. In short, by shifting the focus to soteriology, Melanchthon placed into question the traditional view that John wrote primarily to defend Christ's divinity. His commentary promoted a new understanding of John's purpose, one expressed in Luther's contemporaneous judgment about the priority of John. For Luther, it was not John's more complete orthodox christology but rather his more clear delineation of "how faith in Christ overcomes sin, death, and hell, and gives life, righteousness, and salvation" that made John's Gospel superior to the other three.[58] Not all interpreters followed this new trend, but one who did and who can be said to represent its culmination was John Calvin.

Calvin as a Commentator on the Gospel of John

In both method and substance, Calvin's commentary on John engages both ancient and contemporary trends in interpretation. His historical consciousness pushes him not only to emphasize the mind of the author or, in many cases, the intent of the speaker, Christ, in the narrative, but also to advance the recent shift regarding the central message and purpose of John by explicitly rejecting the traditional readings promoting Christ's divine nature. Instead, Calvin focuses on Christ's salvific mission in human history as the Gospel's major theme.

The mixture of traditional, sixteenth-century, and novel elements can be seen in his stance on the classic questions concerning the uniqueness and purpose of the Gospel of John and its relationship to Matthew, Mark, and Luke. His esteem represents a judgment about the eminence of John's Gospel that was, if not universal, undisputedly long-standing. His understanding of the Gospel's central purpose, however, followed the more recent trend inaugurated by Luther and Melanchthon. In the Argument prefacing the commentary, his definition of the word "gospel" and his delineation of John's uniqueness clearly echo the sentiments expressed in Luther's Preface to the New Testament and also reveal the more critical attitude toward traditional authorities that emerged in the sixteenth century. Calvin acknowledges that the ancients believed that John wrote chiefly to defend the divinity of Christ against Ebion and Cerinthus, but at the same time he downplays

---

[58] WADB 6: 10; LW 35: 362.

the significance of this opinion. Instead, he argues that God foresaw something much more, namely, that when the witness of all four gospels would be gathered into one body, John's account of the purpose for which Christ was manifested would provide the foundation for reading the other three. Drawing Luther's judgment about the clarity of John's expression of the gospel to its logical conclusion, Calvin urges readers of the gospels to learn from John *first*, thus reversing the dominant traditional assumption that John's deeper, mystical teaching was more difficult and his subject matter more advanced.[59]

Similar to Luther as well is the fact that Calvin's understanding of the Gospel's subject matter—namely, not the divinity of Christ but how people are saved by Christ—is profoundly shaped by his interpretation of Paul. Whereas John, for Calvin, provides the key to understanding Matthew, Mark, and Luke, Paul's letter to the Romans unlocks the meaning of the whole of scripture.[60] This conviction can be seen initially in his appeal to two Pauline passages (Rom. 1:16 and 2 Cor. 5:18–20) to define the term "gospel." It also manifests itself throughout the commentary proper as Calvin uses statements or ideas derived from Paul in order to clarify John's meaning or rule out possible misreadings of a passage.

Some of the most prominent examples of this can be seen in his treatment of the topic of faith. The Gospel of John presents Calvin with a more nuanced portrait of faith and coming to faith than do the Pauline epistles, offering a "broader conception of the levels, stages, or types of faith and [a more] complex picture of the role of miracles, signs and external sense perception in arriving at faith."[61] Calvin's concern to delineate the proper character of faith dominates his discussion from beginning to end.[62] In his comments on passages about faith, Calvin emphasizes that faith ultimately comes from hearing, that it does not rest on carnal sight, and that it is certain knowledge

---

[59] Erasmus expresses the traditional view: "No Gospel has given rise to more numerous or more difficult problems concerning the faith, none has been the object of more intense efforts by the greatest intellects of antiquity, none has seen greater disagreement among its interpreters, and this I ascribe not to their stupidity or lack of experience, but either to the obscurity of the language or to the difficulty of the subject-matter" (*Paraphrase*, 3).

[60] OE 13:4 = CO 10/2:403 and OE 13:7 = CO 49:1; English translation as John Calvin, *Commentary on the Epistle of Paul to the Romans*, ed. and trans. John Owen, repr. in *Calvin's Commentaries* (Grand Rapids, MI: Baker Books, 1989), xxiv, xxix.

[61] Barbara Pitkin, *What Pure Eyes Could See: Calvin's Doctrine of Faith in Its Exegetical Context* (New York: Oxford University Press, 1999), 95.

[62] For discussion, see the earlier version of this chapter: Barbara Pitkin, "Calvin as Commentator on the Gospel of John," in *Calvin and the Bible*, ed. Donald K. McKim (Cambridge, UK: Cambridge University Press, 2006), 193–97.

of Jesus as the Christ—all perspectives that reflect his reading of Paul. While giving credit to the development and stages of faith, Calvin nevertheless harmonizes the evangelist's meaning with what he takes to be Paul's view. For example, Calvin argues in his comments on John 20 that the disciple Thomas does not come to believe merely because he sees but rather because he remembers "the doctrine that he had nearly forgotten." Calvin continues:

> Faith cannot flow from a mere experience of things but must draw its origin from the word of God. Christ therefore rebukes Thomas for rendering less honor to his word than he ought, and for binding faith, which is born from hearing and ought to be completely intent on the word, to the other senses.[63]

Other interpreters are not as concerned as Calvin to identify the ground of Thomas's faith in the word that he had earlier heard or to criticize so sharply his desire to see and touch Jesus's wounds. Many refer to Hebrews 11:1 to stress that the object of faith is unseen, but Calvin alone among the commentators I consulted supplements this commonplace with a reference to a genuinely Pauline passage (2 Cor. 5:7) and, importantly, with a specific mention of the fact that faith depends on the "mouth of God."[64] His attention to these matters offers a particularly striking example of how Paul's perspective, to his mind most fully expressed in Romans, functions for him as the hermeneutical key to the whole of scripture.

Calvin's treatment of this same incident also provides an example of another hallmark of his exegesis in general and of John in particular, namely, an interest in drawing out the moral implications of the narratives for the believers of his day. His concern with what earlier interpreters designated the tropological sense is evident throughout his exposition of John, even when he views this expanded meaning as not distinct from but an inherent part of the literal or historical sense.[65]

---

[63] OE 11/2: 301 = CO 47: 445; *Commentary on John*, 2: 278.

[64] OE 11/2: 302 = CO 47: 445; *Commentary on John*, 2: 279.

[65] Calvin occasionally acknowledges a figurative meaning, but even this is tied to (or even stuffed into) this enriched literal-historical sense. For example, in his treatment of the word "wilderness" in John 1:23, Calvin first discusses Isaiah's original meaning, then the sense in which John refers the passage from Is. 40:3 to himself. His main concern is not to lay bare hidden meanings but rather to show that John has not "tortured" the words the prophet spoke concerning a past situation by applying them to his own day. Isaiah, says Calvin, spoke figuratively of the desolation of the church of his own day when he designated it a "wilderness." But inasmuch as the visible wilderness in which John was preaching was "a symbol or an image" of the terrible destitution that took away the hope of liberation (presumably in the world before Christ's advent), the comparison to Isaiah's figurative

One example of Calvin's use of gospel history to identify perpetually relevant lessons can be seen in his explanation of Thomas's behavior. The figure
of Thomas has been subject to a perhaps surprising variety of readings in
the Christian exegetical tradition and, as Glenn Most has shown, in narrative and visual culture more broadly.[66] Rampant diversity characterizes the
explanations of the reasons for his absence, the nature of his doubts, whether
it was seeing Jesus or touching him that gave rise to his confession, and the
overall significance of his story. Common to all interpreters, however, is
the conviction—derived largely from John 20:29–31—that the incident has
broader significance and not only was recorded but also actually happened
for the benefit of later generations of believers. Some, like Chrysostom, see
this in the moral lesson to turn from earthly temptations and vices and fix
our eyes on future glory. Others, like Rupert of Deutz (ca. 1075–1129), find a
more allegorical meaning: Thomas represents the Jewish people, who didn't
believe initially but who, in the fullness of time ("after eight days," John 20:26)
will believe with the Gentiles. Similarly, the assessments of Thomas's character prior to the encounter with Jesus are varied. Chrysostom judges that he
was obstinate because he scrutinized everything and blameworthy because
he considered what the others told him about seeing the Lord to be impossible. Cyril suggests more charitably that "wise Thomas" did not so much dis-
credit what was told him but rather was distracted by grief that he might not
also see the risen Lord.[67]

Calvin follows both Chrysostom's characterization of Thomas as obstinate and his interest in drawing moral lessons from his story. However,
he counters against Chrysostom that it is in fact Thomas's slowness and reluctance to believe (and not his scrutiny) that are blameworthy. Moreover,
where Chrysostom would have his readers learn from Thomas to aim for
higher things, Calvin articulates a more negative lesson: "Besides, the ob-
stinacy of Thomas is an example to show us that this wickedness is entirely
natural to all, to retard themselves of their own accord, when the entrance

wilderness is not forced; in fact, God arranged it such that the people would have before their eyes
(i.e., in the visible wilderness in which John preached) a mirror of Isaiah's prophetic proclamation
(OE 11/1: 42 = CO 47: 22; *Commentary on John*, 1: 59).

[66] Glenn W. Most, *Doubting Thomas* (Cambridge, MA: Harvard University Press, 2007).

[67] John Chrysostom, *Commentary on Saint John the Apostle and Evangelist, Homilies 48–88*, trans.
T. A. Goggin (New York: Fathers of the Church, 1960), 458–69; Rupert of Deutz, *Commentaria in
evangelium Sancti Iohannis*, ed. H. Haacke, vol. 9 of *Corpus Christianorum Continuatio Mediaevalis*
(Turnhout: Brepols, 1969), 775; Cyril of Alexandria, *Commentary on the Gospel According to S. John*,
2 vols. (Oxford: James Parker, 1874) 2: 681.

to faith is opened up."[68] In his comments on verses 27–28, Calvin digresses to explain that all believers are like Thomas, obstinate and contemptuous of God's word until faith—not extinguished but suffocated—suddenly recalls them to their senses. The same thing, he claims, happens to many people. Thomas's example teaches them that they must be on their guard against these errors, and also that ultimately all the elect are protected only by God's "secret bridle," by which he "always cherishes miraculously in their hearts some sparks of faith."[69]

Similar sorts of universal moral lessons run throughout Calvin's commentary on the Fourth Gospel, signaled usually by some phrase such as "this example warns us" or "let us learn from this." For Calvin, the Fourth Gospel conveys its important spiritual and moral truths not in a hidden, mystical way; these are discovered rather through careful attention to the narrative story line   that is, through the history related by the evangelist or the words of Christ he records. In this regard he stands in continuity with the medieval traditions that laid emphasis on the foundational character of the literal sense and, eventually, blurred the distinctions between the levels of meaning. However, the contemporary significance that Calvin finds in the narrative as often as not diverges from the traditional mystical meanings that traditional exegetes also uncovered. For example, in his discussion of the healing at the pool of Bethesda (John 5), Calvin does not mention baptism at all. Departing from the dominant tradition still shaping the interpretations of some of his sixteenth-century contemporaries, he sees the healing pool first as a sign of God's presence for the Jews of Jesus's day, to foster obedience to the law and inspire hope for the approaching time of redemption.[70] Calvin thus attends to the original setting in which Jesus performed this healing miracle and identifies what he takes to be his intent for those of Christ's time. The contemporary significance of the incident is found not in the pool as a type or symbol of Christian baptism, but in the way Christ forgives the weakness of the diseased man, who limits God's assistance to the capacity of his own mind as, Calvin remarks, "nearly all of us are wont to do."[71] As with his characterization of Thomas, Calvin finds common ground in the similar conditions of human nature past and present, emphasizing in this episode

---

[68] OE 11/2: 298 = CO 47: 442; *Commentary on John*, 2: 274, translation altered.

[69] OE 11/2: 300 = CO 47: 444; *Commentary on John*, 2: 276–77.

[70] Farmer, *Gospel of John*, 117–18. The baptismal symbolism is also mentioned by Melanchthon, but not by Bucer.

[71] OE 11/1: 155 = CO 47: 107; *Commentary on John*, 1: 189–90.

the utter weakness and incapacity of human beings and their tremendous need for the salvation that the direct encounter with Christ alone can deliver.

In addition to deriving universal tropological meanings from his historicizing reading of the biblical narrative, Calvin links the Gospel of John to his own day through the occasional polemical comments that emerge in his commentary. Given his understanding of the task of biblical commentary to be the lucid and brief exposition of the mind of the writer, Calvin does not wish to make polemic directed at the contemporary situation a central feature of his exposition. However, where he senses alternative explanations of a passage might challenge his own, he addresses them briefly. For example, at the end of his discussion of the incident with Thomas, he criticizes an alleged Roman Catholic use of John 20:29 to prove the doctrine of transubstantiation.[72] In his comments on John 1:14, he dismisses in one sentence Servetus and Anabaptists for purportedly confusing Christ's divine and human natures.[73] By far the vast majority of these polemical asides aim at Roman theology and practice, thereby making good on Calvin's promise in the dedicatory epistle, that this commentary would prove the "satanic" origins of papal religion. In particular, Calvin redirects the Gospel's criticism of Jewish opponents of Jesus to the pope and Roman Catholic practices.[74] Yet here he is neither more nor less polemical than in his other commentaries.

Calvin's criticisms frequently take the form of complaints that those who are the object of his polemic—usually not identified by name—have misread a particular passage of John or drawn inappropriate conclusions from it. In other words, they have failed to attend to the mind of the biblical author or to Christ's intent as related by the evangelist. Significantly, Calvin does not restrict this charge to his confessional adversaries. Rather, even the interpretations of those whose orthodoxy he acknowledges are occasionally found wanting. For example, Calvin begins his comments on John 3:5, "no one can enter the kingdom of God without being born of water and Spirit," by noting that the passage has been explained in various ways. Some refer water and Spirit to the two parts of regeneration (renunciation of the old man and new life). Others think Christ makes an allegorical contrast between earthly human nature and the purer elements of water and Spirit in order to urge humans to lay aside the mass of the flesh and become more like water and air. Chrysostom (the only interpreter identified by name) refers the water to

---

[72] OE 11/2: 302–3 = CO 47: 446; *Commentary on John*, 2: 280.
[73] OE 11/1: 31 = CO 47: 14; *Commentary on John*, 1: 46.
[74] See the Introduction in OE 11/1: xxvii–xxix.

baptism. According to the notes by Feld, these interpretations can be found in the explanations of this verse by Johannes Brenz (1499–1570), Bullinger, and Bucer.[75] Calvin rejects them all as valid or appropriate explanations of what Christ means here. Instead, he argues, Nicodemus labors under the mistaken idea that departed souls enter into other bodies, and to correct this, Jesus uses "water" as a metaphor for Spirit to say "simply" that spiritual purification and invigoration are necessary for newness of life.[76] Sometimes explicitly and other times implicitly, Calvin thus corrects readings and conclusions he judges to be false when they deviate, in his view, from the plain or genuine sense of the passage.

Calvin's historical consciousness is most evident in the way he engages and reinterprets the christological implications of the Gospel. One of the most striking aspects of his commentary is how he responds to the traditional view that the central purpose of the Gospel of John was to describe and defend Christ's divinity. Other interpreters who shared the newer orientation, such as Melanchthon and Bucer, merely pass over in silence earlier discussions of this topic in their comments on some of the passages traditionally used to promote or delineate Christ's divine nature. Calvin, in contrast, explicitly rejects these traditional interpretations and, moreover, criticizes the exegesis of those who had proffered them.[77] For example, in his comments on John 6:27, "for it is on him that God the Father has set his seal," Calvin complains, "The ancient writers have wrongly twisted this [passage] toward Christ's divine essence, as if he is said to be sealed, because he is the imprint and express image of the Father. For he was not speaking plainly here about his eternal essence but [explaining] what he has been commissioned and enjoined to do, what is his office toward us, and what we ought to seek and hope from him."[78] Calvin voices similar criticisms in his comments on John 5:30, 8:24, 10:30, 14:10–11, 16:15, and 17:21, emphasizing also that Christ's original audience was the Jewish people of his own time. To them, as to Calvin's sixteenth-century readers, Christ proclaims his office as mediator and savior—not his eternal divinity. In his comments on John 5:26, 6:57, 10:38, and 17:1, Calvin does not explicitly criticize earlier interpreters but nevertheless cautions his readers that the passage does not apply to Christ's divine essence alone

---

[75] OE 11/1: 87–88, notes 13, 14, and 15. See also Melanchthon, *Annotationes*, CR 14: 1080.

[76] OE 11/1: 88–89 = CO 47: 56; *Commentary on John*, 1: 110–11.

[77] David C. Steinmetz, *Calvin in Context*, 2nd edition (New York: Oxford University Press, 2010), 211.

[78] OE 11/1:198 = CO 47:140; *Commentary on John*, 1:242, translation altered.

but rather to his manifestation in the flesh. Calvin's judgment that the need to combat heresy had led earlier interpreters of the Fourth Gospel to distort the sense of certain passages was not without precedent.[79] But Calvin alone is concerned to point out these failings consistently throughout his commentary.

Before considering why Calvin might have voiced these concerns, it is important to note that he does not think that all of the traditional appeals to verses in John to prove or defend Christ's divine nature were unfounded. In fact, he begins his commentary by noting that in John 1:1 the evangelist "asserts the eternal divinity of Christ," and Calvin himself finds this teaching sufficient to refute the calumny of Servetus and the Arians.[80] Similarly, in his comments on John 1:14, "and the Speech [sermo] was made flesh," he succinctly explains the two natures doctrine as defined at Chalcedon and shows how these words of the evangelist—which are brief but lucid—fittingly refute the "blasphemies" of Nestorius, on the one hand, and Eutyches, Servetus, and the Anabaptists, on the other.[81] Indeed, Calvin views at least part of Christ's message and mission to be to demonstrate his divine origin and nature, even when these cannot be fully grasped until after his resurrection and ascension. For example, he remarks that with the miracle at Cana (John 2:1–11) Christ gave the first proof of his divinity; that the "object of Christ's discourse" in John 8:12–19 "is to show that all he does and teaches ought to be accounted divine"; and that Christ's declaration "I know whom I have chosen" (John 13:18), which Calvin understands in terms of eternal election, is a clear testimony to his divinity.[82] The culmination of these scattered observations comes in Calvin's comments on Thomas's confession in John 20:28. He links the two parts of Thomas's cry, "My Lord and my God!" to two stages in knowing Christ. When Thomas calls him "Lord," he acknowledges Christ as incarnate mediator, but, "having acknowledged him to be Lord, [he] is immediately and justly carried upwards to his eternal divinity."[83] Calvin

[79] For example, Erasmus, Paraphrase, 12.
[80] OE 11/1: 11–12 = CO 47:1; Commentary on John, 1: 25–26. See also the congrégation on John 1 in CO 47: 469–80; Calvin, Sermons on the Deity of Christ, 18–30.
[81] OE 11/1: 29–31 = CO 47: 13–14; Commentary on John, 1: 44–46.
[82] OE 11/1: 69 = CO 47: 41; Commentary on John, 1: 89; OE 11/1: 268 = CO 47: 194; Commentary on John, 1: 328; OE 11/2: 122 = CO 47: 311; Commentary on John, 2: 64–65. See also his comments on John 7:29, where he remarks that some (i.e., Augustine) refer "I am from him" to Christ's eternal essence and "he has sent me" to Christ's office; Calvin says he does not reject this view, although he does not know if Christ meant to speak so abstrusely, and, moreover, that this would not be a sufficiently strong proof of his eternal divinity against the Arians (OE 11/1: 245 = CO 47: 176; Commentary on John, 1: 300). For Augustine, see Tractates on John 28–54, 32–33 [on John 7:35–36].
[83] OE 11/2: 300 = CO 47: 444; Commentary on John, 2: 277.

concludes his comments by remarking that this "passage is abundantly sufficient for refuting the madness of Arius" and that it declares "the unity of
person in Christ."[84] Clearly the traditional use of passages to infer Christ's
divinity was not, for Calvin, entirely without merit. However, he intentionally and explicitly restricts the number of passages that he thinks can be legitimately interpreted in this way.

The reason for this curtailing becomes clearer when one considers what
Calvin substitutes in place of the traditional inferences of Christ's divinity.
The comments on John 6:27 ("For it is on [the Son of Man] whom the Father
has set his seal") are typical in this regard. There Calvin argues that Christ
does not refer there to his eternal essence but rather to his "office"; in other
places Calvin says that Christ does not refer to his "simple divinity" but
rather to himself insofar as he was manifested in the flesh. One might say
that, for Calvin, the great christological theme of the Fourth Gospel is not
Christ's divinity but Christ incarnate—not Christ's eternal nature but Christ
as historical God-man. Thus, traditional views holding that John focused on
Christ's divinity while the other evangelists focused on his humanity underestimate, to Calvin's mind, the fact that it is the "Word made flesh" that is preeminent in John's account. Although believers will, like Thomas, be carried
upward to confess Christ as God, in order for this to happen, faith must begin
"with that knowledge that is nearer and more easily acquired."[85] Otherwise
they will find themselves like the disciples crossing by boat to Capernaum
in John 6:19, filled with terror at the "simple demonstration of his divinity"
until Christ calms them by his word.[86]

Although Christ's divinity is still a theme for Calvin, this topic cannot be
said to constitute the Fourth Gospel's central purpose, namely, to awaken
faith in Christ the incarnate mediator. Hence, the traditional subject is sub-
ordinated to—or perhaps better, included within—the larger, overarching
theme of Christ as incarnate savior and human salvation in history. We recall from the Argument that the distinguishing feature of John's writing,
according to Calvin, was to exhibit more clearly than the other gospels the
purpose for which Christ was manifested. It is not its deeper grasp of Christ's
person that distinguishes John from the other gospels, but rather its more
complete portrayal of the "doctrine by which the office of Christ, together

---

[84] OE 11/2: 301 = CO 47: 444; *Commentary on John*, 2: 278.
[85] OE 11/2: 301 = CO 47: 444; *Commentary on John*, 2: 277.
[86] OE 11/1: 194 [there verse 20] = CO 47: 136; *Commentary on John*, 1: 236–37.

with the power of his death and resurrection, is unfolded."[87] This means that the evangelist's task was not in the first place to describe and defend Christ's divinity but rather to describe and defend how human beings come to full knowledge of Christ as incarnate mediator *and* as eternal Son. Though this soteriological focus on this understanding follows a sixteenth-century interpretive trend, Calvin's explicit rejection of traditional christological exegesis marks a more definitive development, even a culmination, of this shift in the understanding of the Fourth Gospel's central purpose.

One consequence of this shift of focus can be seen in the way he deals with Christ's humanity in his commentary. Calvin's attention to this theme was not new; even interpreters who found the main purpose of John to be to describe and defend Christ's divinity also addressed Christ's human nature, and, ultimately, became more precise in delineating the relationship between the two. Yet most would likely share Aquinas's judgment that the other evangelists treat principally the mysteries of Christ's humanity, while John, without ignoring these, "especially and above all, makes known the divinity of Christ in his Gospel."[88] A slightly different emphasis can be found in Chrysostom, who claims that in his portrayal of Jesus's tears at the tomb of Lazarus, John actually stresses more than the other evangelists Christ's humanity in his earthly ministry. However, he relates this, says Chrysostom, to make up for the fact the he does not portray Christ's agony on the cross in such humble detail as do the other gospel writers.[89] This view shares with the dominant perspective the assumption that what is most important in passages in which Jesus appears to be ignorant, in which he prays to the Father, and in which he displays human emotions is how they demonstrate that Christ is fully human. For Calvin, however, the demonstration of Christ's true humanity is not necessarily the main point of these passages. This is in part because, in contrast to interpreters of the fourth and fifth centuries, he can simply assume the orthodox interpretation of Christ's two natures. Beyond this, however, his stress on the "office of Christ" more than his person leads him to draw from these passages about Christ's humanity distinctive lessons concerning human nature in general.[90]

---

[87] OE 11/1: 8 = CO 47: vii; *Commentary on John*, 1: 21.

[88] Thomas Aquinas, *Commentum in . . . Joannem*, 280.

[89] See Wiles, *Spiritual Gospel*, 12, referring to Chrysostom's Homily 63, sec. 2; see Chrysostom, *Commentary on John Homilies 48–88*, 182.

[90] See also Barbara Pitkin, "The Spiritual Gospel? Christ and Human Nature in Calvin's Commentary on John," in *The Formation of Clerical and Confessional Identities in Early Modern Europe*, ed. W. Janse and B. Pitkin, *Dutch Review of Church History* 85 (2005) (Leiden: Brill, 2006), 187–204. The following discussion appears in a different context there.

The clearest instance of this can be found in Calvin's comments on Jesus's response to the death of Lazarus in John 11:33–35. Most interpreters held that by his display of emotion Jesus proved his truly human nature, even as they disagreed over the reasons why he was so troubled and offered various explanations of the exemplary purpose of his tears.[91] Although early commentators did not treat these latter themes as the main point of the passage, in exploring them, some of them forged a connection between Jesus's humanity and human nature in general, which becomes prominent in Calvin's interpretation of the passage. For example, Cyril of Alexandria argues that the inclination to tears arises from Jesus's "holy flesh," which in this struggle is reproved by the Holy Spirit. The subjection of Christ's own natural human infirmities to "such feelings only as are pleasing to God" marks a victory and transformation that can be extended to all humans.[92] In the sixteenth century, some interpreters began to argue even more explicitly that the purpose of Jesus's tears was more than a demonstration of his humanity. As Farmer has shown, commentators such as Bullinger, Bucer, and Wolfgang Musculus (1497–1563) focus on Jesus's emotion as an example of the character and limits of proper Christian commiseration and grief.[93]

Building on this interest, Calvin seems to take all of this a step further, touching only implicitly on the point of proving Christ's true humanity in his exposition of the passage. Rather, he begins by picking up earlier arguments that Christ's tears give proof of his genuine sympathy with the mourners and sorrow over the whole human condition. He then addresses a traditional concern over how Christ, as the divine Son of God, could be subject to human passions, qualifying a notion he attributes to Augustine (also promulgated by Erasmus) that Christ "brought groaning and grief upon himself by his own accord," that is, at appropriate times by an act of will. Instead, Calvin argues, by virtue of the incarnation, Christ was from the very beginning subject to human infirmities and feelings, sin only excepted. The point of all this is that believers may know that they "have a mediator, who willingly pardons [their]

---

[91] Erasmus held to this traditional view in his *Paraphrase on John* (144–45), and Farmer notes that this "exegetical commonplace" was also expressed by Zwingli, Oecolampadius, and Bullinger (*Gospel of John*, 163–64). The notes to this passage in Erasmus's *Paraphrase* convey some of the variety of earlier exegetical discussions; see also Wiles, *Spiritual Gospel*, 146–47.
[92] Cyril, *Commentary on the Gospel According to S. John*, 2: 122; cf. discussion in Wiles, *Spiritual Gospel*, 146–47.
[93] Farmer, *Gospel of John*, 163–67.

infirmities, and who is ready to assist those infirmities which he has experienced himself."[94]

At this juncture we see emerging Calvin's focus on what Christ does for humans rather than who he is. His next set of comments leads him to make an important point about the latter; however, this leads him immediately to an extended discussion not of Christ's humanity but rather of human nature itself. Positing an objection that human passions are always sinful, Calvin responds by making an important distinction: "for our affections are sinful because they rush on without restraint, and suffer no limit, but in Christ the affections were adjusted and regulated in obedience to God, and were altogether free from sin."[95] Human feelings are sinful when they are not regulated by true modesty and when they arise from improper motives. To clarify, Calvin adds that this is the condition of fallen human nature; at the creation, he explains, God implanted affections in the first humans that were obedient and submissive to reason. He does not mention the idea of a Second Adam, but that Pauline notion clearly underlies his argument that it was in this orderly way that Christ experienced human affections: "Christ was indeed troubled and vehemently agitated, but in such a way as to keep himself in subjection to the will of the Father."[96] In closing, Calvin echoes a rejection of "the unbending sternness of the Stoics" found also in Bucer and Musculus (but without linking this to Anabaptism, as they do).[97] Rather, he urges his readers to follow Christ as their leader in reining in the passions, "for even Christ took our affections into himself, so that by his power we may subdue everything in them that is sinful."[98] Thus, the point of the passage, for Calvin, becomes the restoration of human nature. While this conclusion bears similarities to that of Cyril cited earlier, there is an important difference: Cyril focused on a conflict within Christ himself, who extends his victory to others. Calvin, rather, shifts the conflict to human beings, who by the present power of Christ dwelling in them are conformed to him and restored to original perfection.

---

[94] OE 11/2: 63 = CO 47: 265; *Commentary on John*, 1: 440. The view of Augustine is found in *Tractates on John 28–54*, 252–53 [on John 11:1–54]; cf. Erasmus, *Paraphrase*, 144. Musculus also alludes to Heb. 4:15 in his comments on the passage (Farmer, *Gospel of John*, 166).

[95] OE 11/2: 63 = CO 47: 265; *Commentary on John*, 1: 440.

[96] OE 11/2: 64 = CO 47: 266; *Commentary on John*, 1: 441.

[97] Farmer, *Gospel of John*, 165, 167.

[98] OE 11/2: 64 = CO 47: 266; *Commentary on John*, 1: 441–42.

Conclusion

At the end of the sixteenth century, the Lutheran theologian Giles Hunnius (1550–1603) attacked Calvin's exegesis of passages in John and other parts of the Old and New Testaments for rejecting the anti-Arian interpretations of the patristic writers, even though, as Hunnius acknowledged, Calvin did not reject the orthodox doctrines of the trinity or Christ's two natures but only some of the traditional interpretations of these passages on which these were based. Hunnius's criticisms sparked a virulent polemical exchange with the Reformed theologian David Pareus (1548–1622) over Calvin's readings and their theological implications.[99] In a study of Calvin's exegesis of the three Johannine passages at stake in the debate and his employment of these passages in the *Institutes*, David Steinmetz shows the complexity of Calvin's handling of these issues in his commentary on John. He concludes that, as Pareus maintained, Calvin's interpretation of John did not mean he opened the door to anti-trinitarianism, engaged in "judaizing" interpretations across the board, or universally undermined the interpretations of the church fathers. What Calvin did was to reject what he considered to be weak or unsustainable exegetical arguments, regardless of their source, in order "to provide the best possible exegetical foundation for the dogmatic claims of the church."[100] Calvin's historicizing approach to the Gospel of John was integral to this process.

The Fourth Gospel was one of the most important books of the Bible for Calvin, and long before he wrote a formal commentary, the dominant theological themes of the Gospel had a profound impact on his theology. Undoubtedly one of the most valuable aspects of his 1553 commentary is the insight it provides into the way Calvin addressed these themes, particularly salvation in Christ, as an exegete striving to lay bare the mind of the biblical author. Beyond this, the commentary is significant as a "proving ground" for Calvin's exegetical method, revealing little of the contentious domestic climate in which it was written and pressing the depth of his commitment to what he takes to be the evangelist's proper meaning. That Calvin's explicit rejection of traditional christological exegesis of certain Johannine passages became itself a source of controversy suggests the singularity of his approach,

[99] For discussion and references to the texts, see Steinmetz, *Calvin in Context*, 207–16.
[100] Steinmetz, *Calvin in Context*, 214.

even among his sixteenth-century contemporaries. For all its perpetuation of traditional attitudes about the special character of the Gospel of John, Calvin's commentary nevertheless offers a genuinely new contribution to the history of Johannine interpretation, one markedly shaped by his historical sensitivities.

4

David, Faith, and the Confusion of History in Calvin's Commentary on the Psalms

It is impossible for us to believe this one to be the literal sense which they call the literal sense, that which makes David a historian rather than a prophet.[1]

Introduction

The book of Psalms is one of the most beloved biblical books throughout the entire history of Christianity. The high regard extended toward the psalter by Christian exegetes in all periods both mirrored and helped to further the profound influence of the Psalms on Christian worship and spirituality; it also contributed to a tradition of interpretation that is quite possibly unlike the exegetical history of any other book of the Bible. The Psalms played a particularly important role in the theology, devotional life, and material culture of the Reformed tradition. This chapter investigates a central feature of John Calvin's contribution to this history by considering his portrayal of David as a paradigm for the faith of sixteenth-century Christians in his 1557 commentary on the Psalms. Furthermore, it sheds light on a peculiar development in Calvin's doctrine of faith that his historicizing engagement with the Psalms occasioned.

Like his exegetical predecessors, Calvin assumed that the Psalms contained a message that could be applied to his contemporaries, that they expressed this message in a beautiful and unparalleled way, and that they provided

---

[1] Jacques Lefèvre d'Étaples complaining in the preface to his commentary on the Psalms about rabbinic interpreters and Nicholas of Lyra's twofold literal sense. Lefèvre, *Quincuplex Psalterium*, 2nd edition (Paris: H. Estienne, 1513), rpt. *Quincuplex Psalterium: Fac-similé de l'édition de 1513* (Geneva: Droz, 1979), Aii *verso*; English translation from Heiko A. Oberman, *Forerunners of the Reformation: The Shape of Late Medieval Thought*, trans. P. L. Nyhus (New York: Holt, Rinehart & Winston, 1966), 300.

Calvin, the Bible, and History. Barbara Pitkin, Oxford University Press (2020). © Oxford University Press.
DOI: 10.1093/oso/9780190093273.001.0001

models for Christian prayer. Yet, at the same time, Calvin also shared with many of his contemporaries and predecessors an appreciation for the "historical" meaning of scripture.[2] With interpreters following Jerome (ca. 347–420), Calvin did not think that David was the author of all of the psalms, since many referred to events that did not occur in David's lifetime. Moreover, Calvin consistently sought to identify the particular historical circumstances that led David to compose his psalms, but this, too, was not without precedent. Even Calvin's insistence on what R. Gerald Hobbs has called the "sufficiency of the historical for Christian exegesis" had its sixteenth-century antecedents, most notably in the work of Martin Bucer (1491–1551).[3]

What is intriguing about Calvin's exegesis is the way he relates his profound historicizing interest to an even stronger desire to retrieve the faith of David as a paradigm for Christian faith. As we shall see in his use of the figure of David in his commentary, Calvin develops a strategy for upholding the exemplary character of the Psalms while also emphasizing their historical nature. In so doing, Calvin represents a trend among some sixteenth-century interpreters who moved away from Jacques Lefèvre d'Étaples's (ca. 1455–1536) proper literal sense toward what looks like a recovery of Nicholas of Lyra's (ca. 1270–1349) *other* literal sense, namely, the historical literal sense that does not apply directly to Christ.[4] According to J. S. Preus, Martin

[2] For discussion of premodern interest in the literal, grammatical, or historical sense(s) beyond the summary in chapter 1, see Henri de Lubac, *Exégèse médiévale: Les quatre sens de l'Écriture*, 4 vols. (Paris: Aubier, 1959–64); James Samuel Preus, *From Shadow to Promise: Old Testament Interpretation from Augustine to the Young Luther* (Cambridge, MA: Harvard University Press, 1969); Beryl Smalley, *The Study of the Bible in the Middle Ages*, 3rd edition (Oxford: Basil Blackwell, 1983); Christopher Ocker, *Biblical Poetics before Humanism and Reformation* (Cambridge, UK: Cambridge University Press, 2002). On Calvin, see Alexandre Ganoczy and Stefan Scheld, *Die Hermeneutik Calvins: Geistesgeschichtliche Voraussetzungen und Grundzüge* (Wiesbaden: Franz Steiner, 1983).

[3] R. Gerald Hobbs, "How Firm a Foundation: Martin Bucer's Historical Exegesis of the Psalms," *Church History* 53, no. 4 (1984): 484. The first edition of Bucer's commentary on the Psalms, *Sacrorum Psalmorum libri quinque* (Strasbourg: G. Andlanus, 1529), was published pseudonymously and went through several subsequent editions. In the preface to his own commentary in 1557, Calvin mentions with approval Bucer's commentary and that of Wolfgang Musculus, *In sancrosanctum Davidis Psalterium commentarii* (Basel: Herwagen, 1551), CO 31: 13, 14. On the interest of certain sixteenth-century interpreters in relating the Hebrew origins of the psalms to apostolic or traditional christological readings, see R. Gerald Hobbs, "Martin Bucer on Psalm 22: A Study in the Application of Rabbinic Exegesis by a Christian Hebraist," in *Histoire de l'exégèse au XVI siècle: Textes du colloque internationale tenu à Genève en 1976*, ed. Olivier Fatio and Pierre Fraenkel (Geneva: Droz, 1978), 144–63; R. Gerald Hobbs, "Hebraica Veritas *and* Traditio Apostolica: Saint Paul and the Interpretation of the Psalms in the Sixteenth Century," in *The Bible in the Sixteenth Century*, ed. David C. Steinmetz (Durham, NC: Duke University Press, 1990), 83–99.

[4] Preus points out the irony in Nicholas of Lyra's theory of the *duplex sensus litteralis*, which Lyra introduced in order to stem the flood of allegorical interpretations of the Old Testament. Instead, it led to the "near suffocation" of the historical-literal meaning in many subsequent exegetes, such as Lefèvre, who relied exclusively on the prophetic-literal sense (*From Shadow to Promise*, 67–71).

Luther (1483–1546) initiated this move from Lefèvre's proper literal sense (i.e., Lyra's prophetic literal sense) to Lyra's historical-literal sense in his first exegetical work on the Psalms, the *Dictata super psalterium* (1513–1515).[5] Preus finds that this shift enables Luther to argue that the "faithful synagogue" is to be taken as the "model and norm" for the faith of the Christian church and individual believers.[6] Similar to his reception of the apostle Paul and his interpretation of the Gospel of John (discussed in chapters 2 and 3), Calvin's approach represents a general sixteenth-century trend inspired by Wittenberg reformers; in this case, his particular resolution of the problem of the historical and exemplary character of the Psalms is strikingly different from that of Luther in the *Dictata* and even in his later *Operationes in psalmos* (1519–1521). Calvin's strategy reveals some of his most deeply held theological assumptions and leads him to play them off against one another in a surprising way.

Calvin and the Psalms

The book of Psalms was exceptionally important for Calvin. Toward no other book of the Bible—not even Romans—did he direct the full range of his theological, rhetorical, administrative, and even artistic energy, starting as early as his arrival in Geneva.[7] On January 16, 1537, the preachers of the newly reformed city, at Calvin's instigation, requested that the Small Council introduce the vernacular psalm singing into the reformed worship service.[8] The main force behind the ensuing task of versifying the psalms and setting them to melodies, which took nearly twenty-five years to complete, was Calvin himself. The first collection appeared in 1539 in Strasbourg, while Calvin was serving as a pastor there. This collection contained nineteen psalms, thirteen of which Calvin took from translations of the French poet Clément Marot (1496–1544), and six of which he versified himself, along with metrical

---

[5] Preus, *From Shadow to Promise*, 142–271, esp. 268–69.

[6] Preus, *From Shadow to Promise*, 217.

[7] See *Le Psautier de Genève: Images commentées et essai de bibliographie* (Geneva: Bibliothèque publique et universitaire, 1986), chaps. 1–2; John Calvin, *Der Psalter auf der Kanzel Calvins*, ed. and intro. E. Mülhaupt (Neukirchen: Neukirchener Verlag, 1959), 8–24; Henri Chaix, *Le Psautier Huguenot: Sa formation et son histoire dans l'Église Réformée* (Geneva: Romet, 1907), chaps. 1–4.

[8] "Articles concernant l'organisation de l'église et du culte a Genève, proposés au conseil par les ministres," OS 1: 375.

settings of the Canticle of Simeon, the Apostles' Creed, and the Decalogue.[9] Psalm-singing was introduced in Geneva upon Calvin's return in 1541. An expanded version of the psalter containing thirty-six psalms was published in the first Genevan liturgical manual in 1542, and the following year a revised metrical psalter consisting of forty-nine psalms and the Canticle of Simeon, all versified by Marot, appeared.[10] Calvin contributed the preface to both of these later publications, commending the practice of congregational singing in the vernacular and applauding the unique suitability of the psalms for this activity. Moreover, he also preached numerous sermons on psalm texts, twenty-eight of which were published during his lifetime.[11] Calvin's manner of preaching on the Psalms underscores further his special regard for them. It was Calvin's custom to preach on the Old Testament on weekdays and on the New Testament on Sundays. He usually preached twice on Sundays in St. Pierre, in the morning and in the afternoon. The fact that he occasionally devoted the afternoon sermon to a psalm, but never to any other Old Testament text, is a compelling indication of the high theological value Calvin placed on them.

Calvin's special attention to the Psalms was not limited to their use in worship, but extended also to his activity as a biblical scholar. Calvin oversaw the revisions to Olivétan's 1535 translation of the Bible into French, undertaking the first revision in 1545 himself. For the second revision, he sought the assistance of the Hebraist Louis Budé (1520–1551), who made numerous improvements in the translation of the psalms.[12] Budé's translation was first published in 1551 by Jean Crespin and appeared both as part of the revised French Bible and as an independent text. In his preface to the latter, Calvin expresses his opinions on the great utility of the book of Psalms. He declares that no book in all of Holy Scripture is as full of the doctrine of God's

---

[9] *Aulcuns pseaulmes et cantiques mys en chant* (Strasburg: [Knobloch], 1539; facsimile, Geneva: A. Jullien, 1919); see Daniel Trocmé-Latter, *The Singing of the Strasbourg Protestants, 1523–1541* (Burlington, VT: Routledge, 2015), 220–23.

[10] *La forme des prières et chants ecclésiastiques* (Geneva: 1542; facsimile, Kassel: Bärenreiter, 1959); Clément Marot, *Cinquante pseaumes de David mis en françoys selon la verité hebraïque: Édition critique sur la texte de l'édition publiée en 1543 à Genève par Jean Gérard*, ed. Gérard Defaux (Paris: Honoré Champion, 1995).

[11] These sermons include two from 1546 on Psalms 115 and 124 (CO 32: 456–80), four published in 1552 on selections from Psalms 16, 27, and 87 (CO 8: 369–452), and twenty-two published in 1554 on Psalm 119 (CO 32: 481–752). For details and a reconstruction of Calvin's preaching on the Psalms, see Elsie Anne McKee, *The Pastoral Ministry and Worship in Calvin's Geneva* (Geneva: Droz, 2016), 469–72, 937–38.

[12] Rodolphe Peter, "Calvin and Louis Budé's Translation of the Psalms," in *John Calvin: A Collection of Distinguished Essays*, ed. G. E. Duffield (Grand Rapids, MI: Eerdmans, 1966), 190–200.

inestimable love for humankind and of God's admonitions against human ingratitude as the psalter.[13]

The following year (1552), Calvin began his lectures on the Psalms, which he completed in 1555 or 1556. These were recorded by a secretarial team consisting of Nicolas Des Gallars (ca. 1520–1581), Jean Budé (1515–1587), and Charles de Jonviller (1517–1590). From 1555 to August 1559 the book of Psalms was the subject of the *congrégations*, the weekly Bible studies held on Fridays and attended by ministers, students, and other interested persons. Concurrently Calvin was composing his commentary on the Psalms, which was published in Latin in 1557 and in French in 1558.[14] This project grew out of his lectures and, Calvin confesses in his preface, was motivated in part by the fear that an auditor's lecture notes might be published under his name without his permission or perhaps even without his knowledge. Yet, Calvin continues, it became clear that this publication was not an entirely superfluous undertaking. Dwelling once again on the unique qualities of the psalter, he notes that the Psalms are full of every precept serving to conform the life of the Christian to holiness, piety, and righteousness, and that their principal intent is to teach and train believers to bear the cross.[15] While other parts of scripture contain God's commandments, the Psalms provide concrete examples for imitation. Consideration of these inspired compositions will awaken human beings most effectually to their own maladies and teach them most clearly concerning their remedy.[16]

Throughout the 1550s, the period during which Calvin preached and lectured on, wrote about, and discussed the Psalms, the Genevan psalter project continued, now in the care of Theodore Beza (1519–1605). Once again,

---

[13] *Les Pseaumes de David traduicts selon la verité hebraïque, avec annotations tresutiles par Loys Budé: Preface de Jehan Calvin, touchant l'utilité des pseaumes, et de la translation presente* (Geneva: J. Crespin, 1551), *. ii *verso*–iii *recto*; e-rara.ch, http://dx.doi.org/10.3931/e-rara-5722; also as an appendix to Peter, "Calvin and Budé's Translation," 201–2.

[14] John Calvin, *In librum Psalmorum Iohannis Calvini commentarius* ([Geneva]: R. Estienne, 1557), CO 31: 13–842; 32: 1–442; John Calvin, *Le livre des Pseaumes exposé par Iehan Calvin* ([Geneva]: C. Badius, 1558), revised edition, *Commentaires de M. Jean Calvin sur le livre des Pseaumes* ([Geneva]: C. Badius, 1561). English translation as John Calvin, *Commentary on the Book of Psalms*, 5 vols., ed. and trans. James Anderson, repr. in *Calvin's Commentaries* (Grand Rapids, MI: Baker Books, 1989); hereafter *Commentary on the Psalms*, followed by volume and page number; translation occasionally altered. On the commentary, see T. H. L. Parker, *Calvin's Old Testament Commentaries* (Edinburgh: T. & T. Clark, 1986), 29–32; Wulfert de Greef, "Calvin as Commentator on the Psalms," trans. R. A. Blacketer, in *Calvin and the Bible*, ed. Donald K. McKim (Cambridge, UK: Cambridge University Press, 2006), 85–106; Wulfert de Greef, *Calvijn en zijn uitleg van de Psalmen: Een onderzoeck naar zijn exegetische methode* (Kampen: Kok, 2006).

[15] CO 31: 19, 20; *Commentary on the Psalms*, 1: xxxix.

[16] CO 31: 17, 18; *Commentary on the Psalms*, 1: xxxvii.

though, it was Calvin who provided the impetus. Shortly after Beza's arrival in Geneva in 1548, Calvin sought his assistance in the completion of the task left unfinished by the death of Marot a few years earlier. Amid his other duties, Beza worked throughout the 1550s on the versification of the remaining psalms. A collection of eighty-three psalms appeared in 1551. After a general revision of the entire collection, the first complete edition of the Genevan psalter with all 150 psalms was published in 1562, just two years before Calvin's death.[17]

Calvin's extended and multifaceted engagement with the book of Psalms played a crucial role in establishing the songbook of Israel as a central vehicle for Reformed piety.[18] What were the reasons for Calvin's twenty-five-year-long preoccupation with this biblical book? His prefaces to the various editions of the Genevan psalter, to Louis Budé's translation, and to his own commentary provide some clues. First, the Psalms teach clearly the human need for God; that is, they provide true self-knowledge, and they urge believers to seek God's aid. Calvin states on several occasions that the Psalms contain an anatomy of all parts of the soul, for in them the diligent reader finds a mirror of his own affections and spiritual maladies. Moreover, readers learn about adversity and hope, they are incited to have compassion on those who suffer around them, and they are inspired by zeal for the house of God. Second, having demonstrated the human need for God, the Psalms instruct those who would have their need met with concrete examples of how to attain this. The Psalms provide examples of the proper form of prayer and show believers the kind of requests they are to make of God.[19] Third, the Psalms demonstrate God's goodness, by which God very sweetly invites human beings to seek and meditate on God's grace. Thus, according to Calvin, the Psalms, when they are read, sung, studied, and explicated, instruct completely about God and about human nature. They provide clear knowledge of God's goodness and human need; they teach and inspire true piety.[20]

---

[17] For an overview, see McKee, *Pastoral Ministry and Worship*, 203–8.

[18] For just two overviews of the importance of the Psalms and the psalter, see Robert M. Kingdon, "Uses of the Psalter in Calvin's Geneva," in *Der Genfer Psalter und seine Rezeption in Deutschland, der Schweiz und den Niederlanden: 16.–18. Jahrhundert*, ed. E. Grunewald, H. P. Jürgens, and J. R. Luth (Tübingen: Max Niemeyer, 2004), 21–32; Barbara B. Diefendorf, "The Huguenot Psalter and the Faith of French Protestants in the Sixteenth Century," in *Culture and Identity in Early Modern Europe (1500–1800): Essays in Honor of Natalie Zemon Davis*, ed. Barbara B. Diefendorf and Carla Hesse (Ann Arbor: University of Michigan Press, 1993), 41–63.

[19] CO 31: 16–18; *Commentary on the Psalms*, 1: xxxvii.

[20] "There is no other book in which there is to be found more express and magnificent commendations, both of the singular liberality of God toward his church, and of all his works; there is no other book in which are recorded so many deliverances, nor one in which the evidences and experiences of the fatherly providence and solicitude, which God exercises toward us, are so

For Calvin, a particular excellence of the Psalms lies in their instruction by way of example. They depict in unparalleled fashion the faith and prayers of the psalmists, who through the exhibition of their own thoughts and affections draw the reader to self-examination and to the exercise of faith. Of course, the most prominent example by far is provided by David. Calvin writes that David is like a mirror in which believers can contemplate all that should lead them to pray well and to praise God when he has heard them.[21] Indeed, Calvin compares his own call and the course of his vocation to that of the great king and prophet, noting that though he falls far short of David's example, he is assured that whatever David suffered was exhibited to Calvin by God as an example for imitation.[22]

Edward Gosselin has demonstrated the prevalence of the idea of the imitation of David among sixteenth-century Protestant exegetes and has sketched the emergence of this concept in the work of three pre-Reformation reformers: Augustine (354–430), Nicholas of Lyra, and Lefèvre. Gosselin argues that Protestant commentators found in David a faith like their own and a historical situation that paralleled theirs, and that they viewed David as a colleague of the reformation faithful.[23] Because they saw in the Psalms and in David in particular the manifestation of the doctrine of promise, Protestant reformers desired conformity with the faith of the historical David—that is, David as an individual living at a particular time and in a particular place— to a degree unparalleled by earlier exegetes. In this, Gosselin detects a shift in the perception not only of David and of the Psalms, but also of the theological validity of what Gosselin designates the grammatical-historical sense of the Old Testament. While interpreters like Lyra and Lefèvre both sought to reconcile the Old and New Testaments and strove to take seriously (each in his own way) the literal sense of the text, their attempts ultimately failed, according to Gosselin, because they did not realize the theological identity of

celebrated. In short, there is no other book in which we are more perfectly taught the right manner of praising God, or in which we are more powerfully stirred up to the performance of this exercise of piety" (CO 31: 19, 20; *Commentary on the Psalms*, 1: xxxviii–xxxix).

[21] *Les Pseaumes de David . . . Preface de Jehan Calvin*, *. iii recto; Peter, "Calvin and Budé's Translation," 202.

[22] CO 31: 19, 21 and 20, 22; *Commentary on the Psalms*, 1: xxxix–xl. On Calvin's portrayal of David's exemplary character, see also G. Sujin Pak, *The Judaizing Calvin: Sixteenth-Century Debates over the Messianic Psalms* (New York: Oxford University Press, 2010), 84–91.

[23] E. A. Gosselin, *The King's Progress to Jerusalem: Some Interpretations of David during the Reformation Period and Their Patristic and Medieval Background* (Malibu, CA: Undena, 1976), 5; see also Preus, *From Shadow to Promise*.

the testaments. For many pre-reformation exegetes, Old Testament persons like David were finally theologically valid only insofar as they prefigured life under the new covenant. With the Protestant reformers' understanding of one gospel or one covenant, the historical David took on different, and, according to Gosselin, greater theological significance. He argues that for exegetes such as Luther, Philip Melanchthon (1497–1560), Calvin, and Beza, David functions as a "type," not in the sense of being an empty figure of things to come but as an example of beliefs and teachings that remain the same under the "new" covenant.[24]

Setting aside for the present objections that one might raise against certain details in Gosselin's argument,[25] it is clear from the discussion above that Calvin views David primarily as an example for imitation and that, according to Calvin, David perceived himself as such. Gosselin is certainly correct in maintaining that the theological presupposition underlying this perception is Calvin's notion that there is ultimately only a single divine covenant, a topic that Calvin explicates most fully in *Institutes* (1559), 2.9–11. Because old and new covenant differ for Calvin only in dispensation but not in substance, David, as an Old Testament figure, can become a paradigm for New Testament faith. This raises several questions. First, there is the question of the very nature of faith: If David presents an example of faith for believers' imitation, what are the characteristics of the faith that he exemplifies? Second, what is the object of David's faith, and is this identical to the object of Christian faith? Third, and most intriguing, is the question of the relationship between the faith exemplified by David and faith that is explicitly christocentric. According to Calvin, Christ is really present to believers under the old dispensation, but only in a shadowy form. Can such faith be truly paradigmatic when Calvin demands in the *Institutes* that true faith must look explicitly to Christ?[26]

These three questions provide guidance for the investigation into Calvin's use of David in his commentary on the Psalms. First, analysis of statements about faith in Calvin's exegesis will provide a characterization of the kind of faith David exemplifies. The argument will demonstrate that faith, as depicted in Calvin's exegesis of select Davidic psalms, is primarily a kind of

---

[24] Gosselin, *King's Progress*, 70.

[25] See the reviews of Gosselin, *King's Progress*, by David Steinmetz, in *Archive for Reformation History: Literature Review* 7 (1978): 31; Hans Möller, in *Theologische Literaturzeitung* 103 (1978): 758–59; Patricia Wilson-Kastner, in *Sixteenth Century Journal* 10, no. 1 (1979): 102.

[26] *Institutes* (1559), 2.6.4; 3.2.1; 3.2.5.

perception that corrects the noetic effect of sin and enables the believer both
to penetrate (to a very small degree) the mysteries of God's providence and
to benefit from affliction and persecution. Second, the discussion will seek to
infer the object of faith on the basis of these findings. Finally, an inquiry into
some of the theological assumptions that Calvin brings to the interpretive
task will illustrate the tensive relationship between the paradigmatic faith of
the historical, biblical figure of David and Calvin's doctrine of faith in Christ.

The Faith of David

We have seen that, for Calvin, the Psalms are primarily concerned with
teaching fallen human beings about their need for God. This need consists of
various elements. The psalmists cry out for themselves and on behalf of God's
people for rescue from their enemies, alleviation of suffering, vengeance on
their persecutors, and God's judgment on the wicked. They also pray for for-
giveness, for the restoration of true worship, and for God's mercy. However,
these elements themselves are not exhaustive of the human need for God that
Calvin finds so preeminently articulated in the Psalms. Rather they merely
express another, and for Calvin more fundamental, human need for noetic
healing, for understanding, or for new perception.

Consideration of what Calvin holds to be the central problem depicted
in the Psalms illustrates this need for perception. Certainly the difficulties
besetting human beings that the Psalms describe, namely, the apparent confusion of history, confounded by the prosperity of the wicked, the persecution of the righteous, and the apparent capriciousness or utter absence of the
deity, are significant issues. Yet, for Calvin, the real problem is not that history
itself is confused, but rather that humans are unable to perceive God's providence under such conditions. Fallen human beings suffer impaired vision
and judge these events according to what Calvin designates the judgment of
the flesh. They are unable to understand that all events take place as a result of
God's determination and that God only appears to be far off; the meaning of
history is inscrutable to fallen eyes. In contrast, believers have the capacity to
judge these same events according to the eye of faith and thereby perceive—
albeit dimly—God's activity in them.[27] This is not a matter of reality versus

---

[27] See, for example, Calvin's comments on Ps. 16:8 and Ps. 37:13 (CO 31: 155, 372; *Commentary on the Psalms,* 1: 228 and 2: 28–29).

illusion. For Calvin, the prosperity of the wicked and the persecution of the righteous are not illusory.[28] The eye of faith does not diminish the reality of events in the world, but rather ascribes to these events new meaning.

Calvin's exegesis of Psalm 12 provides a typical example of this new kind of judgment. According to Calvin, in this psalm David describes the confused state of the world, in which the church is flooded with iniquity. David consoles himself and others in verses 5 and 6 and asserts with confidence the safety of all the godly. He assures them that God has promised deliverance and that God is not deceitful, so they can be certain that God's guardianship of the faithful is active and perpetual, even when sometimes hidden.[29] From David's example, Calvin contends, believers learn that they can and should call on God for succor, even in times of blackest despair. Addressing a similar situation in his comments on Psalm 31:14, Calvin states that David is not so overwhelmed with sorrow "that the hidden light of faith could not shine inwardly in his heart."[30] In contrast to the ungodly, who are deaf, through faith believers can hear God's promise to be gracious and can thereby understand not only that God is sovereign over the confusion of history but also that situations like these are both necessary and beneficial for believers.[31]

If Calvin relates faith in his exegesis of the Psalms directly and primarily to issues of perception, is faith itself then a kind of perception, or is the new capacity to see or hear rather an effect of faith? Calvin's treatment of this theme in the commentary is complex, but if we consider the way that he speaks about faith and especially the metaphors that he employs to characterize it, it appears that while it is certainly true that noetic healing and the ability to ascribe new meaning to world events results from faith, faith also *is* this new perception.[32] Repeatedly Calvin employs images of light and vision to describe the character of faith and depict its activity. He writes that faith illumines the way to God,[33] and he urges his readers to let it shine forth so that they might behold God's heavenly throne, that is, to see that God is present and sovereign over all things and events.[34] He calls faith an "eye" that is

---

[28] See Charles Trinkaus, "Renaissance Problems in Calvin's Theology," *Studies in the Renaissance* 1 (1954): 60–65.

[29] CO 31: 128–31; *Commentary on the Psalms*, 1: 174–78.

[30] CO 31: 307; *Commentary on the Psalms*, 1: 510.

[31] See Calvin's comments in his introduction to Psalm 12 (CO 31: 126; *Commentary on the Psalms*, 1: 171.

[32] Fuller discussion of this, with examples from other parts of the commentary not discussed in this chapter, is in Barbara Pitkin, *What Pure Eyes Could See: Calvin's Doctrine of Faith in Its Exegetical Context* (New York: Oxford University Press, 1999), 98–130.

[33] CO 31: 173; *Commentary on the Psalms*, 1: 266.

[34] CO 31: 123; *Commentary on the Psalms*, 1: 164.

directed to God or, more particularly, to God's providence.[35] He compares faith to a light that God kindles into a brighter flame throughout the life of the believer.[36] And concerning Psalm 138 he writes that the entire office of faith is "to see life in the midst of death and to trust the mercy of God."[37] Faith is thus, at least in part, a gift of supernatural perception that opens godly eyes to God's merciful and just nature and to God's providential activity in the maintenance of the world and the governance of human affairs.[38] The light of faith increases and may at times be diminished. However, faith's illumination is never fully extinguished; indeed, through the experience of affliction, it glows more brightly.

Calvin finds that David, through his words and example, demonstrates how the light of faith constantly guides the life of believers. Many of David's psalms begin with a declaration of trust and confidence in God, after which David recounts a particular trial or temptation.[39] Calvin repeatedly points out that these expressions are undoubted proof of the constancy of David's faith in God's promise. Though beset with spiritual conflicts and outward persecution, David is not swayed by these perils to abandon trust in God, but rather, through faith, recognizes that help must come from God alone. However, David's confidence is not always immediately apparent. Sometimes David begins a psalm abruptly by crying out directly to God. Yet this fact itself, according to Calvin, is evidence that David still perceives and relies on God's providence. Commenting on Psalm 10:1, Calvin writes that, even

---

[35] CO 31: 594; *Commentary on the Psalms*, 2: 434–35.

[36] CO 31: 154–55; *Commentary on the Psalms*, 1: 227.

[37] CO 32: 375; *Commentary on the Psalms*, 5: 204.

[38] Only the faithful can perceive God's providence; see, for example, Calvin's comments on Ps. 8:2 and Ps. 113:1 (CO 31: 89 and 32: 177; *Commentary on the Psalms*, 1: 97; 4: 331). Moreover, Calvin claims at times that God's hand is more apparent in God's works in human history than in the structure of the heavens and earth; see his comments on Ps. 113:7 (CO 32: 179; *Commentary on the Psalms*, 4: 334). This elevation of the revelatory power of history over nature is in tension with the view Calvin expresses elsewhere in his commentary and in other works, like his sermons on Job, that history is far more confused than nature. Susan Schreiner, "Exegesis and Double Justice in Calvin's Sermons on Job," *Church History* 58, no. 3 (1989): 327, notes that Calvin understands Job's vindication to lie in the fact that Job, unlike his friends, did not believe that divine providence was equally discernible in nature and history, but held that providence is more often indiscernible in history. On this relationship between the visibility of providence in nature and history in Calvin's interpretation of the Psalms, see Pitkin, *What Pure Eyes Could See*, 98–130; Barbara Pitkin, "Calvin's Commentary on Psalm 1 and Providential Faith: Reformed Influences on the Psalms in English," in *Crossing Traditions: Essays on the Reformation and Intellectual History in Honour of Irena Backus*, ed. Maria-Cristina Pitassi and Daniela Solfaroli Camillocci (Leiden: Brill, 2018), 164–81. On the issue more broadly, see Trinkaus, "Renaissance Problems," and Susan E. Schreiner, " 'Through a Mirror Dimly': Calvin's Sermons on Job," *Calvin Theological Journal* 21, no. 2 (1986): 175–93.

[39] See, for example, Calvin's comments on Ps. 8:1 and 11:1 (CO 31: 87–88, 120–21; *Commentary on the Psalms*, 1: 93–94, 158–59).

though David complains that God stands far off, David is still fully persuaded of God's presence; otherwise it would have been in vain that he directed his groans and prayers to God at all. Despite the often forsaken tone of his cry and the fact that he accuses God of delaying the fulfillment of God's office, by turning to God and unburdening his troubles, David yields God the honor God deserves.[40] Thus, even though David views events in the world through new eyes, his vision is not yet fully restored and his perception vacillates between the judgment of the eye of sense and that of the eye of faith.

In the Psalms commentary faith illumines God's providential activity. We have seen how the Psalms, according to Calvin, deal principally with the problem of the apparent hiddenness of providence and, with this, the obscurity of God's power, justice, and mercy. Coinciding with these, the temptation to which David is repeatedly subject and which he recounts in his psalms is to think that God has forsaken the church and all creation, that God has forgotten God's promise to protect and nurture the faithful, and that God is not a merciful and omnipotent Father but is rather either a capricious tyrant or a powerless weakling. It is the task of faith to dispel these false impressions and reinforce or restore the perception of God's providence. Calvin describes this activity in his comments on Psalm 10:12. This verse, which is for him the key verse of Psalm 10, reads, "Arise, O Jehovah." Calvin argues that with these words David does not incite God to action, but rather excites his own hope in God. David corrects the "infirmity of sense" under which he suffers; that is, he moves from the judgment of the flesh to the perception of faith. Calvin generalizes from this example for his readers and concludes,

> it is a disease under which mortal human beings in general labor, to imagine, according to the judgment of the flesh, that when God does not execute his judgments, he is sitting idle, or lying at ease . . . But [the faithful] soon shake their minds of that false imagination . . . Of this we have before us a striking example . . . It is therefore a temptation to which all are naturally prone, to begin to doubt the providence of God, when his hand and judgment are not seen. The godly, however, differ widely from the reprobate. The former, by means of faith, check this judgment of the flesh; while the latter indulge themselves in this perverse imagination.[41]

---

[40] CO 31: 108–9; *Commentary on the Psalms*, 1: 133–35.
[41] CO 31: 115–16; *Commentary on the Psalms*, 1: 149–50.

A similar line of argumentation can be found throughout the Psalms commentary, as Calvin underscores faith's clarifying vision and ability to grasp, in part, God's providence amid the confusion of history as the principal theme of many psalms, even those Calvin does not think were authored by David.[42]

When certain psalms move from decrying the confusion of events to declarations of faith, they repeatedly raise up for Calvin the issues of providence and the meaning of history. But beyond simply providing occasions for Calvin to emphasize the necessity of reliance on God's providence (as in the example from Ps. 10:12), the psalm texts also lead Calvin to explore the question of exactly what faith's illumination of providence and history entails. Interesting tensions emerge as Calvin struggles to specify what faith can know or see of God's providential activity and in what sense David's example allows the reformed believer to attribute meaning to the confusion of the sixteenth century. Most often faith appears to be limited only to trust in God's providence and promise, despite all appearances to the contrary. Faith "illuminates" by effecting trust in what at present remains hidden. At other times Calvin hints that believers actually catch a glimpse of God's providential activity. Faith here allows believers to penetrate, if only to a very small degree, the mystery of God's secret providence by making manifest the order that is hidden in the confusion of history. And yet there is a dynamic relationship between the two extremes, with the result that the believer never simply resigns herself to simple trust, but also actively engages in a struggle to perceive.

An instance of the first and more limited kind of perception is found in Calvin's exegesis of Psalm 11, which begins with a declaration of trust in God. Calvin tells his readers that in the first three verses of this psalm, David recounts his spiritual conflicts and severe anxiety under Saul's persecution, when he was advised to give up his hope in God's promise and go into exile. Though David is strongly tempted, Calvin argues, he does not yield, but instead counters the opinion that God's promise will not be fulfilled by declaring in verse 4 that "Jehovah is in the palace of his holiness, Jehovah has his throne in heaven; his eyes behold, and his eyelids consider the children of men." Calvin insists that this declaration is an explicit affirmation of God's providence. Faith affords the view that God is not merely sitting but actively

---

[42] See, for example, his treatment of Psalms 1 and 73 (CO 31: 40–41, 673–74; *Commentary on the Psalms*, 1: 7–8; 3: 120–21). Calvin does not take David to be the author of Psalm 1. For discussion of his development of this theme in his treatment of this psalm and its afterlives in English, see Pitkin, "Calvin's Commentary on Psalm 1."

reigning, and this reassures David of God's favor. David does "see" something, but the vision of God reigning is really only a certainty that God is in control despite all appearances. David does not actually observe the details of the divine activity, but must infer that it must be the case that God is active in human affairs and from this expects that he will restore "order from this miserable state of confusion."[43] Here it seems that what the light of faith corrects is the false impression that God is unfaithful to his promises. Calvin urges his readers to let faith "illuminate for us God's heavenly throne," principally instilling confidence in God's hidden providence.[44]

A more ambiguous view emerges out of the discussion of the perception of faith in Psalm 13, which begins with David crying out that God has forgotten him. Discussing this opening plea, Calvin writes:

> It is not usual for human beings or natural feeling to acknowledge in the midst of our affliction that God cares about us, but by faith we apprehend his invisible providence. Thus David, insofar as he could judge from the actual state of affairs, perceived himself to be deserted by God. At the same time, however, the eye of his mind, guided by the light of faith, penetrated to the grace of God, even though this was hidden in darkness.[45]

By faith David rises above the judgment of the flesh and concludes that his welfare is indeed secure in the hand of God. He accomplishes this by disregarding what is near, namely, his present affliction and persecution; so too, according to Calvin, should believers learn from his example and extend their minds as far as possible in hope.

Yet in his comments on this psalm it remains unclear what Calvin means when he writes that by faith believers "apprehend" God's invisible providence, that they penetrate to the grace of God, or that they should extend their minds beyond the present. Perhaps he intends only to contrast metaphorically the confused and limited sight of the eye of the mind or flesh to the confident and therefore more encompassing scope of the eye of faith. Or can it be that Calvin here hints that believers actually glimpse what God is doing in secret through spiritual eyes? From these and similar passages that treat the confusion of present history, it appears that only the more limited perception

---

[43] CO 31: 123; *Commentary on the Psalms*, 1: 164.

[44] CO 31: 123; *Commentary on the Psalms*, 1: 164. See also Calvin's similar points in his comments on Ps. 33:13 and Ps. 36:5 (CO 31: 331, 361; *Commentary on the Psalms*, 1: 549; 2: 8–9).

[45] CO 31: 132; *Commentary on the Psalms*, 1: 182.

of God's providence is possible. With respect to contemporary affairs, faith is far removed from actual sight, and the best that faith can manage is to see through a mirror dimly.[46] However, elsewhere the psalms texts allow Calvin to speak of a more exact kind of perception. Calvin attributes this more precise discernment not only to David, who is, for Calvin, a prophet, but also to all the faithful. This perception of providence is not dimly through the reflection of a mirror (*speculum*) but from a high watchtower or lookout (*specula*). In distinction to the ambiguous perception described above, it is directed not at God's activity in the present but rather toward that in the future.

The watchtower image, which Calvin derives from Habakkuk 2:1, appears in his discussion of texts such as Psalms 36:12, 37:37, and 73:18 that predict the downfall of the wicked through God's judgment on them.[47] From the clearer vantage point of the watchtower, David obtains views of things previously hidden; he sees that the wicked will fall and that they prosper now only to exercise the faith of believers. A striking example of this appears in Calvin's comments on Psalm 73:18, "surely thou has set them in slippery places; thou shalt cast them down in destruction." Calvin argues that since David's earlier conflicts (detailed in verses 1 through 14) have drawn him closer to God, he now speaks with a composed mind, saying, "I now see, Lord, how you proceed; for, although the ungodly continue to stand for a while yet they are perched on slippery places, that before long they may fall in destruction."[48] Through the eye of faith, David perceives that, though both the godly and the ungodly are subject to uncertainties in the present, it is only the ungodly who are on slippery places. The godly may stumble, but the hand of the Lord supports and sustains them. Yet we note that David does not claim to see this supporting hand in the same way that he glimpses the future destruction of the ungodly and the precarious nature of their present condition.

Like David, the righteous, too, can discern by faith the certain destruction that impends upon the wicked so clearly that they can also perceive the present schemes of the wicked to be doomed.[49] Yet it appears that, regardless of the fact that faith from the watchtower can catch a glimpse of how God

---

[46] Calvin does not indicate the New Testament passages, but he may have in mind 2 Cor. 5:7 and 1 Cor. 13:12. On the centrality of this theme in Calvin's exegesis of Job, see Schreiner, "'Through a Mirror Dimly': Calvin's Sermons on Job."

[47] CO 31: 364–65, 385, 683; *Commentary on the Psalms*, 2: 14–15, 51; 3: 144. On Psalm 73, see Pitkin, *What Pure Eyes Could See*, 126–29.

[48] CO 31: 683; *Commentary on the Psalms*, 3: 144.

[49] See Calvin's comments on Pss. 55:23 and 58:8 (CO 31: 545, 562; *Commentary on the Psalms*, 2: 345, 375).

proceeds, the main consequence of this lofty perspective is the strengthening of trust in present providence that remains hidden. The vision of the future thus both confirms what faith already perceives, namely, that help comes from God alone, and reinforces faith in God's present providential activity.

The eye of faith directed toward the future functions both as an exercise of faith and a support for faith. In this respect it fulfills the same role as the remembrance of God's past mercies and guidance, an activity for which David, once again, provides a model. David boosts his own and his listeners' confidence in God's providence by recounting how this has unfolded itself in the past. Even though such remembrance may, by comparison with the present trials, increase the burden of them, David demonstrates again and again how to gather confidence from such reflection instead.[50] That faith can perceive more order in events past and future than in present affairs is not a cause for despair, but rather a reason for hope. Moreover, though it thus grounds the believer's confidence in present providence, the eye of faith does not provide occasion for smugness. Repeatedly Calvin urges that the fault of his readers' continued blindness is within them. God would make them see his providential care as clearly in daily affairs if only they had eyes pure enough to behold God's judgments occurring in their midst.[51]

In the Davidic psalms Calvin discovers and underscores a view of faith that is characterized by what we might call an existential assurance of God's continuing care. For Calvin, David, unlike Job, does not usually exceed the proper limits of grief, but, except for one instance, gives evidence even in his periods of vacillation of his underlying trust.[52] Yet Calvin is not content simply with a faith that yields to the incomprehensibility of God. Just as God, for Calvin, does not sit idly in heaven looking down from a distance on natural and historical events, from the human side faith is not passive, simply accepting what it cannot see.[53] The faith Calvin finds in David is always

---

[50] See, for example, Calvin's comments on Pss. 4:1, 6:5, 9:13, and 143:5 (CO 31: 59, 76, 104; 32: 402; Commentary on the Psalms, 1: 39–40, 70, 125; 5:253).

[51] See, for example, Calvin's comments on Ps. 37:34 (CO 31: 384; Commentary on the Psalms 2: 50).

[52] For Calvin, David goes dangerously far in expressing his sorrow in Psalm 39 (CO 31: 396–405; Commentary on the Psalms, 2: 71–88). Both David and Job were confronted with what Schreiner calls "the darker side of God's hiddenness" through the inscrutability of God's providence in history ("Exegesis and Double Justice," 338). In his sermons on Job, Calvin finds that Job, however, more often than David, yields to temptation and accuses God of acting capriciously and tyrannically (see, for example, the following passages cited by Schreiner, 334: CO 34: 335–36, 338–42, 345, 357–60; 35: 54–56, 131). For discussion of Calvin's uncomfortable struggle with this aspect of the book of Job, see Schreiner, 332–35.

[53] On Calvin's emphasis on God's "omnioperative character" and its implications for human action and responsibility, see Trinkaus, "Renaissance Problems," 68–79.

active, squinting and straining to overcome human blindness to the order of history, inferring this order from the glimpses from the watchtower of the future judgment of the wicked, from recollection of past experiences of God's faithfulness and mercy, or from the order of nature. Calvin thus reads David's affirmations and appeals alike as expressions of David's confidence in God's providence—as a confidence that becomes increasingly dynamic in character. Faith impels David to seek refuge in God; faith gives voice to his prayer and leads him to praise.

Affliction and persecution, consisting of both inward fears and, more often in the Psalms, outward calamities, serve to further rather than diminish David's faith by exercising faith's dynamic character. On the surface, David's personal afflictions and the persecution of the true church he represents appear to be signs of a history out of control. Yet these miseries themselves provide occasion for David to express his confidence that history *is* ordered, even if this order is not apparent to the eye of the flesh. Moreover, David's sufferings lead him to exercise the eye of faith and to seek to penetrate history's hidden meaning. According to Calvin, affliction is both necessary and beneficial. It forces the godly person into a conflict between the eye of the flesh and the eye of faith and results in a more coherent, yet not completely purified, comprehension of God's providence.

Affliction awakens or increases faith in several ways. Most often it frees one from the allurements of prosperity, which delude the mind into thinking that the self, rather than God, is the cause of good fortune. Calvin finds an example of affliction's purgative role in David's exclamation "You have hidden your face" in Psalm 30:7. In his comments on this passage, Calvin observes:

> Here he confesses that, after he was deprived of God's gifts, this deprivation, like medicine, had purged his mind of perverse confidence. Certainly this is a marvelous and incredible method, that God, hiding his face as if bringing on darkness, illumines the eye of his servant, which saw nothing in the clear light [of prosperity]. However, it is thus necessary that we be shaken violently, in order to drive away the delusions that suffocate faith and stifle our prayers to God and stupefy us with sweet madness.[54]

According to Calvin, suffering also brings awareness both of prior sinfulness and of the need for divine rescue, thereby exercising faith. David realizes

---

[54] CO 31: 297; *Commentary on the Psalms,* 1: 493.

this, and through the eye of faith, he attributes a positive role to his suffering. Recognizing that chastisement itself derives from God's providence, he declares the goodness of his cause and his confidence in the divine call. Through his many conflicts he is led not only to cry out to God for deliverance, that is, to recognize that help comes from God alone. He also intensifies his reliance on the divine promise by cultivating an attitude of patience and, as a result of the triumph of the eye of faith, attains a certain peace.

There is a parallel to this view that affliction and suffering actually lead one to a deeper sense of God's providence in history in Calvin's statements on the visibility of God's providence in nature. For Calvin all creation, but particularly the heavens, manifests the glory of God, not only in its beautiful arrangement but especially in the orderly process of days and seasons and in the fact that the stars and planets remain fixed in the heavens and the tempestuous waters of the sea are restrained. However, fallen human beings are incapable of perceiving God's hand in the orderly processes of nature through the eye of the flesh. Yet the violent disturbances of nature—thunderstorms, earthquakes, and other natural disasters—compel humans, especially those who would stubbornly deny God, to acknowledge his existence.[55] As long as natural events are orderly and the righteous enjoy prosperity, even eyes healed by faith are less likely to acknowledge God's providence and are more likely to attribute the present state of affairs to fortune or to themselves. Disorder is necessary to compel the recognition that it is God who determines both natural events and human affairs; it is God's promise, and not appearances, on which human beings must rely. Appearances change in a moment, but God's promises remain steadfast.

Thus far the discussion has led us to consider the character of the faith that David exemplifies for Calvin. We have seen that the view of faith that Calvin presents in his interpretation of the Davidic psalms is intrinsically linked to issues of providence and perception, that it is both constant trust and inherently active, that it is supported by the memory of past providence, that it benefits from affliction, and that it issues in a clearer vision of nature and history, and in patience, hope, peace of mind, and renewed piety. That all these themes surface in Calvin's discussion comes as no surprise to those familiar with Calvin's *Institutes*, for they are central concerns in his theology. However, because of the specific way that the psalms texts intensify

---

[55] See Calvin's comments on Ps. 29:1–8 (CO 31: 286–89; *Commentary on the Psalms,* 1: 475–80) and *Institutes* (1559), 1.17.1.

the themes of faith, perception, and providence, Calvin sketches in his commentary on the Psalms a more nuanced picture of their interrelationship. Yet while the Davidic psalms are, for Calvin, directly concerned with faith, they do not provide a complete definition of faith. In part this is because, according to Calvin, the Psalms do not primarily convey information about faith, but rather instruct through their depiction of David's faith in action. Thus, Calvin's concern is not to define but rather to describe and thereby lift up David's example for imitation by the godly. Yet in order to comprehend fully the paradigmatic status of David's faith for Christian faith, we must look beneath the prominent themes in the text and probe some of the unspoken, underlying assumptions about the nature of faith that Calvin brings to the interpretive task. First I consider briefly the object of David's faith and then the relationship of David's faith to faith in Christ.

I use the word "object" to refer to faith's foundation or ground, to that to which faith constantly looks and from which it derives its strength.[56] As we have seen, in the Psalms commentary, Calvin depicts faith as looking to God's providence. Yet providence cannot be the proper object of faith, since the perception of providence even by the eye of faith is subject to too much vacillation to produce the kind of certain reliance that Calvin demands. Even the remembrance of God's past deliverances, in which God's providential care is most manifest, is insufficient. For Calvin, the only possible foundation for David's faith is God's word—specifically, God's promise to be favorable. This promise is contained in the covenant with Abraham, in the Mosaic law, and in the particular promise to establish David on the throne of Israel.[57] At several points in his commentary Calvin states explicitly that the word or promise is that upon which faith ultimately relies, and he indicates the content of this promise to be a declaration of God's mercy.[58] This declaration consists for David in the promise that God will never fail or forsake him. To be persuaded of this and to exclaim, as David does in Psalm 31:14, "Thou art my God," is for Calvin the proof of genuine faith.[59]

In order to relate David's faith in the promise that God will be his God to full Christian faith in Christ, we must dig even deeper into the theological presuppositions latent in Calvin's exegesis, and in particular his doctrine of

---

[56] This is consistent with Calvin's use in *Institutes* (1559), 2.6.4 and 3.2.1, 6–7.

[57] On the promise as contained in the law, see especially Calvin's comments on Ps. 19:7–14 (CO 31: 198–207; *Commentary on the Psalms,* 1: 317–33).

[58] See, for example, Calvin's comments on Pss. 26:4, 33:11, and 116:7 (CO 31: 266. 329–30; 32: 194–5; *Commentary on the Psalms,* 1: 441, 547; 4: 363–64).

[59] CO 31: 308; *Commentary on the Psalms,* 1: 510–11.

the one covenant. For Calvin, the Davidic psalms not only speak of events that are, from the perspective of the psalmist, past or present, but also prophesy about the future. Calvin usually focuses his interpretation on what David meant at the time he composed a particular psalm; sometimes he distinguishes what he considers to be the original intent of the psalmist from the meaning applied to the same text by New Testament writers who quote it. In these cases he restricts or limits or even outright rejects traditional readings of passages as literal prophecies fulfilled only in Christ or his future kingdom in order to maintain David's exemplary character.[60] However, though he does it rarely, Calvin also can speak of a particular text as having its primary referent or fulfillment in the future. Under the description of a present situation, David provides a "type" of Christ's future kingdom; in his own person David represents Christ; and, in fact, David says some things about himself and his reign that are most appropriately applied to Christ.[61] Yet as Sujin Pak has demonstrated, Calvin's rendering of these typological or prophetic meanings differs from the traditional christological and trinitarian content emphasized by the antecedent Christian exegetical tradition, including Luther and Bucer.[62] In explaining certain passages as predictions of Christ or, more often, his messianic kingdom, Calvin would not have thought that he was deviating from his ideal of the plain or natural sense of the text, since David, according to Calvin, intended to speak prophetically of the future in these passages. Yet even with this device available to him, Calvin does not often ascribe a prophetic meaning.[63]

Why does Calvin downplay David's prophetic status? I suggest that Calvin's intent is to avoid making David into an anomalous figure removed from his own historical situation. As we have seen, Calvin wants and finds a David as completely entangled in the web of his own history as Calvin's readers are caught up in theirs. Hence David's faith relies on the promise as contained

---

[60] See, for example, Calvin's comments on Ps. 16:8–11 (quoted in Acts 2:30, 13:33) and Ps. 19:4 (quoted in Rom. 10:18) (CO 31: 156–57, 196–98; *Commentary on the Psalms*, 1: 230–32, 314–15). For a discussion of the history of the interpretation of this latter passage, see Hobbs, "Hebraica veritas *and* Traditio Apostolica," 64–97. On Calvin's departure from traditional christological readings of the psalms, see Pak, *Judaizing Calvin*, 79–84. On Calvin's idiosyncratic reading of Psalm 22, see Bernard Roussel, "John Calvin's Interpretation of Psalm 22," in *Adaptations of Calvinism in Reformation Europe: Essays in Honour of Brian G. Armstrong*, ed. Mack P. Holt (Aldershot, UK: Ashgate, 2007), 9–20.

[61] See, for example, Calvin's comments on Pss. 2, 18:37–40, 20:9, and the preface to Ps. 72 (CO 31: 42–43, 187–88, 211–12, 633–64; *Commentary on the Psalms*, 1: 11–12, 294–95, 341–42; 3: 99–100).

[62] Pak, *Judaizing Calvin*, 77–101.

[63] See also Parker, *Calvin's Old Testament Commentaries*, 202–5.

in and conveyed by the vehicles appropriate to the historical period in which David lived, namely, the Mosaic law and the Abrahamic covenant, which, for Calvin, contain Christ in a shadowy yet real way.

However, if we consider in more detail Calvin's notion of one covenant and two dispensations, we find that this idea actually complicates, rather than resolves, the question of the relationship of David's faith in the promise to Christian faith in Christ. In the *Institutes*, Calvin expresses the idea of different dispensations for different ages by arguing that the "old" and "new" covenant differ not in substance but in clarity of manifestation.[64] Faith in both instances is grounded on the word, that is, on the very same promise of grace and mercy. For those under the new dispensation, this word is incarnate in Christ, and therefore Christ is the lens through which they can perceive and receive the divine promise. For those under the old dispensation, the word is present in the Abrahamic covenant and the Mosaic law; the promise received by the Old Testament faithful is exactly the same in substance as that received by later believers, but it is not incarnate in flesh.[65] Yet because the word is, in a sense, sacramentally present in law and covenant, these are a "type" of the incarnation of the word in flesh, containing the reality to which they point.[66] Hence Calvin insists that the ceremonies of the old covenant truly contain Christ, who is the fullest and clearest manifestation of God's saving word.

Behind Calvin's argument for the substantial identity of old covenant and new covenant is a developmental view of humanity and human history, toward which God has accommodated dispensations to evolving human abilities and historical circumstances. The people of Israel under the Mosaic law received the grace of Christ in the testimonies of mercy and favor in the law and covenant. Only when humankind was sufficiently mature did God make the promise clearly manifest in Christ. This historical gradualism enables Calvin to maintain the immutability of God, who accommodates the promise to fit the changing human situation. However, it also creates a problem for the paradigmatic status of David's faith and intensifies the question of how David, living under the old dispensation without clear manifestation of the mystery of Christ, can present Christians with an unequaled

---

[64] *Institutes* (1559), 2.9–10.

[65] On the relationship between the eternal *sermo* by which Old Testament figures knew God and the word incarnate in the flesh, see E. David Willis, *Calvin's Catholic Christology: The Function of the So-called Extra Calvinisticum in Calvin's Theology* (Leiden: Brill, 1966), 69, 109.

[66] Parker, *Calvin's Old Testament Commentaries*, 202.

pattern for imitation. Calvin's retrieval of the exemplary character of David's faith, which is based on his attempt to relate the Mosaic law and the gospel of Christ and to reconcile the Old and New Testaments through the idea of one covenant of grace, thus remains in tension with his gradualist view of history and his developmental notion of humanity.

Consideration of the two ways that Calvin understands the relationship between law and gospel illuminates and perhaps in part accounts for this tension. Calvin has both a broad and a narrow definition of this relationship.[67] In the broad sense, the law is the eternal expression of the divine will, given in grace and containing within it the promise. The gospel, understood in this broad sense, is the promise of mercy and fatherly favor. This appears to be the understanding of law that governs Calvin's exegesis of many of the Davidic psalms. As Calvin notes in his comments on Psalm 19:7,

> Furthermore, under the term "law" [David] not only understands the rule of living righteously or the Ten Commandments, but comprehends the whole covenant by which God had set apart his people from the rest of the world and the whole teaching of Moses . . . These statements by which he commends the law would not be fitting to the Ten Commandments alone unless he added the gratuitous adoption and the promises which depend on it and, in short, the whole body of doctrine in which true religion and piety consists.[68]

According to this broad scheme, law and gospel overlap or are even essentially identical. David's faith is a response to an act of grace (the giving of the law) that discloses the promise (of mercy and divine favor) and can thus function as a paradigm for Christian faith. However, understood in the narrow sense, law and gospel are in a dialectical relationship to one another. Strictly understood, law enjoins works righteousness, whereas gospel is the proclamation of the grace freely offered in Christ. The narrow, dialectical understanding of law and gospel plays no prominent role in Calvin's exegesis of the Psalms, yet it, together with the broad sense, justifies the gradualism

---

[67] *Institutes* (1559), 2.7.2; 2.9.2; 2.11.7.

[68] CO 31: 199; *Commentary on the Psalms*, 1: 318. Calvin underscores the point in his comments on verse 8: "David does not speak simply of the precepts of the moral law but comprehends the whole covenant by which God had adopted the descendants of Abraham to be his peculiar people; and therefore, to the moral law (the rule of living well) he joins the free promises of salvation, or rather, Christ himself, in whom and upon whom this adoption was founded" (CO 31: 201; *Commentary on the Psalms*, 1: 321).

inherent in the idea of one covenant that underlies Calvin's interpretation. The movement from shadow to increasing clarity is a movement from law understood in the broad sense, that is, as containing the gospel, to the gospel understood in the narrow sense, as the proclamation of grace manifest in Christ.[69] This movement creates the tension in Calvin's use of David, since the sixteenth-century Christians who are to imitate his faith, though they have by virtue of their historical situation the advantage of a superior and clearer manifestation of God's mercy and favor, often appear to be so much more blind.

Conclusion

Calvin's exegetical retrieval of the faith of David as an example for imitation by all the godly reflects his theological assumption of the unity of the covenant and also certain tensions inherent in this doctrine. Yet, as we have seen, Calvin appears to ignore the problematic aspects that his formulation of one covenant poses for the paradigmatic status of David's faith and to assert instead the need for a faith just like David's by underscoring the similarity between the situation in which David found himself and the challenges facing sixteenth-century Reformed Christians. Calvin finds in the Psalms a message of comfort for those confounded and tempted by a confused historical situation. This message is so compelling that Calvin is willing to downplay one of his central assumptions about the nature of faith—namely, that it is explicitly christocentric—in order to raise the example of David to prominence.

Calvin could have emphasized David's prophetic ability and argued, as he no doubt assumed, that David did have faith in Christ, whether this was through the law and covenant or by virtue of his prophetic status. Yet Calvin does not stress this as *the* similarity between David and Christian believers. It is here that the difference between the approaches of Luther and Calvin are most pronounced.[70] For Luther, David and later Christians are united by a

---

[69] I am indebted to B. A. Gerrish for this insight (Chicago, January 27, 1988).

[70] For example, in Luther's interpretation of Psalm 122 (given by Preus, *From Shadow to Promise*, 220–25, as an example of Luther's urging the synagogue as a model for faith), Luther says that the synagogue rejoices because entrance into the church has been promised to it and that the church is in solidarity with the synagogue because both await the fulfillment of the promise; according to Preus, both appear explicitly to look to a future Christ. In his comments on verses 1–3, Luther says the synagogue rejoices because it has been promised entrance into the future church, that Christians who have not yet accepted the promises also stand at the gates, and "Jerusalem" is the church militant, still being built by the Word and the gospel (LW 11: 539–40). Calvin's comments on Psalm 122, however,

common faith in Christ, whereas for Calvin, as Bernard Roussel has observed in respect to Calvin's interpretation of Psalm 22, "David and all Christians are contemporaries who all experience the same hope and despair in the presence of their God."[71] Likewise, Calvin could have attributed David's superior vision of the downfall of the wicked to the fact that David possessed the gift of prophecy. Calvin's reluctance to pursue either of these options stems from his unwillingness to risk making a sharp distinction between the faith of David in his historical situation and that of sixteenth-century Christians in theirs. Though these will only be able to follow David at a great distance, they must still be able to follow, otherwise the struggles and victories expressed by David in his psalms will only become occasions for despair. With respect to the question of the perception of providence, Calvin thus blurs the distinction between the prophet and the ordinary, sixteenth-century believer, equipping the faith of the latter with a prophetic glimpse, however slight, into the mystery of God's providence.

Calvin's interest in maintaining the historicity of David is motivated not only by his pastoral concern to console and strengthen his troubled flock by providing them with an example for imitation. In addition, this interest arises out of certain presuppositions about the nature of redemption and its relationship to history or human events and affairs, as opposed to the realm of nature. The Psalms commentary provides a particularly clear example of this aspect of Calvin's historical consciousness. Calvin assumes that history must be meaningful, for it is in history that redemption takes place.[72] For Calvin, all of human history is the site not only of God's providential but also God's redemptive activity. Surprisingly, Calvin implies in the Psalms commentary that it is often history, and not nature, that shows forth God's glory most prominently for human eyes.[73] For instance, Calvin writes concerning

---

focus on how David rejoices upon seeing the readiness of the people to celebrate God's appointing of the present place for the ark of the covenant to rest. The later faithful are to recall this joy and obedience and model themselves on it when they recall that they have *already* received Christ, who has promised to be with them forever (CO 32: 302–3; *Commentary on the Psalms*, 5: 69–72). Discussing verse 4, Calvin relates how the historical particulars of sanctuary, ceremonies, and the monarchy were figures of Christ; he does not attribute to ancient Israel an explicit faith in Christ but rather one mediated by these figures (CO 32: 305; *Commentary on the Psalms*, 5: 74).

[71] Roussel, "John Calvin's Interpretation of Psalm 22," 15.

[72] On Calvin's views on history more broadly, see Josef Bohatec, "Gott und die Geschichte nach Calvin," *Philosophia Reformata* 1, no. 3 (1936): 129–61; Barbara Pitkin, "Calvin, Theology, and History," *Seminary Ridge Review* 12, no. 2 (2010): 1–16.

[73] Or, alternatively, God's providence over nature might be said to be at times subsumed under God's providence over history, since, for Calvin, the maintenance of the natural order is a great instance of God's care for human beings and should incite them to praise. See Calvin's comments on

Psalm 8:1 that, though the whole of nature presents humans "the most abundant matter for showing forth the glory of God," they are undoubtedly more powerfully affected by what they experience themselves. Therefore, David celebrates the special favor that God shows toward human beings, for this "is the brightest mirror in which [they] can behold [God's] glory."[74] Yet, as we have seen, history, though it bears God's promise of grace and mercy, both reveals and conceals God's presence and activity. Through the eye of faith believers glimpse God's glory in history; where history continues to conceal this from them, this very hiddenness spurs faith on in its ongoing struggle to see God.

Pss. 24:2 and 33:7 (CO 31: 244–45, 328; *Commentary on the Psalms,* 1: 402–4, 544) and *Institutes* (1559), 1.14.2. Further discussion in Pitkin, *What Pure Eyes Could See,* 113–30.

[74] CO 31: 88; *Commentary on the Psalms* 1: 93–94. On Calvin's exegesis of this psalm in comparison to Bucer and Jewish exegetes, see Pak, *Judaizing Calvin,* 94–99.

5

Exile in the Mirror of History in Calvin's Commentary on Isaiah

Introduction

In an article first published in 1992, Heiko Oberman posited a "reformation of the refugees" as a new phase in the Reformation, marking a departure from the urban reformation of the 1520s and 1530s that had been the focus of much of twentieth-century scholarship. Oberman contended that Calvin was the instigator of this movement to reform all of Europe, beginning with France, from a base in the city of Geneva, and he drew a connection between this endeavor and Calvin's interpretation of the Bible: "Reading the Scriptures as an exiled refugee in light of his own experience, [Calvin] addressed his listeners and readers not as citizens of Geneva or any other European region, but rather as uprooted wayfarers who had signed up for the hazardous trek to the eternal city."[1] Whether or not and the extent to which Oberman's notion of a "reformation of the refugees" corresponds to the reality of the sixteenth-century Reformed movements is a disputed matter; nevertheless, one cannot deny the fact that a definite consciousness of the contemporary refugee experience has left its imprint on Calvin's work in general and his biblical exegesis in particular.[2] One wonders, in light of Oberman's observation, how this awareness might manifest itself in Calvin's treatment of scriptural references to exile.

[1] Heiko A. Oberman, "*Europa afflicta*: The Reformation of the Refugees," *Archiv für Reformationsgeschichte* 83 (1992): 103; rpt. in *John Calvin and the Reformation of the Refugees* (Geneva: Droz, 2009), 187; see also Heiko A. Oberman, *The Two Reformations: The Journey from the Last Days to the New World*, ed. Donald Weinstein (New Haven, CT: Yale University Press, 2003), 111–16.

[2] On Oberman's concept, see Jane Dempsey Douglass, "Pastor and Teacher of the Refugees: Calvin in the Work of Heiko A. Oberman," in *The Work of Heiko A. Oberman: Papers from the Symposium on His Seventieth Birthday*, ed. Thomas A. Brady et al. (Leiden: Brill, 2003), 51–65; for a confirmation with slight revision of Oberman's views, see Michael Bruening, *Calvinism's First Battleground: Conflict and Reform in the Pays de Vaud, 1528–1559* (Dordrecht: Springer, 2005), 167–263.

Calvin, the Bible, and History. Barbara Pitkin, Oxford University Press (2020). © Oxford University Press.
DOI: 10.1093/oso/9780190093273.001.0001

In order to explore this more closely, this chapter considers the theme of exile in Calvin's exegesis of Isaiah, which was for him the most important of all the prophetic books in the Old Testament. He lectured or preached on the book at three different times between 1546 and 1559, and over the course of his career he engaged the book in various other ways.[3] In 1551 Nicholas des Gallars (1520–1580) published—under Calvin's name and with his approval and cooperation—a exposition of Isaiah compiled from his first cycle of sermons (starting in 1546) and his subsequent lectures (1549–1550); a French translation appeared the following year. This constituted the first of his exegetical publications on the Old Testament. In the second half of the 1550s, Calvin preached on Isaiah again (1556–1559), and at the conclusion of his sermon series, he revised and expanded des Gallars's earlier compilation and republished it as a proper commentary.[4] In January 1564, just a few months before his death, he provided an introduction to Isaiah and an explanation of the first three verses in his last recorded contribution to the weekly Bible studies (congrégations) in Geneva.[5] After he stopped preaching and lecturing in February, Calvin still attended the Friday congrégations when his health permitted; discussing Isaiah in this collaborative setting was his last act of public engagement with scripture.[6]

Calvin's particular interest in the book of Isaiah can be explained first of all through the central themes of the progress of the kingdom of God and the restoration of the church, which were very important to him and which he found expressed in the text and highlighted for his auditors and readers. Scholars have offered different but compatible ways of articulating this distinctive feature of Calvin's reading. Peter Wilcox notes that "missionary and eschatological themes are far more prominent in Calvin's expositions of the Prophets than they are in, for example, the *Institutes*, or Calvin's true 'commentaries.'"[7] This is especially true in the case of the commentary on Isaiah,

---

[3] For a brief summary of Calvin's engagement with Isaiah, see Erik A. de Boer, "Jean Calvin et Ésaïe 1 (1564): Édition d'un texte inconnu, introduit par quelques observations sur la différence et les relations entre congrégation, cours et sermons," *Revue d'histoire et de philosophie religieuses* 80, no. 3 (2000): 372.

[4] John Calvin, *Commentarii in Isaiam prophetam* [revised edition] (Geneva: J. Crespin, 1559), CO 36–37. English translation as John Calvin, *Commentary on the Book of the Prophet Isaiah*, 4 vols., ed. and trans. William Pringle, repr. in *Calvin's Commentaries* (Grand Rapids, MI: Baker Books, 1989); hereafter *Commentary on Isaiah*, followed by volume and page number; translation occasionally altered. See BC 2: 59/1.

[5] See de Boer, "Jean Calvin et Ésaïe 1."

[6] CO 21: 96.

[7] Peter Wilcox, "Calvin as Commentator on the Prophets," in *Calvin and the Bible*, ed. Donald K. McKim (Cambridge, UK: Cambridge University Press, 2006), 130; see also Peter Wilcox, "The Restoration of the Church in Calvin's Commentaries in Isaiah the Prophet," *Archiv für*

in which Calvin, as Amy Plantinga Pauw demonstrates, offers more of an "ecclesiological" than a "christological" reading.[8] Sujin Pak has suggested that Calvin does not follow the traditional christological-prophetic model for reading Old Testament prophecy, but that he "tended to operate with a christological-ecclesial model, in which the Old Testament prophets proclaimed the progress of Christ's kingdom" in history.[9] To be sure, Calvin follows some conventional christological interpretations of select passages in Isaiah, but similar to his handling of traditional messianic passages in the Psalms and christological or trinitarian proof texts in the Gospel of John (see chapters 3 and 4 in this volume), he often criticized or dismissed as illegitimate earlier applications of other prophecies to Christ. Here, as Euan Cameron has noted, Calvin evidences one aspect of his historical sensitivities.[10]

Certainly the book of Isaiah's great concern for true piety, its warnings relating to exile, and its proclamations concerning the captivity as well as the restoration of Israel provide the foundation for Calvin's interest in these themes.[11] It is not surprising *that* Calvin's exegesis engages these topics; nevertheless it is most interesting to see *how* he interprets them. It was certainly no accident that the preacher who had fled his native France began preaching on Isaiah for the second time and began personally preparing a second edition of the commentary in the very years (1556–1559) during which a new

Reformationsgeschichte 85 (1994): 68–96; Peter Wilcox, "'The Progress of the Kingdom of Christ' in Calvin's Exposition of the Prophets," in *Calvinus Sincerioris Religionis Vindex: Calvin as Protector of the Purer Religion*, ed. Wilhelm H. Neuser and Brian G. Armstrong (Kirksville, MO: Sixteenth Century Journal, 1997), 315–22.

[8] Amy Plantinga Pauw, "Becoming a Part of Israel: John Calvin's Exegesis of Isaiah," in *"As Those Who Are Taught": The Interpretation of Isaiah from the LXX to the SBL*, ed. Claire Mathews McGinnis and Patricia K. Tull (Atlanta, GA: Society of Biblical Literature, 2006), 203. On the history of the interpretation of Isaiah, see also John F. A. Sawyer, *The Fifth Gospel: Isaiah in the History of Christianity* (Cambridge, UK: Cambridge University Press, 1996).

[9] G. Sujin Pak, "Contributions of Commentaries on the Minor Prophets to the Formation of Distinctive Lutheran and Reformed Confessional Identities," *Church History and Religious Culture* 92 (2012): 244; see also G. Sujin Pak, *The Reformation of Prophecy: Early Modern Interpretations of the Prophet and Old Testament Prophecy* (Oxford: Oxford University Press, 2018).

[10] Euan Cameron, "Calvin the Historian: Biblical Antiquity and Scriptural Exegesis in the Quest for a Meaningful Past," in *Calvin and the Book: The Evolution of the Printed Word in Reformed Protestantism*, ed. Karen E. Spierling (Göttingen: Vandenhoeck & Ruprecht, 2015), 82–83.

[11] I use "Israel" or "children of Israel" in this chapter to refer collectively to God's chosen people; when I mean the political entity, I use "kingdom of Israel." Calvin often uses the term "Jews" to refer to the people of Isaiah's time; I have not corrected this anachronism in the quotations.

wave of religious refugees swept into the city of his exile, a large number of whom were received into citizenship in Geneva.[12]

The church being restored, which functions as a recurring motif in Calvin's ecclesiological exegesis of Isaiah, must therefore be understood as an "exile church," a congregation of refugees. Wilcox has shown that the theme of the restoration of the church in the Isaiah commentary can be understood in different ways.[13] Similarly the theme of exile can be understood on a number of levels. Calvin explores exile first of all in his references to the situation of contemporary European refugees; second, in his treatment and exposition of the historical exile of Israel; and, third, in the connections he draws between the experience of exile and the doctrine of divine providence. This chapter explores a few examples of Calvin's treatment of each of these three aspects in order to demonstrate how each illuminates a different aspect of his historical consciousness. The conclusion returns to the question of Calvin's own self-awareness as refugee and the mirroring character of history.

Exile in Calvin's Day

Shortly before the publication of the second edition of the commentary on Isaiah, news reached Geneva of the death of the Catholic queen of England, Mary Tudor (1516–1558), and the imminent coronation of her half-sister and successor, the Protestant Elizabeth (1533–1603). Calvin had planned to reuse the original dedication to King Edward (1537–1553), who had died since the publication of the first edition.[14] However, he quickly composed a second dedication to Elizabeth herself (which was inserted into the text at the last minute before the one to Edward), in which he references the contemporary refugee situation.[15] He expresses the hope that his commentary will be restored to its earlier privileges, after having been banned from England along with the entire doctrine of godliness in the recent "wretched and lamentable dispersion."[16] He maintains that, as a "nursing mother" (as Isaiah

---

[12] On this time period and the political importance of the French refugees, see William G. Naphy, *Calvin and the Consolidation of the Genevan Reformation*, revised edition (Louisville, KY: Westminster John Knox, 2003), 208–32.

[13] Wilcox, "Restoration of the Church," 78–94; Wilcox, "Calvin as Commentator on the Prophets," 124–30.

[14] Calvin states this intention in a letter to John Utenhoven in 1557 (CO 16: 673).

[15] CO 17: 413–15; *Commentary on Isaiah*, 1: xvi–xviii. Elizabeth refused the dedication, and Calvin complained about this in a letter to William Cecil in May 1559 (CO 17: 490–92).

[16] CO 17: 414; *Commentary on Isaiah*, 1: xvi.

49:23 designates queens), Elizabeth should gather home to England all the exiles who, on account of their faith, were forced to wander through foreign lands.[17] Although this dedication was written only after completion of the revisions to the commentary, it is important to note that Calvin's correspondence demonstrates his long-standing concern for his religious compatriots who had fled England under Mary.[18] His personal connections to these refugees were strengthened when a group of English and Scottish exiles found their way to Geneva in October 1555, where they produced liturgical manuals and English Bible translations that reflected close connections with the Genevan clergy and publishing projects.[19] In a sense, the Isaiah commentary itself could be counted as one of those exiles driven out of England, and the new dedication referencing these issues serves to heighten this theme.

Of course, Calvin's attention was drawn not only to those Protestants who had fled England and Scotland but also to refugees from France and other countries, such as the group of Protestants from the southern Swiss town of Locarno who sought refuge in Zurich after the Diet of Baden in 1554. In his comments on Isaiah 16:4, Calvin mentions the need to take in and protect all those who have been exiled, especially those fleeing for religious reasons:

> Let us therefore learn from this passage to be kind and dutiful to fugitives and exiles, and especially to believers, who are banished for their confession of the word. No duty can be more pleasing or acceptable to God; and, on the other hand, nothing is more hateful or abominable in his sight than barbarity and cruelty. If we wish to obtain any alleviation of our calamities, let us be kind and compassionate, and not refuse assistance to the needy.[20]

He makes a similar point in his sermon on the same passage, held in March 1557.[21] Max Engammare provides further evidence of the prominence of the

---

[17] CO 17: 415; *Commentary on Isaiah*, 1: xviii.

[18] See, for example, letters from 1554 and 1555 to Heinrich Bullinger (CO 15: 93–96, 123–25), John a Lasco (CO 15: 142–44), the English exiles in Zurich (CO 15: 161–62) and Frankfurt (CO 15: 393–94), and the Reformed congregation in Poitiers (CO 15: 443–45).

[19] For Calvin's influence on the English psalter, see Barbara Pitkin, "Calvin's Commentary on Psalm 1 and Providential Faith: Reformed Influences on the Psalms in English," in *Crossing Traditions: Essays on the Reformation and Intellectual History in Honour of Irena Backus*, ed. Maria-Cristina Pitassi and Daniela Solfaroli Camillocci (Leiden: Brill, 2018), 175–78.

[20] CO 36: 303; *Commentary on Isaiah*, 1: 484.

[21] Jean Calvin, *Sermons sur le Livre d'Esaïe: Chapitres 13–29*, ed. Georges A. Barrios (Neukirchen: Neukirchener Verlag, 1961), SC 2: 111.

theme of contemporary exile in Calvin's sermons on Isaiah and, indeed, in his preaching in general.[22]

Even when Calvin focuses primarily on the situation of the religious refugees of his own day, in the commentary he also treats exile in a broader sense. For example, in his comments on Isaiah 33:20, Calvin reminds his readers that the life of every pious Christian is a kind of exile, and he references their own experience to make his point. He argues that the main complaint of the faithful during the Babylonian captivity concerned the exile from their homeland and the loss of its goods; the notion of Jerusalem as "peaceful habitation" mentioned in Isaiah's prophecy does not mean even for those living today a life free from external expulsion and spiritual wandering:

> Even in the present day this peacefulness is concealed; for we lead an exceedingly wandering and uncertain life, are tossed about by various storms and tempests, are attacked by innumerable enemies, and must engage in various battles, so that there is scarcely a single moment that we are at rest.[23]

The third section, on the experience of exile and divine providence, will return to the extension of the concept of exile beyond the concrete reality of the exiles of Isaiah's time. For now, these examples demonstrate how both the political and personal dimensions of the present experience of religious expulsion and emigration are evident in Calvin's interpretation of this prophetic book. Even though Calvin does not reference the refugee situation of his day in the commentary as often as he does in his sermons on Isaiah, the experience of current exile is noticeably present and binds the commentary's sixteenth-century readers to the words of the prophet and the past experience of the children of Israel.

Exile in the Mirror of the Biblical Past

In order to render this connection between exile at the time of the Babylonian captivity and the situation of religious refugees in the sixteenth century more precise, this section examines Calvin's treatment of Isaiah's warnings

[22] Max Engammare, "'Dass ich im Hause des Herrn bleiben könne, mein Leben lang': Das Exil in den Predigten Calvins," in Calvin und Calvinismus: Europäische Perspektiven, ed. Irene Dingel and Herman J. Selderhuis (Göttingen: Vandenhoeck & Ruprecht, 2011), 229–42.
[23] CO 36: 575; Commentary on Isaiah, 3: 37. See also Pauw, "'Becoming a Part of Israel,'" 205.

concerning exile and the portrayal of the experience of exile in the commentary. As in his other commentaries, Calvin's interpretation reflects his strong interest in the biblical past. This is in part the reason why references to the contemporary situation of exiles are less frequent and explicit than in his sermons. A few examples show, however, that Calvin addresses his readers' current experiences by building bridges between the specific history of the people of Judah addressed by the prophet and his own time through the metaphor of the "mirror" and by making their particular exile and return in the distant past relevant to his day.

Although Calvin casts an eye to his own age in his interpretation of Isaiah, for him it is important to understand and explain the prophet's words in their original historical context. At the very beginning of the commentary he remarks that Isaiah was sent primarily to the inhabitants of Judah, and that all of his prophecies, including those concerning neighboring peoples and lands, were intended for them.[24] They can, of course, be applied to Calvin's time, but only under certain conditions. He argues that it is important to keep in mind the difference between the situation of the people of God living before Christ on the one hand and that of the Christian church on the other—a distinction that Calvin explains more fully in the *Institutes*.[25] For example, right at the beginning of the book, Isaiah reminds his auditors about their special status as God's chosen people and, accordingly, their obligation to honor God; Calvin remarks that Christians are children of God who have an even greater duty, since they have been redeemed through the blood of Christ and have received the gift of the gospel.[26] Another example of this awareness of the difference of times can be seen when Isaiah speaks of the last days in chapter 2, verse 2. According to Calvin, Isaiah refers the people of Judah here to the coming kingdom of Christ, so that they might direct their attention away from their present condition and look toward the future redeemer. Christians, however, living after the incarnation, already inhabit this final age.[27]

Whoever therefore applies the prophet's words to the time after Christ's appearance must attend carefully to the original context, so as not to obscure this key distinction between past and present. Calvin notes in his comments on Isaiah 1:7, 9 that attention to context is generally more difficult when

[24] CO 36: 27–28; *Commentary on Isaiah*, 1: 36–37.
[25] *Institutes* (1559), 2.10–11.
[26] CO 36: 29; *Commentary on Isaiah*, 1: 39–40.
[27] CO 36: 59; *Commentary on Isaiah*, 1: 91.

treating Isaiah and the other prophetic books than when interpreting other books of the Old Testament, since the prophets' proclamations are not necessarily ordered chronologically. They speak at times concerning events that have already taken place, and at others about the present or future events, and sometimes weave these together.[28] Further complicating the interpretive task, for Calvin, is that many of the prophecies are universal and refer to the church in every age. Yet even here Calvin shows his awareness of original context. An example of this can be seen in his comments on Isaiah 49:8, a passage which other Christian commentators had seen as a promise to or prophecy of Christ. Calvin, consistent with his ecclesiological focus, says that Isaiah refers here to Christ particularly as the head of the church and notes that Paul cites this passage and applies it to the whole church in 2 Corinthians 6:2.[29] Calvin then explicates Paul's use of the passage and uses this to determine Isaiah's meaning and its universal application:

> It ought also to be observed that these predictions should not be limited to a certain age, since they belong to the whole church in all ages. For if we begin with the deliverance from Babylon, we must go on to the redemption of Christ, of which it must be regarded as the commencement and the forerunner. And since there are still found among us many remnants of slavery, we must proceed forward to the last day, when everything shall be restored.[30]

As the theme of restoration of the church manifests itself in history unfolding across the ages, Calvin seeks to situate his sixteenth-century readers and their own experience of exile in this process.

Before examining passages that illustrate *how* Calvin achieves this, it is important to lay bare some of the assumptions underlying his concern for original context and respect for the historical past and his equally strong interest in the present condition of the church. Even though Isaiah's prophecies are for the people of Judah, they transcend their particular circumstances to

---

[28] CO 36: 35, 36; *Commentary on Isaiah*, 1: 50, 51.

[29] CO 37: 199–200; *Commentary on Isaiah*, 4: 22–23. Calvin's reading of prophetic passages traditionally applied to Christ's saving work as referring rather to the church of which Christ is the head is widespread in Calvin's interpretation of the prophets. Importantly, as Sujin Pak has argued, in reading them of the church Calvin *was* reading them christologically: "Concerning the classic texts that Christian tradition (and Luther) viewed as literal prophecies of Christ's incarnation, passion, resurrection, and ascension, Calvin repeatedly insisted that these texts should not be confined to Christ alone but extended to the whole church" (*Reformation of Prophecy*, 234).

[30] CO 37: 200; *Commentary on Isaiah*, 4: 22–23.

impart a larger lesson, and some of them, like Isaiah 49:8 (and others), are expressly universal in scope and cannot be restricted to a particular age. For Calvin, what constitutes the hermeneutical key that allows for this extended meaning? In a study of Calvin's treatment of eschatological prophecies about the day of the Lord in the prophets and the Psalms, Richard Muller argues that Calvin's hermeneutic reflects a model of promise and fulfillment, according to which, on one level, Old Testament prophecies are fulfilled in the New Testament. But this fulfillment, though centered on Christ, also extends over the "entire length of Christ's kingdom," and thus any future eschatological referent is always indirect, mediated by earlier partial fulfillments in the history of Israel and the church. According to Muller, this notion of prophecy having multiple fulfillments "provided Calvin with a structure of interpretation within which both a grammatical-historical reading and a strong drive toward contemporary application can function."[31] He draws on Hans-Joachim Kraus's earlier notion of "kerygmatic analogy" to identify ways that Calvin extends the meaning of a text beyond its original context through various strategies, including the notion of a "similitude of times."[32]

Muller's concern is to demonstrate, through analysis of Calvin's actual exegetical practice, that Calvin's interests in original context should not be taken as a "harbinger" of modern historical criticism but rather indicate a working hermeneutic that is not very different from the approaches of other reformers that had their roots in the Middle Ages.[33] While this point is, in my view, undoubtedly correct, Muller attributes to Calvin a view of the literal sense that is too expansive, including "exacting analysis of the original context—[which] becomes the pivot upon which the larger, still literal meaning of the text may be built."[34] Without necessarily ascribing this extended meaning to the literal sense, one can nevertheless affirm the notion of multiple fulfillment of prophecy and, with Wilcox, specify that, in Calvin's exegesis of prophets like Isaiah, prophecy has a triple reference: the imminent historical event, the time of Christ's first appearance, and the whole course of history.[35]

I suggest therefore that it is not an expanded notion of the literal sense but rather a particular concept of sacred history that provides the unifying thread

[31] Richard A. Muller, "The Hermeneutic of Promise and Fulfillment in Calvin's Exegesis of the Old Testament Prophecies of the Kingdom," in *The Bible in the Sixteenth Century*, ed. David C. Steinmetz (Durham, NC: Duke University Press, 1990), 71.

[32] Muller, "Hermeneutic of Promise and Fulfillment," 73–74.

[33] Muller, "Hermeneutic of Promise and Fulfillment," 69; cf. 81–82.

[34] Muller, "Hermeneutic of Promise and Fulfillment," 71.

[35] Wilcox, "Calvin as Commentator on the Prophets," 121.

in Calvin's approach to Isaiah. As Sujin Pak has shown through analysis of a wide range of commentaries on the prophets, Calvin's understanding of sacred history—emphasizing a "continuous history in which all the historical elements of the prophets' own time are significant and useful"—had much in common with the Swiss reformers like Heinrich Bullinger (1504–1575) and distinguished itself from the tendency to separate the history of the prophets from the history of Christ and the gospel that characterized Lutheran exegesis.[36] For Calvin, the original history itself not only is the "primary site of meaning" for Isaiah's (and the other prophets') texts but also functions as "a mirror for the church across time" precisely because of this continuity.[37] According to Pak, Luther, too, employed a mirror metaphor, but saw the Old Testament more as a mirror of doctrine and focused on the biblical figures as exemplars of faith.[38] Indeed, as chapter 4 indicated, in Luther's interpretation of the psalms, David and later Christians share the same faith in Christ. Though Calvin would ultimately agree with this commonality in principle, in contrast, he does not stress faith in Christ as the similarity between David and Christian believers. Instead, Calvin focuses on David's own struggles to perceive and trust in divine providence as a model for how his contemporaries should view the history unfolding around them. In many of his exegetical works, then, Calvin uses the image of the "mirror" to facilitate a distinctive kind of analogical reading that links the past, present, and future of God's people across the ages while also acknowledging more explicitly a difference in times. In the Isaiah commentary, exile is but one aspect of that continuous historical experience.

Calvin's comments on Isaiah 13 provide an example of how the history of ancient Israel functions as a kind of mirror for the later condition of the Christian church. According to Calvin, Isaiah prophesies here concerning the punishment and fall of Babylon in order to comfort the exiles of his day. As these future events unfolded, the faithful would not be confused or disturbed but would rather recognize in them, as in a mirror, the providence of God.[39] Moreover, this mirror would show them something else:

Thus when God threatened such dreadful punishment against the blind Gentiles, the Jews, who had been instructed in the law, might behold as in

---

[36] Pak, *Reformation of Prophecy*, 233; cf. 243–44.
[37] Pak, *Reformation of Prophecy*, 231.
[38] Pak, *Reformation of Prophecy*, 231–32, n79.
[39] CO 36: 256; *Commentary on Isaiah*, 1: 407.

a mirror what they [themselves] had deserved. But the chief design which Isaiah had in view in these predictions was, to point out to the Jews how dear and valuable their salvation was in the sight of God, when they saw that he undertook their cause and revenged the injuries which had been done to them.[40]

In these passages Isaiah's prophecies against Babylon and the future events they foretell both function as mirrors for the people of his own day, reflecting God's providential care back to them. Calvin then maintains that the historical prophecies of Isaiah can further be applied to readers in the sixteenth century, even if God "does not indeed, at the present day, foretell the precise nature of those events which shall befall kingdoms and nations."[41] Whenever Calvin's readers see similar events unfolding in their own historical situation, they should humble themselves before God. Calvin notes that sometimes their own times can help illuminate for them the ancient people's historical experience. For example, he mentions briefly the advance of the Ottoman Turks and contemporary attitudes toward the wartime practices of the Germans, Spanish, and English as present-day examples of the kinds of things that Isaiah relates concerning the historical fall of Babylon.[42]

In Calvin's view, Isaiah's message in chapter 13 relates primarily to the prophet's own contemporaries, providing prophecy as a mirror for them to make sense of their own future history, events which themselves function as mirrors of divine providence. It is by reflecting on that prophecy and the subsequent historical events (now past) that later generations and Calvin's sixteenth-century readers can become more attuned to the workings of divine providence in their own age. Calvin raises a question concerning the accuracy of Isaiah's prediction: Why does Isaiah describe the fall of Babylon in verse 12 as a complete annihilation, when the actual history of the event and even the eyewitness account provided by Daniel suggest otherwise?[43] He rejects the possibility of interpreting Babylon allegorically as all of the reprobate and argues that Isaiah's prediction refers to the literal Babylon, even if its decline was extended over many years. Outlining several stages in this process, he insists on the accuracy of Isaiah's description, since "so

---

[40] CO 36: 257; *Commentary on Isaiah*, 1: 408.

[41] CO 36: 257; *Commentary on Isaiah*, 1: 408.

[42] See comments on Is. 13:5, 17 (CO 36: 260, 267; *Commentary on Isaiah*, 1: 413, 425); in his comments on Is. 22:17, Calvin draws a parallel between Sheban (Is. 22:15) and Thomas More (CO 36: 379; *Commentary on Isaiah*, 1: 131). For more examples, see Cameron, "Calvin the Historian," 83.

[43] CO 36: 264–65; *Commentary on Isaiah*, 1: 420–21.

long as God permitted the city to remain in existence, it presented a shameful and revolting spectacle to the whole world, that the accomplishment of the prophecy might be more evident and more impressive."[44] Although Isaiah, for Calvin, does not write a chronologically ordered historical account, one both can and should see in his testimony a general portrayal of divine providence unfolding itself in the historical process.

In the mirror of the particular historical circumstances addressed by Isaiah, exile is presented as a specific form of chastisement, but one that is designed to instruct the godly. Isaiah depicts exile most often as divine punishment, as can be seen, for example, in Isaiah 5:13. Here Calvin refutes an interpretation that would blame the teachers for the people's ignorance and errors and instead argues that the prophet "charges the people with gross and voluntary ignorance" that justifies their banishment and captivity. Because the prophet speaks in the past tense, Calvin concludes that the divinely imposed captivity has already begun in Isaiah's time, but ventures that it will be fulfilled only with the complete destruction of both of the kingdoms of Israel and Judah.[45] This long period of implementation echoes Calvin's observation in his comments on Isaiah 2:1, that Isaiah and all the prophets who succeeded him were particularly tasked with threatening the people, "until the temple shall be burnt, and the city destroyed, and the Jews be carried into captivity.[46] Even after their return they would continue to experience calamities, and for this reason sorely need the consoling proclamation of restoration and return that Isaiah pronounces in verses 1–4. In his comments on Isaiah 47:6, Calvin underscores that the prophet forewarns that the calamity of exile in Babylon was "a scourge which God inflicted," but that he at the same time offers consolation when God proclaims he will destroy the Babylonians for failing to show compassion.[47] For Calvin, Isaiah's warnings of chastisement—including exile—are intended to stir toward God's people living before the advent of Christ to repentance and foster hope. Yet they mirror a useful lesson for Calvin's readers—namely, that the source of all their misery lies in the misuse of God's word, and godless behavior on the part of sixteenth-century Christians will warrant a penalty similar to that imposed on Isaiah's audience. Despite this warning, Calvin does not speak

---

[44] CO 36: 265; *Commentary on Isaiah*, 1: 422.
[45] CO 36: 111–12; *Commentary on Isaiah*, 1: 177–78.
[46] CO 36: 59; *Commentary on Isaiah*, 1: 91–92; cf. comments on Is. 2:3 (CO 36: 63; *Commentary on Isaiah*, 1: 97).
[47] CO 37: 165; *Commentary on Isaiah*, 3: 453.

often explicitly of the present exile as a punishment, and never of the evangelical exiles of his time as ungodly.

For Calvin, one ought to look especially for the return of the exiles in the mirror of history. He argues already in his comments on Isaiah 1:27 that the restoration of the church, the major theme in Isaiah, consists precisely in the gathering of the refugees who had been so widely dispersed.[48] As Wilcox has shown, in Calvin's view the prophecies concerning this restoration can be understood on two levels: first of all they refer to the actual historical events surrounding the captivity and return from Babylon; second, they relate to the entire course of history from the time of the captivity to the last day—a process whose decisive turning point is reached in the appearance of Christ.[49] Thus, Isaiah 9:2, "the people who walk in darkness will see a great light," does not refer, according to Calvin, *directly* to the coming kingdom of Christ; rather, the prophet understands the return of the exiles to Jerusalem as a prelude to the greater restoration or renewal in Christ and includes all the ages and stages in this process together.[50]

Sometimes, however, Calvin determines that Isaiah does speak only of Christ, as is the case, for example, in Isaiah 11:1, at the head of a chapter that nevertheless also presents exile amid a complex interrelationship between past and present. According to Calvin, "branch" refers only to Christ, and Isaiah goes on to speak of him plainly and without figure.[51] In verse 11, however, the prophet begins to describe the method of restoration: the return from exile prophesied here by Isaiah refers not to the return from Babylon but only to the gathering in of the dispersed remnant through the appearance of Christ and the "sign" of the preached gospel. Yet Isaiah's message to his auditors invites them to hope for this future by recalling a key past experience: "Now, to confirm the hope of the elect people, [Isaiah] recalls to their minds the remembrance of a past deliverance, that they may not doubt that God is as able to deliver them now as their fathers found him to be in Egypt."[52] Just as Isaiah strengthens his auditors' faith by reminding them about their forefathers' and -mothers' redemption out of Egypt, so Calvin encourages his contemporary readers:

---

[48] CO 36: 55; *Commentary on Isaiah*, 1: 82.
[49] Wilcox, "Calvin as Commentator on the Prophets," 127.
[50] CO 36: 190; *Commentary on Isaiah*, 1: 299.
[51] CO 36: 235; *Commentary on Isaiah*, 1: 373.
[52] CO 36: 245; *Commentary on Isaiah*, 1: 389.

Whenever we call to remembrance the deliverances from Babylon and from Egypt, we may be convinced that God is equally able, and will equally assist us at the present day, that he may restore the church to her ancient glory. What he did once and again, he is able to do a third time and a fourth and many times.[53]

In this way, the repeated experiences of exile and return across the ages bind Isaiah's auditors with Calvin's sixteenth-century readers; both discover strength for the present in the mirror of the past.

In his interpretation of Isaiah 11, Calvin does more than remind his readers about distinct, past acts that God repeats again and again. He finds that Isaiah's words in verse 13 point beyond their immediate context to a return that will only be completed far in the future:

I reply, the prophet here includes the whole of Christ's kingdom, and not merely a single age or century. In this world we taste but the beginning of Christ's kingdom; and while the church is harassed by enemies both within and without, still the Lord defends and preserves her, and conquers all her enemies. Besides, this prediction properly belongs to the true and lawful children of Abraham, whom the Lord has purified by the cross and by exile, and has constrained to lay aside ambition and envy; as those who have been tamed in the school of Christ cease to be desirous of renown. Thus the promise which Isaiah makes in this passage has already been in part fulfilled, and is fulfilled every day. But we must proceed in these exercises, and must fight earnestly within and without, till we obtain that everlasting peace which it will be our happiness to enjoy in the kingdom of God.[54]

Insofar as the promised return from exile has only been partially fulfilled, a hope for the future completion is gained through a glance into the looking glass of history. As Calvin concludes his comments on chapter 11, after reminding his readers that Isaiah's audience could perceive the same divine power in their deliverance from Babylon as they saw in the exodus from Egypt, "what the Lord has once performed let us also expect for the future, and for that purpose let us ponder the ancient histories."[55]

---

[53] CO 36: 246; *Commentary on Isaiah*, 1: 390.
[54] CO 36: 247; *Commentary on Isaiah*, 1: 392–93.
[55] CO 36: 250; *Commentary on Isaiah*, 1: 396.

Summing up one can say that the perpetual refugee character of the true church, made up of the true children of Abraham, is constantly before Calvin's eyes in his treatment and exposition of the historical experience of exile in this text—even when Calvin takes pains to explain Isaiah's prophecies in the context of Israel's history. The pious of his day recall themselves to the ancient histories and to promises both fulfilled and yet to be realized in order to nourish hope in a future return out of their own exile. Past, present, and future reflect and illuminate one another in complex mirror images.

The Experience of Exile and the Providence of God

In Calvin's view one needs to understand the concept of exile not simply in connection with the history of Israel but also in light of the entire history of salvation. This perspective yields both a negative as well as a positive dimension to the notion that the church since its very beginnings is a church of refugees. Calvin explores the negative dimension in his comments on Isaiah 51:3, where God promises to make Jerusalem's deserts a "place of delights." Here Calvin finds a reference to paradise, from which the first humans were expelled on account of their sin, going into a kind of exile that characterizes Christian life all the way down to the present. He observes: "Now we, who have been deprived of that blessing which he bestowed on our first parent, are exiles throughout the whole world, and are deprived of that paradise."[56] Exile as punishment means, moreover, that humanity drifts through history without recognizing in its course the providence of God. All disorder in history stems from human sin.

Alternatively, however, exile provides a way back to God, and not just because God redeems the chastised remnant. Insofar as the faithful go into exile willingly, on account of their faith, they cast themselves upon divine providence and give witness to their obedience to God. The figure of Abraham represents the most important example of this more positive experience of exile in the commentary. According to Calvin, Isaiah encourages his auditors not only by reminding them about the redemption that their ancestors experienced when God brought them back from their exile in Egypt. In addition he holds up as an example their father Abraham, who also had to leave his native country, just as they had done. Max Engammare points to

---

[56] CO 37: 228; *Commentary on Isaiah*, 4: 68.

Calvin's portrayal of Abraham elsewhere as a figure of comfort and protection for those who like him have gone into exile in the name of God.[57] In the commentary on Isaiah, there is only one place where Calvin explores this in detail, but this single instance sufficiently demonstrates how the example of Abraham's exile, which he embarked upon through the urgings of divine providence, not only served to comfort the children of Israel at the time of the Babylonian exile but also represents the earthly condition of all of Abraham's true children. Moreover, Calvin's description of Abraham's departure from his homeland in his comments on Isaiah 41:2 hints at his own experience as a religious refugee:

> Moses does not enumerate all the difficulties which Abraham encountered at his departure, but any person may conclude that this journey could not be free from very great annoyances; for it was impossible for him, when he set out, not to draw upon himself the hatred of the nation, and to be universally condemned as a madman for leaving his native land, and relations, and friends, and wandering to an unknown country. After having come into the land of Canaan, he had to do with wicked and cruel men, with whom he could not be agreed, because he was entirely opposed to their superstitions. What Moses relates shows plainly enough that Abraham was never at rest.[58]

It is well known that Calvin was reluctant to speak of himself. Nevertheless, perhaps one can hear in his speculations about Abraham's experience a small echo of what Calvin himself underwent when he left his French homeland, going into exile as a religious refugee.

Conclusion

This investigation of the varied manifestations of the concept of exile in Calvin's commentary on Isaiah yields more certain insight into Oberman's claim by showing *how* Calvin read "the Scriptures as an exiled refugee in light of his own experience."[59] In his commentary on Isaiah, Calvin assumes that

---

[57] Max Engammare, "Une certaine idée de la France chez Jean Calvin l'exilé," *Bulletin de la société de l'histoire du protestantisme français* 155 (2009): 15–27.

[58] CO 37: 35; *Commentary on Isaiah*, 3: 248. See also Calvin's comments on Is. 51:1–2, where Calvin discusses Abraham as an example of faith rather than of exile experience (CO 37: 226–28; *Commentary on Isaiah*, 4: 66–68).

[59] Oberman, "*Europa afflicta*," 103.

exile is no foreign concept to his readers. Even in cases when they did not have to flee from their native country, they probably knew religious refugees and could imagine their life on earth and the history of the church in general as an exile imposed on them by God as punishment for sin and, at the same time, as a "hazardous trek to the eternal city" understood as a return from exile. Was Calvin, then, a kind of exiled prophet for this refugee people? It is interesting to note in connection with this question that the way that Calvin's exposition of what was for him the greatest prophetic book came to be published was similar to the way he envisioned that Isaiah's prophecies themselves were collected and made available: in both cases, the words and teachings were collected and published by others. As Calvin explains in his introduction to his commentary on Isaiah, the prophets wrote down a short summary of the messages they delivered orally and hung them up on the doors of the Temple. After a while these would be removed and stored in the treasury. Still later the prophecies would be gathered and organized as occasion demanded—that is, not necessarily chronologically.[60] Des Gallars, the editor of Calvin's first published exposition of Isaiah, describes in a foreword to his edition a similar process that he adopted for collecting and arranging Calvin's ideas. He describes how he wrote down in Latin at home what seemed important to him in Calvin's sermons and lectures and used this as the basis for constructing the commentary, observing "not that I included everything or followed the same order or method."[61] Even though Calvin himself later expanded the summary put together by des Gallars, the similarity in the process of preparing the first edition contributes to the image of Calvin as a prophet—indeed as an exiled prophet or even as an asylum seeker that has emerged in recent research.[62]

In addition to these multilayered insights into Calvin's own refugee consciousness, there are further intriguing elements of Calvin's treatment of the theme of exile: the complex relationships among exile in the present, exile in

---

[60] CO 36: 24; *Commentary on Isaiah*, 1: xxxii; cf. Calvin's comments on Is. 8:1 (CO 36: 165; *Commentary on Isaiah*, 1: 261). Calvin repeated this point in his lectures on Jeremiah (CO 39: 99–100). Cameron discusses this and points out that Luther makes a similar observation in his preface to Jeremiah; see "Calvin the Historian," 85 and 85n36.

[61] "Nicolaus Gallasius pio Lectori S." (1551), CO 36, Prolegomena. See also Wilcox, "Restoration of the Church," 73–74; Pauw, " 'Becoming a Part of Israel,' " 205.

[62] Max Engammare, "Calvin: A Prophet without a Prophecy," *Church History: Studies in Christianity and Culture* 67 (1998): 643–61; Herman J. Selderhuis, "Calvin as an Asylum Seeker: Calvin's Psalms Commentary as a Reflection of His Theology and as a Source of His Biography," in *Calvin's Books: Festschrift Dedicated to Peter De Klerk on the Occasion of His Seventieth Birthday*, ed. Wilhelm Neuser et al. (Heerenveen: J. J. Groen, 1997), 283–300; Jon Balserak, *John Calvin as Sixteenth Century Prophet* (Oxford: Oxford University Press, 2014); Pak, *Reformation of Prophecy*, esp. 153–77.

the past, exile as punishment for sin, and exile as a path of salvation. Above all, one notes that Calvin's sense for historical anachronism seems not nearly as pronounced as, for example, in his published lectures on Daniel and in his commentary on the last four books of the Pentateuch, which will be the subject of the next two chapters.[63] The contrast to his Daniel lectures is especially striking. As chapter 6 will detail, Calvin insists on a more consistent historical interpretation of Daniel's prophecies in relation to the ancient Israelites' situation up to the appearance of Christ in the first century. His exposition of that biblical book observes the boundary between past and present to a much greater degree, even though the history of Israel still functions as a mirror, in which Calvin's auditors and readers can learn to perceive divine providence in their own time and place.[64]

There is perhaps a simple explanation for the looser relationship between past and present in the Isaiah commentary, namely, that it comes from des Gallars, who notes in his preface: "The perusal of these commentaries will enable you better to understand how well adapted the doctrine of Isaiah is to the present time."[65] Even though Calvin reworked des Gallars's material for the second edition, he was still using as a basis for his commentary a summary of his own sermons and lectures that had been drawn up by someone else. And in the sermons certainly, and also to a degree in the lectures, Calvin tended to pay more attention to contemporary applications of the sacred past.

A little more complicated explanation of the difference lies perhaps in the fact that, as we shall see, Calvin gives Daniel's prophecies a primarily christological interpretation—focusing, however, on Christ's birth, earthly life, and his death and not relating them to his return at the end of days. In the commentary on Isaiah, in contrast, Calvin concentrates on an ecclesiological reading in respect to the church that even after the appearance of Christ finds itself in exile. As Pak has argued, this latter ecclesiological reading still has a christological dimension, but in a different sense from the christological-prophetic mode employed by Luther and other traditional exegetes.[66] In

---

[63] Pauw is correct in noting that Calvin's interpretation nevertheless pays much more attention to historical context than the previous and contemporary interpretive traditions ("'Becoming a Part of Israel,'" 207, 216, 219).

[64] An earlier version of this argument (revised as chapter 6 in this volume) appeared as Barbara Pitkin, "Prophecy and History in Calvin's Lectures on Daniel (1561)," in *Die Geschichte der Daniel-Auslegung in Judentum, Christentum, und Islam: Studien zur Kommentierung des Danielbuches in Literatur und Kunst*, ed. Katharina Bracht and David S. du Toit (Berlin: De Gruyter, 2007), 323–47.

[65] Nicolaus Gallasius pio Lectori S. (1551), CO 36, Prolegomena.

[66] Pak, "Contributions of Commentaries," 244.

the end, one can say that the restoration of the exile church—a process that extends over the entire course of human history—bears witness for Calvin to God's promise never to abandon the church. The need for the church to embrace and trust in this promise at all times explains in part the mirroring of past, present, and future that the concept of exile bridges.

6

Prophecy and History in Calvin's Lectures on Daniel

Introduction

In June 1559, John Calvin began a series of lectures under the auspices of the recently inaugurated Genevan Academy.[1] His topic was the Old Testament book of Daniel, a subject which occupied him until the middle of April 1560. Following his customary practice, he pursued a continuous exposition of the text, delivering his sixty-six lectures extemporaneously. In the early 1550s several of his regular auditors had developed a system for transcribing his oral comments, collating their notes, and preparing a virtually verbatim copy that could be published.[2] It was, then, this transcription of Calvin's lectures that was published in 1561 by the Genevan printer Jean de Laon.[3]

The lectures were in fact Calvin's second full exegetical treatment of this book; in the summer and fall of 1552 he had preached on Daniel during his weekday morning sermons, also following a *lectio continua* format. Like all of Calvin's sermons preached since 1549, these extemporaneously delivered sermons were taken down by a professional scribe.[4] In 1565, a year after Calvin's death, forty-seven of these sermons on the last eight chapters of Daniel were published in La Rochelle, without the authorization of the

[1] The official inauguration was held on June 5, 1559. Karin Maag, *Seminary or University? The Genevan Academy and Reformed Higher Education, 1560–1620* (Brookfield, VT: Ashgate, 1995), 10.

[2] For a description of this process, which was coordinated by Jean Budé and Charles Jonvilier, see Peter Wilcox, "Calvin as Commentator on the Prophets," in *Calvin and the Bible*, ed. Donald K. McKim (Cambridge, UK: Cambridge University Press, 2006), 108–109; on Calvin's auditors, see Peter Wilcox, "The Lectures of John Calvin and the Nature of His Audience, 1555–1564," *Archiv für Reformationsgeschichte* 87 (1996): 136–48.

[3] John Calvin, *Praelectiones in librum prophetiarum Danielis* (Geneva: J. de Laon, 1561), CO 40: 529–722; 41: 1–304. Translations of the lectures appeared in French in 1562 and 1569 and in English in 1570. Two further Latin editions were published in 1571 and 1591. In English in John Calvin, *Commentaries on the Book of the Prophet Daniel*, 2 vols., ed. and trans. Thomas Myers, repr. in *Calvin's Commentaries* (Grand Rapids, MI: Baker Books, 1989); hereafter *Commentaries on Daniel*, followed by volume and page number.

[4] For an account of the origins of this practice, see T. H. L. Parker, *Calvin's Old Testament Commentaries* (Edinburgh: T. & T. Clark, 1986), 10–12.

Calvin, the Bible, and History. Barbara Pitkin, Oxford University Press (2020). © Oxford University Press.
DOI: 10.1093/oso/9780190093273.001.0001

Genevan authorities.[5] Beyond the sermons, an "Argument du livre des Revelations du Prophete Daniel" by Calvin appeared as a preface to the French translation of Philip Melanchthon's (1497–1560) 1543 commentary on Daniel, which was published in Geneva in 1555.[6]

A complete study of Calvin's exegesis of Daniel would need to attend to these sermons and the preface in addition to the lectures. However, because Calvin's lectures represent his most mature and thorough treatment of Daniel, this chapter focuses on the lectures, in order to demonstrate the continuity and discontinuity of Calvin's exegesis of Daniel with earlier and contemporary patterns of interpretation. The first section provides a brief overview of the main features of Calvin's lectures and his novel interpretation of this Old Testament book. Subsequent sections examine in detail Calvin's historicizing treatment of three issues: the four empires, the seventy weeks, and the question of the Antichrist. The conclusion reflects on what Calvin's interpretation of these issues reveals about his understanding of prophecy and history.

Calvin's Exposition of Daniel

Calvin's interpretation of Daniel in his 1561 lectures embraces both the moral and the prophetic elements of this biblical text that constituted two recurring foci of earlier Christian interpreters: for Calvin, Daniel is both an exemplary man of faith and a prophet revealing God's word and plan for the future. Indeed, the story of Daniel remaining true to his faith under hostile political conditions suggests many obvious, pertinent parallels with the religious situation in France at the time of Calvin's lectures. One might expect Calvin to underscore Daniel's steadfast refusal to hide his religious convictions and to explore the question of political loyalty in conditions of religious persecution

---

[5] CO 41: 323–688 and 42: 1–174. In the introduction to Calvin's sermons on Deuteronomy published in 1567, the publisher complains about the unauthorized printing of the sermons on Daniel (BC 3: 67/3).

[6] Philip Melanchthon, *Commentaire de Philippe Melanc[h]thon sur le livre des revelations du Prophete Daniel; item les explications de Martin Luther sur le mesme Prophète adioutées à la fin* ([Geneva]: J. Crespin, 1555); Calvin's preface is reprinted in Hans Volz, "Beiträge zu Melanchthons und Calvins Auslegungen des Propheten Daniel," *Zeitschrift für Kirchegeschichte* 67 (1955–56): 117–8. Within the work, the French translator designates Luther's preface a "commentary" (*Commentaire,* 349, 421). In the "Argument du livre," Calvin does not discuss Melanchthon's or Luther's comments but simply summarizes the book of Daniel itself. This leads Volz to suggest that Calvin's preface was likely an independent piece added by the publisher.

by the state. One might expect this all the more so upon learning that Calvin dedicated his published lectures to his reformed coreligionists living in France, and that the majority of the scholars in his audience were training to return to France as missionaries.[7] However, though Calvin derives lessons for his auditors from the behavior of Daniel and his companions, these moral applications are truly a secondary theme.[8] Instead, Calvin pursues a predominantly prophetic-historical rather than a moral exegesis of the book. In contrast to his treatment of David in his commentary on the Psalms (discussed in chapter 4), Calvin's *main* focus and aim of these lectures is not to urge the imitation of the exemplary Daniel but rather to inculcate what he takes to be the true understanding of Daniel's prophetic message. For Calvin, a proper grasp of these historical prophecies is the necessary precondition for understanding the continued relevance of this Old Testament book for Christian spiritual, moral, and political life.

It is precisely in Calvin's somewhat idiosyncratic rendering of Daniel's prophetic message that most previous studies of his lectures have detected his allegedly distinctive contribution to the history of Danielic exegesis.[9] To summarize these elements briefly, Calvin limits the scope of Daniel's prophecies to the events up through the first century of the common era. Thus, the four monarchies in Daniel 2 and the four beasts in Daniel 7 represent kingdoms and situations that are long past. The little horn in Daniel 7 refers

[7] Wilcox, "Lectures of Calvin," 146.

[8] John Gammie provides a list of places in the *Institutes* (1559) where Calvin draws on Daniel for "pastoral and doctrinal lessons." John Gammie, "A Journey through Danielic Spaces: The Book of Daniel in the Theology and Piety of the Christian Community," *Interpretation* 39 (1985): 154–55. I am grateful to Pete Wilcox for sharing his thoughts on this point.

[9] The most thorough treatment is Machiel A. van den Berg, "Het rijk van Christus als historische realiteit: Calvijns anti-apocalyptische uitleg van het boek Daniël" (Ph.D. diss., University of Utrecht, 2008), https://dspace.library.uu.nl/handle/1874/31558. See also Mario Miegge, *Il sogno del re di Babilonia: Profezia e storia da Thomas Müntzer a Isaac Newton* (Milan: Feltrinelli, 1995), 71–90 and "'Regnum quartum ferrum' and 'lapis de monte': Die kritische Wende in der Danielrezeption im 16. Jahrhundert und ihre Folgen in Theologie und Politik," in *Europa, Tausendjähriges Reich und Neue Welt: Zwei Jahrtausende Geschichte und Utopie in der Rezeption des Danielbuches*, ed. Mariano Delgado, Klaus Koch, and Edgar Marsch (Stuttgart: Kohlhammer, 2003), 239–51; Arno Seifert, *Der Rückzug der biblischen Prophetie von der neueren Geschichte: Studien zur Geschichte der Reichstheologie des frühneuzeitlichen deutschen Protestantismus* (Cologne: Böhlau, 1990), 29–64; Irena Backus, "The Beast: Interpretations of Daniel 7.2–9 and Apocalypse 13.1–4, 11–12 in Lutheran, Zwinglian and Calvinist Circles in the Late Sixteenth Century," *Reformation and Renaissance Review* 3 (2000): 59–77; Walter Käser, "Die Monarchie im Spiegel von Calvins Daniel-Kommentar: Ein historischer Beitrag zur reformierten Lehre vom Staat," *Evangelische Theologie* 11 (1951–52): 112–37; Gammie, "Journey." Euan Cameron analyzes Calvin's historicizing treatment of prophecy in Daniel and in his commentaries on Isaiah and Jeremiah: "Calvin the Historian: Biblical Antiquity and Scriptural Exegesis in the Quest for a Meaningful Past," in *Calvin and the Book: The Evolution of the Printed Word in Reformed Protestantism*, ed. Karen Spierling (Göttingen: Vandenhoeck & Ruprecht, 2015), 77–94.

to Julius Caesar and his successors. Falling within the same time frame, the appearance of the Ancient One, the judgment and open books, and the appearance of the Son of Man in Daniel 7:9–14 refer to Christ's first advent and ascension—not to the final judgment. Finally, the events described in Daniel 8 and 11 concern the rule of Antiochus Epiphanes, the Maccabean Revolt, and ancient Rome, and do not foretell or even typify the future Antichrist.

Calvin's explanation of the prophecies of Daniel as relating entirely—with one exception—to historically past events went completely counter to the dominant Protestant interpretive trend of his day, though it was not entirely without precedent. The prevailing view manifested itself in historical summaries such as the world history known as *Carion's Chronicle* that was edited by Melanchthon[10] and the *Four World Monarchies* by John Sleidan (1506–1556).[11] It also was expressed in Martin Luther's (1483–1546) biblical prefaces and other writings on Daniel,[12] in commentaries on Daniel by John Oecolampadius (1482–1531)[13] and Melanchthon,[14] and in published sermons on Daniel by Heinrich Bullinger (1504–1575).[15] Notably, Sleidan, Melanchthon, and Bullinger were all personal acquaintances of Calvin with

[10] Melanchthon published this first in 1532, and subsequently revised and expanded it, publishing his last edition in 1558 and 1560; the revisions were completed by Casper Peucer. *Chronicon Carionis*, CR 12: 709–1094. See Katharine Firth, *The Apocalyptic Tradition in Reformation Britain, 1530–1645* (Oxford: Oxford University Press, 1979), 15–22; Robin Barnes, *Prophecy and Gnosis: Apocalypticism in the Wake of the Lutheran Reformation* (Stanford, CA: Stanford University Press, 1988), 106–8.

[11] John Sleidan, *De quatuor summis imperiis libri tres* (Strasbourg: Rihel Brothers, 1556); also known in English translation as *A Key to History*.

[12] See Stefan Strohm, "Luthers Vorrede zum Propheten Daniel in seiner Deutschen Bibel," in *Die Geschichte der Daniel-Auslegung in Judentum, Christentum und Islam: Studien zur Kommentierung des Danielbuches in Literatur und Kunst*, ed. Katharina Bracht and David S. du Toit (Berlin: De Gruyter, 2007), 219–44; O. Albrecht, "Luthers Arbeiten an der Übersetzung und Auslegung des Propheten Daniel in den Jahren 1530 und 1541," *Archiv für Reformationsgeschichte* 23 (1926): 1–50.

[13] John Oecolampadius, *In Danielem prophetam Joannis Oecolampadii libri duo* (Basel: J. Bebel, 1530; Basel: T. Wolff, 1530). See van den Berg, "Het rijk van Christus," 135–84, 360–62.

[14] Philip Melanchthon, *In Danielem prophetam commentarius* (Wittenberg: J. Klug, 1543), CR 13: 823–980. See also two letters from Melanchthon to Veit Dietrich, discussing issues surrounding the interpretation of Daniel (CR 3: 545–48 = MBW 2053; CR 3: 557–59 = MBW 2067). On Melanchthon's interpretation of Daniel—along with Proverbs the only Old Testament book on which he published a commentary—see Heinz Scheible, "Melanchthons Verständnis des Danielbuchs," in Bracht and du Toit, *Die Geschichte der Daniel-Auslegung*, 293–322; van den Berg, "Het rijk van Christus," 85–134, 357–60.

[15] Heinrich Bullinger, *Daniel sapientissimus dei propheta, qui a vetustis polyhistor, id est multiscius est dictus, expositus homiliis LXVI* (Zurich: C. Froschauer, 1565). See Daniel Timmerman, "'The World Always Perishes, the Church Will Last Forever': Church and Eschatology in Bullinger's Sermons on the Book of Daniel (1565)," *Zwingliana* 36 (2009): 85–101; Anja-Silvia Göing, "Schulausbildung im Kontext der Bibel: Heinrich Bullingers Auslegungen des Propheten Daniel (1565)," in *Heinrich Bullinger: Life—Thought—Influence*, ed. Emidio Campi and Peter Opitz (Zurich: Theologischer Verlag Zurich, 2007), 437–58; Emidio Campi, "Über das Ende des Weltzeitalters: Aspekte der Rezeption des Danielbuches bei Heinrich Bullinger," in Delgado, Koch, and Marsch, *Europa*, 225–38; cf. Backus, "Beast," 75–76.

whom he corresponded. Their works also emphasized, like Calvin's, the historical dimension and import of Daniel's prophecies. In contrast, however, they understood the four monarchies to comprise a universal world history that was still ongoing in the sixteenth century. Furthermore, they identified the papacy or the Ottoman Turks as the Antichrist prophesied by Daniel, and in so doing viewed Daniel as an eschatological handbook for the end times. This reading of Daniel as a prediction of the entire course of history had deep roots in the Middle Ages, but gained new impetus as a result of the religious and political challenges of the sixteenth century.[16]

In this same situation of religious and political ferment, Calvin's lectures offer an alternative historical reading of the book of Daniel.[17] His approach has been credited with inaugurating a critical shift in the history of Danielic interpretation, a move that, as Mario Miegge and Arno Seifert have argued, saw completion in the work of Emmanuel Tremellius (1510–1580), Jean Bodin (1529–1596), and François De Jon (1545–1602), all of whom limited the historical scope of Daniel's prophecies even further and identified the fourth monarchy not as Rome but as the Seleucid successors of Alexander the Great.[18] However, Calvin's praeteristic and noneschatological reading of Daniel was by no means widely embraced. Indeed, the model represented by Luther, Melanchthon, Bullinger, and others continued to dominate sixteenth-century perspectives and was revitalized in the seventeenth century, particularly in England.[19]

The discussion now turns to Calvin's treatment of three critical issues—the four empires, the seventy weeks, and the question of the Antichrist—in order to shed light on the details of his alternative historical reading and to suggest what is at stake for him in the interpretations he defended. Calvin was profoundly aware that in articulating his positions he was dissenting from the popular view—so aware in fact that he occasionally broke with his general

---

[16] See Cameron, "Calvin the Historian," 87–88. On medieval interpretations of Daniel, see Werner Goez, "Die Danielrezeption im Abendland—Spätantike und Mittelalter," in Delgado, Koch, and Marsch, *Europa*, 176–96; Mark Zier, "The Medieval Latin Interpretation of Daniel: Antecedents to Andrew of St. Victor," *Recherches de théologie ancienne et médiévale* 58 (1991): 43–78; Firth, *Apocalyptic Tradition*, 2–5.

[17] Calvin's reading has also been seen to have significant political implications, although scholars have not agreed about the substance of these. See, e.g., Backus, "Beast," 62, 72; Kaser, "Monarchie." For an overview of the political ramifications of early modern readings of Daniel, see Klaus Koch, "Europabewusstsein und Danielrezeption zwischen 1648 und 1848," in Delgado, Koch, and Marsch, *Europa*, 326–84.

[18] Miegge, "'Regnum quartum ferrum,'" 240, 242; cf. Miegge, *Il sogno*, 69–100. For discussions of this trend, see Koch, "Europabewusstsein," 331–33, 371–72; Seifert, *Rückzug*, 49.

[19] See Firth, *Apocalyptic Tradition*.

humanistic convention of not naming the names of those with whom he disagreed. In them he perceived, I contend, an inappropriate application of biblical prophecy and an inadequate understanding of history. These twin errors signaled, to him, a biblical hermeneutic that was, if not completely wrong, at least suspect in its way of deriving present meaning from the biblical past.

Calvin on the Four Empires in Daniel 2 and 7

In the exegetical traditions to which Calvin's reading of Daniel is indebted, the four monarchies or empires signified in Nebuchadnezzar's dream in Daniel 2 and in Daniel's vision of the four beasts in Daniel 7 had become standard means for marking the divinely appointed ages of history. Moreover, the feet of iron and clay (Dan. 2:32) and the terrible, unnamed fourth beast (Dan. 7:7–12) were almost universally understood to represent the Roman Empire.[20] Diversity, however, characterized the views of the extent to which the prophecies concerning the fourth beast—especially the identity of the "little horn" (Dan. 7:8)—had been fulfilled. Brief consideration of three points raised in Calvin's lectures—the identity and duration of the fourth empire; the identity of the horns of the fourth beast; and the Son of Man and his kingdom—will illustrate his particular contribution to these traditional concerns.

In the first place, Calvin complains about interpreters who fail to embrace the standard identification of the four monarchies with the historically successive Babylonian, Persian, Macedonian, and Roman empires. Jewish interpreters, he charges, confuse the Roman with the Turkish kingdom[21] or include the Greeks under the second empire,[22] thus confounding the Roman with the Greek (i.e., third) kingdom.[23] He also criticizes Christian interpreters who include the Turkish Empire within the Roman, noting that he finds "nothing probable in that opinion."[24]

---

[20] The four-kingdom motif with Rome as the fourth kingdom is also found in 4 Ezra 11–12 (=2 Esdras 11–12), 2 Apocalypse of Baruch, and the *Sibylline Oracles* 4. See John Collins, *Daniel: A Commentary on the Book of Daniel*, vol. 27 of *Hermeneia: A Critical and Historical Commentary on the Bible* (Minneapolis, MN: Fortress, 1993), 84. On the identification of the fourth beast as Rome in later Jewish and Christian interpreters, see Collins, *Daniel*, 113, and Jay Braverman, *Jerome's Commentary on Daniel: A Study of Comparative Jewish and Christian Interpretations of the Hebrew Bible* (Washington, DC: Catholic Biblical Association of America, 1978), 91–94.

[21] Comments on Dan. 2:31 (CO 40: 589; *Commentaries on Daniel*, 1: 162); Comments on Dan. 7:7 (CO 41: 46; *Commentaries on Daniel*, 2: 21).

[22] Comments on Dan. 2:39 (CO 40: 598; *Commentaries on Daniel*, 1: 174–75).

[23] Comments on Dan. 2:44 (CO 40: 604; *Commentaries on Daniel*, 1: 183).

[24] Comments on Dan. 7:7 (CO 41: 46; *Commentaries on Daniel*, 1: 21).

While Luther, Melanchthon, and Sleidan are all possible Christian targets of Calvin's criticism, the source for the allegedly Jewish identification of the four kingdoms is not clear.[25] However, when Calvin begins to discuss the indestructible kingdom that will crush and bring to an end the other four (Dan. 2:44), he indicates that he is responding to information about Isaac Abrabanel's (1437–1508) interpretation of Daniel, which was supplied by one of his auditors, the Hebraist Anthony Cevallerius (Antoine Chevalier, 1523–1572).[26] According to Calvin, Abrabanel had argued that Jesus could not be the king implied as the head of this final, indestructible kingdom. Calvin cites and refutes six points upon which Abrabanel is said to have argued his position.[27] Central to his argument against the views attributed to Abrabanel is a chronological claim that the Roman Empire began when the Romans reduced Greece to a province and, moreover, that it ended in the first century of the common era, after the gospel had begun to be proclaimed. The assumption that the Roman Empire came to an end at the time of the promulgation of the gospel is a repeated theme in Calvin's lectures. Thus while Calvin defends the traditional identification of the fourth empire as Rome, he severely restricts the period of its duration.

This restriction means that, for Calvin, the events prefigured in Nebuchadnezzar's dream and in Daniel's vision relate to imperial Rome and were fulfilled long ago. In his description, the Roman Empire, as the fourth, terrible, and nameless beast, enjoyed an amazing geographic range attained through immense cruelty. The iron teeth symbolize its audacity and insatiable greed, which Calvin greatly details. The beast was slain (Dan. 7:11) when foreigners assumed positions of leadership after the death of Nero; Calvin argues that although the Roman Empire continued in name, this once powerful and oppressive regime had ceased to flourish.[28] Thus the purpose of

---

[25] According to Melanchthon, the fact that the statue in Nebuchadnezzar's dream had feet mixed of iron and clay signified the "regna nata post dissipatam monarchiam, videlicet Francicium, Hispanicum, Germanicum, Sarracenicum, Turcicum" (CR13: 833). In the second book of *De quatuor summis imperiis [The Four World Monarchies]*, Sleidan understood the Turkish Empire to be the continuation of the Eastern Roman Empire. See also Werner Goez, *Translatio imperii: Ein Beitrag zur Geschichte des Geschichtsdenkens und der politischen Theorien im Mittelalter und in der frühen Neuzeit* (Tübingen: J. C. B. Mohr, 1958).

[26] See Miegge, *Il sogno*, 76; cf. Backus, "Beast," 71n31; and Wilcox, "Calvin on the Prophets," 119.

[27] Comments on Dan. 2:44 (CO 40: 604–6; *Commentaries on Daniel*, 1: 183–87). See also Calvin's further criticisms of Abrabanel in his comments on Dan. 7:27 (CO 41: 83–85; *Commentaries on Daniel*, 2: 74–77). On Abrabanel, see Stefan Schorch, "Die Auslegung des Danielbuches in der Schrift 'Die Quellen der Erlösung' des Don Isaak Abravanel (1437–1508)," in Bracht and du Toit, *Die Geschichte der Daniel-Auslegung*, 179–98.

[28] Comments on Dan. 7:11 (CO 41: 57–58; *Commentaries on Daniel*, 2: 37–38).

the prophecy of the four kingdoms was to sustain the Jewish faithful through various trials until the promised redeemer would appear.

According to Daniel's vision in chapter 7, the distinguishing feature of the last beast is its numerous horns (Dan. 7:7–8). For Calvin these do not symbolize specific rulers or kings but rather stand as a general symbol of Rome's popular form of government—he observes, "the prophet simply means that the Roman Empire was complex, being divided into many provinces, and these provinces were governed by leaders of great weight at Rome, whose authority and rank were superior to others."[29] The small horn that arises and supplants three others represents Julius Caesar and his successors, and not the pope or the Turk, as Calvin alleges other interpreters erroneously claim when they assume that Daniel is speaking about the whole course of Christ's kingdom.[30] That three horns are taken away refers to the consolidation of power under Augustus and not, Calvin charges, to a dispersion that happened three hundred to five hundred years after the death of Christ.[31] Finally, the loud speech of the little horn indicates the Caesars' vastly inflated sense of pride and their dictatorial usurpation of power.

Calvin's identification of the horns of the beast is put to the test when Daniel later relates that he beheld the little horn making war with the saints (Dan. 7:21). Surprisingly, here Calvin says that "many" other interpreters refer this to Antiochus Epiphanes, on account of his extreme hostility and cruelty toward the Jews. Moreover, he acknowledges that "many think his image to have been exhibited to the prophet as the little horn."[32] Conceding that this opinion is plausible, Calvin insists that the best explanation of the passage can only be found in the continued and professed war carried out against the church after Christ was made manifest to the world: when Judea was laid waste by Titus; "the Jews were stabbed and slaughtered like cattle

---

[29] Comments on Dan. 7:7 (CO 41: 49; *Commentaries on Daniel*, 2: 25). See also Calvin's comments on Dan. 7:23 (CO 41: 73–74; *Commentaries on Daniel*, 2: 62). On the rejection of the traditional view of Jerome by Andrew of St. Victor, see Beryl Smalley, *The Study of the Bible in the Middle Ages*, 3rd edition (Oxford: Basil Blackwell, 1983), 128–29; cf. Collins, *Daniel*, 119.

[30] Comments on Dan. 7:8 (CO 41: 50–51; *Commentaries on Daniel*, 2: 26–27). In his biblical preface to Daniel, Luther identified the small horn in chapter 7 as Mohammed or the Turk (WADB 11: 2). Similarly, Melanchthon identified the small horn in Daniel 7 as the Turk and not the papacy and explained in detail how the details of the passage fit the Muslim expansion (CR 13: 860). On these interpretations and those of Oecolampadius, Bullinger, and George Joye, see Euan Cameron, "The Bible and the Early Modern Sense of History," in *The New Cambridge History of the Bible*, vol. 3, *From 1450 to 1750*, ed. Euan Cameron (Cambridge, UK: Cambridge University Press, 2016), 671–2; cf. Backus, "Beast," 66–67.

[31] Comments on Dan. 7:8 (CO 41: 51–52; *Commentaries on Daniel*, 2: 28). See also Calvin's comments on Dan. 7:19–20 (CO 41: 69–70; *Commentaries on Daniel*, 2: 55–56).

[32] Comments on Dan. 7:21 (CO 41: 70; *Commentaries on Daniel*, 2: 56).

throughout the whole extent of Asia"; and, eventually, the "cruelty of the Caesars embraced all Christians."[33] In his comments on Daniel 7:24, Calvin underscores his view that what is said concerning the little horn only makes sense when it is referred collectively to the Caesars, through whose cunning the effigy of the republic was preserved.[34]

Consistent again with this identification of the little horn, Calvin understands the words spoken against the most high God (Dan. 7:25) to be the edicts promulgated by the Caesars, demanding that Christians be punished. The cryptic words "for a time, times, and half a time" (Dan. 7:25) mean that the end of this persecution was known only to God. Calvin rejects the view that a "time" is a year and that the prophecy refers to the forty-two months (or three and a half years) mentioned in Revelation 13:5.[35] Thus like the prophecy of the four kingdoms, the prophecy of the little horn was meant to confirm the faith of God's people at the time when the gospel was first being proclaimed, and to give solace to the prophet Daniel by showing that God would protect the church when the prophecy of the kingdoms was being realized.

A final element in Calvin's treatment of the four kingdoms is his discussion of the appearance of the Son of Man and the kingdom that is handed over to his saints. Discussing Daniel's vision of the Ancient of Days ascending the throne (Dan. 7:9–10), Calvin stresses that this means that God's perpetual judgment became conspicuous; this exhibition was fitting, since this vision refers to the supreme manifestation of God's power and justice, namely, to the advent of Christ. From the very outset Calvin underscores that the vision refers to Christ's first appearance, and that those who extend this prophecy to his second advent are completely wrong.[36] The "Son of Man" is Christ, who appears to Daniel "like" or "as" a human being even though he had not yet become incarnate. Calvin cites Irenaeus and Tertullian by name to support his understanding that this vision consisted of a symbol of Christ's future flesh.[37] That this Son of Man came to the Ancient of Days and received an everlasting kingdom (Dan. 7:13–14) refers to Christ's ascension and the

---

[33] Comments on Dan. 7:21 (CO 41: 71; *Commentaries on Daniel*, 2: 57). Despite Calvin's claim, the identification of the little horn as Antiochus Epiphanes was not widespread. Jerome points to this as the view of Porphyry. He rejects this opinion and refers it to a future, insignificant king of Rome. Jerome also identifies this king as the "son of perdition" of 2 Thessalonians 2 (Braverman, *Jerome's Commentary on Daniel*, 77).

[34] Comments on Dan. 7:24 (CO 41: 74–75; *Commentaries on Daniel*, 2: 62–63).

[35] Comments on Dan. 7:25 (CO 41: 78–79; *Commentaries on Daniel*, 2: 68–69).

[36] Comments on Dan. 7:9 (CO 41: 53; *Commentaries on Daniel*, 2: 31).

[37] Comments on Dan. 7:13 (CO 41: 60; *Commentaries on Daniel*, 2: 40–41).

commencement of his reign—not to its close, "as many interpreters force and strain this passage."[38]

Though Calvin acknowledges that what is prophesied of Christ's kingdom has not yet been completely fulfilled, he insists that the judgment and the handing over of the kingdom to the saints (Dan. 7:27) is concurrent with the death of the fourth beast—and thus took place in Christianity's earliest days, with the preaching and promulgation of the gospel. Calvin is aware that this view breaks with tradition:

> This does not seem to have been accomplished yet; and hence, many, nay, almost all, except the Jews, have treated this prophecy as relating to the last day of Christ's advent. All Christian interpreters agree in this. But as I have shown before, they pervert the proper meaning of the prophet.[39]

Traditional interpreters have been misled by the present obscurity of Christ's kingdom, which is spiritual and not visible to carnal eyes. In addition, they have been confused by the fact that though Daniel emphasizes the beginning of the reign of the saints, he also embraces the whole of Christ's kingdom in his vision. Calvin notes,

> Thus the prophet heard from the angel concerning the saints who are pilgrims in the world, and yet shall enjoy the kingdom and possess the greatest power under heaven. Hence also we correctly conclude that this vision ought not to be explained of the final advent of Christ, but of the intermediate state of the church. The saints began to reign under heaven, when Christ ushered in his kingdom by the promulgation of his gospel.[40]

Thus consistent with his treatment of the four kingdoms and the horns of the beast, Calvin's interpretation of the Son of Man and the inauguration of the reign of the saints understands these prophecies to have been fulfilled long ago.

Calvin's praeteristic and noneschatological view of the four monarchies was a minority view but not unique among his contemporaries. For example, Andreas Osiander's (1498–1552) *Conjectures on the Last Days*

[38] Comments on Dan. 7:14 (CO 41: 63; *Commentaries on Daniel*, 2: 45).
[39] ". . . genuinum prophetae sensum"; Comments on Dan. 7:27 (CO 41: 82; *Commentaries on Daniel*, 2: 72).
[40] Comments on Dan. 7:27 (CO 41: 84; *Commentaries on Daniel*, 2: 74).

(1544) also saw the prophecy of the four kingdoms as completely fulfilled, although Osiander set the destruction of Daniel's fourth beast in the fourth century, with the emergence of Christian rulers such as Constantine. More significantly, Osiander identified the little horn as Julius Caesar, though he also signaled his reluctant dissent from the opinion of "certain men of great name."[41] However, Osiander put his vision of the four kingdoms as a particular rather than a universal world history to a quite different use than Calvin did. Daniel's prophecies may have been fulfilled, but those of Revelation, in which Osiander perceived a second Roman dominion, and other texts provided him enough information to calculate the date for Christ's return sometime in the near future. In the end, Osiander crafted a world history, of which Daniel's prophecies were a piece, if not the whole story. Calvin, however, emphasized the series of events prophesied by Daniel as a particular and past historical occurrence.

Calvin on the Seventy Weeks in Daniel 9:24–27

Calvin's lack of interest in historical calculations and future eschatological projections is even more evident in his four lectures on the prophecy of the seventy weeks at the end of Daniel 9. This time his praeteristic reading of the prophecy is not unusual; most Christian interpreters viewed the seventy weeks as a prediction of events up to and surrounding Christ's first advent.[42] Where they disagreed was over the determination of the starting and ending points of the period covered in the prophecy and how to reckon the years. Thus, in contrast to the four monarchies, Daniel's seventy weeks served more "as a source for chronological speculation than for imminent expectation."[43]

[41] Andreas Osiander, *Coniecturae de ultimus temporis, ac de fine mundi, ex sacris literis* (Nuremberg: Johann Petreius, 1544), d ii *recto*–d ii *verso*; in English as Andreas Osiander, *Conjectures of the End of the World*, trans. G. Joye (Antwerp, 1548). On Osiander's *Conjectures*, see Seifert, *Rückzug*, 50–52; Barnes, *Prophecy and Gnosis*, 128–30; Firth, *Apocalyptic Tradition*, 61–65. According to Backus, Nikolaus Selneccer explicitly rejected the identification of the little horn as Julius Caesar in his 1567 commentary on Daniel (Backus, "Beast," 63).

[42] Although a minority followed Irenaeus and Hippolytus and extended or applied the final week to the last judgment, as Collins notes, "the church fathers generally sought the culmination of this period in the career of Christ" (*Daniel*, 356). For fuller discussion, see Franz Fraidl, *Die Exegese der siebzig Wochen Daniels in der alten und mittleren Zeit* (Graz: Leuschner & Lubensky, 1883); Louis E. Knowles, "The Interpretation of the Seventy Weeks of Daniel in the Early Fathers," *Westminster Theological Journal* 7, no. 2 (1945): 136–60; Lester L. Grabbe, "The Seventy-Weeks Prophecy (Daniel 9:24–27) in Early Jewish Interpretation," in *The Quest for Context and Meaning: Studies in Biblical Intertexuality in Honor of James A. Sanders*, ed. Craig Evans and Shemaryahu Talmon (Leiden: Brill, 1997), 595–611.

[43] Collins, *Daniel*, 116.

Careful determination of the time was important because Christian interpreters understood this passage as a central prophecy of Jesus Christ. Moreover, they frequently felt the need to defend this conviction by detailing their calculations in response to challenges from religious outsiders, such as the pagan philosopher Porphyry (ca. 234–305) and Jewish interpreters.

Calvin, however, does not share this traditional concern for exact chronology and appears to worry that interpreters' efforts to establish this precisely detract from the main point of the prophecy. Nevertheless, he must address the question of chronology in some detail in order to refute interpretations that he deems false. The most immediate object of his polemic is Jewish interpretations that deny the text prophesies Christ, and here again he complains primarily about Abrabanel. Yet he also criticizes Jerome (ca. 347–420) for not judging the relative validity of the Greek, Latin, and Jewish interpretations that he merely reports. More subtly, Calvin also disparages the calculations of such contemporaries as Oecolampadius and Melanchthon. Very uncharacteristically for Calvin, he explicitly names those with whom he disagrees, even though he acknowledges this runs counter to his usual method. He apologizes at the outset: "I do not usually refer to conflicting opinions, because I take no pleasure in refuting them, and the simple method which I adopt pleases me best, namely, to expound what I think delivered by the Spirit of God."[44] Calvin's alternative historical approach to the question of the seventy weeks can be seen in his comments on others' interpretations of this passage; in his solution to the problem of chronology; and, finally, in his understanding of the main purpose of this prophecy.

Calvin's opening comments on Daniel 9:24 echo the warnings of interpreters from Jerome to Oecolampadius about the difficulty of these verses. He confesses that he must thus necessarily refute the various views of others in order to explain its meaning.[45] He begins with Jewish interpreters, whom he charges with both ignorance and impudence. Although Jerome reported that the Jews of his day, like their Christian counterparts, understood this passage as a prophecy of the messiah, Calvin finds that Jerome was not discriminating enough in his report. According to Calvin, Jewish interpreters make three crucial errors: two substantive and one chronological. First,

---

[44] CO 41: 167; *Commentaries on Daniel*, 2: 195–96.

[45] "This passage has been variously treated, and so distracted, and almost torn to pieces by the various opinions of interpreters, that it might be considered nearly useless on account of its obscurity"; Comments on Dan. 9:24 (CO 41: 167; *Commentaries on Daniel*, 2: 195). For Jerome's caveat, see Braverman, *Jerome's Commentary on Daniel*, 95; on Oecolampadius, see Ernst Staehelin, *Das theologische Lebenswerk Johannes Oekolampads* (Leipzig: M. Heinsius, 1939), 564.

Calvin alleges that all the rabbis referred this passage to the continual punishment that God would inflict on the Jews after their return from captivity—
hence they understood this as a prophecy of the calamities that the people
would endure over 490 years, culminating in the destruction of the second
temple. Second, he charges that they date the starting point of the seventy
weeks with the destruction of the first temple and close the period with the
destruction of the second. Not only does this computation make the time
period too long, but it also, complains Calvin, blames Daniel for being so
misled as to think that God would show mercy to the captives. In his lengthy
polemic against Abrabanel in his forty-ninth lecture, Calvin charges: "Now,
that dog and others like him are not ashamed to assert that Daniel was a bad
interpreter of this part of Jeremiah's prophecy, because he thought the punishment completed, although some time yet remained."[46] Finally, Calvin
alleges that Jewish exegetes misinterpret the reference to Christ—some understand this as a general reference to the priests; some refer it to specific
high priests such as Zerubbabel or Joshua,[47] and some, like Abrabanel, refer
it to Agrippa.[48]

After exposing the "foolish corruptions" of the rabbis on the seventy
weeks, Calvin reports the opinions of Christian commentators with whom he
also disagrees. Drawing explicitly on Jerome for the ancient writers, Calvin
criticizes by name the interpretations of Eusebius, Africanus, Nicholas of Lyra,
Hippolytus, and Apollinaris.[49] He then excuses himself from treating the remaining commentators and his contemporaries—save two. Oecolampadius,
he notes, rightly admonishes his readers to set this period within a calculation of the years since the beginning of creation. However, Calvin contends

---

[46] Comments on Dan. 9:24 (CO 41: 169; *Commentaries on Daniel*, 2: 198). On Abrabanel's interpretation, see Fraidl, *Die Exegese der siebzig Wochen*, 132–34.

[47] Cf. Zech. 4:14.

[48] Comments on Dan. 9:25 (CO 41: 173–74; *Commentaries on Daniel*, 2: 205). This was also the
view of Rashi (Fraidl, *Die Exegese der siebzig Wochen*, 128) and was reported by Nicholas of Lyra; see
Mark Zier, "Nicholas of Lyra on the Book of Daniel," in *Nicholas of Lyra: The Senses of Scripture*, ed.
Philip D. W. Krey and Lesley Smith (Leiden: Brill, 2000), 183.

[49] Calvin criticizes Eusebius for referring "Christ" to the priests and for understanding Aristobulus
as the one who was slain; Africanus for using lunar years and dating from Darius, the son of Hystaspes
(actually, Africanus dated from the twentieth year of Artaxerxes, but Melanchthon says that these are
the same person [CR 13: 885]); Nicholas of Lyra for using lunar years; Hippolytus for locating the
seven weeks in the time that followed Christ's death and resurrection; Apollinaris for beginning at
Christ's birth and extending the prophecy to the end of the world; and Eusebius again for extending
the last week up to the end of the world. Comments on Dan. 9:25 (CO 41: 175; *Commentaries on
Daniel*, 2: 207–8). Not all of the portrayals are accurate reflections of the ancient writers' interpretations, and they are probably not gleaned from study of the original texts. In addition to Jerome,
Oecolampadius could have also been the source for Calvin's views of the patristic writers.

that even this broader approach will not satisfy, since the scriptures' account
of the years after the fall of the first temple is sketchy, and readers are left to
other sources of information. Then he claims that Melanchthon, "who excels
in genius and learning and is happily versed in the studies of history," makes
two calculations, neither of which Calvin completely approves.[50] Does the
inability of Christians to agree on the meaning of the seventy weeks suggest
that their reading of scripture falls short of divine truth—as Calvin claims
Abrabanel has charged? No, Calvin responds—even if all these Christian
interpretations are false, as he willingly concedes.[51]

As one can gather from the discussion of Calvin's comments on others'
interpretations, Calvin sets his own resolution of the problem of chronology
within the context of a lengthy protest concerning the futility of precise
calculations. He insists simply that the starting point of the seventy weeks
must be the Persian monarchy, with the culmination of the sixty-ninth week
in the baptism of Christ. The problem is that secular history, which must fill
in the gaps left by the scriptures, posits roughly 550 years from the reign of
Cyrus to the advent of Christ.[52] Moreover, the Persians, unlike the Greeks,
were not precise in their histories.[53] However, he argues, the inability to make
an exact calculation does not render Christian teaching uncertain any more
than discrepancies in the narratives of profane historians require one to reject the entire history as fabulous.[54] Any studious person ought to be able to
sit and compare the Greek and Latin histories, weigh the evidence, and come
to the conclusion that there is no better way to express the period stretching
from Cyrus to Christ than the seventy weeks of the prophecy. Though Calvin
thus excuses himself from reckoning the years individually, he does provide a
general outline for his auditors.

Calvin designates Cyrus's edict as both the termination of Jeremiah's seventy years and the starting point for Daniel's first seven weeks, which comprehend the three-year period in which the foundations for the temple were laid
and the forty-six years which were required to complete the building.[55] The
sixty-two weeks begin at the time of Darius, son of Hystaspes, and extend to

[50] Comments on Dan. 9:25 (CO 41: 176; *Commentaries on Daniel*, 2: 209). For Melanchthon's detailed calculations, see CR 13: 881–89.
[51] Comments on Dan. 9:25 (CO 41: 175; *Commentaries on Daniel*, 2: 208).
[52] Comments on Dan. 9:24 (CO 41: 169; *Commentaries on Daniel*, 2: 199).
[53] Comments on Dan. 9:25 (CO 41: 177; *Commentaries on Daniel*, 2: 211). Cf. Melanchthon, who
also blames the Persians; CR 13: 882.
[54] Comments on Dan. 9:25 (CO 41: 176; *Commentaries on Daniel*, 2: 209).
[55] Comments on Dan. 9:24–25 (CO 41: 169, 178, 183; *Commentaries on Daniel*, 2: 199, 212, 219.

the baptism of Christ, which Calvin claims encompasses roughly 480 years.[56] He appears to view the seventieth week as the period including and immediately after Christ's earthly ministry. In his view, it is Christ who confirms the covenant in this last week (Dan. 9:27) with the preaching of the gospel, which renewed the covenant with the Jews and began to call the gentiles to salvation. Christ also made the sacrifice and offering cease at the time of his resurrection, when the validity of the rites of the Mosaic law had ceased.[57] Thus presumably this half of the week is the last half, with Christ's earthly life constituting the first half. The prophecy of the abomination he refers again to the time after the resurrection, when the Jews were summoned to repentance but rejected Christ. The "decreed end" falls outside of the seventy weeks' time, since Calvin sees this prophecy fulfilled in destruction of the Temple by Titus.[58]

What does all this suggest about Calvin's understanding of the purpose of the prophecy of the seventy weeks? The main concern underlying Calvin's computation is not that the years must be precisely accounted for lest the prophecy be in vain. Rather, the bottom line for him is that the period extending from Jeremiah's prophecy of seventy years and Daniel's seventy weeks must be continuous and without interruption, otherwise the prophecy fails to achieve its purpose. Daniel's seventy weeks begin when the seventy years of captivity come to an end. The fact that there appear to be more years than are accounted for by the seventy weeks of years leads interpreters to posit gaps at various points. But this is just as problematic from Calvin's perspective as Jewish interpretations that include Jeremiah's seventy years within Daniel's seventy weeks. Both strategies miss what Calvin thinks is an essential chronological and substantive connection between the two prophecies. Expressing astonishment that even Christian interpreters have failed to consider how Daniel alludes here to Jeremiah's prophecy, Calvin formulates his understanding of the purpose of this prophecy:

> For the prophet here compares God's grace with his judgment, as if he had said, the people have been punished by an exile of seventy years, but now their time of grace has arrived. Nay, the day of their redemption has dawned, and it shone forth with continual splendor, shaded, indeed, with a

---

[56] Comments on Dan. 9:25 (CO 41: 176; *Commentaries on Daniel*, 2: 209).
[57] Comments on Dan. 9:27 (CO 41: 187–89; *Commentaries on Daniel*, 2: 225–27).
[58] Comments on Dan. 9:27 (CO 41: 190; *Commentaries on Daniel*, 2: 229).

few clouds, for 490 years until the advent of Christ . . . We now understand why the angel does not use the reckoning of years, or months, or days, but weeks of years, because this has a tacit reference to the penalty which the people had endured according to the prophecy of Jeremiah.[59]

For Calvin, this prophecy of future events is *not* for the purpose of calculation but rather for consolation, with the message that God is following up a period of "sorrowful darkness" with "one of favor of sevenfold duration," culminating in the appearance of Christ.[60]

Similar to the prophecy of the four monarchies, the prophecy of the seventy weeks was intended to console the ancient faithful as they waited for and witnessed the advent of Christ. In contrast to a minority of Christian interpreters, Calvin's reading of the seventy weeks is historical and noneschatological in that he finds that both prophecies were fulfilled at or around the time of Christ's first advent. A further dimension of the alternative character of his historical reading can be seen in his reluctance to square the prophecy with actual history, in contrast to the majority of Christian interpreters whose general views on the starting and ending points of the period he shares. Even though, as Euan Cameron has pointed out, Calvin shows elsewhere in the commentary a fascination with the historical details of the Hellenistic-Maccabbean period of Jewish history, for Calvin, the prophecy of the seventy weeks does not provide an exact historical account of future events, for its purpose and truth lie in more than mere chronology.[61] Such prophecies are prophetic interpretations of history, for the purpose of consolation of the ancient faithful.

Calvin on the Question of the Antichrist in Daniel 8:23–25 and 11:36–45

Turning finally to the question of the Antichrist in Daniel 8 and 11, we find here, as with the four monarchies, that Calvin's treatment of this theme once again runs counter to the dominant interpretive patterns of his Christian predecessors and contemporaries. Earlier we saw that Calvin rejected interpretations of the little horn in Daniel 7:7 as the pope or the Turk; similarly,

---

[59] Comments on Dan. 9:24 (CO 41: 170; *Commentaries on Daniel*, 2: 200).
[60] Comments on Dan. 9:24 (CO 41: 170; *Commentaries on Daniel*, 2: 200).
[61] Cameron, "Calvin the Historian," 91–92.

he denied that the last king of Daniel 7:24–25 was the Antichrist.[62] In his comments on Daniel 8:23–25 and Daniel 11:36–45, Calvin explicitly refutes, at times by name, those who relate these prophecies in any way— even through typology—to the Antichrist. Calvin's vehement and consistent reading of these two passages in terms of the history of Antiochus IV Epiphanes, on one hand, and ancient Rome, on the other, not only goes against traditional Christian readings, revitalized in Calvin's day in part through Martin Luther's biblical preface to Daniel.[63] Calvin's interpretation in his lectures also contradicts two passages in his own *Institutes*, where he alleges that Daniel speaks of the Antichrist directly or in the person of Antiochus.[64] Consideration of Calvin's comments on the king of bold countenance (Dan. 8:23–25) and the king who shall act as he pleases (Dan. 11:36–45) will demonstrate the thoroughness of his historical reading of Daniel in his lectures. At the same time, these comments will press the limits of a strictly historical interpretation and position us to entertain the question of Calvin's view of the ongoing relevance of this Old Testament book for the Christians of his day.

Calvin reads Daniel 8 and the king of bold countenance entirely as a prophecy of the fall of the Persian Empire to the Greeks. In contrast to the prophecy of the seventy weeks, this is an account that he finds so clear and consistent with profane history that he judges that Daniel "narrates things exactly as if they had already been fulfilled."[65] The he-goat in Daniel's vision represents Alexander the Great, and the four horns in verse 8 are his successors. The little horn in Daniel 8:9 is Antiochus IV Epiphanes. Because his tyranny over the people of God was so cruel, Calvin finds this extensive warning to have been especially useful and necessary.[66] He avoids elevating this historical crisis to the eschatological level by downplaying the

[62] "Those who understand this of Antichrist think their opinion confirmed by the conduct of other tyrants who carried on their warfare against God with arms and violence, but not by words. But the prophet does not speak so subtly here" (CO 41: 76; *Commentaries on Daniel*, 2: 65).

[63] See Strohm, "Luthers Vorrede"; Albrecht, "Luthers Arbeiten." Luther's views would have been known in Geneva through the French translation of Luther's preface that appeared in the volume containing the French translation of Melanchthon's commentary on Daniel.

[64] *Institutes* (1559), 4.2.12 and 4.7.25. Calvin added the latter reference to the image of the Antichrist described in the person of Antiochus to the 1559 edition. On Calvin's understanding of the Antichrist, see Heinrich Berger, *Calvins Geschichtsauffassung* (Zurich: Zwingli Verlag, 1955), 73–92.

[65] Comments on Dan. 8:21 (CO 41: 115; *Commentaries on Daniel*, 2: 120). Cf. Jerome's response to Porphyry: "For so striking was the reliability of what the prophet foretold that he could not appear to unbelievers as a predicter of the future but as a narrator of things past" (Braverman, *Jerome's Commentary on Daniel*, 15–16).

[66] Comments on Dan. 8:9 (CO 41: 97–99; *Commentaries on Daniel*, 2: 95–96).

apocalyptic overtones of the angel's explanation in verse 17. For Calvin, this simply means that the vision will be completed according to God's timetable.[67]

Calvin's rejection of an eschatological reading in terms of the Antichrist first becomes explicit in his reading of Daniel 8:20–25. At this point he apparently interrupted his reading of the passage after verse 23, with its reference to the king of bold countenance. Calvin interpolates: "Hence Luther, indulging his thoughts too freely, refers this passage to the masks of the Antichrist— but we will see this later."[68] In his comments on the angel's revelation about the king itself, Calvin summarizes a number of opinions—all anonymous— concerning the meaning of the various statements about the king's character and all reading the prophecy in light of Antiochus. Concluding his comments on Antiochus's demise, he makes good on his promise to address the interpretation he attributes to Luther. First he chastises those who omit all discussion of Antiochus and act as if the angel describes the future devastation of the church after the coming of Christ and the promulgation of the gospel. For Calvin, the meaning of this prophecy is so clear that even children can see it, and to deny its historical reference to the time of Antiochus is to deprive scripture of its authority. No more sound is the reasoning of those more modest and considerate interpreters who see in Antiochus a figure of the Antichrist.[69] Distinguishing his own approach from this latter one, Calvin allows that one might *adapt* the prophecy to the present use of the church by applying what is said of Antiochus by analogy to the Antichrist:

[67] For a different view, see Luther's marginal comment in the German Bible, "des endes. Das zeigt er an, Das Epiphanes nicht allein gemeinet wird in diesem Gesichte, sondern auch der Endechrist" (WADB 11:2). Cf. Oecolampadius: "Non est autem ut haec in consummationem seculi reijcias, sicut quidam hinc occasionem sumunt, quasi in ipsißima antichristi secula ista referantur" (*In Danielem prophetam*, f. 100 recto).

[68] CO 41: 114; *Commentaries on Daniel*, 2: 119. Oecolampadius, referring to Luther's writing against Catharinus (WA 7: 722–77), is a likely source for Calvin's charge (Oecolampadius, *In Danielem prophetam*, f. 101 recto; cf. Staehelin, *Lebenswerk*, 563n1). This interpretation is not in Luther's preface to Daniel or in the marginal comments in the German Bible (which Calvin would have known through the Latin or, more immediately, the French translation); Luther's brief comments on chapter 8 dwell on the cruelty of Antiochus toward the Jews and their religion, and he concludes that many ancient doctors have seen Antiochus as a figure of the Antichrist. The view of "larvis Antichristi" is likewise not expressed in Melanchthon's commentary on this passage, although he does understand under the Roman papacy the entire Roman episcopacy, not just the pope (CR 13: 871).

[69] A long-standing Christian tradition, at least as ancient as Jerome; more recently exemplified by Oecolampadius (*In Danielem prophetam*, f. 100 verso) and Melanchthon, who "accommodated" what was said of Antiochus to the Antichrist manifest in the Roman papacy and took this to be the prophet's intention. Melanchthon also criticized on Paul's authority (2 Thess. 2) those who simply restricted this to Antiochus (CR 13: 870).

Some think this prophecy refers to Antichrist, thus they pass by Antiochus, and describe to us the appearance of Antichrist [*faciem Antichristi*], as if the angel had shown Daniel what should happen after the second renovation of the church. The first restoration took place when liberty was restored to the people, and they returned from exile to their native land, and the second occurred at the advent of Christ. These interpreters suppose this passage to show that devastation of the church which should take place after the coming of Christ and the promulgation of the gospel. But as we have previously seen, this is not a suitable meaning, and I am surprised that men versed in the scriptures should so pour forth clouds upon clear light. For, as we said yesterday, nothing can be clearer, or more perspicuous, or even more familiar, than this prophecy. And what is the tendency of ascribing so violently to Antichrist what even mere children clearly see to be spoken of Antiochus, except to deprive scripture of all its authority? Others speak more modestly and more considerately, when they suppose the angel to treat of Antiochus for the purpose of depicting in his person the figure of Antichrist. But I do not think this reasoning sufficiently sound. I desire the sacred oracles to be treated so reverently, that no one may introduce any variety according to the will of man, but simply hold what is positively certain. It would please me better to see anyone wishing to adapt [*aptare*] this prophecy to the present use of the church and to apply to Antichrist by analogy [*per anagogem*] what is said of Antiochus. We know that whatever happened to the church of old, belongs also to us, because we have fallen upon the fullness of times.[70]

Thus Calvin distinguishes what he takes to be the simple, genuine sense of the prophecy from later applications. Interpretation in the lectures focuses on the meaning of the text in its original context—application to the present is a different and subsequent step.

Calvin's reading of the king who acts as he pleases (Dan. 11:36–45) goes even further in ruling out reference to the Antichrist and offering an uncommon historical interpretation of the prophecy. Calvin understands the last three chapters of Daniel as a single visionary event, with chapter 10 as

---

[70] Comments on Dan. 8:24–25 (CO 41: 121–22; *Commentaries on Daniel*, 2: 128–29). This is an interesting contrast to Nicholas of Lyra, who in his *Postilla* introduced the notion of a twofold literal sense in his comments on Daniel 8, and repeated this in his comments on Dan. 11:21 and in his preface to the corrected second edition (Zier, "Nicholas of Lyra," 191–92); see also Philip D. W. Krey, "Nicholas of Lyra's Commentary on Daniel in the Literal Postill (1329)," in Bracht and du Toit, *Die Geschichte der Daniel-Auslegung*, 199–215.

a preface to the more detailed vision of events leading up to the manifestation of Christ and then extended, very briefly, to the day of final resurrection. Even with this eschatological *terminus*, in Calvin's view Daniel's vision
is concerned primarily with the renovation of the church at the first advent
of Christ. As in chapter 8, Calvin downplays the eschatological import of
Daniel 10:14, where the angel tells Daniel he will explain what will happen
at the end of days. Calvin remarks, "the scriptures, in using this phrase, 'the
last days,' or 'times,' always point to the manifestation of Christ, by which the
face of the world was renewed."[71] Also similar to his interpretation of Daniel
8, Calvin remarks that this detailed account seems "like a historical narrative
under the form of an enigmatic description of events then future."[72]

In his comments on chapter 11, Calvin notes that scripture does not need
to provide all the historical details of these events; nevertheless, he appears
to find the details illuminating, and thus supplies much relevant background
information for understanding the rise and fate of Antiochus—particularly
concerning his military campaigns. At times, however, Calvin refers his
auditors to the "writings of the historians" or the Books of the Maccabees for
an even fuller account.[73] In this regard his approach is very similar to that of
Melanchthon, who also supplied a rich historical context for readers of his
commentary. When he came to verse 36, the king who shall do as he pleases,
however, Melanchthon pursued his commentary on two levels: after a long
excursus on the Antichrist, he continued his historical discussion of the
events as they applied to Antiochus, but at the same time he accommodated
each verse to the Antichrist, because, he says, this "history of Antiochus is the
image and prophecy of the Antichrist."[74]

Unlike Melanchthon and other interpreters, Calvin does not relate
the end of chapter 11 to the Antichrist in any way at all. Moreover, while
Melanchthon had criticized those who read these verses *only* to Antichrist
and not to Antiochus as well, Calvin rejects all who interpret these verses
in reference to either. Signaling again his awareness that his opinion goes

---

[71] Comments on Dan. 10:14 (CO 41: 208; *Commentaries on Daniel*, 2: 255); cf. Richard A. Muller,
"The Hermeneutic of Promise and Fulfillment in Calvin's Exegesis of the Old Testament Prophecies
of the Kingdom," in *The Bible in the Sixteenth Century*, ed. David C. Steinmetz (Durham, NC: Duke
University Press, 1990), 70. This is in contrast to Jerome, who understood this verse to refer to the end
of the world (Braverman, *Jerome's Commentary on Daniel*, 115). Cf. also Calvin's comments on Dan.
11: 35 (CO 41: 264–65; *Commentaries on Daniel*, 2: 337); comments on Dan. 11:40 (CO 41: 279–80;
Commentaries on Daniel, 2: 357).

[72] Comments on Dan. 11:2 (CO 41: 217; *Commentaries on Daniel*, 2: 268).

[73] See, e.g., Calvin's comments on Dan. 11:30 (CO 41: 252; *Commentaries on Daniel*, 2: 319).

[74] CR 13: 951; cf. CR 3: 545–46 = MBW 2053.

against the "the consent of the majority,"[75] he notes at the start the obscurity of the passage and the variety of interpretations, which necessity compels him to address. Jewish interpreters are not agreed among themselves; some interpret this passage of Antiochus, and others of the Romans. Christian interpreters present "much variety," though most see this prophecy fulfilled in the Antichrist. The more moderate among these "suppose Antichrist to be obliquely hinted at, while they do not exclude Antiochus as the type and image of the Antichrist." This opinion, Calvin admits, has great probability, but he "does not approve of it and can easily refute it." Since the events narrated do not fit the historical occurrences of Antiochus and the Maccabean period, Calvin ultimately judges that "the angel, when saying a 'king shall do anything' does not allude to Antiochus, for history refutes this."[76]

According to Calvin, then, the events prophesied by the angel in Daniel 11:36–45 refer to the Roman Empire, from the earliest days of the republic down to its demise, in Calvin's view, in the first century. He acknowledges that some Jewish interpreters also understood the prophecy this way, but he criticizes those who extend it down to present times.[77] The Romans, he judges, were so vain and proud as to make themselves superior to all deities, while maintaining the pretense of piety. Moreover, they lacked all natural affection, "loving neither their wives nor the female sex." Calvin explains in great detail how all of the predictions in verses 36–45 were fulfilled by Roman expansion, until they began to suffer military losses and saw their empire diminished about the time of the promulgation of the gospel.

Similar to his understanding of the seventy weeks, Calvin's underlying concern is the continuity of the period covered in the consoling prophecy delivered to Daniel: "Let us remember, then, that the angel is not now speaking of Antiochus, nor does he make a leap forwards to Antichrist, as some think, but he means a perpetual series. Thus the faithful would be prepared for all assaults on their faith, if this rampart had not be interposed."[78] When

---

[75] "I must, however, refer briefly to opinions received by the consent of the majority, because they occupy the minds of many, and thus close the door to the correct interpretation" (CO 41: 265; *Commentaries on Daniel*, 2: 338). For Melanchthon, see CR 13: 951.

[76] Comments on Dan. 11:36 (CO 41: 266; *Commentaries on Daniel*, 2: 339). Similarly, Calvin remarks in his comments on Dan. 11:37, "I do not wonder at those who explain this prophecy of Antiochus, experiencing some trouble with these words, for they cannot satisfy themselves, because this prediction of the angel's was never accomplished by Antiochus, who did neither neglect all deities nor the god of his fathers. Then, with regard to the love of women, this will not suit this person." He also details why these also cannot be referred to Mohammed or the pope (CO 41: 270; *Commentaries on Daniel*, 2: 345–46).

[77] Comments on Dan. 11:36 (CO 41: 265; *Commentaries on Daniel*, 2: 338).

[78] Comments on Dan. 11:36 (CO 41: 269; *Commentaries on Daniel*, 2: 344).

the angel suddenly jumps forward to the final resurrection in Daniel 12:2, Calvin asks rhetorically why he passes over "the intermediate time, during which many events might be the subject of prophecy?" The answer is that the angel wishes to support the elect in the hope of promised salvation amid the ongoing turmoil of the church. But this is the only point of eschatological concern in Calvin's entire series of lectures, and Calvin pointedly refuses to engage in any calculations concerning when this might be. In short, Calvin does not think that Daniel is referring to the Antichrist and only very briefly to the end of time and the final resurrection. If, however, this passage is not for calculating the timing of the events of the last day—wherein lies its relevance for Calvin's auditors and their future parishioners? Let me conclude with a few reflections on this issue.

Conclusion

Calvin's interpretation of the four empires, the seventy weeks, and the question of the Antichrist in his *Lectures on Daniel* offers a distinctive historicizing reading of the Danielic prophecies and prophetic visions—a reading that consciously breaks with the dominant interpretive trends of Calvin's day. His at times idiosyncratic interpretation of these passages sheds further light on his understanding of prophecy, history, and the best way to derive present meaning from the biblical past.

First, these lectures show the complexity of Calvin's view of prophecy. Whereas in his commentary on Isaiah (discussed in chapter 5), Calvin more often allowed for multiple fulfillments of some prophecies over the life of God's people and the course of history, his reading of Daniel's christological prophecies is more restrictive. For Calvin, Daniel is not useful for calculating the end times, because in his view the book's prophecies are intended, in the first place, for the consolation of the ancient faithful. The prophecies of these events may be loose and general—as in the case of the seventy weeks—or they may be remarkably specific, as in the case of the predictions concerning Antiochus or Julius Caesar. In either case, two concerns consistently shape Calvin's reading of them. First, the events foretold in Daniel are long past, for they are prophecies of the Old Testament that have been fulfilled in Christ's first advent. Second, in order to maximize the consoling effect of the message, Calvin insists on the unbroken continuity of the predicted events, from the time of Daniel to the fulfillment in the manifestation of Christ and the gospel. Although the precision and accuracy of the predictions can serve to comfort the faithful, for Calvin, the unbroken chain of events is a more powerful testimony to God's merciful care of his people until the coming of Christ—which is, for Calvin, the common message underlying all the prophecies. However, it is important to underscore the fact that in Calvin's view the events prophesied by Daniel are laid out in an unbroken sequence, but they are by no means comprehensive, embracing all of world history.

This point leads to a second consideration, which concerns Calvin's view of history and the relationship of his historicizing reading of Daniel to previous and contemporary exegesis. Calvin's interpretation of Daniel is allied with other historicizing approaches that value the events described in scripture as individual historical occurrences, whose validity was distinct from additional levels of meaning that they may be perceived to represent, for instance, figuratively, typologically, or morally.[79] Yet Calvin appears to exhibit a stronger historical awareness than those whose views he criticizes, even allies like Oecolampadius and Melanchthon. He consistently complains that interpreters who lack what we would call historical distance pervert the plain and simple meaning of the text. For Calvin, the prophecies of Daniel were a comfort to the ancient faithful in *their* particular trials; they proclaimed God's merciful care in *their* concrete historical circumstances. To be sure, this represents a furthering of earlier historical approaches (such as that of Nicholas of Lyra or Melanchthon) and must be seen in continuity with the broader trends outlined in chapter 1 and as another instance of Calvin following recent shifts in exegetical approaches to logical conclusions.[80] Yet there can be no doubt that Calvin inaugurates a critical shift in Danielic interpretation, one that throws his uncompromising sense of history into relief.

That the ancient prophecies were issued and fulfilled and, according to Calvin, are to be understood as comforts to the ancient faithful leads us, finally, to Calvin's views on the relevance of the book of Daniel for later generations. The proper interpretation of Danielic prophecies in Calvin's lectures

[79] On this trend, see Barnes, *Prophecy and Gnosis*, 100–103.

[80] Cf. Muller, who sees Calvin's method as a development of Melanchthon's historical emphases ("Hermeneutic of Promise and Fulfillment," 81); see also the broader analysis of Lutheran and Reformed views in G. Sujin Pak, "Contributions of Commentaries on the Minor Prophets to the Formation of Distinctive Lutheran and Reformed Confessional Identities," *Church History and Religious Culture* 92 (2012): 237–60. Thompson suggests that Calvin's treatment of prophecy "recalls the double literal sense" of Nicholas of Lyra. John L. Thompson, "Calvin as a Biblical Interpreter," in *The Cambridge Companion to John Calvin*, ed. Donald K. McKim (Cambridge, UK: Cambridge University Press, 2004), 69. On Nicholas of Lyra and Melanchthon, see Krey, "Nicholas of Lyra's Commentary"; Scheible, "Melanchthons Verständnis."

involves understanding and explaining their significance in their original, past context. It is remarkable that his vision of how to equip his auditors for missionary work involves a rich historical grounding in and appreciation of the scriptural past. Yet as he details in his comments on Daniel 8:24, he does not reject—he even welcomes—an application or adaptation of the situation of the "church of old" to present use. And throughout the lectures, he derives many moral, doctrinal, even political lessons for his auditors in just this way.[81] However, this application of the ancient prophecies to the present day is *"per anagogem"*; they are analogies drawn by the interpreter, which Calvin sees as extensions of the prophet's original meaning and not inherent in it. Analogies are possible, for Calvin, precisely because of the continuity of historical development that he insists is present in the Danielic prophecies, which means that, in his view, people living in different periods in history can find themselves in similar situations. At least in part because of the connectedness of historical events, the past is a mirror in which one can perceive "the perpetual condition of the church."[82] One might characterize Calvin's alternative historical approach to the book of Daniel as *"ad historiam pro ecclesia."*[83] His praeteristic and noneschatological approach yields an interpretation of Daniel as past history that nevertheless speaks to the church in all ages.

[81] For a particularly striking example, that points to the similarity of circumstances, see his comments on Dan. 11:35 (CO 41: 263–65; *Commentaries on Daniel*, 2: 332–34).

[82] Comments on Dan. 8:24, 25 (CO 41: 122; *Commentaries on Daniel*, 2: 130–31).

[83] Cf. Melanchthon's letter to Veit Dietrich: "Haec verba vel maxime me moverunt, quod ait, 'non curabit Deum Patrum suorum,' ut ad Ecclesiam putarim referendum esse hunc locum. Et tamen ad historiam etiam quadrat" (CR 3: 558 = MBW 2067).

7

Biblical Exegesis and Early Modern Legal History in Calvin's Mosaic Harmony

Introduction

Many of the other chapters in this book demonstrate ways in which Calvin's emphasis on a historical reading of the Bible, particularly of the Old Testament, both is in continuity with and also distinguishes itself from broader trends in Christian biblical interpretation in the late medieval period and in the sixteenth century. This chapter focuses on another essential context for understanding Calvin's historical hermeneutic. Before Calvin read the biblical commentaries of his contemporaries and the patristic masters such as Augustine (354–430) or John Chrysostom (ca. 347–407), and before he availed himself of the new critical tools for biblical interpretation that gave ready access to a more historical and literal reading of scripture, such as Augustinus Steuchus's *Recognitio Veteris Testamenti ad Hebraicam Veritatem* (1529, 1531) and Sebastian Münster's *Hebraica Biblia* (1534–1535, 1546), Calvin cut his interpretive teeth as a law student in the French school of historical jurisprudence.[1] The concrete ways in which the legal training to which Calvin was exposed and how the skills he acquired shaped his approach to the Bible constitute a crucial element in his historicizing hermeneutic.[2]

---

[1] On Calvin's use of Steuchus, Münster, and other sources in his commentary on Genesis, see Anthony N. S. Lane, *John Calvin: Student of the Church Fathers* (Edinburgh: T. & T. Clark, 1999), 205–38.

[2] One of the few previous investigations of this topic is Michael L. Monheit, "Passion and Order in the Formation of Calvin's Sense of Religious Authority" (Ph.D. diss., Princeton University, 1988). Basil Hall notes that the origins of Calvin's methods as a biblical commentator stemmed from "Budé and the men who were his disciples" and not the "school of Lefèvre and his disciples at Meaux." Basil Hall, "John Calvin, the Jurisconsults, and the *Ius Civile*," in *Studies in Church History*, vol. 3, *Papers Read at the Third Winter and Summer Meetings of the Ecclesiastical History Society*, ed. G. J. Cuming (Leiden: Brill, 1966), 211. On the effects of Calvin's legal training for his theology and reforming work in general, see also Christoph Strohm, "Sixteenth-Century French Legal Education and Calvin's Legal Education," trans. Barbara Pitkin, in *Calvin and the Early Reformation*, ed. Brian C. Brewer and David M. Whitford (Leiden: Brill, 2020), 44–57.

Calvin, the Bible, and History. Barbara Pitkin, Oxford University Press (2020). © Oxford University Press.
DOI: 10.1093/oso/9780190093273.001.0001

One commentary in particular suggests itself as especially fruitful terrain for an investigation into the relationship between French legal humanism and Calvin's biblical interpretation, namely, his penultimate and, with respect to format, his most unusual work of biblical exegesis: the commentary on the last four books of the Pentateuch, published in Latin in 1563 and in French the following year.[3] The intermingling of narrative and legal material in these four books inspired Calvin to apply his historical hermeneutic more broadly and more creatively in order to explain the meaning and significance of the Mosaic histories and prescriptions for the ancient Israelites, on the one hand, and for pious readers living in the sixteenth century, on the other. The investigation will show that Calvin's unusual arrangement of the material in this commentary and his attention to the affiliation between law and history occasioned by the subject matter of Exodus, Leviticus, Numbers, and Deuteronomy resonate with what Anthony Grafton has described as a "new key" of history reading and writing and reveal Calvin engaging his generation's quest for historical method.[4]

While matters surrounding arrangement of historical material and the integration of legal and historical method do not exhaust by any means the questions faced by historians in the sixteenth century, they were undoubtedly central issues for anyone seeking to read or write—not to mention teach—about the past. Considering Calvin's attention to each of these concerns in his commentary will enrich the understanding of his historical approach to biblical interpretation and his view of history unfolded in previous chapters by shedding light on the place of his vision among historians of his day. In order to situate Calvin's ideas more concretely, in each case his treatment will be viewed through the lens of a contemporary theorist whose innovative approach to the topic reflected and shaped contemporary developments in the study of history. Though both of these conversation partners, namely, François de Connan (1508–1551) and François Baudouin (1520–1573), come from the pool of Calvin's acquaintances, the reason for their selection is not because their works had any direct influence on Calvin's commentary per

---

[3] John Calvin, *Mosis libri quinque cum commentariis: Genesis seorsum, reliqui quatuor in formam harmoniae digesti* (Geneva: H. Estienne, 1563); commentary on the last four books in CO 24–25; Jean Calvin, *Commentaires sur les cinq livres de Moyse: Genese est mis à part, les autres quatres livres sont disposez en forme d'Harmonie* (Geneva: F. Estienne, 1564). English translation as John Calvin, *Commentaries on the Four Last Books of Moses, Arranged in the Form of a Harmony*, 4 vols., ed. and trans. Charles William Bingham, repr. in *Calvin's Commentaries* (Grand Rapids, MI: Baker Books, 1989); hereafter *Commentaries on the Mosaic Harmony*, followed by volume and page number.

[4] Anthony Grafton, *What Was History? The Art of History in Early Modern Europe* (Cambridge, UK: Cambridge University Press, 2007), 21.

se, but rather because these writings represent broader trends, resonances of which can be heard in the commentary on Exodus through Deuteronomy. The lens of contemporary historical scholarship reveals in Calvin's commentary a less traditional and more nuanced reading of the biblical past than that found in other Christian interpretations of these biblical books, one in which the new attitudes and approaches to history that emerged among the professional historians of his day can be detected.

Calvin, Connan, and the Question of Arrangement

Calvin's commentary on the last four books of the Pentateuch, commonly called the "Mosaic Harmony" or simply "Mosaic," was published with a revised version of his Genesis commentary, which had first appeared nearly a decade earlier. The most striking feature of the commentary on Exodus, Leviticus, Numbers, and Deuteronomy is Calvin's rearrangement of the historical narrative and legal material, a move that reflects the systematic treatment of these books in the *congrégations* (the weekly Bible studies in Geneva) starting in 1559. It also echoes the method of his last commentary on the New Testament, which had united the material in Matthew, Mark, and Luke into a single narrative.[5] However, the reorganization of the material in his Mosaic commentary was far more extensive, radical, and, in the history of interpretation, apparently unprecedented.[6] While earlier exegetes had produced harmonies of the gospels or used the Decalogue as method for organizing biblical precepts, no one had gone as far as Calvin. He separated out the

---

[5] See *Vie de Calvin* (CO 21: 90); cf. T. H. L. Parker, *Calvin's Old Testament Commentaries* (Edinburgh: T. & T. Clark, 1986), 31–32. For further details on the production and character of this commentary, see BC 2: 63/16; Erik A. de Boer, "*Harmonia legis*: Conception and Concept of John Calvin's Expository Project on Exodus–Deuteronomy (1559–63)," *Church History and Religious Culture* 87 (2007): 173–201; Erik A. de Boer, *Genevan School of the Prophets: The congrégations of the Company of Pastors and Their Influence in 16th Century Europe* (Geneva: Droz, 2012), 48–50, 163–87; Raymond A. Blacketer, *The School of God: Pedagogy and Rhetoric in Calvin's Interpretation of Deuteronomy* (Dordrecht: Springer, 2006), 127–70; Raymond A. Blacketer, "Calvin as Commentator on the Mosaic Harmony and Joshua," in *Calvin and the Bible*, ed. Donald K. McKim (Cambridge, UK: Cambridge University Press, 2006), 30–52; I. John Hesselink, *Calvin's Concept of the Law* (Allison Park, PA: Pickwick, 1992), 15–17. The harmony on the Synoptic Gospels had appeared in 1555, also following upon treatment of the material in a harmonizing format in the *congrégations*.

[6] Darlene Flaming mentions the gospel harmonies of Augustine, Bucer, and Osiander ("Calvin as Commentator on the Synoptic Gospels," in McKim, *Calvin and the Bible*, 136). Blacketer notes the use of the Decalogue to categorize biblical legislation by Philo and Rabbi Saadiah Gaon and Philip Melanchthon's use of the Decalogue to organize the material in his Proverbs commentary ("Calvin as Commentator on the Mosaic Harmony and Joshua," 41–42). Further discussion of Calvin's sources in de Boer, *Genevan School*, 178–83.

historical narrative concerning the exodus and journey to the promised land
from the legislation imparted by Moses and then substantially restructured
both bodies of material. He rearranged all of the precepts, not only following
a traditional practice of classifying them as moral, ceremonial, or judicial,
but also distributing related precepts under one of the Ten Commandments
or placing them in a preface on the dignity of the law or in two concluding
sections on the summary of the law (e.g., Deut. 6:5, 10:12–13; Lev. 19:18) and
the sanctions of the law—passages that relate to blessings and curses associ-
ated with the keeping of the covenant. He also included an excursus on the
use of the law, in which he discussed no passages from the Pentateuch but
rather drew on Paul to depict and underscore the theological use of the law.[7]
Even the narrative exposition had to be tidied up considerably, especially the
events related after the giving of the law at Sinai in Exodus 20.[8] Thus, in its
final form, the commentary for the most part follows the narrative of Exodus
up through the preparations at Sinai in chapter 19, to which Calvin adds
a few verses from the next chapter and from Deuteronomy 5. Then comes
the exposition of the Law—restructured according to the precepts of the
Decalogue—and, following this, the more streamlined exposition of events
that occurred after Sinai.

What motivated Calvin to depart so radically from his own customary
pattern of continuous exposition of the biblical text aimed specifically at
unfolding the mind of the biblical author? In his introduction, he defends
himself against charges of trying to improve on Moses's account, declaring
that he hopes only to aid the reader in understanding each of the four books
separately by providing this compendium. Thus, it is evident, as Raymond
Blacketer notes, that "concern for the right order of teaching . . . drives his unusual method."[9] Though a wish to aid the unpracticed reader also determined
his decision to treat Matthew, Mark, and Luke in a harmony, there Calvin
only wanted to arrange the material into one "unbroken chain" or "single picture" to make it easier for the reader to perceive similarities and differences.[10]

[7] Calvin makes similar points in his comments on Ex. 19:1–2 (CO 24: 192–94; *Commentaries on the Mosaic Harmony*, 1: 313–16).

[8] For a summary of the rearrangement of the narrative sections, see Parker, *Calvin's Old Testament Commentaries*, 94–95.

[9] Blacketer, "Calvin as Commentator on the Mosaic Harmony and Joshua," 40; de Boer traces the roots of this motive in the *congrégation* on Ex. 1:1–8 and demonstrates how the *congrégations* func-tioned as an "incubator" for Calvin's plan (*Genevan School*, 163–87).

[10] John Calvin, *Harmonia ex tribus Evangelistis composita, adiuncto seorsum Johanne* ([Geneva]: R. Estienne, 1555), CO 45: 4; English translation as John Calvin, *Commentary on the Harmony of the Evangelists, Matthew, Mark and Luke*, 3 vols., ed. and trans. William Pringle, repr.

Since in the case of the *Mosaic Harmony*, the pedagogical concern leads to such a markedly different and innovative exegetical strategy, it is worthwhile to reflect further on the ramifications of and possible unspoken reasons for Calvin's decision as well.

A first consideration has to do with the notion of this particular commentary as a systematic "compendium" for reading scripture—in this case, the books Exodus through Deuteronomy. Calvin did not typically think of biblical commentaries as providing a compendium of *doctrine*, as that was rather the purpose of the *Institutes*. A concern for consolidated teaching certainly led him to comment on the Synoptic Gospels through parallel accounts in his harmony of Matthew, Mark, and Luke, and he did designate this digest a "compendium" of the three histories.[11] In all other cases, however, Calvin thought the best pedagogical approach was to treat each of the biblical books separately, even when he might have done otherwise—as he could have, for example, with the Pauline epistles. It is perhaps fruitful to speculate why Calvin did not think that the disparate doctrine of the Pauline epistles should be subjected to systematic treatment in a commentary, whereas he obviously thought that the teaching of Moses in Exodus through Deuteronomy should be. One could conjecture that Calvin's commentary on Romans provided a "compendium" for reading the remaining Pauline epistles—for as noted in earlier chapters, Calvin certainly viewed Romans as the key to the other letters and, indeed, the hermeneutical entrance to all of scripture. If he did not judge Genesis to be like Romans in providing a systematic orientation for the remaining books by the same biblical author, then this might help explain why Calvin adopted a novel teaching method in this commentary.

The question remains, of course, as to why Calvin didn't just leave it up to the *Institutes* to provide the necessary orientation, especially because the *Institutes* has a discussion of the Decalogue and the divisions of moral, ceremonial, and judicial law.[12] Blacketer has suggested that one reason for Calvin going against his earlier practice of avoiding topical digressions within a

in *Calvin's Commentaries* (Grand Rapids, MI: Baker Books, 1989), 3: xl. See de Boer, *Genevan School*, 154–59, 170–76.

[11] CO 45: 4; Calvin, *Commentary on the Harmony of the Evangelists*, 3: xl.

[12] *Institutes* (1559), 2.8 and 4.20.14–16; for a study of the structural and methodological relationship between the *Institutes* and this commentary, see Richard Neugebauer, "Exegetical Structure in the *Institutes of the Christian Religion* and the Biblical Commentaries of John Calvin: A Study of the *Commentary on the Four, Last Books of Moses Arranged in the Form of a Harmony*" (M.A. thesis, Columbia University, 1968).

commentary may be that he knows as he is writing this commentary that he will not make any further revisions to the *Institutes*.[13] De Boer has argued that Calvin intended to produce a "harmony of the law" as a counterpart to his earlier harmony of the gospel.[14] A further reason for Calvin's unusual approach is political, and I have explored elsewhere the impact of the current historical-political context on the unusual shape of commentary.[15] Clearly Calvin's expressed rationale—namely, that the commentary provides a reorganized, topical compendium to orient the unpracticed reader—offers an important but not exhaustive explanation for his experimental procedure.

In thinking about the reasons for Calvin's unusual presentation of the material, therefore, we must also make note of the fact that his unconventional approach reflects some rather traditional assumptions. In the first place is a long-standing Jewish idea that all biblical and Talmudic law is connected to the revelation at Sinai, either because all law was received by Moses there or because all the biblical commandments—according to later tradition, numbered 613—are contained in some way in the Decalogue.[16] Medieval Christian interpretive traditions also viewed the Ten Commandments as the expression of natural, moral law and thus as the basis for all divine law. For example, the fifteenth-century exegete Denis the Carthusian (1401/2–1471) noted in his commentary on Leviticus that the ceremonial laws he thought were especially the topic of Leviticus were all implicitly and virtually included in the first three precepts of the Decalogue (that is, the moral law), and, similarly, the judicial laws were virtually and implicitly comprehended in the remaining seven.[17] In keeping with this spirit of the Ten Commandments as a principle for categorizing other laws and precepts, Philip Melanchthon (1497–1560) produced a commentary on Proverbs that used the Decalogue to structure and interpret the text, and Blacketer finds that this may have

---

[13] Blacketer, "Calvin as Commentator on the Mosaic Harmony and Joshua," 41. De Boer discusses the changes to the discussion of the Decalogue in the 1559 *Institutes* ("*Harmonia legis*," 187).

[14] De Boer, *Genevan School*, 172–76.

[15] Barbara Pitkin, "Calvin and Politics According to the Mosaic Harmony (1563 | 1564): Text, Paratext, and Context," in *Calvin frater in Domino*, ed. Arnold Huijgen and Karin Maag (Göttingen: Vandenhoeck & Ruprecht, 2020), 37–56.

[16] See Scott M. Langston, *Exodus through the Centuries* (Oxford: Blackwell, 2006), 194; Blacketer also discusses in detail the exegetical background and possible sources for Calvin's approach (*School of God*, 127–38, and "Calvin as Commentator on the Mosaic Harmony and Joshua," 42–43).

[17] Denis the Carthusian, *Enarratio in Leviticum*, in vol. 2 of *D. Dionysii Cartusiani opera omnia*, 42 vols. in 44 (Monstrolii: S. M. de Pratis, 1847), 133. For a brief overview of some of the other medieval views of the Decalogue as a summary of Christian life, see Langston, *Exodus through the Centuries*, 196–202.

been the likely inspiration for Calvin's approach.[18] A predecessor in the reorganization of both the legal and historical material lies in the *Jewish Antiquities*. Josephus (ca. 37–100) condensed, reordered, and supplemented the Mosaic legislation and also recast the narrative covering the accounts in Exodus, Leviticus, Numbers, and Deuteronomy. Like Calvin, he also repeatedly stressed that these rearrangements did not signal any deficiency in the scriptural material.[19] The *Antiquities*, however, were, in contrast to Calvin's *Mosaic Harmony*, not a work of biblical commentary but an early attempt at historical writing that drew heavily on scripture.

Nevertheless, the fact remains that structurally Calvin did something no other Christian commentator had done before with these books of the Bible. Interestingly, his unprecedented approach has parallels in the new strategies arising from a growing demand for a more erudite and critical approach to history. De Boer has noted the importance of the context of the study of Roman law for Calvin's concept of law in general.[20] Schooled in law at the preeminent French institutions of Orléans and Bourges, Calvin was well acquainted with the new approaches to and uses of the past pioneered by humanist scholars such as Guillaume Budé (1467/8–1540), who revolutionized the study of Roman law and history in France with his critical, philological studies of legal texts combined with analysis of material culture, such as coins and inscriptions.[21] In the first half of the sixteenth century, these developments in historical scholarship in France were, as elsewhere in Europe, both experimental and limited in scope, but they laid a foundation for the more sweeping and systematic new histories that would appear later

---

[18] Three editions appeared in 1529, 1550, and 1555; see Blacketer, *School of God*, 137–38, and "Calvin as Commentator on the Mosaic Harmony and Joshua," 44; Robert Stupperich, "Melanchthons Proverbien-Kommentare," in *Der Kommentar in der Renaissance*, ed. August Buck and Otto Herding (Boppard: Harald Boldt, 1975), 21–34; Nicole Kuropka, *Philipp Melanchthon: Wissenschaft und Gesellschaft* (Tübingen: Mohr Siebeck, 2002), 90–133.

[19] Josephus, *Jewish Antiquities, Books I–IV*, ed. and trans. H. St. J. Thackeray (Cambridge, MA: Harvard University Press, 1978).

[20] De Boer, "*Harmonia legis*," 185–86; in the revised version of this discussion appearing in *Genevan School* (172–74), de Boer expands this observation by incorporating findings from my original 2010 article on which the current chapter is based.

[21] Donald R. Kelley, *Foundations of Modern Historical Scholarship: Language, Law, and History in the French Renaissance* (New York: Columbia University Press, 1970), 53–86. See also Josef Bohatec, *Budé und Calvin: Studien zur Gedankenwelt des französischen Frühhumanismus* (Graz: Böhlaus, 1950). Budé's most important works were his *Annotationes in Pandectas* (1508) and *De Asse et partibus ejus libri quinque* (Paris, 1528). On the former, see Julian H. Franklin, *Jean Bodin and the Sixteenth-Century Revolution in the Methodology of Law and History* (New York: Columbia University Press, 1963), 18–27.

in the century.[22] In tracing some of the key stages in the emergence of the innovative theories of history promulgated by, for example, Étienne Pasquier (1529–1615), Jean Bodin (1529/30–1596), and Henri La Popelinière (1541–1608), George Huppert points to some of the salient features of this new orientation to the past.[23] Among these were first a common dissatisfaction with the traditional chronicles, which were perceived as lacking in critical method; second, an emulation of classical historians and broader familiarity with the ancient world, which formed the focus of humanist education; third, textual critical attitudes and techniques and a focus on the political past mediated by historical writing in Renaissance Italy; and, finally, the impress and influence of current legal scholarship, which in many ways constituted the incubator for the new approaches through its highly developed, critical use of original sources and nonliterary artifacts and "rigorous criteria of proof."[24] That Calvin shared these same interpretive values is more than evident in his commentary on Seneca's *De Clementia* (1532), and the lasting influence of his formation in legal humanism can be seen not only in his biblical hermeneutics but also in his shaping of ecclesiastical and civic law in Geneva.[25]

Legal humanism subjected the standard collection of classical Roman law, the *Corpus iuris civilis*—compiled and synthesized under the emperor Justinian I (ca. 482–565) in the sixth century and the object of extensive medieval commentary or glossing—to strict philological and textual analysis in order to identify the interpolations and adaptations of the sixth-century compilers and opinions of later scholastic commentators. One of the results of these efforts to restore Roman law to its original grandeur by stripping it of later accretions was a heightened sense that France had its own historical and legal traditions, which not only demanded critical investigation but also

---

[22] A classic formulation of the issue is J. G. A. Pocock, "Introductory: The French Prelude to Modern Historiography," in *The Ancient Constitution and the Feudal Law*, 2nd edition (Cambridge, UK: Cambridge University Press, 1987), 1–29.

[23] George Huppert, *The Idea of Perfect History: Historical Erudition and Historical Philosophy in Renaissance France* (Urbana: University of Illinois Press, 1970).

[24] Huppert, *Idea of Perfect History*, 24.

[25] On Calvin's textual interpretation in the Seneca commentary, see Michael L. Monheit, "Young Calvin, Textual Interpretation and Roman Law," *Bibliothèque d'Humanisme et Renaissance* 59, no. 2 (1997): 276–82. Basil Hall notes the similarity between instructions on how to interpret Roman civil law of Matteo Gribaldi (a jurist from Toulouse who stayed briefly in Geneva during Calvin's time there) and Calvin's ideal of lucid brevity ("John Calvin, the Juriconsults, and the *Ius Civile*," 214–15). For discussions of Calvin's involvement in establishing a legal code in Geneva, see Josef Bohatec, "Calvin et la procédure civile à Genève," *Revue historique de droit français et étranger*, 4th series, 17 (1938): 229–303; W. Stanford Reid, "John Calvin, Lawyer and Legal Reformer," in *Through Christ's Word: A Festschrift for Dr. Philip E. Hughes*, ed. Philip Edgcumbe Hughes, W. Robert Godfrey, and Jesse L. Boyd (Phillipsburg, NJ: Presbyterian and Reformed, 1985), 158–64.

might be more relevant for the French context than the laws from imperial Rome.[26] This complicated the picture further and rendered even more urgent the need for new synthetic schemes.

To the extent that roots of the late sixteenth century's quest for an adequate, systematic, and scientific approach to the past lie in the fertile soil of the reformed study of law in France, it is here that one must look to uncover the seedbed of Calvin's innovative organizational endeavor.[27] In the course of his legal studies, Calvin himself had studied briefly under the Italian jurist Andrea Alciato (1492–1550), frequently claimed as the founder of the leading school of historical study of law and legal institutions in France. Furthering the agendas of Italian humanists, such as Lorenzo Valla (ca. 1407–1457), and others, such as Budé, who had begun viewing Roman law in a historical context, Alciato's lectures focused on philological explanations and textual criticism instead of the traditional medieval glosses of the legal code.[28] Most significantly, he inspired a new generation of disciples, including Connan, François Hotman (1524–1590), Baudouin, as well as Jacques Cujas (1522–1590), François le Douaren (1509–1559), and Hugues Doneau (Donnellus) (1527–1591), all of whom influenced both the study and practice of law and the field of history. Some of the most prominent, midcentury jurists not only used philological and historical analysis to interpret Roman and French customary laws, but also endeavored to meet the demand for reorganizing and systematizing these materials. First among them was Connan, who, according to Kelley, "seemed to be more disturbed by the chaotic arrangement of the Digest than by its textual condition."[29] Indeed, Connan's 1553 commentary on the *Corpus iuris civilis* offers an intriguing comparison to Calvin's *Mosaic Harmony*.[30]

[26] For fuller discussion, see Donald R. Kelley, "Legal Humanism and the Sense of History," *Studies in the Renaissance* 13 (1966): 184–99.

[27] On these connections and the search for a new, critical theory of history in general, see Kelley, *Foundations*; Huppert, *Idea of Perfect History*; Grafton, *What Was History?*; William J. Bouwsma, "Gallicanism and the Nature of Christendom," (1971), repr. in *A Usable Past: Essays in European Cultural History* (Berkeley: University of California Press, 1990), 308–24.

[28] For details see Kelley, *Foundations*, 87–115; Quirinus Breen, *John Calvin: A Study in French Humanism*, 2nd edition ([Hamden, CT]: Archon Books, 1968), 44–49.

[29] Kelley, *Foundations*, 102. Kelley notes that important examples of this tendency are the works of François Le Douaren (1509–1599), Hugues Doneau (1527–1591), Nikolaus Vigelius (1529–1600). Bodin viewed Budé, Alciato, and Connan as the "chief representatives of the new jurisprudence" (*Foundations*, 137n48). On Doneau, see Franklin, *Jean Bodin*, 27–35.

[30] François de Connan, *Commentariorum iuris civilis libri X*, 2 vols., ed. Barthélemy Faye (Paris: J. Kerver, 1553); republished with expansions by François Hotman in 1557.

Before undertaking this comparison, it is worthwhile to consider Calvin and Connan's early personal connections and Connan's subsequent career. Connan and Calvin may have met as students in Paris or perhaps only in 1528 in Orléans, where the two were allied with fellow students François Daniel and Nicholas Du Chemin, studying law and hearing the lectures of the renowned Pierre de l'Éstoile (1480–1537). Soon thereafter all four transferred to the University of Bourges to hear Alciato.[31] When a pseudonymous polemical writing appeared in 1529 ridiculing de l'Éstoile's approach to interpreting sections of the civil law, Du Chemin composed a defense of their old teacher, entitled *Antapologia*.[32] Though written by July 1529, it was only published in 1531.[33] Calvin took charge of seeing the publication through the press in Paris in March 1531, and he composed a prefatory letter to Connan, dated March 6, that appeared as his first printed work.[34] In the letter Calvin speculates that the pseudonymous author may be none other than Alciato, and his comments to Connan not only imply Connan's affinity for Alciato but also hint at a difference of opinion among the fellow students toward their professors. Defending Du Chemin's criticism of Alciato and expressing his belief that even Alciato will not object and instead yield to respect for the truth, Calvin writes:

---

[31] Alciato came to the University of Bourges in 1529; around or shortly after the same time Calvin, Connan, François Daniel, and Nicholas Du Chemin transferred to Bourges from Orléans in order to hear Alciato's lectures. There is some disagreement among scholars as to the precise chronology, and uncertainty about the dates is noted by Emile Doumergue, who suggests that Calvin went to Bourges after the vacation in September 1529. Emile Doumergue, *Jean Calvin: Les hommes et les choses de son temps*, 7 vols. (Lausanne: Georges Bridel, 1899–1927), 4:141. Doumergue's supposition is echoed in John Calvin, *Calvin's Commentary on Seneca's De Clementia*, ed. and trans. Ford Lewis Battles and André Malan Hugo (Leiden: Brill, 1969), 11 (Calvin is immatriculated at Bourges in the fall of 1529). See also Breen, *John Calvin*, 44 (Calvin went to Bourges in the spring of 1529); Reid, "John Calvin, Lawyer and Legal Reformer," 150 (Calvin went to Bourges in 1529 or 1530); Kelley, *Foundations*, 100 (Calvin's stay at Bourges was in 1530–1531). For a concise but thoroughly documented discussion of Calvin's legal training and a summary and evaluation of existing literature on its significance for his theology and reforming work, see Christoph Strohm, *Ethik im frühen Calvinismus: Humanistische Einflüsse, philosophische, juristische und theologische Argumentationen sowie mentalitätsgeschichtliche Aspekte am Beispiel des Calvin-Schülers Lambertus Danaeus* (Berlin: De Gruyter, 1996), 223–28; see also Strohm, "Sixteenth-Century French Legal Education."

[32] For analysis of this episode, see Monheit, "Young Calvin," 267–76; Michael L. Monheit, "Guillaume Budé, Andrea Alciato, Pierre de l'Éstoile: Renaissance Interpreters of Roman Law," *Journal of the History of Ideas* 58, no. 1 (1997): 21–40; but cf. also Strohm, *Ethik*, 225–26; Hall, "John Calvin, the Juriconsults, and the *Ius Civile*," 210.

[33] Breen, *John Calvin*, 52, gives this date for the composition of the treatise.

[34] CO 9: 785–86; English translation in Calvin, *Calvin's Commentary on Seneca's De Clementia*, 385–87, and in Breen, *John Calvin*, 53–55 (though note the author's comments about the translation in the errata noted at the front of the second edition). Sadly this is the only piece of correspondence that survives between the two, even though Calvin refers to Connan's "many letters" in his prefatory epistle.

This I wanted to be said, so that by the same effort I might clear myself both with Alciatus and with you; for I was afraid that out of sheer zeal for Alciatus you might be more inclined toward the opposition, and might reproach me for not standing on Alciatus's side. For I know with what enthusiasm you used to speak of him—doubtless as a most grateful student of the best of teachers.[35]

Calvin reminds Connan that he has expressed a positive evaluation of de l'Éstoile in a recent conversation and in many letters. He also defends Du Chemin's learning and "precise judgment" and ends with a flattering appeal to Connan's deeper appreciation of the secrets of the law, which Calvin believes should lead him to a favorable judgment of the treatise. All in all, one has the sense that Calvin glosses over the seriousness of their disagreement in a bid to win the agreement of someone whose opinion, he seems to think, carries a lot of weight. This attitude is suggested also by the reference to Connan the following year in the preface to the commentary on Seneca. Here Calvin claims that he ran the commentary by several friends to get their opinion of his work, but he singles out only Connan by name, writing, "And most particularly did I set store by the opinion of my friend Connan, a man of prudence and learning, by whose judgment I stand or fall."[36]

After this Calvin and Connan appear to have gone their separate ways, and no further evidence of personal contact between the two exists. From 1539 until his death in 1551, Connan held appointments as a royal advisor in Paris. His duties included offering political and legal advice and serving as the king's representative in implementing policies, collecting taxes, and the like in the provinces.[37] Somehow he also found time to compose his ten books of commentary on the *Corpus iuris civilis*, in which he employed an innovative method that involved massive reorganization of the material contained in this compilation of legislation.[38] Connan took as his basic structure the

---

[35] CO 9: 786; Calvin, *Calvin's Commentary on Seneca's De Clementia*, 386.
[36] Calvin, *Calvin's Commentary on Seneca's De Clementia*, 6–7.
[37] For details see Christoph Bergfeld, *Franciscus Connanus (1508–1551): Ein Systematiker des römischen Rechts* (Cologne: Böhlau, 1968), 7–20. The main source for Connan's biography is the prefatory epistle to Connan, *Commentarium iuris civilis,* written by the editor, Louis Le Roy (Ludovicus Regius).
[38] This collection contained four distinct bodies of legislation: the *Codex Iustinianus,* which was a compilation of imperial laws; the *Digest* or *Pandects,* which contained extracts from the writings of Roman jurists writing between the mid-first century BCE and the end of the third century CE, organized into fifty books; the *Institutes,* a textbook for law students, consisting of fragments from earlier textbooks, and especially the Institutes of Gaius; the *Novellae,* or new laws (known in the sixteenth century as "Authenticum"), which included imperial laws promulgated between 535 and 565, after the formal approval of the second edition of the *Codex* in 534.

order of topics in the *Institutes*, the third part of the body of law, which was intended as a textbook for introducing students to the legislation in the parts known as the *Codex* and the *Digest*. His first book forms an introduction that investigates and defines key terms and concepts, such as *ius* and *iustitia*, discusses the sources of law, and provides an overview of the legal and constitutional history of Rome. The remaining nine books mostly discuss topics in the order supplied by the *Institutes*, with the exception of marriage law in book 8 and inheritance law in books 9–10. Connan used the laws supplied by the *Institutes* to structure the discussion, and then brought in passages from the *Codex* or the *Digest* that related to the object at hand. He also cited relevant examples from other classical literature to explain their meaning. This was, apparently, no mere antiquarian enterprise, but an attempt to reformulate Roman law and heighten its utility for French legal scholarship. Louis Le Roy (1510–1577), the editor of this posthumously published work, understood Connan to have been independently furthering the goals of the classical jurists and offering a remedy for the present times.[39]

Le Roy was obviously enthusiastic about Connan's attempt to find a new system for presenting, studying, and engaging Roman law. At least some of his contemporaries appear to have agreed. François Hotman justified his reedition of the work in 1557 by saying that he had heard it praised so much but had found it so hard to obtain a copy that he had decided to edit it himself.[40] Bodin made use of the work in his writings and mentions Connan favorably in his groundbreaking *Methodus ad facilem historiarum cognitionem (Method for the Easy Comprehension of History)* (1566).[41] The work was reissued several times before the early seventeenth century and continued to be influential into the eighteenth century, although it was already surpassed in the sixteenth by the more refined systems of Doneau and Nikolaus Vigelius (1529–1600).[42] The significance of Connan's work for our purposes is as representative of a broader trend toward method, system, and

[39] For detailed discussion of Connan's commentary, see Bergfeld, *Franciscus Connanus*, 23, 45–145, 152. The work remained incomplete, due to his death in 1551.

[40] Bergfeld, *Franciscus Connanus*, 21.

[41] Jean Bodin, *Method for the Easy Comprehension of History*, trans. Beatrice Reynolds (New York: Octagon, 1966), 5; cf. Bergfeld, *Franciscus Connanus*, 44; on Bodin and Connan, see Jean Moreau-Reibel, *Jean Bodin et le droit public comparé dans ses rapports avec la philosophie de l'histoire* (Paris: J. Vrin, 1933), 19–33.

[42] Bergfeld, *Franciscus Connanus*, 21, 208–9. Hugues Doneau (Hugo Donellus), *Commentariorum de iure civili libri viginti octo* (1589–); on Doneau's commentary, see Franklin, *Jean Bodin*, 30–35. Nikolaus Vigelius, *Methodus Universi iuris civilis* (1561); see Harold J. Berman, *Law and Revolution*, vol. 2, *The Impact of the Protestant Reformations on the Western Legal Tradition* (Cambridge, MA: Harvard University Press, 2003), 124–25.

critical interpretation in approaching the past—a trend perpetuated just a decade later in the historical arena by, for example, Baudouin's *De institutione historiae universae* (Institution of universal history) (1561) and Bodin's *Method*.

One can only guess at Calvin's reaction to the innovative approach taken by his former university classmate and the man whose judgment he claims, in his preface to Du Chemin's *Antapologia* and his own commentary on Seneca, to have held so dear. There is a heavily used copy of his commentary listed in the library catalogue of the Genevan Academy, but given the large number of trained lawyers in Geneva, one cannot assume that only Calvin would have been attracted to it.[43] Whether or not Calvin knew the work himself, his novel approach to the organization of the historical and legal material in his Mosaic commentary reflects the same impulses that drove the systematizing endeavor represented by Connan's commentary on Roman civil law: to provide a logical and orderly presentation for teaching and, ultimately, for reevaluation and retrieval of past legislation. Inasmuch as Calvin extended this principle not just to the legal material but to the historical material as well, one is led to consider more broadly the systematizing, synthetic impulse.

Law, History, and the Quest for Historical Method

In the middle of the sixteenth century some French jurists began expanding the focus of their work beyond recovery and representation of Roman legal traditions and raised questions about how to arrive at the most perfect and complete understanding of the past in a broader sense. What would be the best way to integrate all of the insights about ages gone by into a coherent whole? Theorists such as Baudouin and Bodin were motivated by a concern for a more universal history, desiring either to go beyond the particular traditions of different peoples to more coherent representations of these products of individual cultures or, alternatively, to define the particularity of one culture's past and character in all its exquisite complexity. While the concern for a critical and universal view of the past was by no means novel, the intensity of interest in a more systematic way of dealing with historical

---

[43] Alexandre Ganoczy, *La bibliothèque de l'académie de Calvin: Le catalogue de 1572 et ses enseignements* (Geneva: Droz, 1969), 275; see Strohm, *Ethik*, 230–32.

sources reflects the new status that history as a discipline had assumed in educated circles and in educational curricula.[44] Heightened appreciation for the past nurtured in the legal faculties of France gave way to new questions about how to deal with the increasing wealth of historical artifacts and data—how to read, interpret, evaluate, and transmit historical knowledge. New experimental schemes aimed not only at comprehending the legacy of the past but also at proposed ways to move beyond the mere presentation of recovered sources to identify principles for their interpretation and potential ongoing relevance.[45] Charles H. Parker has suggested several ways in which Calvin's *Institutes* reflect these impulses; the *Mosaic Harmony* reveals the ways in which they impacted not only his historical approach to theology but also his interpretation of scripture.[46]

Beyond the division and arrangement of the material explored earlier, there are a number of ways in which these concerns with the acquisition, evaluation, organization, and transmission of the past have left their imprint on Calvin's commentary. First, this interest can be seen in his treatment of Moses as the author of the four books and his ongoing concern to explain Moses's motives, purposes, and methods. In Calvin's view, Moses is both a legislator and a historian, composing this record of the events and the divine regulations especially for the Israelites and their posterity. As is typical in his other biblical commentaries, Calvin attends to the human author's reasons for writing as he does. For example, he begins the commentary by explaining briefly Moses's design in choosing this starting point; he refers repeatedly to the fact that Moses wrote as he did in accommodation to what Calvin designates as the rude capacity of his original audience; finally, he attributes the disconnected arrangement of the material to the human author. True, Moses relates divine mandates and he is more than an earthly lawgiver— in contrast, Calvin says, to Lycurgus or Solon.[47] He can also speak of the Holy Spirit as a narrator or as dictating to Moses what would be useful to

---

[44] As Franklin observes, "in the later Renaissance the commitment to this enterprise was new in the degree of its intensity. Political and social thought was now more heavily oriented towards historical examples and comparisons than in any period of classical antiquity. And whereas the ancients had never generally assumed that the study of the past should have equal weight with philosophy or rhetoric in the curriculum of education, in the sixteenth century a systematic study of the entire realm of history was all but universally regarded as a fundamental goal of education" (*Jean Bodin*, 84).

[45] See Franklin, *Jean Bodin*, 85.

[46] Charles H. Parker, "Bourges to Geneva: Methodological Links between Legal Humanists and Calvinist Reformers," *Comitatus: A Journal of Medieval and Renaissance Studies* 20, no. 1 (1989): 63–65.

[47] CO 24: 613; *Commentaries on the Mosaic Harmony*, 3: 22.

relate.[48] Nevertheless, these facts do not diminish for Calvin the significance of Moses's role as the one who crafts the presentation, leaving out things he judges to be unnecessary or repeating material that Calvin's readers might judge superfluous.[49] He underscores that Moses is not writing a comprehensive history and is thus selective with the material he supplies.[50] At the same time, he argues that Moses takes pains to supply proper evidence to prove the veracity of the events he relates. For example, Calvin underscores the proofs that show that Moses's account of the final plague, the slaying of the Egyptians' firstborn males, is true, whereas the demonically inspired fables found in secular histories tried to bury the memory of this significant event; he makes a similar argument against some profane writers' explanations of the rescue at the Red Sea.[51] Calvin is concerned to present Moses's account as a reliable if also selective and somewhat disorganized presentation of Israel's past.

Second, for Calvin the history related by Moses not only is addressed to the ancient Israelites and their posterity but also provides valuable and essential lessons for later generations of Jews and Christians, including Calvin's own. Fundamentally, he is always concerned first to understand these events as they pertain to Moses and the children of Israel. For example, in his explanation of the burning bush in Exodus 3, Calvin can identify the angel appearing to Moses as the pre-incarnate Eternal Son, justifying this by Paul's statement that Christ was the leader of his people in the desert (1 Cor. 10:4); hence the christological reading is not, for Calvin, anachronistic. He rejects as too forced earlier allegorical views of the bush as Christ's body or the thorns as signifying Israel's stubbornness. Instead, he offers the "natural sense" that the vision is like Abraham's in Genesis 15:17. In both cases, then, the meaning of the vision is that "God will not permit his people to be extinguished in

---

[48] For an example of the Spirit dictating see Calvin's comments on Ex. 3:1 (CO 24: 34; *Commentaries on the Mosaic Harmony*, 1: 59). Marten Woudstra discusses further ways that Calvin attends to the human author, treats the text as a literary composition, and is concerned with the grammatical, historical, and geographical details therein: Marten Woudstra, "Calvin Interprets What 'Moses Reports': Observations on Calvin's Commentary on Exodus 1–19," *Calvin Theological Journal* 21, no. 2 (1986): 151–74; see esp. 154–60.

[49] For example, see Calvin's comments on Ex. 37:1–39 (CO 25: 66; *Commentaries on the Mosaic Harmony*, 3: 305).

[50] See Calvin's comments on Ex. 14:13 (CO 24: 151; *Commentaries on the Mosaic Harmony*, 1: 245) and Ex. 16:4 (CO 24: 166; *Commentaries on the Mosaic Harmony*, 1: 270).

[51] See Calvin's comments on Ex. 12:29 (CO 24: 137–38; *Commentaries on the Mosaic Harmony*, 1: 224–25) and Ex. 14:28 (CO 24: 155; *Commentaries on the Mosaic Harmony*, 1: 252). Recounting the latter event and the singing of the song that memorialized it in Exodus 15, Calvin emphasizes the importance of eyewitnesses to verify Moses's account.

darkness." There is a "similitude" or symbolic character to the vision—namely, that Israel is like the bush, and the fire is like the tyrannical oppression that would have consumed them had God not intervened: "Thus was the cruelly afflicted people aptly represented, who, though surrounded by flames, and feeling their heat, yet remained unconsumed, because they were guarded by the present help of God."[52] Hence in the first place Calvin relates the vision to the particular situation of Moses and the Israelites in Egypt. That does not prevent him from drawing lessons from the history for his sixteenth-century readers, but he urges his readers to respect the priority of the "natural sense" before making connections to their own situation through "anagoge" or a principle of the "similitude of times." As previous chapters have demonstrated, this respect of the pastness and particularity of the past is a prominent feature of Calvin's biblical exegesis in general, and while this approach is in continuity with traditions emphasizing the priority of the literal or historical sense in Christian biblical interpretation, it also represents another point of intersection with more recent humanistic concerns with reading the past on its own terms before reaping examples for the present day.

Third, Calvin not only organizes the legal material systematically but interprets it in a historically contextual way. This is most clear in his application of the traditional Christian distinction between the universally binding moral law, on the one hand, and the ceremonial and political or judicial laws, on the other. Traditionally this distinction allowed Christian interpreters to separate out the cultic and political elements of Israelite law that were abrogated or superseded by Christ (at least according to the literal sense) from the perpetual commandments of God that continued in force. Calvin had used the distinction in this way in the *Institutes*.[53] Here he employs this distinction to structure his presentation of the law, discussing each of the precepts in the Decalogue in turn according to the following pattern: first he cites and discusses the commandment as expressed in Exodus 20 and Deuteronomy 5. He then cites and explains other passages that he considers to be "expositions" of the same precept and in this sense still perpetually

---

[52] Comments on Ex. 3:2 (CO 24: 36; *Commentaries on the Mosaic Harmony*, 1: 62). He similarly criticizes allegorical interpretations of the command that Moses take off his shoes in his comments on Ex. 3:4 (CO 24: 37; *Commentaries on the Mosaic Harmony*, 1: 63). For a summary of other Jewish and Christian interpretations, see Langston, *Exodus through the Centuries*, 45–52.

[53] *Institutes*, 4.20.15. On the use of this distinction by medieval scholastic theologians, see Otto Hermann Pesch, "Sittengebote, Kultvorschriften, Rechtssatzungen," in *Thomas von Aquino: Interpretation und Rezeption: Studien und Texte*, ed. W. Eckert (Mainz: Matthias-Grünewald, 1974), 488–518.

binding. Following this, he treats verses that he considers to be cultic or political supplements or appendices to the commandment under consideration: regulations governing ceremony, ritual, the priesthood, and purity, as well as the civil laws covering punishments for violating the commandment (e.g., stoning for blasphemy, a violation of the second commandment; the *lex talionis*). He views most of the ceremonial and political regulations as completely peculiar to their time and culture and largely as a special instance of God's accommodation to the particular—and sometimes, in Calvin's judgment, rude—capacity of Israel in those days, with the end result being, in the words of David F. Wright, "a gain in historical realism."[54] Indeed, Calvin's collection of all the laws having to do with the construction of the tabernacle, the priesthood, and the various types of offerings and sacrifices as supplements to the second commandment allows a logically organized and remarkably robust picture of the religious practices of ancient Israel as portrayed in the biblical text to emerge. It is important to note that Calvin understands the ceremonies of Mosaic religion as types having a substance that transcends their external manifestation, so that while the external forms have ceased, their inner meaning remains valid for Christian believers. But he does not often make this point explicitly in his treatment of the details of Israelite religious practice, focusing instead on what they were to teach the Israelites themselves.

Fourth, in explaining the cultic and political laws Calvin not only focuses on the original context of these traditions but also employs at times a comparative method to elucidate them and highlight the ways that features of biblical law either are similar to pagan legal codes or represent a unique tradition. For example, in the appendices to the commandment to honor one's parents, Calvin discusses passages that prescribe capital punishment for smiting or cursing parents (Ex. 21:15, 17; Lev. 20:9; Deut. 21:18–21) and compares these regulations to Roman law. Detailing the particular form of capital punishment for this crime prescribed by a Roman law, the origins of which he had discussed in his commentary on Seneca, Calvin maintains that

---

[54] "In this commentary Calvin displays at times a remarkably sharp insight into the circumstances of Israelite life, from its religious and material environment to its group dynamics and social psychology." David F. Wright, "Calvin's Pentateuchal Criticism: Equity, Hardness of Heart, and Divine Accommodation in the Mosaic Harmony Commentary," *Calvin Theological Journal* 21, no. 1 (1986): 46. Wright finds that Calvin expands his principle of divine accommodation in order to come "to terms with textual contexts that are in his view incompatible with true religion and natural equity as they stand, that require some kind of explanation or qualification lest they be thought to embody the perfect will of God" (36).

Roman legislation required death only for parricide, whereas God's law goes farther in condemning all who are violent or abusive toward parents.[55] At the same time, he argues, God's law is milder and more just in requiring that evidence in such a trial come from both the father and the mother, whereas Roman law required only testimony of the father and was therefore more open to abuse.[56] The prohibition against murder in the sixth commandment also provides opportunity for comparison. Discussing the apparently slight punishments for inflicting physical injury (Ex. 21:18), Calvin refers to the small fine imposed by the Twelve Tables for unjust beatings. That God avenges the death of a servant at the master's hand leads Calvin to contrast the justice of Exodus 21:20 to the "gross barbarism" of the power of life and death over servants granted to the *paterfamilias* by the rule of *patria potestas* of Rome and other peoples.[57] Yet in respect to the command to put conquered peoples to death (Deut. 20:13, 16–17), it is Moses's law that appears more inhumane than the commands of profane writers to spare the conquered. Calvin expresses great reservation about the command to annihilate non-Canaanite cities, but argues that with respect to the Canaanites the Israelites were actually carrying out God's judgment, and hence the exception to the common laws of war was justified.[58] Discussing penalties for murders committed with intent versus those resulting from accident in his comments on Numbers 35:16–18, Calvin notes that these kinds of distinctions are familiar from the *lex cornelia*, and he relates opinions of the ancient jurists Martianus, Paulus, and Ulpian on this matter that are cited in the *Digest*.[59] He thinks such similarities are in part due to the fact that other nations borrowed from the Mosaic legislation—a point he makes explicitly in discussing the penalties for stealing livestock (Ex. 22:1–4) in the political supplements to the eighth commandment. Here he argues at some length that Solon and the Decemvirs (who, according to legend, compiled the Twelve Tables from

[55] CO 24: 607; *Commentaries on the Mosaic Harmony*, 3: 13. Calvin alludes to a law concerning the unique mode of punishment for the crime of parricide. Calvin also refers to this "Cornelian law" in his commentary on Seneca and refutes that it was promulgated by Sulla (82 BCE). He cites Cicero to argue that the law goes back to the "ancestors" and was only called back into use by Pompey. He also refers to Zasius's text-critical work on this law and explains how this punishment came to be applied to this crime (Calvin, *Calvin's Commentary on Seneca's De Clementia*, 139* and 252–55). See also Blacketer, *School of God*, 259–60.

[56] CO 24: 608; *Commentaries on the Mosaic Harmony*, 3: 15. Calvin's reference is to the absolute power of fathers as head of the household (*paterfamilias*), including the right of life and death, granted by the Roman law of *patria potestas*. See also Blacketer, *School of God*, 261–62.

[57] CO 24: 624; *Commentaries on the Mosaic Harmony*, 3: 40.

[58] CO 24: 632; *Commentaries on the Mosaic Harmony*, 3: 53.

[59] CO 24: 638: *Commentaries on the Mosaic Harmony*, 3: 63–64.

Solonic legislation) made changes for the worse in assigning a harsher penalty to thieves caught with the goods (*furtum manifestum*) than to those who had disposed of them (*furtum nec manifestum*). God, in contrast, decrees harsher punishment for those who are so hardened that they kill or sell the stolen animal. If the thief is not able to make restitution, he is to be sold, and Calvin notes this was also the custom of Rome. But whereas both Moses and the Twelve Tables permit the slaying of a thief if the robbery occurs at night, the Twelve Tables extend this to crimes committed in daylight when the thief is armed. God, however, condemns to death those who avenge these crimes by killing the thief.[60] These kinds of comparisons, with references, for example, to legislation in the Twelve Tables, the *Digest*, or *lex cornelia*, are found most often in Calvin's treatment of the political or judicial supplements outlining the civil penalties attached to the second table of the Decalogue. They reveal both his sense of the particularity of individual cultures and a notion of similarities across legal traditions, whether he attributes these to derivation (Greek and Roman traditions drawing on Mosaic law) or to common, universal principles of natural law reflected in particular legal codes.

Finally, there are limits to Calvin's historical contextualization of the legal material, and this signals his interest in discerning universal principles of ongoing relevance. For one, the very fact that he considers the precepts of the Decalogue universally valid expressions of a perfect rule of life virtually prevents any effort to contextualize the Ten Commandments in Exodus or Deuteronomy themselves or the passages that immediately follow as "expositions" of each commandment. A rare instance in which Calvin relates such a law to Israel's particular situation is his discussion of the prohibition against adopting practices attributed to the Canaanites, such as divination, magic, and witchcraft (Deut. 18:9–14), which he regards as one of the expositions of the first commandments. Here he draws a general lesson for his readers, but also describes why these specific prohibitions were especially necessary for Israel.[61] For the most part, however, his discussion of the commandments and the verses he considers to be further expositions of them focuses on the eternally binding doctrine that they express. Another factor limiting appreciation of any historical situation in which the laws were articulated lies in Calvin's redistribution of the laws under one of the precepts of the Decalogue or in one of the excurses preceding or following them. Even

---

[60] CO 24: 687–90; *Commentaries on the Mosaic Harmony*, 3: 140–43.
[61] CO 24: 265–70; *Commentaries on the Mosaic Harmony*, 1: 423–33.

though there is a "gain in historical realism" in the sense of how the commandments relate to Israel's cultic and political life, there is at the same time
little to no indication of much variety with respect to development, time,
or even literary context for the moral precepts. For example, when Calvin
discusses the repetition of a commandment in Deuteronomy, he does not
reflect on the circumstances in which Moses repeated the law, having only
mentioned this briefly right before his discussion of the first commandment.[62] Similarly, when he cites, for example, verses from Leviticus 19, 20,
and 21 in his preface to the law, he gives no indication that in the original
context these exhortations serve to underscore the covenantal relationship
at the conclusion of or in the midst of various other precepts.[63] It is true that,
now located in the preface where all the verses extolling the law are gathered,
they serve in a sense as a general commendation of all the entire body of law
that follows. The schematic rearrangement and classification thus serve to
isolate the moral precepts and envelope them—not at all surprisingly—with
an ahistorical aura.

To be sure, Calvin's interpretation of the moral laws could be quite nuanced
and complex, as John Thompson has shown with regard to Calvin's evolving
engagement with the seventh commandment in several treatments of the
Pentateuch.[64] Nevertheless, we can hardly expect Calvin to have engaged in
rich historical contextualization of laws he considered eternal and universal
expressions of the divine will. While his failure to do so falls short of modern
historical methods, his handling of this issue very much reflects concerns
and issues current in the historical methods developing in his own day. In
short, Calvin's culling of the universal from the particular and his use of this
distinction to structure his discussion of the legal material and, in a sense,
to orient the presentation of the historical narrative, echoes desires of some
of his contemporaries to determine principles for coming to terms with the
increasing amount of historical data presenting itself to sixteenth-century
students and scholars of the past.

Calvin's attempt to supply an orderly elucidation of divine law not only
within its historical context but also transcending it takes on new urgency when viewed through the lens of a quest for an integrated, universal

---

[62] CO 24: 259–60; *Commentaries on the Mosaic Harmony*, 1: 416–17.

[63] See comments on Lev. 19:36–37, 20:8, and 22:31–22 (CO 24: 211–13; *Commentaries on the Mosaic Harmony*, 1: 342–44).

[64] John L. Thompson, "Second Thoughts about Conscience: Nature, the Law, and the Law of Nature in Calvin's Pentateuchal Exegesis," in *Calvinus Pastor Ecclesiae*, ed. Herman J. Selderhuis and Arnold Huijgen (Göttingen: Vandenhoeck & Ruprecht, 2016), 123–46.

history, of the type proposed by Calvin's former secretary and later adversary, Baudouin. While Calvin's *Mosaic Harmony* is clearly not an attempt to write a universal history, it can be seen to weigh in on some of the central questions that both motivated and impelled that endeavor: What are the principles for interpreting the past? And to what extent can the particular histories of specific peoples supply categories and principles for determining values of others? Calvin published his Mosaic commentary at the high point of his personal and professional animosity toward Baudouin.[65] Did his sharp dis- agreement with Baudouin in the early 1560s over the future of Christianity and the best way to deal with religious schism—colored by much personal invective—also reveal their shared preoccupation with questions of histor- ical method? While complete investigation of this topic lies outside the scope of the present study, brief consideration of Baudouin's writings, and espe- cially his proposal for uniting law and history, which Kelley has designated as "the first serious attempt in France to formulate a definition of history— indeed to promote history from an art to a science by organizing it in a meth- odological way," provides an interesting lens through which to view Calvin's simultaneous historicizing and universalizing of Israel's story in his *Mosaic Harmony*.[66]

Before outlining Baudouin's program, one might consider briefly the per- sonal connections linking him to Calvin. Like Connan and Calvin, Baudouin was a product of the new wave of legal humanism, which he studied at the University of Louvain and furthered through contacts in Paris after 1539. He began corresponding with Calvin no later than 1545, writing from Paris, where he started lecturing on civil law the following year.[67] In Paris

---

[65] Doumergue credits Baudouin with writing the opening chapter of the "Calvin legend" (*Jean Calvin*, 1: 150–61); however, Irena Backus traces Baudouin's influence on the life of Calvin written by his disciple, Jean-Papire Masson, which followed Baudouin's criteria for history and resulted in a fairly objective—if at the same time negative—portrait of Calvin. See Irena Backus, "Roman Catholic Lives of Calvin from Bolsec to Richelieu: Why the Interest?," in *John Calvin and Roman Catholicism: Critique and Engagement, Then and Now*, ed. Randall C. Zachman (Grand Rapids, MI: Baker Academic, 2008), 32–46; cf. Irena Backus, *Life Writing in Reformation Europe: Lives of Reformers by Friends, Disciples, and Foes* (Aldershot, UK: Ashgate, 2008), 125–86.

[66] Kelley, *Foundations*, 116.

[67] For more details about this period, Baudouin's correspondence with Calvin, and his stays in Geneva, see Kelley, *Foundations*, 122–28; Michael Erbe, *François Bauduin (1520–1573): Biographie eines Humanisten* (Gütersloh: Gütersloher Verlagshaus Mohn, 1978), 46–57. There are twenty-three known letters from Baudouin to Calvin: fourteen written between July 1545 and May 1548; five written from Bourges between November 1550 and September 1552; three written from Strasbourg in 1555–1556; and one written as the introduction to his final polemical response to Calvin and Beza (November 1563). In Paris in the 1540s, Baudouin held his lectures through the faculty of canon law, since officially the teaching of Roman law had been banned at Paris by decree of Pope Honorius III in 1219.

he had served as assistant to the jurist Charles Du Moulin (1500–1566) and met Hotman, both of whom became adherents of Reformed Christianity.[68] Baudouin shared these evangelical sympathies, and in 1545 was banned from his native town, Arras, because of them. After visiting Calvin in Geneva briefly in August or September 1545, he returned to Paris via Strasbourg (and possibly Basel), continued writing to Calvin, and eventually joined him in Geneva two years later. During the summer and fall of 1547, Baudouin lived in Calvin's house and served as one of his secretaries. By November he had moved to Lyon, where he worked as a proofreader for the printer Sebastian Gryphius, and in May of the following year he received a call to an appointment to the legal faculty of the University of Bourges, as the successor to Du Moulin, and continued publishing commentaries on Roman civil law.[69] He held this position until January 1555, when faculty jealousies and politics that played out in student uprisings led to his departure.[70] Passing again through Geneva, Baudouin took positions in Strasbourg and then in Heidelberg, where, in addition to lectures on law, he offered lectures on history and wrote his treatise on universal history, which was published in 1561.[71] This was the same year that the already strained relationship between Baudouin and Calvin exploded over an incident connected with the Colloquy of Poissy in the fall and resulted in an intense battle in print.[72] During this time Baudouin returned to France, and in July 1563 he reaffiliated with the Roman Catholic church.

At the end of his biography of Baudouin, Michael Erbe notes that until quite recently Baudouin was remembered more as a jurist and less as a theorist of history or a proponent of religious tolerance or conciliation; at the same time, however, his influential publications in the field of jurisprudence

---

[68] On Du Moulin and his relationship to Baudouin, see Erbe, *François Bauduin*, 37–38. On Baudouin's early connections to Hotman, see 52–53. On Baudouin and religious reform, see Joseph Duquesne, "François Bauduin et la Réforme," *Bulletin de l'Academie delphinale* 5th series, 9 (1917): 55–108; Mario Turchetti, *Concordia o Tolleranza? François Bauduin (1520–1573) e i "Moyenneurs"* (Geneva: Droz, 1984).

[69] For a list of publications, see Erbe, *François Bauduin*, 210–39; see also Kelley, *Foundations*, 118–20.

[70] On the conflict between Baudouin and his earlier mentor, Le Douren, see Erbe, *François Bauduin*, 78–80.

[71] François Bauduin, *De institutione historiae universae et ejus cum iurisprudentia conjunctione* (Paris: A. Wechelus, 1561); for an overview, see Franklin, *Jean Bodin*, 116–36.

[72] See Richard Stauffer, "Autour du Colloque de Poissy: Calvin et le *De officio pii ac publicae tranquillitatis vere amantis viri*," in *Actes du colloque L'Amiral de Coligny et son temps* (Paris: Société de l'histoire du protestantisme français, 1974), 135–53, repr. in *Interprètes de la Bible: Études sur les réformateurs du XVIe siècle* (Paris: Beauchesne, 1980), 249–67; Turchetti, *Concordia o Tolleranza*, 233–390. Erbe traces the original literary conflict between Baudouin and Calvin and its afterlife in the writings of their disciples (*François Bauduin*, 122–74).

are as significant for his view of history and historical method as his 1561 treatise.[73] Indeed, in early 1556, Matthias Flacius Illyricus (1520–1575) wrote to Baudouin to get his opinion on the proposed plan for writing the first Protestant church history (commonly known as the Magdeburg Centuries) and invited him to join the project. Though Baudouin did not accept, he nevertheless wrote three letters advising the centuriators about the endeavor, formulating ideas that would appear again in his 1561 treatise.[74] In these writings one can identify several essential features of his view of the past and his method for the acquisition, evaluation, organization, and transmission of historical knowledge and begin to appreciate the significance of his proposal for a universal historical method achieved through an alliance of law and history, not just enabling a more accurate restoration of the past but also revealing principles relevant for understanding the present.

First is Baudouin's concern to establish a reliable historical account. In his first letter to Flacius, he lavishes attention on the issue of determining the accuracy of sources, which he thinks is similar to determining what happened from witness accounts in legal cases, though in the case of history it is far more difficult.[75] The historian cannot just rely on the authority of the witness but has to use all available witnesses and testimony critically in order to determine the fact.[76] He takes up this problem also in his *De institutione historiae universae*, where he both urges caution in accepting past accounts wholesale and also warns against complete skepticism; the key is to apply to humanist textual critical methods and grasp the difference between primary and secondary accounts or evidence in determining the past. Franklin notes that in this discussion developments in historical jurisprudence supply two of Baudouin's key criteria for determining authenticity: first, he calls for critical editions, in short, "the humanist technique of emendation which had been so successfully applied to the textual correction of the *Corpus Juris*." Second, he makes analogies to the use of oral and written testimony in legal cases to propose a hierarchy of evidence from primary and secondary sources.[77] Indeed, as Backus shows, Baudouin passed on his passion for attending to evidence and ensuring reliable accounts to his student, Jean-Papire Masson

[73] Erbe, *François Bauduin*, 186–87.
[74] See Gregory B. Lyon, "Baudouin, Flacius, and the Plan for the Magdeburg Centuries," *Journal of the History of Ideas* 64, no. 2 (2003): 253–72. Baudouin's letters from June, August, and September 1556 are printed in Erbe, *François Bauduin*, 262–76, nn9, 11, and 12.
[75] For a discussion, see Lyon, "Baudouin, Flacius," 265–68.
[76] Lyon, "Baudouin, Flacius," 265.
[77] Franklin, *Jean Bodin*, 127–30, quote from 127; cf. Kelley, *Foundations*, 132.

(1544–1611), who adhered to them in creating the first objective biography of Calvin, one that rejected both the negative myths propagated by Jerome Bolsec (d. ca. 1584) and other Roman Catholic opponents as well as the overly idealized portraits of Theodore Beza (1519–1605) and Nicolas Colladon (1530–1586).[78]

Second, in Baudouin's case, concern to attend to the credibility of the sources aimed at something larger than simply accurate reconstruction of the past. As Gregory Lyon puts it, the "past must be understood on its own terms, and completely, in order to understand the principles that might apply to the present."[79] On one hand, these principles might pertain to laws that continue to be valid. For example, in his *Justinian, or the New Law* (1560), Baudouin sought to separate out those aspects of Roman law that were of mere "antiquarian interest" relating only to the history of the times from what possessed continuing "legal authority."[80] As a sign of how Roman law, historically understood, might furnish principles of continued relevance, Baudouin's response to Calvin's anonymously published attack on George Cassander's (1513–1566) irenic *De officio pii* (1561), in which Calvin erroneously attacked Baudouin as the author and accused him of being an "unreliable mediator" in religious matters and a Nicodemite to boot, took the form of a commentary on Roman law governing libel.[81] On the other hand, these principles might refer to ways in which past legislation, policies, or events might serve as models for the present. In his important work treating the ecclesiastical and secular legislation of Constantine the Great (1556) and his *History of the Disputation of Carthage* (1566), Baudouin noted examples for resolving or at least addressing the present religious discord.[82] Baudouin's vision of using the past to address the religious problems of his day through concord and religious dialogue culminated in this latter work, in which he compared the disputation between Donatist and Catholic

---

[78] Backus, "Roman Catholic Lives," 32–46.

[79] Lyon, "Baudouin, Flacius," 270.

[80] Kelley, *Foundations*, 120; François Baudouin, *Iustinianus, sive de iure novo, commentariorum libri IIII* (Basel: J. Oporinus, 1560). On this text and Baudouin's hermeneutic in general, see Hans Erich Troje, "'Peccatum Triboniani': Zur Dialektik der 'Interpretatio duplex' bei François Baudouin," *Studia et Documenta Historiae et Iuris* 36 (1970): 341–58; cf. Erbe, *François Baudouin*, 104–5.

[81] Calvin's treatise is *Responsio ad versipellem quendam mediatorem* ([Geneva]: J. Crespin, 1561), CO 9: 525–60; Baudouin responded in François Baudouin, *Ad leges de famosis libellis et de calumniatoribus* (Paris: A. Wechelus, 1562). See Turchetti, *Concordia o Tolleranza*, 342–47.

[82] Erbe, *François Baudouin*, 93–94. Duquesne views this work as the beginning of his evolution away from Calvin ("François Baudouin et la Réforme," 89), although cf. Erbe, 94n70. On François Baudouin, *Constantinus Magnus, sive de Constantini Imp. legibus ecclesiasticis atque civilibus, commentariorum libri duo* (Basel: J. Oporinus, 1556), see Turchetti, *Concordia o Tolleranza*, 103–22.

bishops convened by the emperor Honorarius in 411 to the recent colloquies of Regensburg (1541) and Poissy (1561) in order to determine the best model for establishing religious dialogue and achieving church unity.[83] Invoking as an interpretive principle the "similitude of times," Baudouin was able thus to combine a strong interest in accurate reconstruction of the past with a method for using the past to address present concerns. He was, as Backus says, "a firm believer in . . . the capacity of historical situations, if correctly analyzed and studied in context, to yield a message that would make history instructive for the future."[84]

Third, distinguishing Baudouin's way of conceiving of how the past can furnish models for later generations is his call for the disciplines of law and history to work together to achieve the dual goals of accurate reconstruction of the past based on critically examined evidence and identification of lasting principles culled from history for the present. In his advice to Flacius and the centuriators, Baudouin suggested that before discussing the "internal development" of ecclesiastical doctrines and ceremonies, "church history should first make use of legal treatises and secular histories in order to contextualize the status and condition of the church within each century."[85] Similarly, his wide-ranging work on Roman law suggests that, in contrast to Connan, for example, he perceived the main problem of the *Corpus iuris civilis* not to be the disorderly arrangement but rather the limitation of its scope. In other words, what was wanting in understanding Roman law was the broader context that would take into account Roman legislation not contained in the *Corpus* and the conditions of the times from which all laws originated.[86] These ideas about taking a broader historical view to Roman law were fleshed out in lectures on historical method that he held in Heidelberg beginning in 1559 alongside his regular lectures on the *Digest* and the *Codex*.[87] Building on insights expressed already in his 1555 inaugural address at the Academy in Strasbourg and developed presumably in these lectures, in his *De institutione historiae universae* Baudouin expounds his vision for what Kelley has termed a "permanent alliance" between law and history, fused together into "a single

---

[83] Erbe, *François Bauduin*, 163–65.
[84] Backus, "Roman Catholic Lives," 34; cf. Lyon, "Baudouin, Flacius," 256. Baudouin refers to Cicero's idea of history as "magistra vitae" in *De institutione historiae universae*, 16.
[85] Lyon, "Baudouin, Flacius," 254; cf. 262–63; Erbe, *François Bauduin*, 266.
[86] See Franklin, *Jean Bodin*, 42–46.
[87] Erbe, *François Bauduin*, 109; on Baudouin's topical approach to the *Digest* and *Codex* in these lectures, see 99–101.

cultural science."[88] Ideally such an "integral" or perfect history would be universal in the sense of including not just Roman laws but also ecclesiastical history and legislation as well as the history and laws of the Hebrews and other cultures, although it does not include for the present purposes what Baudouin designates natural history.[89] Only such a contextualizing universal history could reveal the guiding principles for proper human action in the public arena.

Many of the lessons Baudouin was drawing from the past pertained to the religious crisis of his day and include not only the examples for reestablishing religious concord or unity mentioned earlier but also a principled rejection of coercion of heretics and the death penalty for heresy gleaned from his examination of the religious legislation of imperial Rome.[90] This points to a final, noteworthy element of his proposal, namely, that universal history, as he understands it, has an important theological dimension.[91] In fact, he begins his treatise on history by articulating a view of divine providence that sounds very similar to Calvin's doctrine: Humans have been created by God and placed into the amphitheater of this world in order to be spectators not only of things presented to their eyes but also of those things comprehended by memory; indeed, they should be not just spectators but actors and even judges on this stage.[92] Moreover, Baudouin, like Calvin, holds that God's providence in human affairs is a more pronounced revelation of providence, although he seems more optimistic than the latter about the human ability to make use of this testimony: "For here [in history] no less than there [in nature] we will be drenched in sense and wonder of things divine if we are not blind and stupid. Indeed, God attends and governs here to a much greater degree."[93] Kelley has thus designated him "a Christian humanist in the style of Erasmus" and suggested that it was in fact his experience of religious crisis with its attendant political pressure that propelled him from a "naïve humanist view" to his mature "reflections upon the nature and method of

[88] Kelley, *Foundations*, 122; for details, see 130–36; cf. also Franklin, *Jean Bodin*, 46. On the inaugural address in Strasbourg, published as François Baudouin, *Iuris civilis schola Argentinensis* (Strasbourg: W. Rihel, 1555), see Erbe, *François Bauduin*, 82–85.

[89] Baudouin, *De institutione historiae universae*, 2–3.

[90] François Baudouin, *Ad edicta veterum principum Romanorum de Christianis* (Basel: J. Oporinus, 1557); cf. Mario Turchetti, "Calvin face aux tenants de la concorde (moyenneurs) et aux partisans de la tolérance (castellionistes)," in *Calvin et ses contemporains*, ed. Olivier Millet (Geneva: Droz, 1998), 47.

[91] Erbe, *François Bauduin*, 109; cf. Troje, " 'Peccatum Triboniani,' " 356.

[92] Baudouin, *De institutione historiae universae*, 1; cf. Franklin, *Jean Bodin*, 116–17.

[93] Baudouin, *De institutione historiae universae*, 5.

history."[94] Here we might add that it was also during his years of growing alienation from Calvin and his reform that Baudouin's views on the joining of jurisprudence, history, and theology in universal history took shape, first in Strasbourg and then in Heidelberg. This alliance manifests itself on a number of levels, ranging from the subject matter to the goal of historical investigation. Universal history thus involves a synthesis of sacred and secular history and divine and human law, achieved through an alliance of critical juristic and historical methods. Also, via the principle of the similitude of times it yields principles of lasting import and relevance, in particular, addressed to the religious situation in Baudouin's day. Finally, and most importantly perhaps, it has as its goal the recognition of divine providence.[95]

Baudouin's conception of universal history may have been the first but was certainly not the only nor was it the most influential theory of history and historical method to emerge in the middle of the sixteenth century. One might mention two important, virtually simultaneous proposals that sprang up from the same seedbed of legal humanism. One is Bodin's *Method*, which advanced a theory of history that Kelley has described as both more universal and more eclectic than Bauduoin's.[96] A different kind of approach manifested itself in Pasquier's encyclopedic *Recherches de la France* (Researches in French history and literature), the first volume of which was published in 1560. Less overtly theoretical than Baudouin's and Bodin's treatises and focused on French history and institutions, the *Researches* were no less concerned with questions of evidence and other issues of historical method; this lifelong project was, moreover, also forged in the crucible of religious conflict.[97] These three jurists-turned-historians disagreed on many things, including whether human history is a story of fall or progress and the role of divine providence in its course.[98] Yet their projects represent a common effort to further and broaden the lessons of historical jurisprudence in order to develop a more scientific approach to the past, even when they proposed different ways for achieving this.

These new approaches to history on the foundation of jurisprudence testify to a broad interest among Calvin's contemporaries and countrymen in a set of issues and strategies, echoes of which can be heard in the *Mosaic*

[94] Kelley, *Foundations*, 122.
[95] Baudouin, *De institutione historiae universae*, 9.
[96] Kelley, *Foundations*, 136.
[97] On Pasquier, see Kelley, *Foundations*, 271–300; Huppert, *Idea of Perfect History*, 28–71.
[98] For a comparison of the approaches of Baudouin, Bodin, and Pasquier, see Huppert, *Idea of Perfect History*, 59–61.

Harmony: concern for the reliability of the historical account and the testimony of the historian; a comparative perspective on the material that
assumes the particularity of individual cultures and their distinct traditions
and seeks to establish these through contextualization; a simultaneous interest in uncovering principles from history that transcend their own context and can through the similitude of times serve as permanent guides for
human action; a cooperative endeavor between the disciplines of jurisprudence and history; and, finally, a theological dimension profoundly shaping
history itself and the task of the historian. Although one would not consider
Calvin's commentary a genre of universal history and certainly not a theory
of history, it reflects contemporary assumptions about these matters and
through its own eclectic and unusual approach it embodies these to a certain
degree.

His approach, at the very least, reflects the orientation of and in all likelihood set a pattern for later efforts to deal with pentateuchal material by other
Reformed jurists and theologians.[99] In 1577 Beza published an examination
of Mosaic legislation, which he proposed to order thematically by grouping
the laws into the categories of moral, ceremonial, and political laws and distributing them among the commandments of the Decalogue.[100] In the same
year the Reformed jurist, pastor, and theologian Lambert Danaeus (1530–
1595), then teaching in Geneva, published his *Ethics*, in which he also engaged Calvin's use of the moral, civil, and judicial division of the laws and,
moreover, undertook a thorough comparison between the Mosaic legislation and the *Corpus iuris civilis*. Danaeus drew on a fourth-century collation
of Roman and Mosaic law published in 1573 with a commentary by Pierre
Pithou (1539–1596), a French Reformed jurist who, like Baudouin, sought
an alliance between law and history.[101] Christoph Strohm has suggested that
all of these aimed to recover a more robust and positive application of the
judicial laws of the Old Testament for current law and ethics. The extent to
which this is in continuity with or marks rather a drawing back from Calvin's
own historicizing approach invites further investigation.

---

[99] On the material touched on here, see Strohm, *Ethik*, 264–74.

[100] Theodore Beza, *Lex Dei moralis, ceremonialis, et politica, ex libris Mosis excerpta, et in certas
classes distributa* ([Geneva]: P. de Saint-André, 1577); see de Boer, *Genevan School*, 183–84.

[101] On Pithou, see Kelley, *Foundations*, 241–70; see also de Boer, *Genevan School*, 184.

Conclusion

While the question of the full impact of Calvin's pioneering approach to the interpretation of the last four books of the Pentateuch must be left for another day, the implications of his unusual method for understanding his own historicizing interpretation of the Bible can be briefly summarized in closing. First, these findings suggest that Calvin's historicizing hermeneutic and exegetical work need to be viewed not only through the lens of the history of biblical interpretation but also in light of the broader efforts to deal with the legacies of past ages undertaken by Calvin's contemporaries, particularly in the area of early modern legal history. Surely the integration of legal and historical material in this particular commentary makes for especially pronounced connections to developments in contemporary fields of law and history; nevertheless this perspective suggests a fruitful context for viewing and understanding the deep historical sensibilities Calvin evidences in his interpretation of the Bible more generally—an appreciation for the integrity of the past that often distinguishes his readings from those of other exegetes.

Second, the novelty of Calvin's approach in his *Mosaic Harmony* also demonstrates and invites further reflection on a subtle development in his biblical hermeneutic. In seeking to explain Calvin's rearrangement of the biblical material for his commentary, Blacketer and de Boer have rightly underscored how pedagogical concerns justified Calvin's break with his customary pattern of continuous, verse-by-verse explanation of the text. In addition, de Boer notes that Calvin introduces the idea of a distinction between "history" and "doctrine" in a *congrégation* on John 1 in 1550 as a way of distinguishing the greater emphasis in John on doctrine from the greater prominence given to history in the other three canonical gospels.[102] In invoking this distinction again in explaining the reasons for his rearrangement of the material in the commentary and in structuring his presentation along these lines, Calvin reiterates the idea of "history" and "doctrine" as two integral but also distinct components of scripture. The interpreter needs to grasp the difference between them, for while both history and doctrine are relevant for later generations of the faithful, the examples of history are not always and certainly not immediately applicable, whereas the doctrine or the laws of faith may have more universal and immediate application—though these, too, frequently need to be understood within a particular historical context

---

[102] De Boer, *Genevan School*, 174; cf. CO 47: 467–68.

before their meaning for later believers can be apprehended. Calvin's commentary on the last four books of the Pentateuch testifies to the increasingly precise articulation and application of this principle in his mature exegesis.

Beyond these implications for understanding his biblical hermeneutic and possible development within his historicizing approach to scripture, Calvin's interest in more formalized approaches to accessing historical knowledge to which this commentary bears witness opens a window to consideration of Calvin's views on the historical enterprise more generally. Although Calvin did not write a treatise on historical method or a universal history, he did weigh in on two of the most significant works of the new Protestant historiography of his day. In the 1540s, John Sleidan (1506–1566) solicited Calvin's advice on writing what was to become the first history of the Protestant church, which Calvin supplied, along with material for the project.[103] In February 1557, Calvin responded somewhat belatedly to an inquiry from Casper von Nidbruck (ca. 1525–1557) about the plan for the Magdeburg Centuries.[104] Though Calvin's reply to Nidbruck arrived too late to have any influence on the project and is far less detailed than the earlier letters from Baudouin to Flacius on the same matter, his comments on and suggestions for the project address key questions for contemporary history writing. He applauds the proposal of the centuriators, but modestly apologizes that he is not really the right person to provide a detailed assessment of such an ambitious project. All the same, he raises some key criticisms concerning the approach. On the one hand, he questions the distribution of the volumes by centuries as unpractical, arguing that sometimes a single decade has more significant material than an entire century. On the other, he thinks that the topical organization within each century is useful but ultimately can lead to needless repetition that will tire and bore the reader. He suggests instead that the author not hold slavishly to the order of individual topics, but instead keep related events together for the sake of a clearer presentation. Calvin's judgment about the utility of the division into centuries and the *loci* ordering of historical events within centuries stands in stark contrast to Baudouin's approval of these two strategies in his letters to Flacius.[105] Finally, Calvin urges that a

---

[103] John Sleidan, *De statu religionis et reipublicae, Carolo Quinto Caesare, commentarii* (Strasbourg: W. Rihel, 1555); see Alexandra Kess, *Johann Sleidan and the Protestant Vision of History* (Burlington, VT: Ashgate, 2008), 2, 48–51.

[104] CO 20: 448–50. See Barbara Pitkin, "Calvin, Theology, and History," *Seminary Ridge Review* 12, no. 2 (2010): 1–16.

[105] Heinz Scheible, *Die Entstehung der Magdeburger Zenturien: Ein Beitrag zur Geschichte der historiographischen Methode* (Gütersloh: Gütersloher Verlagshaus Gerd Mohn, 1966), 48.

chapter outlining the purpose and intention of the authors be placed at the beginning to guide the reader.

As this chapter has demonstrated, all three of these considerations—concern to avoid artificial structuring of historical material, clear presentation that will not tire and bore the reader, and a guiding and explicit purpose for the narrative structure—decisively shaped Calvin's innovative approach to the last four books of the Pentateuch when the project began in the Genevan *congrégations* just two years later. The impact of this novel method was initially felt by the participants in these meetings, which constituted the workshop in which Calvin crafted his unusual commentary. Yet these participants were no passive auditors, but rather active contributors to a dialogue about the best way to approach, organize, and derive meaning from this body of material. There is almost no way to assess the impact of Calvin's approach on his dialogue partners, although the next chapter will explore a related issue: how Calvin as a preacher sought to affect his auditors. For now, it is worth underscoring the communal nature of the process of historical reflection underlying the *Mosaic Harmony*—like that which yielded the Magdeburg Centuries—as one more way in which Calvin's most unusual biblical commentary can be seen in light of the creative and experimental proposals for interpreting the past that emerged over the course of the sixteenth century.

8

The Consolation of History in Calvin's Sermons on Second Samuel

Introduction

On Saturday, May 23, 1562, John Calvin ascended the pulpit in the cathedral of Saint Pierre in Geneva and inaugurated a series of eighty-seven sermons on Second Samuel.[1] From his opening words, he underscored the exemplary character of the actions and events related in this biblical book and sought to shape his community's response to the civil war raging in France by urging them to imitate David. Upon hearing of the death of Saul and Jonathan on the battlefield, David humbled himself, fasted, and prayed. Calvin urged his congregation:

> We really do need this admonition, for we can see how God is afflicting this poor world today. Even people who are strangers to us are still related to us, because we are all made in the image of God and have a common nature, which should be a mutual bond of love and brotherhood. Then there is a far closer union between us and the suffering believers who are scattered here and there in all churches that God has chastened on every side. Indeed, we see troubles everywhere: we see fires burning; we hear that the throats of poor innocent people have been cut; that they have been subjected to mockery and contempt, and that they are being led to the slaughter. We see the enemies of truth ready to annihilate everything, and we do not know what God is intending to do. Nevertheless, see how his sword is unsheathed. The fire, as I have said, is kindled and we do not know how far it will burn.[2]

---

[1] On the location, see Elsie McKee, "Calvin and His Colleagues as Pastors: Some New Insights into the Collegial Ministry of Word and Sacraments," in *Calvinus Praeceptor Ecclesiae: Papers of the International Congress on Calvin Research*, ed. Herman J. Selderhuis (Geneva: Droz, 2004), 19–20, 28.

[2] John Calvin, *Predigten über das 2. Buch Samuelis*, ed. Hanns Rückert (Neukirchen: Neukirchener Verlag, 1961), SC 1: 6. Partial English translation as John Calvin, *Sermons on 2 Samuel: Chapters 1–13*, ed. and trans. Douglas Kelly (Carlisle, PA: Banner of Truth, 1992), 10; hereafter *Sermons on Second Samuel*. Calvin uses the image of the unsheathed sword and burning fires repeatedly throughout these sermons. It likely derives from Ezekiel, which uses the imagery in chapters 5, 20, and 21. Calvin

Calvin, the Bible, and History. Barbara Pitkin, Oxford University Press (2020). © Oxford University Press.
DOI: 10.1093/oso/9780190093273.001.0001

Over the next eight months, the political subject matter of Second Samuel provided Calvin the preacher with abundant opportunities to address questions of fundamental concern to the inhabitants of Geneva during the first war of religion. In the sacred history of David's interactions and battles with Saul's supporters, Abner and Ishboseth, and the later rebellion of David's own son, Absalom, Calvin found larger lessons about when war is justified and when it is not, the reasons for war, and proper conduct during wartime.

In his pioneering study of Geneva's involvement in the events leading up to the French wars, Robert Kingdon demonstrated the ways in which the city—despite its professed neutrality—was heavily involved in the promotion and spread of Calvinism in France and, ultimately, in the first war itself. He notes, "though the appearance of neutrality was maintained, the government allowed and at times encouraged the sending of small groups of men, large sums of money, and substantial quantities of gunpowder to the forces fighting for the Calvinist faith"—all with the knowledge and tacit approval of the town's pastors.[3] Publicly, however, Geneva's officials and especially the ministers advocated more spiritual means of supporting the Huguenot armies. Upon receipt of the declaration of war issued by the Huguenot leader Louis, the prince of Condé (1530–1569), in April 1562, the town council wrote to Bern and explained its "plan to redouble prayers and increase sermon attendance in order to invoke the aid of the Almighty for this cause." The Bernese responded and urged "the Genevans to order even more prayers."[4] Without discounting in the least Geneva's clandestine material support, in order to grasp the full extent of the town's reaction to the war, one needs to attend as well to the heightened spiritual focus adopted as a response. Recent studies have demonstrated the connections between Calvin's exegetical lectures and commentaries and the situation in France from 1555 to 1563, but the sermons in particular offer an important resource for exploring the spiritual response to the war, or at the very least, the ideals, mindsets, and emotions that the town's principal preacher, Calvin,

---

preached sermons on Ezekiel from late 1552 to early 1554 and began lecturing on Ezekiel just as he was finishing up his sermons on Second Samuel in January 1563. On Calvin's interpretation of Ezekiel, see Erik A. de Boer, *John Calvin on the Visions of Ezekiel: Historical and Hermeneutical Studies in John Calvin's "sermons inédits," Especially on Ezek. 36–48* (Leiden: Brill, 2004).

[3] Robert M. Kingdon, *Geneva and the Coming of the Wars of Religion in France, 1555–1563* (Geneva: Droz, 1956), 124.

[4] Kingdon, *Geneva*, 116.

endeavored to evoke.[5] In his sermons especially Calvin sought to shape the response of ordinary Genevans to the events unfolding in their midst by appealing to biblical history to illuminate the present.

Scholars have examined the sermons on Second Samuel for insight into Calvin's views on civil disobedience and the right of private resistance, arguing that they signal a subtle but unmistakable radicalizing of his earlier position on active resistance that foreshadows directions subsequently developed by monarchomach theorists such as Theodore Beza (1519–1605) and François Hotman (1524–1590).[6] While the broader relationship between Calvin and Beza has been the subject of many studies, less explored are the connections between Calvin and Hotman. Virtually all of the scholarship on Calvin and his fellow jurist, religious refugee, and erstwhile secretary has focused on this important question of civil resistance. Although some have used Calvin's Second Samuel sermons to argue for continuity between Calvin's and Hotman's views on this issue, scholars disagree over the extent to which Calvin's views evolved or not over the course of his career and whether he ultimately extended the right of active resistance to tyranny from lower magistrates to private citizens and thus paved the way for later Huguenot political theory. Ralph Keen has argued against J. W. Allen, Quentin Skinner, and others that Calvin qualified his earlier position on absolute obedience. Keen draws on the 1559 *Institutes* and the sermons on First Samuel, which Calvin preached from August 1561 to May 1562, and briefly on the lectures on Daniel published in 1561 to underscore the consistency he finds in Calvin's doctrine of political obedience.[7] In contrast, Max Engammare has

    [5] Raymond Blacketer, "The Moribund Moralist: Ethical Lessons in Calvin's Commentary on Joshua," in *The Formation of Clerical and Confessional Identities in Early Modern Europe*, ed. Wim Janse and Barbara Pitkin, *Dutch Review of Church History* 85 (2005) (Leiden: Brill, 2006), 149–68; Jon Balserak, *Establishing the Remnant Church in France: Calvin's Lectures on the Minor Prophets, 1556–1559* (Leiden: Brill, 2011); Barbara Pitkin, "Calvin and Politics According to the Mosaic Harmony (1563 | 1564): Text, Paratext, and Context," in *Calvin frater in Domino*, ed. Arnold Huijgen and Karin Maag (Göttingen: Vandenhoeck & Ruprecht, 2020), 37–56.

    [6] See Friedrich Kleyser, "Calvin und Franz Hotman," in *Geschichtliche Kräfte und Entscheidungen: Festschrift zum fünfundsechzigsten Geburtstage von Otto Becker*, ed. Martin Göhring and Alexander Scharff (Wiesbaden: Franz Steiner, 1954), 47–64; Willem Nijenhuis, "The Limits of Civil Disobedience in Calvin's Latest Known Sermons: The Development of His Ideas of the Right of Civil Resistance," in *Ecclesia Reformata: Studies on the Reformation* (Leiden: Brill, 1994), 2: 73–97. Douglas Kelly summarizes some of the themes found in them in "Varied Themes in Calvin's 2 Samuel Sermons and the Development of His Thought," in *Calvinus Sincerioris Religionis Vindex: Calvin as Protector of the Purer Religion*, ed. Wilhelm H. Neuser and Brian G. Armstrong (Kirksville, MO: Sixteenth Century Journal, 1997), 209–24. On Hotman, see Donald R. Kelley, *François Hotman: A Revolutionary's Ordeal* (Princeton, NJ: Princeton University Press, 1973).

    [7] Ralph Keen, "The Limits of Power and Obedience in the Later Calvin," *Calvin Theological Journal* 27 (1992): 252–76.

argued for more continuity between Calvin's right of resistance articulated in his sermons and the theories of the monarchomachs, including Hotman.[8] Part of the difficulty, of course, is determining not only what Calvin wrote or said publicly about the issue but also his motives and activities in regard to the war behind the scene, an issue opened up by Kingdon in his *Geneva and the Coming of the Wars of Religion*.

Nonetheless, insight—however complex—into Calvin's ideas about civil resistance is not all that the sermons on Second Samuel reveal about Calvin's attitudes toward the contemporary historical-political situation. Consideration of some of these other elements can reveal much not only about Calvin's political thought but also about his response to the war in general and, importantly, his engagement with the biblical past to make sense of that experience. His efforts to shape his congregation's intellectual and emotional response to the crisis constituted a potentially potent force in Geneva's involvement in the war and also, I suggest, represented a theological strategy that reveals a distinct historical vision that the experience of the war itself reinforced. One application of that historical vision can be seen in a little-known text by Calvin's disciple Hotman.

The meaning and normativity of the past was one of the most pressing intellectual and practical issues of the age in which Calvin and Hotman lived; the outbreak of repeated religious warfare in France and elsewhere only rendered that issue more urgent.[9] Viewing Calvin and Hotman through the lens of reading and interpreting the past instead of the more familiar context of political theory yields insights not only into their own conceptions of history but also into their efforts to use the past to shape Protestant responses to and memory of the events unfolding in their midst. This concluding chapter focuses on two works produced during the early stages of the French religious wars that shed light on this shared endeavor: Calvin's sermons on Second Samuel, preached during the first war (1562–1563) and Hotman's *Consolatio è sacris litteris* (Consolation drawn from sacred scripture), composed during

[8] Max Engammare, "Calvin monarchomaque? Du soupçon à l'argument," *Archiv für Reformationsgeschichte* 89 (1998): 207–26.

[9] On the development of historical thought in the sixteenth century, see, for example, Anthony Grafton, *What Was History? The Art of History in Early Modern Europe* (Cambridge, UK: Cambridge University Press, 2007); Donald R. Kelley, *Foundations of Modern Historical Scholarship: Language, Law, and History in the French Renaissance* (New York: Columbia University Press, 1970). On the role of religious schism in historical thought, see Irena Backus, *Historical Method and Confessional Identity in the Era of the Reformation (1378–1615)* (Leiden: Brill, 2003); Geoffrey Dipple, *"Just as in the Time of the Apostles": Uses of History in the Radical Reformation* (Kitchener, Ontario: Pandora Press, 2005).

the third war (1568–1570).[10] These two mid-sixteenth-century journeys into Israel's history yield important insight into an as yet relatively unexplored dimension of Reformed reactions to the religious wars, namely, the uses of sacred history to make sense of the present crisis.[11]

Calvin's Sermons on Second Samuel

At the outset it is important to note that the use of the past to illuminate the present was a common tactic in Calvin's preaching and—as previous chapters in this volume have demonstrated—in his exegesis in general. Moreover, Calvin had been addressing the tumultuous religio-political situation in contemporary France and applying his historicizing hermeneutic in lectures, sermons, and commentaries at the end of the 1550s and in the early 1560s.[12] However, the sermons on Second Samuel are the only sermons preached in their entirety after the outbreak of actual warfare, and, especially in light of their subject matter, they constitute an intriguing source for assessing Calvin's use of the sacred past in light of the present crisis.

Throughout the sermons Calvin has two primary concerns: first, to explain the events related in the text and, second, to help his auditors understand what they should learn from them. While many of the lessons are of a general spiritual or moral nature and concern attitudes and behaviors that would befit a Christian living at any time, Calvin also makes explicit and frequent references to the violence of the present war and his listeners' experience of it. His ability to draw lessons from a historical consideration of the events in Second Samuel rests on assumptions he holds about the overall purpose of scripture, the kind of history it relates, and how to distinguish elements of perpetual significance from anachronistic aspects related to the history of Israel. Consideration of how these three assumptions manifest themselves in his preaching provides a window for viewing his use of the text to address the crisis of present history.

---

[10] François Hotman, *Consolatio è sacris litteris: Nunc demum edita* (Lyon [i.e., Geneva]: F. Le Preux, 1593). This treatise was published posthumously by Hotman's son Jean.

[11] Danièle Fischer has examined the historical elements in Calvin's sermons, including those on Second Samuel; my analysis concurs with much of hers, although I find her claim that history, for Calvin, has an allegorical sense to be an inaccurate formulation. See Danièle Fischer, "L'Élément historique dans la predication de Calvin: Un aspect original de l'homilétique du Réformateur," *Revue d'histoire et de philosophie religieuses* 64 (1984): 376.

[12] See, e.g., Blacketer, "The Moribund Moralist"; Balserak, *Establishing the Remnant Church*; Pitkin, "Calvin and Politics."

THE CONSOLATION OF HISTORY 201

For Calvin, the purpose of scripture is to provide instruction, and, as previous chapters have shown, one of the primary ways that its historical narratives achieve this aim is through the use of example. In Calvin's sermons, David reprises his role as example for present believers. The characters in Second Samuel, and especially David, serve as both positive and negative role models for Reformed Christian behavior. For example, when commenting in a June sermon on how David seeks the counsel of God about returning to Judah (2 Sam. 2:1), Calvin tells his listeners that they, too, need to seek God's guidance, which will come to them through scripture and the blessing of the Spirit: "So let us be aware that we must diligently read and have our ears wide open from morning until evening to the exposition of Holy Scripture; in addition, unless God gives us his Spirit, we will still be confused, as experience teaches us." He also stresses the importance of paying attention during sermons in order to profit from God's word: "There are many who will return from the sermon much more ignorant than if they had not come, because they are only interested in ceremony and come out of duty. They even bring books with them to make a good show. But they only mutter without any understanding, and derive no profit from the word of God, because they have not applied their spirit to it."[13]

At other times the biblical characters provide decidedly bad role models that should be shunned rather than imitated. Calvin thinks that David, after a good start, shows excessive grief at the end of chapter 1, and he warns against following David's example. In a sermon on chapter 2, Calvin criticizes Abner and Joab for seeming to make light of battle and treating it like a game (2 Sam. 2:14). Though war, he notes, is sometimes unavoidable, it is nonetheless to be detested, and excessive violence should be avoided. Calvin then bemoans the conduct of some of those fighting in France:

And moreover, when we are involved [in war], we must be very careful to pray to God that he will govern the hearts of his own—for today we see once again that in the army marshaled under the name of Jesus Christ and of the Gospel, there are many rascals among the troops. Some of them are there to strip and pillage, and others to commit many outrages; some to satisfy their appetite for vengeance; others to murder no matter how; and still others for publicity.[14]

[13] SC 1: 29; *Sermons on Second Samuel*, 51.
[14] SC 1: 42; *Sermons on Second Samuel*, 72.

Reports of violence and pillaging among Huguenot troops—some of it involving Reformed ministers sent out from Geneva—had been reaching the city in recent months, and Calvin had written a blistering letter to the ministers of Lyon in May chastising them for allowing and even participating in violence in the course of the Protestant takeover of the city.[15] Such behavior was not limited to the common soldiery; in a later sermon he notes that one sees often how contemporary princes engage in pillage, murder, and the like, even toward their own subjects.[16]

Calvin's vision of scripture's pedagogical purpose infuses his presentation of biblical history in these sermons with a patently presentist focus. While he clearly treats the narrative of Second Samuel as a chronicle of actual events, he often comments that a particular episode was written down especially "for us" or "for our benefit" and contends that it is through preaching that its effect is felt. A particularly direct statement of this appears in his sermon on the way that God leads David to victory over the Philistines (2 Sam. 5:17–25):

> We see, then, how God has placed here before our eyes a mirror of his admirable providence . . . This was not written for David, nor for those of his time. It is for our use and instruction. God certainly did all that is quoted here for the salvation of his people at that time, but to whom is the Holy Scripture addressed? It is not for the dead, therefore, it is for us.[17]

Calvin appeals here to one of his favorite metaphors for scripture—the mirror—to link past events to the present and underscore God's unrelenting care for his people. To illustrate how God now restrains the enemies of the church when believers are weak just as he once frustrated the Philistines when David was vulnerable, Calvin vividly recalls the situation in France in the mid-1530s, possibly in the aftermath of the Placards Affair (October 1534). He describes how God blinded the eyes of those intent on abolishing the church of God so that they were not able to exterminate the believers.[18] "Therefore," he concludes, "we have to read this history not only to consider the narrative but also to profit from it ourselves when we compare it to all the experiences that God has given us of his liberality."[19]

---

[15] Letter of May 9, 1562, CO 19: 409–11; see Kingdon, *Geneva*, 110–11.
[16] SC 1: 244; cf. *Sermons on Second Samuel*, 417.
[17] SC 1: 121; cf. *Sermons on Second Samuel*, 210.
[18] SC 1: 122; cf. *Sermons on Second Samuel*, 211.
[19] SC 1: 123; cf. *Sermons on Second Samuel*, 212.

This last comment points to a further significant element in Calvin's understanding of how scripture attains its purpose. To understand the lessons of scripture, one needs not only to study it or hear it preached and have the illumination of the Holy Spirit; that, Calvin remarks, provides only the "pure doctrine," knowledge of which must be confirmed by actual experience:

> Let us always march forward and let us advance in the knowledge of God. However, let us also note that experience and practice increase our knowledge, which we will not have in the simple word of God. For example, when God tells us that he wants to be our Father, we receive it and do not doubt that he will make us feel the reality. However, we have only the pure doctrine, and we must add faith to what God proposes, which all may be hidden from us . . . Therefore, whenever God has spoken to us, we ought to be persuaded and resolved that his word is infallible truth. Nevertheless, we may not have experienced how he wants to help us, how he cares for us and is our Father, in order to keep us safe. We may not have felt it. Well, if he sends us afflictions and then, after we have called on him, he shows mercy towards us, and the outcome proves that our resting on his promises was not in vain. This is how we know, namely through the experienced outcome, according to God's giving us the means to do so.[20]

Present events—and in this case, the experience of wartime affliction—enable a fuller grasp of scriptural teaching by causing the faithful to feel the truth of God's persistent care. The movement between past and present in Calvin's sermons is a two-way street, with the history of Israel providing examples for the present and present events confirming the doctrinal lesson gleaned from the sacred past, shaping believers' minds and hearts.

Calvin's assumptions about the pedagogical purpose of scripture are closely connected to his views on the kind of history that can be found in scripture. For Calvin, the biblical account is in the first place selective, relating only what is necessary for human salvation. He tells his listeners that there were once many other written accounts, such as the book from which David quotes in 2 Samuel 2. While these would no doubt be useful, God has allowed these fuller histories to be lost to punish human laziness.[21] Nevertheless, the sacred history that remains is clearly superior to secular history, precisely

---

[20] SC 1: 116; cf. *Sermons on Second Samuel*, 201.
[21] SC 1: 12; cf. *Sermons on Second Samuel*, 19–20.

because of the unique character of its effective instruction. Commenting on a verse that attributes David's military success to God, Calvin draws this contrast between sacred and profane accounts of the past:

> We see how the sacred history is not like all the chronicles and profane histories that have been compiled by unbelievers. For in those, a great deal will be said about the braveries and virtues of men, and then at the same time about their good fortune. The pagans certainly knew that if fate were not in their favor, then there would be no use in industry, in force, in virtue and in everything that one can do. Therefore, they clearly confessed that it was necessary for God to bless and for victories to come from on high, but only in a confused manner. For they still held on to this good fortune, which seemed to be a goddess to them, and they thought that they could keep her up their sleeve . . . But we see how this [account] is not merely a simply cold and useless recitation which allows the braveries of David to be known. Rather, it offers at the same time instruction so as to make us follow it. The point is that we, knowing that the hand of God guided him, will desire the same thing.[22]

For Calvin, sacred history has a purpose superior to that of the accounts of profane writers, which enables it alone to speak to the present and, indeed, with the illumination of the Spirit and the confirmation of experience, not merely to *impart* information about the past but to *imprint* the lessons of biblical history on human hearts and shape their desires and motivations.

In addition to awakening his listeners' desire for divine guidance in their own times, Calvin also advocates a wide variety of specific behaviors relating to wartime conduct. These include not engaging in unnecessary violence, pillaging, and bloodshed—as we saw earlier—and also doing good to enemies and trying to win them over, engaging in prayer and begging for mercy, and leaving to the proper authorities the task of purging idols. At the same time, however, he urges his listeners to be willing to punish evil and root out scandal, pulling up the bad weeds when God gives grace and liberty to do so.[23] Yet there are also aspects of the biblical narrative that he judges have no immediate relevance for sixteenth-century Christians, although they were perhaps perfectly acceptable in ancient Israel: for example, dancing, musical

---

[22] SC 1: 241–42; cf. *Sermons on Second Samuel*, 414.
[23] See, for example, SC 1: 128, 107; cf. *Sermons on Second Samuel*, 222, 186.

instruments, and the use of elephants in warfare. A final consideration in this section is thus how Calvin distinguishes anachronistic aspects like these that pertain only to the history of Israel from elements of perpetual significance.

For Calvin, the key to making this distinction lies in the same principle that makes sacred history unique: in contrast to profane history, biblical history gives effective instruction because it has a typological character. Calvin works with a traditional understanding of the Old Testament—in particular the reign of David—as a type of the kingdom of Christ. As previous chapters have shown, his use of typology involves a vision of the past that has its own historical integrity, while at the same time, for him, the past is intimately or even substantively joined to the present through divine providence and the underlying unity of sacred history. Calvin's characterization of the double grace of justification and sanctification as distinct but not separate is perhaps a helpful analogy for envisioning the relationship between what are for him two dispensations of one divine covenant, two periods of the history of the one church whose decisive turning point is the appearance of Jesus Christ and the inauguration of his kingdom.[24] Just as justification and sanctification are each distinct moments in the spiritual life of every believer that together constitute the fullness of the effects of faith, the two dispensations of Old and New Testament are distinct but inseparable periods in the historical life of the church and are both essential components of its redemption.

Just as Calvin lifted up David living under the old dispensation as an example for the faith of the believers of his day in his commentary on the Psalms (discussed in chapter 4), Calvin's version of the typological reading here likewise allows him both to uphold the integrity of ancient Israel's religion and history and also to distinguish elements that are not relevant for his present situation. In David's day, the faithful apprehended the kingdom of Christ through the reign of David and his descendants, as well as through the law, the prophets, and religious ceremonies, all of which Calvin values, even as he considers some practices to be accommodations to the relative immaturity of those living before Christ. The history of Israel and its political and religious institutions pointed the ancient faithful to Christ and the biblical narrative of this history still is of great value to believers living in the age in which the substance of the type has arrived. Nevertheless, certain aspects belonging to what Calvin views as the first dispensation of religion are no longer necessary

---

[24] See *Institutes* (1559), 3.11.11. On Calvin's view of church history, see Barbara Pitkin, "Calvin, Theology, and History," *Seminary Ridge Review* 12, no. 2 (2010): 1–16.

206 CALVIN, THE BIBLE, AND HISTORY

or in force; they would be superfluous now.[25] For example, Calvin explains that the priestly ephod, which David consulted when seeking guidance from God, is no longer needed; moreover, the fact that God no longer makes himself known by revelations and prophets is no disadvantage.[26] Though sixteenth-century Reformed Christians find it strange, David's dancing before the ark was done "in accordance with the times."[27] These anachronistic elements are not simply discarded, for like the ceremonial elements of the Mosaic legislation, their spiritual function was real in their time and place. But with the coming of the reality to which they pointed, they are no longer in use, and Calvin makes his congregation aware of their superfluity so that they will focus on applying the proper lessons they should learn.

Typology also allows Calvin to establish the perpetual significance of other events by relating them as types that are fulfilled in the reign of Christ and the Christian church. One such matter in these sermons is the experience of affliction and suffering brought on by war. Again and again he stresses that this experience is perpetual, even for those living after the appearance of Christ in the flesh. In a July sermon he observes, "Although we are today in the kingdom of our Lord Jesus Christ . . . still there is no difference between us and those of olden times when it comes to battles and afflictions of the church."[28] Precisely because of this continuity in sacred history, the history of Israel functions as a mirror reflecting and imparting meaning to the present condition of the church. At the same time, the conflict occurs on a new level—the earthly conflict under the reign of David transcends itself and plays itself out in the spiritual reign of Christ. In the sermon on the battle between Abner and Joab, Calvin stresses that the war is lamentable and scandalous, but he also points out that what pertains to David's earthly kingdom is accomplished today in Christ's spiritual reign: "although those who have been baptized in his name may take up arms against one another, still we must not be appalled, as are many who do not know which way to turn." Deploring contentions and debates between Christians, they must

---

[25] SC 1: 154–55; cf. *Sermons on Second Samuel*, 266. On Calvin's views on divine accommodation, particularly with respect to Old Testament legislation and worship, see Jon Balserak, *Divinity Compromised: A Study of Divine Accommodation in the Thought of John Calvin* (Dordrecht: Springer, 2006), 67–83.

[26] Calvin discussed this part of the priestly garments in his sermon on 1 Samuel 23, but reminds his auditors of that in sermons on Second Samuel; see SC 1: 29, 125; cf. *Sermons on Second Samuel*, 50–51, 217.

[27] SC 1: 155; cf. *Sermons on Second Samuel*, 266.

[28] SC 1: 178; cf. *Sermons on Second Samuel*, 307.

nevertheless be sure to choose the right side and, if assailed, fight valiantly for God.[29] Calvin stresses that ultimately these afflictions are trials from God, and the example of David teaches that the proper response is to endure temptations patiently and resist them.

Criticizing Abner's characterization of battle as a game as presumptuous and cruel, Calvin links this attitude to the opponents of the Huguenot forces. The same, he says, can be said of the enemies of the gospel today, who "when they burn [the poor Christians], they do it, so to speak, with extra large bonfires; and everyone who comes to watch it triumphs over it, rejoicing with hearty laughter." It is as if they are joined together with Abner, and if God had not restrained them, they would have wiped entire towns and cities—Geneva included—off the map. In their "games," they employ such cruelty that human blood is "poured out like the blood of cattle and sheep at a slaughterhouse."[30] Calvin finds that Joab, too, is at fault for engaging in battle and causing bloodshed. Shunning Joab's example, he urges his listeners to detest these wars and combats which arise because of religion, and when they are constrained to fight, to keep themselves under control, never seek to shed human blood, and rather to pursue their enemies' good and peace. Urging moderation, he counsels, "Therefore, let us learn today, as far as possible to hold ourselves back, so that battles will not be cruel, and blood will not flow without good and just occasion."[31]

These examples of the lessons Calvin draws in his preaching on Second Samuel reveal something of the way that he sought to shape Reformed responses to the crisis of religious war. He presented sacred history as a distinctive record of the past that, by virtue of its unique character and purpose, spoke through its chronicle of prior events to the present situation. The events in Second Samuel justified the present war, as lamentable as it truly was, and provided examples of wartime conduct to be imitated as well as avoided. The turn to the biblical past provided moreover a unique source of consolation, acquired not merely through reading scripture and hearing it expounded in sermons, but especially, Calvin suggests, through comparing it to present experience. This historical vision, in which biblical history becomes a living and lived lesson, constitutes one of the key spiritual weapons in Geneva's

---

[29] SC 1: 38; cf. *Sermons on Second Samuel*, 66.
[30] SC 1: 41; cf. *Sermons on Second Samuel*, 71.
[31] SC 1: 43; cf. *Sermons on Second Samuel*, 74.

multifaceted response to the war, situating Reformed believers in a meaningful if tragic sequence of events experienced as the unfolding of divine providence.

Hotman's Consolation Drawn from Sacred Scripture

Like Calvin, François Hotman was a religious refugee who fled France several times for the sake of his Reformed faith. He served as Calvin's secretary in the late 1540s and spent more time in Geneva in the 1550s; throughout this period, Calvin was active in helping him secure teaching appointments, and the two men also corresponded regularly. Although Hotman was not a pastor and did not generally write works of biblical interpretation, his *Consolatio* constitutes a fitting complement to Calvin's sermons on Second Samuel. To be sure, the *Consolatio* represents a quite different approach to the biblical material, but one that was shaped by the same Reformed religious orientation and aimed at a similar goal of marshaling biblical history to generate a response to and sustain faith during a time of religious civil war. Hotman's text exemplifies the kind of historical vision applied to the situation of religious warfare that emerges in Calvin's sermons on Second Samuel. The comparison is apt not only because of their personal connections, but also because Hotman shared with Calvin training in the French school of historical jurisprudence and, in Donald Kelley's words, had "a profound appreciation for history."[32] A brief overview of the various ways this appreciation manifested itself in Hotman's major publications reveals something of the extent and character of his historical sensitivities and also provides a helpful backdrop for viewing his singular engagement with biblical history as a response to the civil wars at the end of the 1560s.

Many—perhaps most—of Hotman's publications focus on aspects of Roman civil law, including philological studies and various commentaries on, reference tools for, and editions of the *Corpus iuris civilis*. A number of these

---

[32] Kelley, *Foundations*, 107. On Hotman, see also Kelley, *François Hotman*, and the earlier biographical studies by Rodolphe Dareste, *Essai sur François Hotman* (Paris: Auguste Durand, 1850), "François Hotman: Sa vie et sa correspondance," *Revue historique* 2 (1876): 1–59, 367–435, and "Hotman: D'après de nouvelles lettres des années 1561–1563," *Revue historique* 97 (1908): 297–315. Dareste's "Dix ans de la vie de François Hotman (1563–1573)," *Bulletin de la société de l'histoire du protestantisme français* 25 (1876): 529–44, is an extract from his "François Hotman: Sa vie." Jacques Pannier, "Hotman en Suisse (1547–1590)," *Zwingliana* 7 (1940): 137–72, draws closely on Dareste's studies. See also David Baird Smith, "François Hotman," *Scottish Historical Review* 13 (1916): 328–65.

originated during his years in Strasbourg in the latter 1550s. These writings bear witness not only to his strong interest in historical contexts but also, as Kelley has argued, to his concern for questions of contemporary relevance and the extent to which ancient legal traditions might apply to the present.[33] His practical, presentist approach to the past also emerges in his first significant piece of ecclesiastical polemic from 1553, in which he turned to the early church to attack the idea of papal primacy on both theological and historical grounds.[34] One of the key elements of his case there involves arguing for the fundamental equality and independence of the ancient patriarchal sees—invoking, in essence, a principle of cultural relativity. This same ideal, applied to contemporary events, manifested itself in contentions advanced in propaganda linked to Hotman justifying the failed conspiracy of Amboise (March 1560) by arguing that the Guises were tyrannical foreigners who had violated French customary traditions.[35] In all these writings, Hotman assumed the relevance of the past in general for the present; the question that came to dominate his writings was rather *which* elements of the past were most applicable and authoritative? Like Calvin and many other theorists of his age, Hotman thus wrestled with the question of anachronism, seeking ways to affirm the uniqueness of different historical periods and cultural situations while at the same time finding continuity between past and present.

Over the next decade, coinciding with the outbreak of the civil wars, Hotman's appreciation for the uniqueness of distinct social contexts and periods in history deepened and expressed itself in a marked shift in his attitude toward the relevance of Roman legal traditions for contemporary France. Containing what Kelley has described as "clear and direct a statement of historical relativism as one can find in the sixteenth century," Hotman's *Antitribonian*—written in French in 1567—paved the way for a heightened emphasis on indigenous traditions as the sole basis for addressing the present

[33] Kelley, *François Hotman*, 183–91; for a chronological listing of Hotman's publications, see 353–59.

[34] François Hotman [F. Vilierius, pseud.], *De statu primitivae ecclesiae* (Hieropolis [Geneva]: J. Crespin, 1553); see Kelley, *François Hotman*, 67–68; Frédéric Gabriel, "De statu primitivae ecclesiae: Histoire, chrétienté et réforme chez les civilistes de l'école de Bourges (Douaren, Bauduin, Hotman)," in *Bourges à la renaissance, hommes de lettres, hommes de lois*, ed. Stéphan Geonget (Paris: Klincksieck, 2011), 243–60.

[35] Most notably, an account of the conspiracy attributed to Hotman appearing in both Latin and French and the anonymous pamphlet, *Letter to the Tiger of France*; [François Hotman?], *Tumultus ambosianus* (N.p., 1560); in French, [François Hotman?], *Le tumulte d'Amboise* (N.p. 1560); [François Hotman], *Epistre envoiee au tigre de la France* (N.p., 1560). See Kelley, *François Hotman*, 114–20.

political crisis.[36] Around the same time, Hotman began writing his influential *Francogallia*, in which he turned to the national constitutional history of France to lay the foundations for an elective monarchy and the right of the estates to remove a tyrant.[37] He did not refer to the recent political events and religious violence in the text itself, but the inflammatory implications of his seemingly antiquarian study were clear from the preface; after it was published, it was read as a "tract for the times."[38] Though he continued to lecture and publish on Roman civil law until the end of his life, in Hotman's view the idealized past in which to seek the solution to the present political crisis lay in French—not Italian—legal and institutional history.

Hotman first published *Francogallia* in 1573, only after the renewal of violence and war following St. Bartholomew's Day the previous year. In the wake of that watershed, he published at least two polemical pamphlets chronicling recent events: an account of the massacre itself and a life of Gaspard de Coligny (1519–1572), whose assassination sparked the escalation of violence.[39] Along with his writings about the Conspiracy of Amboise and the many descriptions of the political and religious situation found in his letters, his efforts to render an account of current events can be seen as further byproducts of his deep historical interests in general and his increasing concern for French past and present in particular. Not just recovering a usable past but also fashioning the historical memories of his contemporaries was part of Hotman's broad historical program.

Paul-Alexis Mellet has underscored recently that the years between 1567 and 1572 were extremely important for Hotman's intellectual development.[40] During this time he reexamined the *Corpus iuris civilis*, engaged French feudal law, and wrote his crucial texts, *Antitribonian* and *Francogallia*. These

---

[36] Kelley, *Foundations*, 111. Hotman wrote his *Antitribonian* in 1567, but it was first published over a decade after his death. François Hotman, *Antitribonian ou discours d'un grand et renomme jurisconsulte de nostre temps* (Paris: J. Perier, 1603). See Kelley, *Foundations*, 106–12; Paul-Alexis Mellet, "'Une sophisterie de chaffoureur': Histoire des institutions et enseignement du droit chez Hotman," in *Bourges à la renaissance, hommes de lettres, hommes de lois*, ed. Stéphan Geonget (Paris: Klincksieck, 2011), 225–41.

[37] François Hotman, *Francogallia*, ed. Ralph Giesey and John H. M. Salmon (Cambridge, UK: Cambridge University Press, 1972). See also Kelley, *Foundations*, 204–11; Kelley, *François Hotman*, 239–47. It appears Hotman had finished most of the *Francogallia* by August 1568: "Editors' Introduction" to Hotman, *Francogallia*, 38. See also Ralph Giesey, "When and Why Hotman Wrote the *Francogallia*," *Bulletin d'humanisme et renaissance* 29 (1967): 581–611.

[38] Hotman, *Francogallia*, "Editors' Introduction," 72; cf. 62; see also Scott Manetsch, *Theodore Beza and the Quest for Peace in France, 1572–1598* (Leiden: Brill, 2000), 66.

[39] François Hotman [E. Varamundus Frisius, pseud.], *De furoribus gallicis* (Edinburgh [Basel], 1573); [François Hotman], *Gasparis Colinii Castellonii . . . vita* (N.p., 1575). See Kelley, *François Hotman*, 230–38.

[40] Mellet, "'Une sophisterie de chaffoureur,'" 229.

endeavors, however, represented no isolated scholarly undertaking, for Hotman was living in France at the time and experienced firsthand the entirety of the second and third wars and the start of the fourth. For nearly three years he was in exile from Bourges, where he had his university appointment. In the summer of 1567 his library was pillaged; soon thereafter he left for Paris. After the second war erupted, he went to Orléans to support Condé's operations, staying on after the war ended the following March. When the third war broke out in the fall of 1568, Hotman fled from Orléans to Sancerre, where he appears to have remained until the end of the war some two years later.[41] When that city fell under siege, Hotman wrote a treatise on sacred history from the creation to Ezra's reading of the law to the exiles returned to Jerusalem from Babylon (Nehemiah 8). His *Consolatio* thus represents his turn to biblical history and constitutes a further aspect of this crucial period in the development of his attitude toward the past and its relevance. Although there are important differences between Hotman's text and Calvin's sermons on Second Samuel, striking commonalities unite them, and these commonalities yield important insights into French Reformed attitudes toward and uses of the scriptural past during the civil wars. In order to uncover these, the discussion will outline first the main differences between Hotman's project and Calvin's sermons and then explore how Hotman engages sacred history to make it meaningful for the present crisis of religious war.

Aside from the obvious difference in genre, two key aspects of Hotman's treatise distinguish it from Calvin's sermons. First, Hotman considers a much larger sweep of the biblical narrative in a mere 179 pages and goes into far less detail about particular incidents. He looks back on sacred history through

---

[41] The literature evidences and perpetuates a discrepancy with respect to his stay in Sancerre. Hotman left Bourges for Paris around the time the second war erupted (September 1567) and then went to Orléans, where he remained after the Peace of Longjumeau (March 1568) ended that phase of the conflict. After the third war broke out the following autumn, he fled to Sancerre. Apparently based on a letter he wrote to Jerome Zanchi in 1579 and cited by Dareste, Hotman is assumed to have remained in Sancerre for roughly two and a half years and then spent another seven months in La Charité—a period of just over three years (Dareste, "François Hotman," 50, 52; Pannier, "Hotman," 162; Kelley, *François Hotman*, 198, 201). This itinerary, however, seems impossible, since (as these sources also note) Hotman was back teaching in Bourges in the fall of 1570. Perhaps recognizing that the math does not quite work, David B. Smith has Hotman fleeing to Sancerre at the outbreak of the second war and remaining there for three years ("François Hotman," 342–43). Yet there may be another way to resolve this discrepancy. In the excerpt from the letter, Hotman refers to his *wife's* recollection of the hardships she bore throughout two years and seven months in Sancerre and another seven months in La Charité. Might it be the case that Hotman moved his wife to one of these safe cities when he left Bourges for Paris in 1567, kept her in these strongholds throughout the second war and in the precarious months that followed, and then joined her in Sancerre in October 1568? In that case, it would be Claude Hotman and in all likelihood her numerous offspring who spent circa three years in the Huguenot refuges, whereas François himself spent only two.

a wide-angle lens, whereas Calvin places a particular period of that past under the microscope. Calvin scrutinizes the changing events and shifting motives of the biblical characters, while Hotman focuses on broader, general, and recurring themes. The most prominent of these is a repeating cycle of periods of defection from and reestablishment of true religion, which he uses to structure his summary of biblical history and give coherence to this large body of material. He suggests that the initial institution of religion was in the Garden of Eden, with all of creation designated a gift for Adam's use and en-joyment so that he might exhibit piety toward God. The first defection comes in the fall, and, following this, the establishment of the first church and sacri-ficial rituals that point to Christ. The circumstances leading to the flood mark the second depravation of religion, and the church is instituted for a second time with the renewal of sacrifices by Noah. The third defection occurs with the tower of Babel; the third establishment of religion with Abraham. All in all, Hotman traces twenty-three periods of defection and reinstitution of reli-gion from creation to the return from Babylon. In addition, he strives for pre-cision in determining the number of years each period lasted, likely drawing on a chronology, *Epitome temporum et rerum* (1565), prepared by Heinrich Bullinger (1504–1575) to date the events Hotman discusses from the time of creation.[42]

Second, Hotman is much more sparing in his applications of biblical lessons to the present, and when he does make them, these are much less direct or explicit than in Calvin's sermons. Similar to his approach in the *Francogallia*, he does not refer to current politics, the violence of the pres-ent civil war, or the current religious turmoil in commenting on the biblical narrative. In contrast to Calvin's treatment, biblical characters are not lifted up as examples of good or bad behavior, but their actions function rather as

---

[42] See Hotman, *Consolatio*, 9–10, 14, 16–17, 21, 27, 30, 34. Hotman's calculations reflect his consul-tation of Heinrich Bullinger's chronology and account of biblical history, *Epitome temporum et rerum ab orbe condito ad excidium usque ultimum urbis Hierosolymorum sub Imperatore Vespasiano*, in *Daniel sapientissimus dei propheta* (Zurich: C. Froschauer, 1565). In a letter to Bullinger in February 1572, Hotman wrote that while in Sancerre, he had found this chronology to be a great consola-tion (cited in Dareste, "François Hotman," 52; cf. Dareste, "Dix ans," 540). Hotman does not slav-ishly follow Bullinger's calculations, but he is clearly referencing them; in addition, he occasionally reflects Bullinger's language; see, for example, their similar comments on the calamity of civil war in Hotman, *Consolatio*, 86, and Bullinger, *Epitome*, 28 *verso*. Note that *Epitome* is attached to Bullinger's *Sermons on Daniel*, which were preached between May 1563 and June 1565 and first published in August 1565. On Bullinger's sermons, see Emidio Campi, "Über das Ende des Weltzeitalters: Aspekte der Rezeption des Danielbuches bei Heinrich Bullinger," in *Europa, Tausendjähriges Reich und Neue Welt: Zwei Jahrtausende Geschichte und Utopie in der Rezeption des Danielbuches*, ed. Mariano Delgado, Klaus Koch, and Edgar Marsch (Stuttgart: Kohlhammer, 2003), 225–38.

the catalysts for each defection and as the means by which God restores the church. For the most part Hotman provides a reasonably concise narrative summary of the events of biblical history without a lot of explanation; on occasion he refers to pagan or early Christian writers to fit the narrative into a larger theological or historical framework or when he disagrees with their positions.[43] Rarely, he digresses to emphasize a point of wider significance. For example, in his discussion of the creation of humanity, he includes a rather long discussion of the excellence of human nature as created, followed by a detailed treatment of the doctrine of the trinity.[44] He concludes his discussion of the fall with an explanation of how Christ is the one who can reconcile humanity and God and makes reference to Christ's restoring and preserving the church throughout the entire text.[45] Beyond these theological framings, Hotman displays his sensitivity to cultural relativity in a chapter on how the form or condition of religion changed over time, from few to many ceremonies, from a single family to an entire people, and so forth, but this too is designed largely to prepare the way for understanding the next defection from religion under the judges.[46] After one extremely uncharacteristic digression on Jephthah's vow (Judges 11), Hotman makes a singular explicit connection to the present, bemoaning the Israelites' relapse into "worship of invented gods" and commenting that this is not surprising, as the same thing is seen today.[47]

Despite these differences in genre, approach, and method evident in Calvin's sermons and Hotman's meditation on biblical history, there are, nevertheless, some striking similarities between these two endeavors and their effort to shine the light of the past on the present and make it meaningful. These similarities can be seen first through examination of Hotman's purpose in writing the treatise and, second, through closer consideration of the overall effect of his organization of sacred history into ages of restoration of

---

[43] See, e.g., Hotman, *Consolatio*, 12, 29, 38, 52, 63–64. Despite these references, it is difficult to determine Hotman's sources, beyond the Bible itself and Bullinger's *Epitome*. Hotman's library had been pillaged before the second war, and it is hard to know what material he might have had at his disposal in Sancerre. The assertion often repeated in the literature that he had *only* the Bible and some works by Augustine goes back at least to his first biographer, Pierre Nevelet, but I have not been able to confirm where, if at all, Hotman himself or perhaps his son, Jean, made this claim. See Pierre Nevelet, "Elogium Franc. Hotmani IC" [1592], in *Franc. Hotmani iuriconsulti operum tomus primus [-tertius]*, 3 vols. (Lyon: Vignon & Stoer, 1599–1600), 1: ix; cf. Dareste, "François Hotman," 52; Kelley, *François Hotman*, 200).

[44] Hotman, *Consolatio*, 3–6.

[45] Hotman, *Consolatio*, 15–16; cf. 17.

[46] Hotman, *Consolatio*, 70–72.

[47] Hotman, *Consolatio*, 86–87.

and defection from true religion. For although Hotman did not draw explicit connections between past and present in his narrative, he intended the book to have immediate and ongoing relevance, and, moreover, that appears to be how his son and editor, Jean, understood his father's purpose when he made the text available to a wider public. Similar to the way that Calvin the preacher urged his listeners to draw on their own experience to derive meaning from scripture in time of war, Hotman's project in its larger context represents an appeal to the reader to engage the biblical past through the lens of present experience in order to draw the connections that will yield consolation in troubled times. For both, biblical history comes alive through the experience of wartime affliction.

First, just as is the case in the *Francogallia*, Hotman's introduction sets the tone and makes it clear that this interpretation of the past is no mere antiquarian study. He prefaces his *Consolatio* with a heartrending account of his personal experience, describing the loss of his library and household goods, his flight with his wife and seven children to Sancerre, and a narrowly repulsed attempt to breach the walls by the Catholic forces laying siege to the city. During the attack, his wife was recovering from childbirth, and Hotman describes how she watched their eight-day-old son expire, and then succumbed herself to a dangerous illness that lasted many months. Exacerbating these personal afflictions was the "flame of civil war, consuming all of France like a destructive fire." He therefore resolved to reveal the source of the consolation that sustained him amid these trials, so that his children and friends would know where to seek a remedy when finding themselves in similar situations. He explains:

> Therefore, I took up sacred scripture, and though I had read through it many times on many occasions, I nevertheless had not ever read it so diligently and attentively or observed it so carefully. Moreover, in order to impress deeper on my mind the memory of those things that seemed to me most memorable and suited for comforting the soul, I wrote a daily summary of them for myself.[48]

---

[48] Hotman, *Consolatio*, "Praefatio auctoris." Jean Hotman also discusses the conditions under which the treatise was written in the dedicatory epistle he penned when he published the *Consolatio* in 1593. He dedicated the treatise to his cousin and father's namesake, François Hotman (Hotman, *Consolatio*, "Epistola"). On Hotman's time in Sancerre, see Dareste, "Dix ans"; Kelley, *François Hotman*, 197–202.

He notes that he focused especially on the vicissitudes of religion, the times when piety was recently flourishing and yet shortly thereafter seemed to be stained and extinguished by impure and contaminating superstitions. Hotman intends his narrative to serve as an aid to his loved ones and as a means to their own consolation in troubled times.

The fact that the written narrative itself is so sparing with respect to present applications of the biblical lessons may seem incongruous with this professed purpose, but in fact in leaving the reader to make the connections, Hotman may have been intentionally following a common strategy. Bullinger's *Epitome* also urges the reader to apply the lessons of the scriptural history it summarizes while only rarely making explicit connections itself.[49] Moreover, the lack of explicit consolations in the text did not deter Hotman's son and editor, who articulated his grasp of his father's intent in the dedicatory letter he wrote for the publication three years after Hotman's death. Describing the conditions under which the book was written in 1568, Jean Hotman indicates that his father wrote the book as a private exercise in which he examined the perennial tribulations of humankind since the fall and the cycle of defection and reintegration of the people of Israel. Observing these events and referring them to the present state of the church of Christ, his father "found rest in the goodness and providence of the one Lord." In Jean's view, this exercise not only benefited his father; he claims that his father intended his *Consolatio* as a kind of inheritance for his family.[50] And while he clearly thinks that the content conveys a consoling message, it seems also that Jean envisions the work's value to lie as much in the fact that it supplies a model for reflection on the biblical past, and wishes that others would follow his father's lead and seek in sacred scripture a remedy for current ills. When viewing Hotman's text as an invitation to and model for seeking consolation in scripture, one can detect a strong similarity to Calvin's urging his listeners to examine scripture through the lens of their own experience.

The second point of connection to Calvin's sermons and his theology more generally lies in the theme of divine providence over history that dominates both of these treatments of the biblical past. Calvin drew out this theme through such tactics as typology, the use of the mirror image, and calls for

[49] "I do not think that the knowledge of the bare history is useful to the reader, unless we, applying this to ourselves, learn and hold fast to the godly use of them and to the amendment of our life" (Bullinger, *Epitome*, 2 recto).

[50] Hotman, *Consolatio*, "Epistola." On Jean's editions of his father's works, see Kelley, *François Hotman*, 325–26.

appropriate analogies to drive home the point that the biblical narrative was no simple account of events but a divinely orchestrated testament to divine providence throughout all ages—even in times of turmoil and war. Hotman achieves the same aim through his organization of sacred history up to the return from Babylon as a series of twenty-three cycles of defection from and restoration to true religion. He begins the *Consolatio* with a detailed consideration of the days of creation, the creation of humanity, and the trinity, which lays the theological foundation for a providential view of history: God as active creator manifest in creation, humanity as created for worshiping the triune God; Christ as the source of redemption from every lapse. Then Hotman begins tracing this ebb and flow of true piety across the course of sacred history in which human actions are catalysts for divine activity, restoring the church after every fall.

Although Calvin's sermons on Second Samuel and Hotman's *Consolatio* thus share a common emphasis on divine providence as a central theme and a historical vision that locates the meaning of history in God's providential care revealed in scripture, the fact remains that Calvin and Hotman take different routes to this same end. One question that remains concerning Hotman's approach is the background to his concept of cycles of apostasy and reintegration. In developing the framework of cycles of defection from and restoration to true religion, Hotman echoes a strategy for understanding history that was widespread in his age. As Geoffrey Dipple has noted, various Radical reformers such as Pilgram Marpeck (d. 1556), the authors of the sixteenth-century *Hutterite Chronicle*, and Dirk Philips (1504–1568) include in their historical visions an understanding of Old Testament history as a "repeated pattern" or "alternating episodes" of fidelity and apostasy or, like the Melchiorite David Joris (ca. 1501–1566), "saw human history as marked by a series of falls and restitutions."[51] Closer to home, in his dedicatory preface to the volume containing his *Epitome*, Bullinger describes his purpose "not so much as a reckoning of times and events from the creation of the world, to the destruction of the city of Jerusalem, as a perennial series and various falls of our true faith or religion."[52] As noted, Hotman utilized Bullinger's text in preparing his *Consolatio*, but whereas Bullinger does not enumerate the exact falls and restitutions, Hotman does. The overall effect of his more precise tracing of this pattern serves to heighten the overall theme

---

[51] Dipple, *"Just as in the Time of the Apostles,"* 148, 155, 165, 239.
[52] Bullinger, *Daniel sapientissimus dei propheta*, "Praefatio," n.p.

of God's orderly providence and, presumably, the consolation derived from recognition of it.

In the context of the intentions laid out in the preface, Hotman's discussion of the purpose of human creation at the start of the treatise, and the prayer attributed to him that is appended to the end of the published edition, the implications are clear: consolation comes not just from the words of scripture but from the *experience* of reading it, meditating on it, and, in Hotman's case, writing about it. Hotman does not make the lessons explicit, I suggest, because he expects that consolation comes through the experience of discovering them for oneself—and that is the legacy he seeks to pass on. Though Hotman's comments on the biblical history do not share Calvin's *explicit* presentist focus, his emphasis on experience has a clear affinity to Calvin's efforts to help his congregation feel the reality and engage the lessons of the Bible gleaned from the past of ancient Israel, viewed through the lens of their present experience of affliction.

Conclusion

In December 1571, Hotman, now finally back living in Bourges, wrote a letter to the Zurich pastor Rudolph Gwalther (1519–1586) in which he gives a picture of the state of the church in France. On the one hand, he notes the miraculous reestablishment of the Reformed church and a resurgence of true piety; on the other, the danger that still threatens. "We find ourselves," he says, "between the hammer and the anvil." He continues:

> What can I tell you? Up to the present day I have heard many excellent sermons in Geneva and Strasbourg; I have read many books by Luther, Bullinger, Calvin, Gwalther, but, believe me, I have not found a better school for piety than the cross and that word from Paul, who promises us the consolation of the Holy Spirit to help us to bear our afflictions.[53]

For both Calvin and Hotman, the consolation of the Holy Spirit came through the avenue of sacred history, which they viewed afresh through the experience of the cross—the affliction of the religious wars. The biblical past and the experience of war combined to forge a key spiritual weapon in the

---

[53] Quoted in Dareste, "Dix ans," 540, and "François Hotman," 53.

Calvinist arsenal: a historical vision of the present tied into God's providence and sacred history across the ages.

When the proverbial hammer fell to the anvil with the St. Bartholomew's Day Massacre just months after Hotman's letter, he found himself fleeing again, this time to Geneva. He published his more well-known treatises which, along with other writings by other adherents of the Reformed faith, not only provided a clearly articulated theoretical basis for active political resistance but also sought to "fashion Huguenot memory" of recent events.[54] These important texts can be seen as marking a new stage in Reformed efforts to make sense of the present through the lens of the past.

---

[54] See Manetsch, *Theodore Beza*, 51–73; quote from 57.

Epilogue

Toward Calvin's Sense of History

In early February 1564, Calvin preached his last sermon, bringing to an end nearly three decades of work in which the public interpretation of the Bible held a central position. It is fitting, in light of the trajectory traced through the chapters of this book, that his last weekday sermon was on 1 Kings (on Wednesday, February 2), and his last Sunday sermon on the harmony of the gospels (on February 6).[1] Though the exact texts upon which he preached are not known, it is significant that his last preaching cycle on the Old Testament was part of a series following the sermons on Second Samuel, in which Calvin continued directly engaging the history of ancient Israel for his Genevan congregation. Yet, as the studies in the preceding chapters have demonstrated, Calvin's historical consciousness shaped his engagement with scripture in all its genres over the entire course of his career. It is possible that with his turn to biblical books containing more historical narrative in the 1550s and 1560s, Calvin refined his historicizing approach, and that his work on the Old Testament in particular enabled him to sharpen the implements in his exegetical toolkit to reconstruct a past with its own integrity and remoteness that was nevertheless profoundly meaningful and relevant for Calvin and his contemporaries. Future scholarship may pursue that notion. I do not explore here the possibility of development in Calvin's hermeneutic, but rather reflect on what his historicizing approach to scripture, evidenced in his actual engagement with the biblical writings, figures, and themes examined in this book's chapters, might contribute to an understanding of Calvin's sense of history more broadly.

The scholarly world still awaits a comprehensive examination of Calvin's understanding of history, despite earlier calls for it and efforts to produce it. In his important study of the emergence of new forms of historical thinking

---

[1] CO 21: 96. After retiring from preaching, Calvin continued to attend the Friday *congrégations* and follow their discussion of Isaiah, health permitting.

Calvin, the Bible, and History. Barbara Pitkin, Oxford University Press (2020). © Oxford University Press.
DOI: 10.1093/oso/9780190093273.001.0001

among sixteenth-century Italian and especially French schools of jurisprudence, Donald Kelley drew attention to the need for a study of Calvin's
historical thought. Kelly's observation appears in a footnote to a paragraph
mentioning Calvin's discussion of the history of the church in the 1543
Institutes, which Kelley provides as an example of Calvin as "the man who
did most to formulate and to publicize the Protestant interpretation of ecclesiastical history."[2] There Kelley notes the insufficiency to meet this task of
the one existing monograph at the time, Heinrich Berger's study of Calvin's
concept of history, published in German in 1955.[3] I judge Josef Bohatec's earlier investigation (again, in German), "Gott und die Geschichte nach Calvin,"
published in 1936, to have made a more promising start, but as a long essay
on Calvin's philosophy (or better, theology) of history it was able to touch
only on some, but not nearly all, of the essential features of Calvin's historical consciousness. Bohatec, too, noted the lack of a monograph on this "important" topic.[4] Danièle Fischer's unpublished French doctoral thesis is still
the most complete study to date, tackling key elements of Calvin's historical
thought and their various contexts, covering the formation of his views,
his use of tradition, and a wide range of Calvin's works. However, this over
one-thousand-page thesis is not widely available and, in its unrevised form,
cannot represent the final word on this subject.[5] Irena Backus and Claude-
Gilbert Dubois treat aspects of Calvin's approach to the past in the context of
larger analyses of historical method, but do not offer thorough accounts of
his thoughts on the topic.[6]

What might the studies of Calvin's historicizing exegesis in this book contribute to the understanding of Calvin's historical thought more broadly?
Is it possible to position Calvin among the trends in historical thought
and scholarship of his day? Was Calvin a "historian" as well as pastor, theologian, biblical scholar, and church reformer? Euan Cameron has rightly
underscored that, unlike some of his contemporaries, Calvin was not a historian in the sense of someone who used historical sources to write an account
of a past time; nonetheless, he notes, certain aspects of Calvin's thought—his

[2] Donald R. Kelley, *Foundations of Modern Historical Scholarship: Language, Law, and History in the French Renaissance* (New York: Columbia University Press, 1970), 157 and 157n14.
[3] Heinrich Berger, *Calvins Geschichtsauffassung* (Zurich: Zwingli Verlag, 1955).
[4] Josef Bohatec, "Gott und die Geschichte nach Calvin," *Philosophia Reformata* 1, no. 3 (1936), 131.
[5] Danièle Fischer, "Jean Calvin, historien de l'église: Sources et aspects de la pensée historique, et de l'historiographie du Réformateur" (Ph.D. diss., University of Strasbourg, 1980).
[6] Irena Backus, *Historical Method and Confessional Identity in the Era of the Reformation (1378–1615)* (Leiden: Brill, 2003), 63–129; Claude-Gilbert Dubois, *La conception de l'histoire en France au XVIe siècle (1560-1610)* (Paris: A. G. Nizet, 1977), 466–84.

resistance to the idea that the meaning of providence was manifestly trans-
parent, his heightened sense of historical anachronism, his fascination with
historical details and figures, his sometimes strong judgments about the political past—show him to be, in particular ways, quite historically minded.[7]
One could add that Calvin's intense interest in contemporary events and his
conviction that the past, properly understood, could inform the present situation and shed some light on God's inscrutable providence also resonated
with the projects of some—but by no means all—contemporary historians
and historical theorists. The sixteenth century witnessed great experimenta-
tion not only in religious doctrines, institutions, and practices but also in historical thought and method. In this time of flux and change, there were both
writers of history and readers of history, and Calvin falls more squarely in the
latter camp. The case studies in this book have focused on how he engaged
with the biblical past as a reader of history to make meaning for the present.
While they do not offer a comprehensive portrait of his historical thought,
they demonstrate that the *sine qua non* for understanding Calvin's broader
concept of history lies in grasping the historical consciousness manifested in
his engagement with the biblical past.

One contribution of these linked case studies of Calvin's actual exegesis
is their nuanced insight into his understanding of the Bible as a historical
document and source. For Calvin, the Bible is the record of God's communi-
cations to his people, which he willed to have written down over time as the
normative foundation for the teaching and collective life of future generations. In the *Institutes,* Calvin outlines the stages by which God's word, which
was communicated to the patriarchs in "secret revelations," was "set down
and sealed in writing": first the law; then the prophets, who interpreted the
law and added predictions of future events; then the histories, composed
by the prophets under the guidance of the Holy Spirit; the psalms; and, finally, the writings of the apostles.[8] The Bible is thus a product of history, at
least in the sense of emerging over time in various historical settings, even
if, to be sure, through divine providence. As to its contents, Calvin stresses
that it does not offer a universal history, and that its primary goal is not to
offer an account of the past for its own sake, but rather to provide a selective
record of God's dealing with humanity in the past so as to guide his people

---

[7] Euan Cameron, "Calvin the Historian: Biblical Antiquity and Scriptural Exegesis in the Quest
for a Meaningful Past," in *Calvin and the Book: The Evolution of the Printed Word in Reformed
Protestantism,* ed. Karen E. Spierling (Göttingen: Vandenhoeck & Ruprecht, 2015), 79–81.
[8] *Institutes* (1559), 4.8.5–9.

in the present. For Calvin, then, scripture is the most important and only normative source for knowledge about the sacred past, and since each of the biblical writers wrote out of and for a particular context, their writings must also be grasped and interpreted historically and contextually before drawing any universal lessons. For this purpose, the interpreter must avail himself or herself of all available tools, including extrabiblical and even non-Christian ones, in order to understand the contexts of the biblical history. Of course, an awareness of history, geography, and the like, as well as the use of previous exegetical traditions, had long been essential for Christian interpreters, and recent developments in philology and rhetoric and new knowledge about past times inspired many of Calvin's contemporaries to broader engagements with historical context so as to unlock the meaning of scripture. But Calvin's commitment to the historicity of the Bible was unparalleled for a Christian interpreter of his age, and led him, as these studies have shown, to sometimes surprising or at least unconventional exegetical moves or conclusions.

The chapters that make up this book have confirmed and expanded earlier work on Calvin's sometimes idiosyncratic interpretations or his emphasis on a more historicizing reading of passages that earlier and contemporary Christian interpreters often viewed through a more overtly Christian doctrinal lens. One of the more fascinating elements of his approach, and one that reveals much about his sense of history and the historical task, is how he squares his historicizing convictions with his search for contemporary religious meaning. To be sure, Calvin still interpreted the Bible from a Christian perspective, but he sometimes shifted the emphasis away from traditional approaches to finding Christ in scripture. This was especially the case in his interpretation of the Old Testament, but also emerges in his handling of parts of the New Testament. He downplays David's prophetic status in his commentary on the Psalms, stresses the references of Isaiah's prophecies to the people of ancient Israel before exploring their multiple fulfillment in the sacred history of the church, and limits the scope of Daniel's prophecies of Christ to Christ's first advent. Even in his commentary on John, he restricts the number of passages that he thinks proclaim Christ's divinity and shifts the focus of the evangelist to Christ's historic mission. His unprecedented rearrangement of the narrative and legislation in his *Mosaic Harmony* was, in the end, an effort to make Moses's meaning more accessible and intelligible to the sixteenth-century Christian reader, even if this also, at times, eclipsed the original setting of some of the moral law.

Yet it was precisely through this attention to the mind of the biblical author and the historical setting of the various books of the Bible that Calvin strove to uncover God's intention for his people in the remote past and across the ages. To arrive at the ultimate meaning of a passage required, for Calvin, discriminating between what pertained particularly to a passage's original context and what broader meaning it bore for later generations of the faithful. Again, this was no new challenge. Christian exegetes for over a millennium and a half had developed many strategies for distinguishing which forms of biblical religion, ethical mandates and practices, and even beliefs had been superseded from those which, properly understood, remained binding on Christian believers. Calvin's strategy, though, gave decisive weight to a biblical passage's original setting and the human author's intention and offered distinct ways for relating these to scripture's later readers. For Calvin, often (though not always) the peculiarities of the biblical past were not identified and then sidelined as irrelevant or transformed through allegory, but instead became the very locus for finding contemporary relevance. Calvin frequently invoked the metaphor of the "mirror" to encourage his readers and auditors to find illumination of their own situation in the biblical past; similarly, he lifted up biblical figures and situations as examples—positive or negative— for those living in his own day. Occasionally he spoke of these situations and individuals as types, without diminishing their importance to their original time and place. He also held that some passages of the Bible indeed foretold future events and read some prophecies as having multiple fulfillments in the life of God's people as a way of underscoring the connection between past and present. Alternatively, he could invoke the notion of analogy or anagogy as a strategy for the interpreter to apply the insights from the past to the present, even when this application was not expressly intended by the original biblical author. All of these interrelated strategies allowed Calvin to preserve the integrity of the past while also finding universal relevance.

A further contribution of these studies lies in the insight they provide, through examination of his working hermeneutic, into his concept of history itself. Underlying Calvin's method of relating the original context and setting of scripture to the historical conditions and demands of his own age are key assumptions about the ultimate nature of history as process over time. For Calvin, the sacred history related in scripture is connected to the present through God's providence. Even though times and circumstances change, this history is unified, unbroken, and continuous, and Calvin finds that there are similar situations that arise to confront God's people across the ages. Biblical figures can function as examples, biblical history can serve as a mirror, multiple historical fulfillments of prophecy are possible, and analogies can be drawn by interpreters because of the unity of sacred history (here referring to the history of God's covenantal people), testified to in scripture and experienced in the lives of later believers, including those in Calvin's day. Because the meaning of contemporary history and God's ways therein are obscure to fallen humans, even to those viewing with the eye of faith, the past becomes a clearer demonstration of providence through this principle of the "similitude of times." Again, Calvin was not unique in stressing this unity, which resonates with the emphasis on the covenant in Reformed theologians like John Oecolampadius (1482–1531) and Heinrich Bullinger (1504–1575). Moreover, some other early modern interpreters were interested in using historical scholarship to demonstrate the fulfillment of past prophecy to refute skeptics and strengthen believers.[9] Embracing these trends, Calvin's exegesis evidences a concept of history that is not focused just on the past but also seeks to make meaning of the historical present, a project that reflects his understanding of the purpose of history.

Calvin was not much interested in some of the problems that occupied many historians of his day. He eschewed preoccupation with biblical chronology, reckoning the age of the world, and speculating about the ages or phases of history or when it might come to an end, even though some of his contemporaries found these useful topics for building up present faith. Yet he was curious about classical history and utilized secular historians to illuminate the Bible's historical settings. Even though he wrote no treatise on church history, in his theological and polemical writings in particular he left hints about his understanding of the history of the church, where things had gone wrong, and why the present reform was justified. Moreover, he distinguished between profane histories and sacred history, by which he meant here the scriptural record. A final contribution of this study to Calvin's broader sense of history is the evidence it provides as to what kind of historical writing he found valuable and why and how he related it to other forms of historical work.

Calvin focused his historical skills on the interpretation of scripture because he was convinced that only sacred history could truly be, as claimed by the Ciceronian dictum, the teacher of life: *historia magistra vitae*. In his

---

[9] Euan Cameron, "The Bible and the Early Modern Sense of History," in *The New Cambridge History of the Bible*, vol. 3, *From 1450 to 1750*, ed. Euan Cameron (Cambridge, UK: Cambridge University Press, 2016), 667–68.

comments on Romans 4:23, Calvin claims that this phrase from a pagan author truly expresses the purpose of history, but that only scripture can fulfill this office: only scripture prescribes rules for testing all other histories and making them profitable, and it alone provides clear moral instruction. Calvin then points out what is to him the most important element: "But as to doctrine, which it especially teaches, it possesses this peculiarity: that it clearly reveals the providence of God, his justice and goodness towards his own people, and his judgments on the wicked." He explains that the proper way to use the "sacred histories" is to draw sound doctrine from them, i.e., instruction on how to live, strengthen faith, and serve God, for which purpose the examples of the saints (like Abraham, the subject of Paul's observation in this section) will be useful. "What will serve to confirm faith is the help which God ever gave them, the protection which brought comfort in adversities, and the paternal care which he ever exercised over them."[10]

These comments, stemming largely from the 1540 edition of the commentary, represent Calvin's effort to explain Paul's claim that the story of Abraham's faith being reckoned as righteousness related in Genesis 15 was written down not for Abraham's sake, but for the sake of later believers. Kelley has suggested that Calvin here evidences a negative view of history, saying in essence that not history, but "sola scriptura" is the mistress of life.[11] The studies in this book suggest that this formulation risks misrepresenting what is really at stake for Calvin. Calvin is not opposing scripture and history, but is rather elevating the sacred history related in scripture over profane histories not written for the express purpose of setting down and sealing God's words and ways in writing. As he reminded his congregation when preaching on 2 Samuel 8, sacred history is superior to chronicles and histories compiled by unbelievers because of its unique and effective instruction: its power, through the illumination of the Spirit, not only to impart but to imprint the lessons of the past on the heart. Scripture contains a special kind of written history, but as we have seen, profane histories and secular knowledge all aid in understanding sacred history, so that it might achieve its unique purpose.

Calvin did not espouse a negative view of history—not as historical record, and not as temporal process. What he sought was a proper understanding of the purpose of historical writing—sacred and secular—and a conception of

---

[10] OE 13: 98 = CO 49: 86; in English, John Calvin, *Commentary on the Epistle of Paul to the Romans*, ed. and trans. John Owen, repr. in *Calvin's Commentaries* (Grand Rapids, MI: Baker Books, 1989), 182–83.

[11] Kelley, *Foundations*, 157n14.

the flow of history under the guidance of divine providence. Calvin's historicizing interpretation of scripture aimed above all else to console his readers
and auditors that all history is in God's hands and ultimately meaningful.
Because of the difficulty of grasping divine providence in the theater of history, as also in the spectacle of nature, the Bible and history, for Calvin, went
hand in hand.

Bibliography

Primary Literature

Aulcuns pseaulmes et cantiques mys en chant. Strasburg: [Knobloch], 1539. Facsimile, Geneva: A. Jullien, 1919.

Augustine. *Tractates on the Gospel of John 1–10*. Translated by J. W. Rettig. Washington, DC: Catholic University of America Press, 1988.

Augustine. *Tractates on the Gospel of John 28–54*. Translated by J. W. Rettig. Washington, DC: Catholic University of America Press, 1993.

Baudouin, François. *Ad edicta veterum principum Romanorum de Christianis*. Basel: J. Oporinus, 1557.

Baudouin, François. *Ad leges de famosis libellis et de calumniatoribus*. Paris: A. Wechelus, 1562.

Baudouin, François. *Constantinus Magnus, sive de Constantini Imp. legibus ecclesiasticis atque civilibus, commentariorum libri duo*. Basel: J. Oporinus, 1556.

Baudouin, François. *De institutione historiae universae et ejus cum iurisprudentia conjunctione*. Paris: A. Wechelus, 1561.

Baudouin, François. *Iuris civilis schola Argentinensis*. Strasbourg: W. Rihel, 1555.

Baudouin, François. *Iustinianus, sive de iure novo, commentariorum libri IIII*. Basel: J. Oporinus, 1560.

Beza, Theodore. *Lex Dei moralis, ceremonialis, et politica, ex libris Mosis excerpta, et in certas classes distributa*. [Geneva]: P. de Saint-André, 1577.

Bodin, Jean. *Method for the Easy Comprehension of History*. Translated by Beatrice Reynolds. New York: Octagon, 1966.

Bucer, Martin [Aretius Felinus, pseud.]. *Sacrorum Psalmorum libri quinque*. Strasbourg: G. Andlanus, 1529.

Bullinger, Heinrich. *Daniel sapientissimus dei propheta, qui a vetustis polyhistor, id est multiscius est dictus, expositus homiliis LXVI*. Zurich: C. Froschauer, 1565.

Bullinger, Heinrich. *Epitome temporum et rerum ab orbe condito ad excidium usque ultimum urbis Hierosolymorum sub Imperatore Vespasiano*. In *Daniel sapientissimus dei propheta*. Zurich: C. Froschauer, 1565.

Calvin, Jean. *Commentaires sur les cinq livres de Moyse: Genese est mis à part, les autres quatres livres sont disposez en forme d'Harmonie*. Geneva: F. Estienne, 1564.

Calvin, Jean. *Deux congrégations et exposition du catéchisme*. Edited by Rodolphe Peter. Paris: Presses Universitaires de France, 1964.

Calvin, Jean. *Institution de la religion chrestienne*. 5 vols. Edited by Jean-Daniel Benoit. Paris: J. Vrin, 1957–63.

Calvin, Jean. *Sermons sur le Livre d'Esaïe: Chapitres 13–29*. Edited by Georges A. Barrios. Neukirchen: Neukirchener Verlag, 1961. SC 2.

Calvin, John. *Advertissement du profit qui reviendroit à la Chrestienté s'il se faisoit inventaire des reliques*. Geneva: J. Girard, 1543. CO 6: 405–52. Also in *"La vraie piété": Divers traités de Jean Calvin et Confession de foi de Guillaume Farel.* Edited by Irena Backus and Claire Chimelli, 153–202. Geneva: Labor et Fides, 1986.

Calvin, John. *Calvin: Commentaries.* Edited by Joseph Hartounian. Philadelphia: Westminster, 1958.

Calvin, John. *Calvin's Commentaries.* 22 vols. Grand Rapids, MI: Baker Books, 1989.

Calvin, John. *Calvin's Commentary on Seneca's De Clementia.* Edited and translated by Ford Lewis Battles and André Malan Hugo. Leiden: Brill, 1969.

Calvin, John. *Commentaries on the Book of the Prophet Daniel.* 2 vols. Edited and translated by Thomas Myers. Reprint in *Calvin's Commentaries.* Grand Rapids, MI: Baker Books, 1989.

Calvin, John. *Commentaries on the Epistle of Paul [sic] the Apostle to the Hebrews.* Edited and translated by John Owen. Reprint in *Calvin's Commentaries.* Grand Rapids, MI: Baker Books, 1989.

Calvin, John. *Commentaries on the Epistle of Paul to the Ephesians.* Edited and translated by William Pringle. Reprint in *Calvin's Commentaries.* Grand Rapids, MI: Baker Books, 1989.

Calvin, John. *Commentaries on the Four Last Books of Moses, Arranged in the Form of a Harmony.* 4 vols. Edited and translated by Charles William Bingham. Reprint in *Calvin's Commentaries.* Grand Rapids, MI: Baker Books, 1989.

Calvin, John. *Commentarii in epistolam ad Hebraeos.* Geneva: J. Girard, 1549. OE 19 = CO 55: 5–198.

Calvin, John. *Commentarii in epistolam Pauli ad Ephesios.* In *Commentarii in quatuor Pauli epistolas: ad Galatas, ad Ephesios, ad Philippenses, ad Colossenses,* 105–202. Geneva: J. Girard, 1548. OE 16: 151–292 = CO 51: 141–240.

Calvin, John. *Commentarii in epistolam Pauli ad Romanos.* Strasbourg: W. Rihel, 1540. OE 13 = CO 49: 1–292.

Calvin, John. *Commentarii in Isaiam prophetam.* [Revised edition.] Geneva: J. Crespin, 1559. CO 36–37.

Calvin, John. *Commentariorum in Acta Apostolorum liber I.* Geneva: J. Crespin, 1552. OE 12/1 = CO 48: 1–317.

Calvin, John. *Commentariorum in Acta Apostolorum liber posterior.* Geneva: J. Crespin, 1554. OE 12/2 = CO 48: 317–574.

Calvin, John. *Commentary on the Acts of the Apostles.* 2 vols. Edited by Henry Beveridge and translated by Christopher Fetherstone. Reprint in *Calvin's Commentaries.* Grand Rapids, MI: Baker Books, 1989.

Calvin, John. *Commentary on the Book of Psalms.* 5 vols. Edited and translated by James Anderson. Reprint in *Calvin's Commentaries.* Grand Rapids, MI: Baker Books, 1989.

Calvin, John. *Commentary on the Book of the Prophet Isaiah.* 4 vols. Edited and translated by William Pringle. Reprint in *Calvin's Commentaries.* Grand Rapids, MI: Baker Books, 1989.

Calvin, John. *Commentary on the Epistle of Paul to the Romans.* Edited and translated by John Owen. Reprint in *Calvin's Commentaries.* Grand Rapids, MI: Baker Books, 1989.

Calvin, John. *Commentary on the Gospel of John.* 2 vols. Edited and translated by William Pringle. Reprint in *Calvin's Commentaries.* Grand Rapids, MI: Baker Books, 1989.

Calvin, John. *Commentary on the Harmony of the Evangelists, Matthew, Mark and Luke.* 3 vols. Edited and translated by William Pringle. Reprint in *Calvin's Commentaries.* Grand Rapids, MI: Baker Books, 1989.

Calvin, John. *Defensio sanae et orthodoxae doctrinae de servitute & liberatione humani arbitrii, adversus calumnias Alberti Pighii Campensis.* Geneva: J. Girard, 1543. CO 6: 225–404.

Calvin, John. *Der Psalter auf der Kanzel Calvins.* Edited and introduction by E. Mülhaupt. Neukirchen: Neukirchener Verlag, 1959.

Calvin, John. *Harmonia ex tribus Evangelistis composita, adiuncto seorsum Johanne.* [Geneva]: R. Estienne, 1555. CO 45, 47.

Calvin, John. *In evangelium secundum Johannem, commentarius Johannis Calvini.* [Geneva]: R. Estienne, 1553. OE 11/1 and 11/2 = CO 47: 1–458.

Calvin, John. *In librum Psalmorum Iohannis Calvini commentarius.* [Geneva]: R. Estienne, 1557. CO 31: 13–842; 32: 1–442.

Calvin, John. *Institutes of the Christian Religion: 1536 Edition.* Revised edition. Translated and annotated by Ford Lewis Battles. Grand Rapids, MI: Eerdmans, 1986.

Calvin, John. *Institutio christianae religionis nunc vere demum suo titulo respondens.* Strasbourg: W. Rihel, 1543.

Calvin, John. *Le livre des Pseaumes exposé par Iehan Calvin.* [Geneva]: C. Badius, 1558. Revised edition, *Commentaires de M. Jean Calvin sur le livre des Pseaumes.* [Geneva]: C. Badius, 1561.

Calvin, John. *Mosis libri quinque cum commentariis: Genesis seorsum, reliqui quatuor in formam harmoniae digesti.* Geneva: H. Estienne, 1563. CO 23–25.

Calvin, John. *The Necessity of Reforming the Church.* In vol. 1 of *Tracts and Treatises on the Reformation of the Church.* Translated by Henry Beveridge and edited by Thomas Torrance, 123–234. Grand Rapids, MI: Eerdmans, 1958.

Calvin, John. *Praelectiones in librum prophetiarum Danielis.* Geneva: J. de Laon, 1561. CO 40: 529–722; 41: 1–304.

Calvin, John. *Predigten über das 2. Buch Samuelis.* Edited by Hanns Rückert. Neukirchen: Neukirchener Verlag, 1961. SC 1.

Calvin, John. *Responsio ad versipellem quendam mediatorem* [Geneva]: J. Crespin, 1561. CO 9: 525–60.

Calvin, John. *Sermons on Galatians.* Translated by Kathy Childress. Edinburgh: Banner of Truth, 1997.

Calvin, John. *Sermons on the Deity of Christ and Other Sermons.* Edited and translated by L. Nixon. 1950. Reprint, Audubon, NJ: Old Paths Publications, 1997.

Calvin, John. *Sermons on 2 Samuel: Chapters 1–13.* Edited and translated by Douglas Kelly. Carlisle, PA: Banner of Truth, 1992.

Calvin, John. *Sermons sur l'Epistre aux Galates* Geneva: F. Perrin, 1563. CO 50: 269–696.

Calvin, John. *Supplex exhortatio ad invictissimum caesarem Carolum quintum et illustrissimos principes aliosque ordines spirae nunc imperii conventum agentes. Ut restituendae ecclesiae curam serio velint suscipere. Eorum omnium nomine edita qui Christum regnare cupiunt* [Geneva]: [J. Girard], 1543. CO 6: 453–534.

Calvin, John. *Three French Treatises.* Edited by Francis M. Higman. London: Athlone, 1970.

Calvin, John, and Pierre Viret. *Deux epistres: L'une demonstre comment Jesus Christ est la fin de la loy; l'autre pour consoler les fideles qui souffrent persecution* [Geneva]: [J. Girard], 1543.

Chrysostom, John. *Commentary on Saint John the Apostle and Evangelist, Homilies 1–47.* Translated by T. A. Goggin. New York: Fathers of the Church, 1957.

Chrysostom, John. *Commentary on Saint John the Apostle and Evangelist, Homilies 48–88.* Translated by T. A. Goggin. New York: Fathers of the Church, 1960.

Connan, François de. *Commentariorum iuris civilis libri X.* 2 vols. Edited by Barthélemy Faye. Paris: J. Kerver, 1553.

Cyril of Alexandria. *Commentary on the Gospel According to S. John.* 2 vols. Oxford: James Parker, 1874.

Denis the Carthusian. *Enarratio in evangelium secundum Joannem.* In vol. 12 of *D. Dionysii Cartusiani opera omnia,* 42 vols. in 44. Monstrolii: S. M. de Pratis, 1901.

Denis the Carthusian. *Enarratio in Leviticum.* In vol. 2 of *D. Dionysii Cartusiani opera omnia,* 42 vols. in 44. Monstrolii: S. M. de Pratis, 1847.

Erasmus, Desiderius. *Paraphrase on John.* Translated and annotated by J. E. Phillips. Vol. 46 of *Collected Works of Erasmus.* Toronto: University of Toronto Press, 1991.

Eusebius. *The History of the Church from Christ to Constantine.* Revised edition. Translated by G. A. Williamson. New York: Penguin, 1989.

Hotman, François. *Antitribonian ou discours d'un grand et renomme jurisconsulte de nostre temps.* Paris: J. Perier, 1603.

Hotman, François. *Consolatio è sacris litteris: Nunc demum edita.* Lyon [i.e., Geneva]: F. Le Preux, 1593.

Hotman, François [E. Varamundus Frisius, pseud.]. *De furoribus gallicis.* Edinburgh [Basel], 1573.

Hotman, François [F. Vilierius, pseud.]. *De statu primitivae ecclesiae.* Hieropolis [i.e., Geneva]: J. Crespin, 1553.

[Hotman, François]. *Epistre envoiee au tigre de la France.* N.p., 1560.

Hotman, François. *Francogallia.* Edited by Ralph Giesey and John H. M. Salmon. Cambridge, UK: Cambridge University Press, 1972.

[Hotman, François]. *Gasparis Colinii Castellonii . . . vita.* N.p., 1575.

[Hotman, François?]. *Le tumulte d'Amboise.* N.p. 1560.

[Hotman, François?]. *Tumultus ambosianus.* N.p., 1560.

Irenaeus. "An Exposition of the Faith: Selections from the Work *Against Heresies* by Irenaeus, Bishop of Lyon." Edited and translated by Edward Rochie Hardy. In *Early Christian Fathers.* Edited by Cyril C. Richardson, 343–98. Philadelphia: Westminster, 1953.

Jerome. *Against Jovinianus.* In *St. Jerome: Letters and Select Works.* Nicene and Post Nicene Fathers, series 2, vol. 6. Grand Rapids, MI: Eerdmans, 1996.

Jerome. *On Illustrious Men.* Translated by T. P. Halton. Washington, DC: Catholic University of America Press, 1999.

Josephus. *Jewish Antiquities, Books I–IV.* Edited and translated by H. St. J. Thackeray. Cambridge, MA: Harvard University Press, 1978.

La forme des prières et chants ecclésiastiques. Geneva, 1542. Facsimile, Kassel: Bärenreiter, 1959.

Lefèvre d'Étaples, Jacques. *Quincuplex Psalterium.* 2nd edition. Paris: H. Estienne, 1513. Reprint, *Quincuplex Psalterium: Fac-similé de l'édition de 1513.* Geneva: Droz, 1979.

Le Psautier de Genève: Images commentées et essai de bibliographie. Geneva: Bibliothèque publique et universitaire, 1986.

Les Pseaumes de David traduicts selon la verité hebraïque, avec annotations tresutiles par Loys Budé: Preface de Jehan Calvin, touchant l'utilité des pseaumes, et de la translation presente. Geneva: J. Crespin, 1551.

Marot, Clément. *Cinquante pseaumes de David mis en françoys selon la verité hebraïque: Édition critique sur la texte de l'édition publiée en 1543 à Genève par Jean Gérard.* Edited by Gérard Defaux. Paris: Honoré Champion, 1995.

Melanchthon, Philip. *Chronicon Carionis* [1558–60]. CR 12: 709–1094.

Melanchthon, Philip. *Commentaire de Philippe Melanc[h]thon sur le livre des revelations du Prophete Daniel; item les explications de Martin Luther sur le mesme Prophète adioutées à la fin.* [Geneva]: J. Crespin, 1555.

Melanchthon, Philipp. *Commentarii in epistolam Pauli ad Romanos.* In *Römerbrief-Kommentar 1532.* Edited by Rolf Schäfer. Vol. 5 of *Melanchthons Werke in Auswahl.* Edited by Robert Stupperich. Gütersloh: Gerd Mohn, 1965.

Melanchthon, Philip. *In Danielem prophetam commentarius.* Wittenberg: J. Klug, 1543. CR 13: 823–980.

Melanchthon, Philip. *Loci communes rerum theologicarum seu hypotyposes theologicae* [1521]. CR 21: 81–227.

Melanchthon, Philip. *Loci communes theologici.* Translated by Lowell J. Satre. In *Melanchthon and Bucer.* Edited by Wilhelm Pauck, 3–152. Philadelphia: Westminster, 1969.

Musculus, Wolfgang. *In sacrosanctum Davidis Psalterium commentarii.* Basel: Herwagen, 1551.

Oecolampadius, John. *In Danielem prophetam Joannis Oecolampadii libri duo.* Basel: J. Bebel, 1530; Basel: T. Wolff, 1530.

Origen. *Commentary on the Gospel According to John, Books 1–10.* Translated by R. E. Heine. Washington, DC: Catholic University of America Press, 1989.

Osiander, Andreas. *Coniecturae de ultimus temporis, ac de fine mundi, ex sacris literis.* Nuremberg: Johann Petreius, 1544.

Osiander, Andreas. *Conjectures of the End of the World.* Translated by G. Joye. Antwerp, 1548.

Rupert of Deutz. *Commentaria in evangelium Sancti Iohannis.* Edited by H. Haacke. Vol. 9 of *Corpus Christianorum Continuatio Mediaevalis.* Turnhout: Brepols, 1969.

Sleidan, John. *De quatuor summis imperiis libri tres.* Strasbourg: Rihel Brothers, 1556.

Sleidan, John. *De statu religionis et reipublicae, Carolo Quinto Caesare, commentarii.* Strasbourg: W. Rihel, 1555.

Thomas Aquinas. *Commentum in Matthaeum et Joannem Evangelistas.* Vol. 10 of *Sancti Thomae Aquinatis Doctoris Angelici Ordinis Praedicatorum opera omnia.* Parma: P. Fiaccadori, 1861. Reprint, New York: Musurgia, 1949.

Secondary Literature

Albrecht, O. "Luthers Arbeiten an der Übersetzung und Auslegung des Propheten Daniel in den Jahren 1530 und 1541." *Archiv für Reformationsgeschichte* 23 (1926): 1–50.

Augustijn, Cornelis. "Calvin in Strasbourg." In *Calvinus Sacrae Scripturae Professor: Calvin as Confessor of Holy Scripture.* Edited by Wilhelm H. Neuser, 166–77. Grand Rapids, MI: Eerdmans, 1994.

Backus, Irena. "The Beast: Interpretations of Daniel 7.2–9 and Apocalypse 13.1–4, 11–12 in Lutheran, Zwinglian and Calvinist Circles in the Late Sixteenth Century." *Reformation and Renaissance Review* 3 (2000): 59–77.

Backus, Irena. "Calvin and the Greek Fathers." In *Continuity and Change: The Harvest of Late Medieval and Reformation History*. Edited by R. J. Bast and A. C. Gow, 253–76. Leiden: Brill, 2000.

Backus, Irena. "Calvin's Judgment of Eusebius of Caesarea: An Analysis." *Sixteenth Century Journal* 22, no. 3 (1991): 419–37.

Backus, Irena. "Church, Communion, and Community in Bucer's Commentary on the Gospel of John." In *Martin Bucer: Reforming Church and Community*. Edited by D. F. Wright, 61–71. Cambridge, UK: Cambridge University Press, 1994.

Backus, Irena. *Historical Method and Confessional Identity in the Era of the Reformation (1378–1615)*. Leiden: Brill, 2003.

Backus, Irena. "L'Exode 20, 3–4 et l'interdiction des images: L'emploi de la tradition patristique par Zwingli et par Calvin." *Nos Monuments d'art et d'histoire* 35 (1984): 319–22.

Backus, Irena. *Life Writing in Reformation Europe: Lives of Reformers by Friends, Disciples, and Foes*. Aldershot, UK: Ashgate, 2008.

Backus, Irena, ed. *The Reception of the Church Fathers in the West: From the Carolingians to the Maurists*. 2 vols. Leiden: Brill, 1997.

Backus, Irena. "Roman Catholic Lives of Calvin from Bolsec to Richelieu: Why the Interest?" In *John Calvin and Roman Catholicism: Critique and Engagement, Then and Now*. Edited by Randall C. Zachman, 25–58. Grand Rapids, MI: Baker Academic, 2008.

Backus, Irena, and Claire Chimelli, eds. *"La vraie piété": Divers traités de Jean Calvin et Confession de foi de Guillaume Farel*. Geneva: Labor et Fides, 1986.

Balserak, Jon. *Divinity Compromised: A Study of Divine Accommodation in the Thought of John Calvin*. Dordrecht: Springer, 2006.

Balserak, Jon. *Establishing the Remnant Church in France: Calvin's Lectures on the Minor Prophets, 1556–1559*. Leiden: Brill, 2011.

Balserak, Jon. *John Calvin as Sixteenth Century Prophet*. Oxford: Oxford University Press, 2014.

Barnes, Robin. *Prophecy and Gnosis: Apocalypticism in the Wake of the Lutheran Reformation*. Stanford, CA: Stanford University Press, 1988.

Berger, Heinrich. *Calvins Geschichtsauffassung*. Zurich: Zwingli Verlag, 1955.

Bergfeld, Christoph. *Franciscus Connanus (1508–1551): Ein Systematiker des römischen Rechts*. Cologne: Böhlau, 1968.

Berman, Howard J. *Law and Revolution*, vol. 2, *The Impact of the Protestant Reformations on the Western Legal Tradition*. Cambridge, MA: Harvard University Press, 2003.

Blacketer, Raymond A. "Calvin as Commentator on the Mosaic Harmony and Joshua." In *Calvin and the Bible*. Edited by Donald K. McKim, 30–52. Cambridge, UK: Cambridge University Press, 2006.

Blacketer, Raymond A. "The Moribund Moralist: Ethical Lessons in Calvin's Commentary on Joshua." In *The Formation of Clerical and Confessional Identities in Early Modern Europe*. Edited by Wim Janse and Barbara Pitkin, 149–68. *Dutch Review of Church History* 85 (2005). Leiden: Brill, 2006.

Blacketer, Raymond A. *The School of God: Pedagogy and Rhetoric in Calvin's Interpretation of Deuteronomy*. Dordrecht: Springer, 2006.

Bohatec, Josef. *Budé und Calvin: Studien zur Gedankenwelt des französischen Frühhumanismus*. Graz: Böhlaus, 1950.

Bohatec, Josef. "Calvin et la procédure civile à Genève." *Revue historique de droit français et étranger*, 4th series, 17 (1938): 229–303.

Bohatec, Josef. "Gott und die Geschichte nach Calvin." *Philosophia Reformata* 1, no. 3 (1936): 129–61.

Bouwsma, William J. "Gallicanism and the Nature of Christendom." 1971; reprint in *A Usable Past: Essays in European Cultural History*, 308–24. Berkeley: University of California Press, 1990.

Braverman, Jay. *Jerome's Commentary on Daniel: A Study of Comparative Jewish and Christian Interpretations of the Hebrew Bible.* Washington, DC: Catholic Biblical Association of America, 1978.

Breen, Quirinus. *John Calvin: A Study in French Humanism.* 2nd edition. [Hamden, CT]: Archon Books, 1968.

Brey, Steven P. "Origen's Commentary on John: Seeing All Creation as Gospel." Ph.D. diss., University of Notre Dame, 2003.

Bruening, Michael. *Calvinism's First Battleground: Conflict and Reform in the Pays de Vaud, 1528–1559.* Dordrecht: Springer, 2005.

Cameron, Euan. "The Bible and the Early Modern Sense of History." In *The New Cambridge History of the Bible*, vol. 3, *From 1450 to 1750*. Edited by Euan Cameron, 657–85. Cambridge, UK: Cambridge University Press, 2016.

Cameron, Euan. "Calvin the Historian: Biblical Antiquity and Scriptural Exegesis in the Quest for a Meaningful Past." In *Calvin and the Book: The Evolution of the Printed Word in Reformed Protestantism.* Edited by Karen E. Spierling, 77–94. Göttingen: Vandenhoeck & Ruprecht, 2015.

Campi, Emidio. "Über das Ende des Weltzeitalters: Aspekte der Rezeption des Danielbuches bei Heinrich Bullinger." In *Europa, Tausendjähriges Reich und Neue Welt: Zwei Jahrtausende Geschichte und Utopie in der Rezeption des Danielbuches.* Edited by Mariano Delgado, Klaus Koch, and Edgar Marsch, 225–38. Stuttgart: Kohlhammer, 2003.

Casteel, Theodore W. "Calvin and Trent: Calvin's Reaction to the Council of Trent in the Context of His Conciliar Thought." *Harvard Theological Review* 63 (1970): 91–117.

Chaix, Henri. *Le Psautier Huguenot: Sa formation et son histoire dans l'Église Réformée.* Geneva: Romet, 1907.

Chaix, Paul. *Récherches sur l'imprimerie à Genève de 1550 à 1564: Étude bibliographique, économique et littéraire.* Geneva: Slatkine, 1978.

Collins, John. *Daniel: A Commentary on the Book of Daniel.* Vol. 27 of *Hermeneia: A Critical and Historical Commentary on the Bible.* Minneapolis, MN: Fortress, 1993.

Dareste, Rodolphe. "Dix ans de la vie de François Hotman (1563–1573)." *Bulletin de la société de l'histoire du protestantisme français* 25 (1876): 529–44.

Dareste, Rodolphe. *Essai sur François Hotman.* Paris: Auguste Durand, 1850.

Dareste, Rodople. "François Hotman: Sa vie et sa correspondance." *Revue historique* 2 (1876): 1–59, 367–435.

Dareste, Rodolphe. "Hotman: D'après de nouvelles lettres des années 1561–1563." *Revue historique* 97 (1908): 297–315.

Daussy, Hugues. "L'action diplomatique de Calvin en faveur des Églises réformées de France (1557–1564)." *Bulletin de la société de l'histoire du protestantisme français (1903–)* 156 (2010): 197–209.

de Boer, Erik A. "Calvin and Colleagues: Propositions and Disputations in the Context of the *congrégations* in Geneva." In *Calvinus Praeceptor Ecclesiae.* Edited by Herman J. Selderhuis, 331–42. Geneva: Droz, 2004.

de Boer, Erik A. "The *congrégation*: An In-Service Theological Training Center for Preachers to the People of Geneva." In *Calvin and the Company of Pastors.* Edited by David L. Foxgrover, 57–87. Grand Rapids, MI: Calvin Studies Society, 2004.

de Boer, Erik A. *Genevan School of the Prophets: The congrégations of the Company of Pastors and Their Influence in 16th Century Europe.* Geneva: Droz, 2012.

de Boer, Erik A. "*Harmonia legis*: Conception and Concept of John Calvin's Expository Project on Exodus–Deuteronomy (1559–63)." *Church History and Religious Culture* 87 (2007): 173–201.

de Boer, Erik A. "Jean Calvin et Ésaïe 1 (1564): Édition d'un texte inconnu, introduit par quelques observations sur la différence et les relations entre congrégation, cours et sermons." *Revue d'histoire et de philosophie religieuses* 80, no. 3 (2000): 371–95.

de Boer, Erik A. *John Calvin on the Visions of Ezekiel: Historical and Hermeneutical Studies in John Calvin's "sermons inédits," Especially on Ezek. 36–48.* Leiden: Brill, 2004.

de Boer, Erik A. "The Presence and Participation of Laypeople in the *congrégations* of the Company of Pastors in Geneva." *Sixteenth Century Journal* 35, no. 3 (Fall 2004): 651–70.

de Greef, Wulfert. *Calvijn en zijn uitleg van de Psalmen: Een onderzoeck naar zijn exegetische methode.* Kampen: Kok, 2006.

de Greef, Wulfert. "Calvin as Commentator on the Psalms." Translated by R. A. Blacketer. In *Calvin and the Bible.* Edited by Donald K. McKim, 85–106. Cambridge, UK: Cambridge University Press, 2006.

de Greef, Wulfert. "Das Verhältnis von Predigt und Kommentar bei Calvin, dargestellt an dem Deuteronomium-Kommentar und den -Predigten." In *Calvinus Servus Christi.* Edited by Wilhelm H. Neuser, 195–204. Budapest: Presseabteilung des Ráday-Kollegiums, 1988.

de Greef, Wulfert. *The Writings of John Calvin, Expanded Edition: An Introductory Guide.* Translated by Lyle D. Bierma. Louisville, KY: Westminster John Knox, 2008.

de Kroon, M. "Bucer und Calvin: Das Obrigkeitsverständnis beider Reformatoren nach ihrer Auslegung von Römer 13." In *Calvinus servus Christi.* Edited by Wilhelm H. Neuser, 209–24. Budapest: Presseabteilung des Ráday-Kollegiums, 1988.

de Lubac, Henri. *Exégèse médiévale: Les quatre sens de l'Écriture.* 4 vols. Paris: Aubier, 1959–64.

DeVries, Dawn. "Calvin's Preaching." In *The Cambridge Companion to John Calvin.* Edited by Donald K. McKim, 106–24. Cambridge, UK: Cambridge University Press, 2004.

Diefendorf, Barbara B. "The Huguenot Psalter and the Faith of French Protestants in the Sixteenth Century." In *Culture and Identity in Early Modern Europe (1500–1800): Essays in Honor of Natalie Zemon Davis.* Edited by Barbara B. Diefendorf and Carla Hesse, 41–63. Ann Arbor: University of Michigan Press, 1993.

Dipple, Geoffrey. *"Just as in the Time of the Apostles": Uses of History in the Radical Reformation.* Kitchener, Ontario: Pandora Press, 2005.

Douglass, Jane Dempsey. "Pastor and Teacher of the Refugees: Calvin in the Work of Heiko A. Oberman." In *The Work of Heiko A. Oberman: Papers from the Symposium on His Seventieth Birthday.* Edited by Thomas A. Brady et al., 51–65. Leiden: Brill, 2003.

Doumergue, Emile. *Jean Calvin: Les hommes et les choses de son temps.* 7 vols. Lausanne: Georges Bridel, 1899–1927.

Dubois, Claude-Gilbert. *La conception de l'histoire en France au XVIe siècle (1560–1610).* Paris: A. G. Nizet, 1977.

Duquesne, Joseph. "François Bauduin et la Réforme." *Bulletin de l'Académie delphinale* 5th series, 9 (1917): 55–108.

Eire, Carlos M. N. *War against the Idols: The Reformation of Worship from Erasmus to Calvin*. Cambridge, UK: Cambridge University Press, 1986.

Ellwein, Eduard. *Summus Evangelista: Die Botschaft des Johannesevangeliums in der Auslegung Luthers*. Munich: Chr. Kaiser, 1960.

Engammare, Max. "Calvin: A Prophet without a Prophecy." *Church History: Studies in Christianity and Culture* 67 (1998): 643–61.

Engammare, Max. "Calvin monarchomaque? Du soupçon à l'argument." *Archiv für Reformationsgeschichte* 89 (1998): 207–26.

Engammare, Max. "'Dass ich im Hause des Herrn bleiben könne, mein Leben lang': Das Exil in den Predigten Calvins." In *Calvin und Calvinismus: Europäische Perspektiven*. Edited by Irene Dingel and Herman J. Selderhuis, 229–42. Göttingen: Vandenhoeck & Ruprecht, 2011.

Engammare, Max. "Le Paradis à Genève: Comment Calvin prêchait-il la chute aux Genevois?" *Études théologiques et religieuses* 69 (1994): 329–47.

Engammare, Max. "Une certaine idée de la France chez Jean Calvin l'exilé." *Bulletin de la société de l'histoire du protestantisme français* 155 (2009): 15–27.

Erbe, Michael. *François Bauduin (1520–1573): Biographie eines Humanisten*. Gütersloh: Gütersloher Verlagshaus Mohn, 1978.

Essary, Kirk. *Erasmus and Calvin on the Foolishness of God: Reason and Emotion in the Christian Philosophy*. Toronto: University of Toronto Press, 2017.

Farmer, Craig. "Changing Images of the Samaritan Woman in Early Reformed Commentaries on John." *Church History* 65, no. 3 (1996): 365–75.

Farmer, Craig. *The Gospel of John in the Sixteenth Century: The Johannine Exegesis of Wolfgang Musculus*. New York: Oxford University Press, 1997.

Farmer, Craig. "Wolfgang Musculus's Commentary on John: Tradition and Innovation in the Story of the Woman Taken in Adultery." In *Biblical Interpretation in the Era of the Reformation: Essays Presented to David C. Steinmetz in Honor of His Sixtieth Birthday*. Edited by Richard A. Muller and John L. Thompson, 216–40. Grand Rapids, MI: Eerdmans, 1996.

Farrar, Frederic W. "Calvin as an Expositor." *The Expositor*, 2nd series, 7 (1884): 426–44.

Farrar, Frederic W. *History of Interpretation: Eight Lectures Preached before the University of Oxford in the Year MDCCCLXXXV*. London: Macmillan, 1886.

Ficker, Johannes. *Die Anfänge der akademischen Studien in Straßburg*. Strasbourg: Heitz, 1912.

Firth, Katharine. *The Apocalyptic Tradition in Reformation Britain, 1530–1645*. Oxford: Oxford University Press, 1979.

Fischer, Danièle. "Jean Calvin, historien de l'église: Sources et aspects de la pensée historique, et de l'historiographie du Réformateur." Ph.D. diss., University of Strasbourg, 1980.

Fischer, Danièle, "L'Élément historique dans la prédication de Calvin: Un aspect original de l'homilétique du Réformateur." *Revue d'histoire et de philosophie religieuses* 64 (1984): 365–86.

Fischer, Danielle. "L'histoire de l'église dans la pensée de Calvin." *Archiv für Reformationsgeschichte* 77 (1986): 79–125.

Fisher, Jeff. *A Christoscopic Reading of Scripture: Johannes Oecolampadius on Hebrews*. Göttingen: Vandenhoeck & Ruprecht, 2016.

Flaming, Darlene K. "Calvin as Commentator on the Synoptic Gospels." In *Calvin and the Bible*. Edited by Donald K. McKim, 131–63. Cambridge, UK: Cambridge University Press, 2006.

Fraidl, Franz. *Die Exegese der siebzig Wochen Daniels in der alten und mittleren Zeit.* Graz: Leuschner & Lubensky, 1883.

Franklin, Julian H. *Jean Bodin and the Sixteenth-Century Revolution in the Methodology of Law and History.* New York: Columbia University Press, 1963.

Froehlich, Karlfried. "Which Paul? Observations on the Image of the Apostle in the History of Biblical Exegesis." In *New Perspectives on Historical Theology: Essays in Memory of John Meyendorff.* Edited by Bradley Nassif, 279–99. Grand Rapids, MI: Eerdmans, 1996.

Gäbler, Ulrich. "Bullingers Vorlesung über das Johannesevangelium aus dem Jahre 1523." In *Heinrich Bullinger, 1504–1575: Gesammelte Aufsätze zum 400. Todestag.* Edited by U. Gäbler and E. Herkenrath, 13–27. Zurich: Theologischer Verlag, 1975.

Gabriel, Frédéric. "De statu primitivae ecclesiae: Histoire, chrétienté et réforme chez les civilistes de l'école de Bourges (Douaren, Bauduin, Hotman)." In *Bourges à la renaissance, hommes de lettres, hommes de lois.* Edited by Stéphan Geonget, 243–60. Paris: Klincksieck, 2011.

Gammie, John. "A Journey through Danielic Spaces: The Book of Daniel in the Theology and Piety of the Christian Community." *Interpretation* 39 (1985): 144–56.

Ganoczy, Alexandre. "Calvin als paulinischer Theologe: Ein Forschungsansatz zur Hermeneutik Calvins." In *Calvinus Theologus.* Edited by Wilhelm H. Neuser, 39–69. Neukirchen: Neukirchener Verlag, 1976.

Ganoczy, Alexandre. *Calvin: Théologien de l'église et du ministère.* Paris: Editions du Cerf, 1964.

Ganoczy, Alexandre. *La bibliothèque de l'académie de Calvin: Le catalogue de 1572 et ses enseignements.* Geneva: Droz, 1969.

Ganoczy, Alexandre. *The Young Calvin.* Translated by David Foxgrover and Wade Provo. Philadelphia: Westminster John Knox, 1987.

Ganoczy, Alexandre, and Stefan Scheld. *Die Hermeneutik Calvins: Geistesgeschichtliche Voraussetzungen und Grundzüge.* Wiesbaden: Franz Steiner, 1983.

Gerrish, B. A. "The Word of God and the Words of Scripture: Luther and Calvin on Biblical Authority." In *The Old Protestantism and the New: Essays on the Reformation Heritage,* 51–68. Edinburgh: T. & T. Clark, 1982.

Giesey, Ralph. "When and Why Hotman Wrote the *Francogallia.*" *Bibliothèque d'humanisme et renaissance* 29 (1967): 581–611.

Gilmont, Jean-François. "Les sermons de Calvin: De l'oral à l'imprimé." *Bulletin de la société de l'histoire du protestantisme français* 141 (1995): 145–62.

Girardin, Benoît. *Rhétorique et théologique: Calvin, le commentaire de l'Épître aux Romains.* Paris: Beauchesne, 1979.

Göing, Anja-Silvia. "Schulausbildung im Kontext der Bibel: Heinrich Bullingers Auslegungen des Propheten Daniel (1565)." In *Heinrich Bullinger: Life—Thought—Influence.* Edited by Emidio Campi and Peter Opitz, 437–58. Zurich: Theologischer Verlag Zurich, 2007.

Goez, Werner. "Die Danielrezeption im Abendland—Spätantike und Mittelalter." In *Europa, Tausendjähriges Reich und Neue Welt: Zwei Jahrtausende Geschichte und Utopie in der Rezeption des Danielbuches.* Edited by Mariano Delgado, Klaus Koch, and Edgar Marsch, 176–96. Stuttgart: Kohlhammer, 2003.

Goez, Werner. *Translatio imperii: Ein Beitrag zur Geschichte des Geschichtsdenkens und der politischen Theorien im Mittelalter und in der frühen Neuzeit.* Tübingen: J. C. B. Mohr, 1958.

Gordon, Bruce. "The Bible in Reformed Thought, 1520–1750." In *The New Cambridge History of the Bible*, vol. 3, *From 1450 to 1750*. Edited by Euan Cameron, 462–88. Cambridge, UK: Cambridge University Press, 2016.

Gosselin, E. A. *The King's Progress to Jerusalem: Some Interpretations of David during the Reformation Period and Their Patristic and Medieval Background*. Malibu, CA: Undena, 1976.

Goumaz, Louis. *Timothee, ou le ministère évangélique: D'après Calvin et ses commentaires sur le Nouveau Testament*. Lausanne: Editions la Concorde, 1948.

Grabbe, Lester L. "The Seventy-Weeks Prophecy (Daniel 9:24–27) in Early Jewish Interpretation." In *The Quest for Context and Meaning: Studies in Biblical Intertextuality in Honor of James A. Sanders*. Edited by Craig Evans and Shemaryahu Talmon, 595–611. Leiden: Brill, 1997.

Grafton, Anthony. *What Was History? The Art of History in Early Modern Europe*. Cambridge, UK: Cambridge University Press, 2007.

Hall, Basil. "John Calvin, the Jurisconsults, and the *Ius Civile*." In *Studies in Church History*, vol. 3, *Papers Read at the Third Winter and Summer Meetings of the Ecclesiastical History Society*. Edited by G. J. Cuming, 202–16. Leiden: Brill, 1966.

Hazard, Mark. *The Literal Sense and the Gospel of John in Late Medieval Commentary and Literature*. New York: Routledge, 2002.

Hesselink, I. John. *Calvin's Concept of the Law*. Allison Park, PA: Pickwick, 1992.

Higman, Francis. *La diffusion de la réforme en France, 1520–1565*. Geneva: Labor et Fides, 1992.

Hill, Charles E. *The Johannine Corpus in the Early Church*. New York: Oxford University Press, 2004.

Hobbs, R. Gerald. "Hebraica Veritas and Traditio Apostolica: Saint Paul and the Interpretation of the Psalms in the Sixteenth Century." In *The Bible in the Sixteenth Century*. Edited by David C. Steinmetz, 83–99. Durham, NC: Duke University Press 1990.

Hobbs, R. Gerald. "How Firm a Foundation: Martin Bucer's Historical Exegesis of the Psalms." *Church History* 53, no. 4 (1984): 477–91.

Hobbs, R. Gerald. "Martin Bucer on Psalm 22: A Study in the Application of Rabbinic Exegesis by a Christian Hebraist." In *Histoire de l'exégèse au XVIe siècle: Textes du colloque internationale tenu à Genève en 1976*. Edited by Olivier Fatio and Pierre Fraenkel, 144–63. Geneva: Droz, 1978.

Holder, R. Ward. "Calvin as Commentator on the Pauline Epistles." In *Calvin and the Bible*. Edited by Donald K. McKim, 224–56. Cambridge, UK: Cambridge University Press, 2006.

Holder, R. Ward. "Calvin's Exegetical Understanding of the Office of Pastor." In *Calvin and the Company of Pastors*. Edited by David Foxgrover, 179–209. Grand Rapids, MI: Calvin Studies Society, 2004.

Holder, R. Ward. *John Calvin and the Grounding of Interpretation: Calvin's First Commentaries*. Leiden: Brill, 2006.

Holder, R. Ward. "Paul as Calvin's (Ambivalent) Pastoral Model." *Dutch Review of Church History* 84 (2004): 284–98.

Holtrop, P. C. *The Bolsec Controversy on Predestination, from 1551 to 1555*. 2 vols. Lewiston, ME: Edwin Mellen, 1993.

Huppert, George. *The Idea of Perfect History: Historical Erudition and Historical Philosophy in Renaissance France*. Urbana: University of Illinois Press, 1970.

Jarrott, C. A. L. "Erasmus' *In Principio Erat Sermo*: A Controversial Translation." *Studies in Philology* 61 (1964): 35–40.

Käser, Walter. "Die Monarchie im Spiegel von Calvins Daniel-Kommentar: Ein historischer Beitrag zur reformierten Lehre vom Staat." *Evangelische Theologie* 11 (1951–52): 112–37.

Kealy, Sean P. *John's Gospel and the History of Biblical Interpretation*. 2 vols. Lewiston, ME: Edwin Mellen, 2002.

Keen, Ralph. "The Limits of Power and Obedience in the Later Calvin." *Calvin Theological Journal* 27 (1992): 252–76.

Kelley, Donald R. *Foundations of Modern Historical Scholarship: Language, Law, and History in the French Renaissance*. New York: Columbia University Press, 1970.

Kelley, Donald R. *François Hotman: A Revolutionary's Ordeal*. Princeton, NJ: Princeton University Press, 1973.

Kelley, Donald R. "Legal Humanism and the Sense of History." *Studies in the Renaissance* 13 (1966): 184–99.

Kelly, Douglas. "Varied Themes in Calvin's 2 Samuel Sermons and the Development of His Thought." In *Calvinus Sincerioris Religionis Vindex: Calvin as Protector of the Purer Religion*. Edited by Wilhelm H. Neuser and Brian G. Armstrong, 209–23. Kirksville, MO: Sixteenth Century Journal, 1997.

Kess, Alexandra. *Johann Sleidan and the Protestant Vision of History*. Burlington, VT: Ashgate, 2008.

Kingdon, Robert M. *Geneva and the Coming of the Wars of Religion in France, 1555–1563*. Geneva: Droz, 1956.

Kingdon, Robert M. "Uses of the Psalter in Calvin's Geneva." In *Der Genfer Psalter und seine Rezeption in Deutschland, der Schweiz und den Niederlanden: 16.–18. Jahrhundert*. Edited by E. Grunewald, H. P. Jürgens, and J. R. Luth, 21–32. Tübingen: Max Niemeyer, 2004.

Klepper, Deeana Copeland. "Theories of Interpretation: The *quadriga* and Its Successors." In *The New Cambridge History of the Bible*, vol. 3, *From 1450 to 1750*. Edited by Euan Cameron, 418–38. Cambridge, UK: Cambridge University Press, 2016.

Kleyser, Friedrich. "Calvin und Franz Hotman." In *Geschichtliche Kräfte und Entscheidungen: Festschrift zum fünfundsechzigsten Geburtstage von Otto Becker*. Edited by Martin Göhring and Alexander Scharff, 47–64. Wiesbaden: Franz Steiner, 1954.

Knowles, Louis E. "The Interpretation of the Seventy Weeks of Daniel in the Early Fathers." *Westminster Theological Journal* 7, no. 2 (1945): 136–60.

Koch, Klaus. "Europabewusstsein und Danielrezeption zwischen 1648 und 1848." In *Europa, Tausendjähriges Reich und Neue Welt: Zwei Jahrtausende Geschichte und Utopie in der Rezeption des Danielbuches*. Edited by Mariano Delgado, Klaus Koch, and Edgar Marsch, 326–84. Stuttgart: Kohlhammer, 2003.

Koen, Lars. *The Saving Passion: Incarnational and Soteriological Thought in Cyril of Alexandria's Commentary on the Gospel According to St. John*. Stockholm: Almqvist & Wiksell, 1991.

Kok, Joel E. "Heinrich Bullinger's Exegetical Method: The Model for Calvin?" In *Biblical Interpretation in the Era of the Reformation: Essays Presented to David C. Steinmetz in Honor of His Sixtieth Birthday*. Edited by Richard A. Muller and John L. Thompson, 241–54. Grand Rapids, MI: Eerdmans, 1996.

Kok, Joel E. "The Influence of Martin Bucer on John Calvin's Interpretation of Romans: A Comparative Case Study." Ph.D. diss., Duke University, 1993.

Kraus, Hans-Joachim. "Calvin's Exegetical Principles." *Interpretation* 31 (1977): 8–18.

Krey, Philip D. W. "Nicholas of Lyra's Commentary on Daniel in the Literal Postill (1329)." In *Die Geschichte der Daniel-Auslegung in Judentum, Christentum und Islam: Studien zur Kommentierung des Danielbuches in Literatur und Kunst.* Edited by Katharina Bracht und David S. du Toit, 199–215. Berlin: De Gruyter, 2007.

Kuropka, Nicole. *Philipp Melanchthon: Wissenschaft und Gesellschaft.* Tübingen: Mohr Siebeck, 2002.

Lambert, Thomas Austin. "Preaching, Praying, and Policing the Reform in Sixteenth-Century Geneva." Ph.D. diss., University of Wisconsin–Madison, 1998.

Lane, Anthony N. S. *John Calvin: Student of the Church Fathers.* Edinburgh: T. & T. Clark, 1999.

Langston, Scott M. *Exodus through the Centuries.* Oxford: Blackwell, 2006.

Lyon, Gregory B. "Baudouin, Flacius, and the Plan for the Magdeburg Centuries." *Journal of the History of Ideas* 64, no. 2 (2003): 253–72.

Maag, Karin. *Seminary or University? The Genevan Academy and Reformed Higher Education, 1560–1620.* Brookfield, VT: Ashgate, 1995.

Madigan, Kevin. *Olivi and the Interpretation of Matthew in the High Middle Ages.* Notre Dame, IN: University of Notre Dame Press, 2003.

Manetsch, Scott. *Theodore Beza and the Quest for Peace in France, 1572–1598.* Leiden: Brill, 2000.

McKee, Elsie. "Calvin and His Colleagues as Pastors: Some New Insights into the Collegial Ministry of Word and Sacraments." In *Calvinus Praeceptor Ecclesiae: Papers of the International Congress on Calvin Research.* Edited by Herman J. Selderhuis, 9–42. Geneva: Droz, 2004.

McKee, Elsie Anne. "Calvin's Exegesis of Romans 12:8—Social, Accidental, or Theological?" *Calvin Theological Journal* 23 (1988): 6–18.

McKee, Elsie Anne. "Calvin's Teaching on the Elder Illuminated by Exegetical History." In *John Calvin and the Church: A Prism of Reform.* Edited by Timothy George, 147–55. Louisville, KY: Westminster John Knox, 1990.

McKee, Elsie Anne. *Elders and the Plural Ministry: The Role of Exegetical History in Illuminating John Calvin's Theology.* Geneva: Droz, 1988.

McKee, Elsie Anne. *John Calvin on the Diaconate and Liturgical Almsgiving.* Geneva: Droz, 1984.

McKee, Elsie Anne. "Les anciens et l'interprétation de I Tim 5, 17 chez Calvin: Une curiosité dans l'histoire de l'exégèse." *Revue de théologie et de philosophie* 120 (1988): 411–17.

McKee, Elsie Anne. *The Pastoral Ministry and Worship in Calvin's Geneva.* Geneva: Droz, 2016.

Mellet, Paul-Alexis. "'Une sophisterie de chaffoureur': Histoire des institutions et enseignement du droit chez Hotman." In *Bourges à la renaissance, hommes de lettres, hommes de lois.* Edited by Stéphan Geonget, 225–41. Paris: Klincksieck, 2011.

Miegge, Mario. *Il sogno del re di Babilonia: Profezia e storia da Thomas Müntzer a Isaac Newton.* Milan: Feltrinelli, 1995.

Miegge, Mario. "'Regnum quartum ferrum' und 'lapis de monte': Die kritische Wende in der Danielrezeption im 16. Jahrhundert und ihre Folgen in Theologie und Politik." In *Europa, Tausendjähriges Reich und Neue Welt: Zwei Jahrtausende Geschichte und Utopie in der Rezeption des Danielbuches.* Edited by Mariano Delgado, Klaus Koch, and Edgar Marsch, 239–51. Stuttgart: Kohlhammer, 2003.

Millet, Olivier. *Calvin et la dynamique de la parole: Étude de rhétorique réformée.* Paris: Honoré Champion, 1992.

Millet, Olivier. "Les *Loci communes* de 1535 et l'*Institution de la Religion chrétienne* de 1539–1541, ou Calvin en dialogue avec Melanchthon." In *Melanchthon und Europa,* part 2, *Westeuropa.* Melanchthon-Schriften der Stadt Bretten 6. Edited by Günter Frank and Kees Meerhoff, 85–96. Stuttgart: Thorbecke, 2002.

Minnis, A. J., and A. B. Scott, eds. *Medieval Literary Theory and Criticism, c. 1100–c. 1375: The Commentary Tradition.* Oxford: Clarendon Press, 1988.

Moehn, Wilhelmus H. Th. "Calvin as Commentator on the Acts of the Apostles." In *Calvin and the Bible.* Edited by Donald K. McKim, 199–223. Cambridge, UK: Cambridge University Press, 2006.

Moehn, Wilhelmus H. Th. *God Calls Us to His Service: The Relation between God and His Audience in Calvin's Sermons on Acts.* Geneva: Droz, 2001.

Monheit, Michael L. "Guillaume Budé, Andrea Alciato, Pierre de l'Éstoile: Renaissance Interpreters of Roman Law." *Journal of the History of Ideas* 58, no. 1 (1997): 21–40.

Monheit, Michael L. "Passion and Order in the Formation of Calvin's Sense of Religious Authority." Ph.D. diss., Princeton University, 1988.

Monheit, Michael L. "Young Calvin, Textual Interpretation and Roman Law." *Bibliothèque d'Humanisme et Renaissance* 59, no. 2 (1997): 263–82.

Moreau-Reibel, Jean. *Jean Bodin et le droit public comparé dans ses rapports avec la philosophie de l'histoire.* Paris: J. Vrin, 1933.

Most, Glenn W. *Doubting Thomas.* Cambridge, MA: Harvard University Press, 2007.

Möller, Hans. Review of *The King's Progress to Jerusalem: Some Interpretations of David during the Reformation Period and Their Patristic and Medieval Background,* by E. A. Gosselin. *Theologische Literaturzeitung* 103 (1978): 758–59.

Muller, Richard A. "Biblical Interpretation in the Era of the Reformation: The View from the Middle Ages." In *Biblical Interpretation in the Era of the Reformation: Essays Presented to David C. Steinmetz in Honor of His Sixtieth Birthday.* Edited by Richard A. Muller and John L. Thompson, 3–22. Grand Rapids, MI: Eerdmans, 1996.

Muller, Richard A. "The Hermeneutic of Promise and Fulfillment in Calvin's Exegesis of the Old Testament Prophecies of the Kingdom." In *The Bible in the Sixteenth Century.* Edited by David C. Steinmetz, 68–82. Durham, NC: Duke University Press, 1990.

Muller, Richard A. "*Ordo docendi*: Melanchthon and the Organization of Calvin's *Institutes,* 1536–1539." In *Melanchthon in Europe: His Work and Influence beyond Wittenberg.* Edited by Karin Maag, 123–40. Grand Rapids, MI: Baker, 1999.

Muller, Richard A. "'Scimus enim quod lex spiritualis est': Melanchthon and Calvin on the Interpretation of Romans 7.14–23." In *Philip Melanchthon (1497–1560) and the Commentary.* Edited by Timothy J. Wengert and M. Patrick Graham, 216–37. Sheffield, UK: Sheffield Academic Press, 1997.

Muller, Richard A., and John L. Thompson, eds. *Biblical Interpretation in the Era of the Reformation: Essays Presented to David C. Steinmetz in Honor of His Sixtieth Birthday.* Grand Rapids, MI: Eerdmans, 1996.

Naphy, William G. *Calvin and the Consolidation of the Genevan Reformation.* Revised edition. Louisville, KY: Westminster John Knox, 2003.

Naphy, William G. "Calvin and Geneva." In *The Reformation World.* Edited by Andrew Pettegree, 309–22. London: Routledge, 2000.

Neugebauer, Richard. "Exegetical Structure in the *Institutes of the Christian Religion* and the Biblical Commentaries of John Calvin: A Study of the *Commentary on the Four,*

Last Books of Moses Arranged in the Form of a Harmony." M.A. thesis, Columbia University, 1968.

Nevelet, Pierre. "Elogium Franc. Hotmani IC" [1592]. In *Franc. Hotmani iuriconsulti operum tomus primus [-tertius].* 3 vols., 1:vi–xiii. Lyon: Vignon & Stoer, 1599–1600.

Nijenhuis, Willem. "The Limits of Civil Disobedience in Calvin's Latest Known Sermons: The Development of His Ideas of the Right of Civil Resistance." In *Ecclesia Reformata: Studies on the Reformation,* 2: 73–94. Leiden: Brill, 1994.

Oberman, Heiko A. "*Europa afflicta:* The Reformation of the Refugees." *Archiv für Reformationsgeschichte* 83 (1992): 91–111. Reprint in *John Calvin and the Reformation of the Refugees,* 177–94. Geneva: Droz, 2009.

Oberman, Heiko A. *Forerunners of the Reformation: The Shape of Late Medieval Thought.* Translated by P. L. Nyhus. New York: Holt, Rinehart & Winston, 1966.

Oberman, Heiko A. *The Two Reformations: The Journey from the Last Days to the New World.* Edited by Donald Weinstein. New Haven, CT: Yale University Press, 2003.

Ocker, Christopher. *Biblical Poetics before Humanism and Reformation.* Cambridge, UK: Cambridge University Press, 2002.

Opitz, Peter. "The Exegetical and Hermeneutical Work of John Oecolampadius, Huldrych Zwingli, and John Calvin." In vol. 2 of *Hebrew Bible / Old Testament: The History of Its Interpretation.* Edited by Magne Saebø, 407–51. Göttingen: Vandenhoeck & Ruprecht, 2008.

Pak, G. Sujin. "Contributions of Commentaries on the Minor Prophets to the Formation of Distinctive Lutheran and Reformed Confessional Identities." *Church History and Religious Culture* 92 (2012): 237–60.

Pak, G. Sujin. *The Judaizing Calvin: Sixteenth-Century Debates over the Messianic Psalms.* New York: Oxford University Press, 2010.

Pak, G. Sujin. *The Reformation of Prophecy: Early Modern Interpretations of the Prophet and Old Testament Prophecy.* New York: Oxford University Press, 2018.

Pannier, Jacques. "Hotman en Suisse (1547–1590)." *Zwingliana* 7 (1940): 137–72.

Parker, Charles H. "Bourges to Geneva: Methodological Links between Legal Humanists and Calvinist Reformers." *Comitatus: A Journal of Medieval and Renaissance Studies* 20, no. 1 (1989): 59–70.

Parker, T. H. L. *Calvin's New Testament Commentaries.* 2nd edition. Louisville, KY: Westminster John Knox, 1993.

Parker, T. H. L. *Calvin's Old Testament Commentaries.* Edinburgh: T. & T. Clark, 1986.

Parker, T. H. L. *Calvin's Preaching.* Louisville, KY: Westminster John Knox, 1992.

Pauw, Amy Plantinga. "'Becoming a Part of Israel': John Calvin's Exegesis of Isaiah." In *"As Those Who Are Taught": The Interpretation of Isaiah from the LXX to the SBL.* Edited by Claire Mathews McGinnis and Patricia K. Tull, 201–22. Atlanta, GA: Society of Biblical Literature, 2006.

Pesch, Otto Hermann. "Sittengebote, Kultvorschriften, Rechtssatzungen." In *Thomas von Aquino: Interpretation und Rezeption: Studien und Texte.* Edited by W. Eckert, 488–518. Mainz: Matthias-Grünewald, 1974.

Peter, Rodolphe. "Calvin and Louis Budé's Translation of the Psalms." In *John Calvin: A Collection of Distinguished Essays.* Edited by G. E. Duffield, 190–209. Grand Rapids, MI: Eerdmans, 1966.

Pitkin, Barbara. "Calvin and Politics According to the Mosaic Harmony (1563 | 1564): Text, Paratext, and Context." In *Calvin frater in Domino.* Edited by Arnold Huijgen and Karin Maag, 37–56. Göttingen: Vandenhoeck & Ruprecht, 2020.

Pitkin, Barbara. "Calvin as Commentator on the Gospel of John." In *Calvin and the Bible*. Edited by Donald K. McKim, 164–98. Cambridge, UK: Cambridge University Press, 2006.

Pitkin, Barbara. "Calvin on the Early Reformation." In *Calvin and the Early Reformation*. Edited by Brian C. Brewer and David M. Whitford, 200–24. Leiden: Brill, 2020.

Pitkin, Barbara. "Calvin's Commentary on Psalm 1 and Providential Faith: Reformed Influences on the Psalms in English." In *Crossing Traditions: Essays on the Reformation and Intellectual History in Honour of Irena Backus*. Edited by Maria-Cristina Pitassi and Daniela Solfaroli Camillocci, 164–81. Leiden: Brill, 2018.

Pitkin, Barbara. "Calvin's Mosaic Harmony: Biblical Exegesis and Early Modern Legal History." *Sixteenth Century Journal* 41, no. 2 (2010): 441–66.

Pitkin, Barbara. "Calvin's Reception of Paul." In *A Companion to Paul in the Reformation*. Edited by R. Ward Holder, 267–96. Leiden: Brill, 2009.

Pitkin, Barbara. "Calvin, Theology, and History." *Seminary Ridge Review* 12, no. 2 (2010): 1–16.

Pitkin, Barbara. "Exil im Spiegel der Geschichte: Calvins Jesajakommentar (1559)." In *Calvin und Calvinismus: Europäische Perspektiven*. Edited by Irene Dingel and Herman Selderhuis, 215–28. Göttingen: Vandenhoeck & Ruprecht, 2011.

Pitkin, Barbara. "Imitation of David: David as a Paradigm for Faith in Calvin's Exegesis of the Psalms." *Sixteenth Century Journal* 24, no. 4 (1993): 843–63.

Pitkin, Barbara. "John Calvin and the Interpretation of the Bible." In vol. 2 of *A History of Biblical Interpretation*. Edited by Alan J. Hauser and Duane F. Watson, 341–71. Grand Rapids, MI: Eerdmans, 2009.

Pitkin, Barbara. "John Calvin, François Hotman, and the Living Lessons of Sacred History." In *Politics, Gender, and Belief: The Long-Term Impact of the Reformation*. Edited by Amy Nelson Burnett, Kathleen Comerford, and Karin Maag, 19–44. Geneva: Droz, 2014.

Pitkin, Barbara. "John Calvin's Vision of Reform, Historical Thinking, and the Modern World." In *The Oxford Handbook of Calvin and Calvinism*. Edited by Bruce Gordon and Carl R. Trueman. New York: Oxford University Press, forthcoming.

Pitkin, Barbara. "Prophecy and History in Calvin's Lectures on Daniel (1561)." In *Die Geschichte der Daniel-Auslegung in Judentum, Christentum und Islam: Studien zur Kommentierung des Danielbuches in Literatur und Kunst*. Edited by Katharina Bracht und David S. du Toit, 323–47. Berlin: De Gruyter, 2007.

Pitkin, Barbara. "The Protestant Zeno: Calvin and the Development of Melanchthon's Anthropology." *Journal of Religion* 84 (2004): 345–78.

Pitkin, Barbara. "Seeing and Believing in the Commentaries on John by Martin Bucer and John Calvin." *Church History* 68, no. 4 (1999): 865–85.

Pitkin, Barbara. "The Spiritual Gospel? Christ and Human Nature in Calvin's Commentary on John." In *The Formation of Clerical and Confessional Identities in Early Modern Europe*. Edited by W. Janse and B. Pitkin, 187–204. *Dutch Review of Church History* 85 (2005). Leiden: Brill, 2006.

Pitkin, Barbara. *What Pure Eyes Could See: Calvin's Doctrine of Faith in Its Exegetical Context*. New York: Oxford University Press, 1999.

Pocock, J. G. A. "Introductory: The French Prelude to Modern Historiography." In *The Ancient Constitution and the Feudal Law*. 2nd edition, 1–29. Cambridge, UK: Cambridge University Press, 1987.

Preus, James Samuel. *From Shadow to Promise: Old Testament Interpretation from Augustine to the Young Luther*. Cambridge, MA: Harvard University Press, 1969.

Puckett, David L. *John Calvin's Exegesis of the Old Testament*. Louisville, KY: Westminster John Knox, 1995.

Rabil, Albert, Jr. "Erasmus' Paraphrase of the Gospel of John." *Church History* 48 (1979): 142–55.

Reid, Jonathan. *King's Sister—Queen of Dissent: Marguerite of Navarre (1492–1549) and Her Evangelical Network*. 2 vols. Leiden: Brill, 2009.

Reid, W. Stanford. "John Calvin, Lawyer and Legal Reformer." In *Through Christ's Word: A Festschrift for Dr. Philip E. Hughes*. Edited by Philip Edgcumbe Hughes, W. Robert Godfrey, and Jesse L. Boyd, 149–64. Phillipsburg, NJ: Presbyterian and Reformed, 1985.

Roussel, Bernard. "John Calvin's Interpretation of Psalm 22." In *Adaptations of Calvinism in Reformation Europe: Essays in Honour of Brian G. Armstrong*. Edited by Mack P. Holt, 9–20. Aldershot, UK: Ashgate, 2007.

Sawyer, John F. A. *The Fifth Gospel: Isaiah in the History of Christianity*. Cambridge, UK: Cambridge University Press, 1996.

Schaff, Philip. "Calvin as a Commentator." *Presbyterian and Reformed Review* 3 (1892): 462–69.

Scheible, Heinz. *Die Entstehung der Magdeburger Zenturien: Ein Beitrag zur Geschichte der historiographischen Methode*. Gütersloh: Gütersloher Verlagshaus Gerd Mohn, 1966.

Scheible, Heinz. "Melanchthons Verständnis des Danielbuchs." In *Die Geschichte der Daniel-Auslegung in Judentum, Christentum und Islam: Studien zur Kommentierung des Danielbuches in Literatur und Kunst*. Edited by Katharina Bracht and David S. du Toit, 293–322. Berlin: De Gruyter, 2007.

Scheld, Stefan. "Die missionarische Verkündigung des Paulus in Calvins Kommentar der Apostelgeschichte." In *Creatio ex amore: Beiträge zu einer Theologie der Liebe*. Edited by Thomas Franke, Markus Knapp, and Johannes Schmid, 312–28. Würzburg: Echter, 1989.

Schilling, Johannes. "Melanchthons loci communes deutsch." In *Humanismus und Wittenberger Reformation*. Edited by Michael Beyer and Günther Wartenberg, 337–52. Leipzig: Evangelische Verlagsanstalt, 1996.

Schorch, Stefan. "Die Auslegung des Danielbuches in der Schrift 'Die Quellen der Erlösung' des Don Isaak Abravanel (1437–1508)." In *Die Geschichte der Daniel-Auslegung in Judentum, Christentum und Islam: Studien zur Kommentierung des Danielbuches in Literatur und Kunst*. Edited by Katharina Bracht and David S. du Toit, 179–98. Berlin: De Gruyter, 2007.

Schreiner, Susan E. "Exegesis and Double Justice in Calvin's Sermons on Job." *Church History* 58, no. 3 (1989): 322–38.

Schreiner, Susan E. "'Through a Mirror Dimly': Calvin's Sermons on Job." *Calvin Theological Journal* 21, no. 2 (1986): 175–93.

Schreiner, Susan E. *Where Shall Wisdom Be Found? Calvin's Exegesis of Job from Medieval and Modern Perspectives*. Chicago: University of Chicago Press, 1994.

Seifert, Arno. *Der Rückzug der biblischen Prophetie von der neueren Geschichte: Studien zur Geschichte der Reichstheologie des frühneuzeitlichen deutschen Protestantismus*. Cologne: Böhlau, 1990.

Selderhuis, Herman J. "Calvin as an Asylum Seeker: Calvin's Psalms Commentary as a Reflection of His Theology and as a Source of His Biography." In *Calvin's Books: Festschrift Dedicated to Peter De Klerk on the Occasion of His Seventieth Birthday*. Edited by Wilhelm Neuser et al., 283–300. Heerenveen: J. J. Groen, 1997.

Smalley, Beryl. *The Gospels in the Schools, c. 1100–c. 1280*. London: Hambledon Press, 1985.

Smalley, Beryl. *The Study of the Bible in the Middle Ages*. 3rd edition. Oxford: Basil Blackwell, 1983.

Smith, David Baird. "François Hotman." *Scottish Historical Review* 13 (1916): 328–65.

Smith, Lesley. *The Glossa Ordinaria: The Making of a Medieval Bible Commentary*. Leiden: Brill, 2009.

Spicq, C. *Esquisse d'une histoire de l'exégèse latine au moyen âge*. Paris: J. Vrin, 1944.

Spierling, Karen E. *Infant Baptism in Reformation Geneva: The Shaping of a Community, 1536–1564*. Aldershot, UK: Ashgate, 2005. Reprint, Louisville, KY: Westminster John Knox, 2009.

Staehelin, Ernst. *Das theologische Lebenswerk Johannes Oekolampads*. Leipzig: M. Heinsius, 1939.

Stauffer, Richard. "Autour du Colloque de Poissy: Calvin et le *De officio pii ac publicae tranquillitatis vere amantis viri.*" In *Actes du colloque L'Amiral de Coligny et son temps*, 135–53. Paris: Société de l'histoire du protestantisme français, 1974. Reprint in *Interprètes de la Bible: Études sur les réformateurs du XVIe siècle*, 249–67. Paris: Beauchesne, 1980.

Steenkamp, J. J. "Calvin's Exhortation to Charles V (1543)." In *Calvinus Sincerioris Religionis Vindex: Calvin as Protector of the Purer Religion*. Edited by Wilhelm H. Neuser and Brian G. Armstrong, 309–14. Kirksville, MO: Sixteenth Century Journal, 1997.

Steinmetz, David C. *Calvin in Context*. 2nd edition. New York: Oxford University Press, 2010.

Steinmetz, David C. "Divided by a Common Past: The Reshaping of the Christian Exegetical Tradition in the Sixteenth Century." *Journal of Medieval and Early Modern Studies* 27 (1997): 245–64.

Steinmetz, David C. Review of *The King's Progress to Jerusalem: Some Interpretations of David during the Reformation Period and Their Patristic and Medieval Background*, by E. A. Gosselin. *Archive for Reformation History: Literature Review* 7 (1978): 31.

Strohm, Christoph. *Ethik im frühen Calvinismus: Humanistische Einflüsse, philosophische, juristische und theologische Argumentationen sowie mentalitätsgeschichtliche Aspekte am Beispiel des Calvin-Schülers Lambertus Danaeus*. Berlin: De Gruyter, 1996.

Strohm, Christoph. "Sixteenth-Century French Legal Education and Calvin's Legal Education." Translated by Barbara Pitkin. In *Calvin and the Early Reformation*. Edited by Brian C. Brewer and David M. Whitford, 44–57. Leiden: Brill, 2020.

Strohm, Stefan. "Luthers Vorrede zum Propheten Daniel in seiner Deutschen Bibel." In *Die Geschichte der Daniel-Auslegung in Judentum, Christentum und Islam: Studien zur Kommentierung des Danielbuches in Literatur und Kunst*. Edited by Katharina Bracht and David S. du Toit, 219–44. Berlin: De Gruyter, 2007.

Stupperich, Robert. "Melanchthons Proverbien-Kommentare." In *Der Kommentar in der Renaissance*. Edited by August Buck and Otto Herding, 21–34. Boppard: Harald Boldt, 1975.

Thompson, John L. "Calvin as a Biblical Interpreter." In *The Cambridge Companion to John Calvin*. Edited by Donald K. McKim, 58–73. Cambridge, UK: Cambridge University Press, 2004.

Thompson, John L. "Calvin's Exegetical Legacy: His Reception and Transmission of Text and Tradition." In *The Legacy of John Calvin*. Edited by D. L. Foxgrover, 31–56. Grand Rapids, MI: CRC Product Services, 2000.

Thompson, John Lee. *John Calvin and the Daughters of Sarah: Women in Regular and Exceptional Roles in the Exegesis of Calvin, His Predecessors, and His Contemporaries.* Geneva: Droz, 1992.

Thompson, John L. "Second Thoughts about Conscience: Nature, the Law, and the Law of Nature in Calvin's Pentateuchal Exegesis." In *Calvinus Pastor Ecclesiae.* Edited by Herman J. Selderhuis and Arnold Huijgen, 123–46. Göttingen: Vandenhoeck & Ruprecht, 2016.

Timmerman, Daniel. "'The World Always Perishes, the Church Will Last Forever': Church and Eschatology in Bullinger's Sermons on the Book of Daniel (1565)." *Zwingliana* 36 (2009): 85–101.

Torrance, Thomas F. *The Hermeneutics of John Calvin.* Edinburgh: Scottish Academic Press, 1988.

Trinkaus, Charles. "Renaissance Problems in Calvin's Theology." *Studies in the Renaissance* 1 (1954): 59–80.

Trocmé-Latter, Daniel. *The Singing of the Strasbourg Protestants, 1523–1541.* Burlington, VT: Routledge, 2015.

Troje, Hans Erich. "'Peccatum Triboniani': Zur Dialektik der 'Interpretatio duplex' bei François Baudouin." *Studia et Documenta Historiae et Iuris* 36 (1970): 341–58.

Turchetti, Mario. "Calvin face aux tenants de la concorde (moyenneurs) et aux partisans de la tolérance (castellionistes)." In *Calvin et ses contemporains.* Edited by Olivier Millet, 43–56. Geneva: Droz, 1998.

Turchetti, Mario. *Concordia o Tolleranza? François Bauduin (1520–1573) e i "Moyenneurs."* Geneva: Droz, 1984.

Van den Berg, Machiel A. "Het rijk van Christus als historische realiteit: Calvijns anti-apocalyptische uitleg van het boek Daniël." Ph.D. diss., University of Utrecht, 2008. https://dspace.library.uu.nl/handle/1874/31558.

van Oort, Johannes. "John Calvin and the Church Fathers." In *The Reception of the Church Fathers in the West: From the Carolingians to the Maurists,* 2 vols. Edited by Irena Backus, 2: 661–700. Leiden: Brill, 1997.

Van Stam, Frans Pieter. "Der Autor des Vorworts zur Olivetan-Bibel *A tous amateurs* aus dem Jahr 1535." *Nederlands archief voor kerkgeschiedenis / Dutch Review of Church History* 84 (2004): 248–67.

Volz, Hans. "Beiträge zu Melanchthons und Calvins Auslegungen des Propheten Daniel." *Zeitschrift für Kirchengeschichte* 67 (1955–56): 93–118.

Walchenbach, John. "John Calvin as Biblical Commentator: An Investigation into Calvin's Use of John Chrysostom as an Exegetical Tutor." Ph.D. diss., University of Pittsburgh, 1974.

Weisheipl, James A. "The Johannine Commentary of Friar Thomas." *Church History* 45 (1976): 185–95.

Wendel, François. *Calvin: Origins and Development of His Religious Thought.* Translated by Philip Mairet. 1963. Reprint, Durham, NC: Labyrinth, 1987.

Wengert, Timothy J. "The Biblical Commentaries of Philip Melanchthon." In *Philip Melanchthon (1497–1560) and the Commentary.* Edited by Timothy J. Wengert and M. Patrick Graham, 106–48. Sheffield, UK: Sheffield Academic Press, 1997.

Wengert, Timothy J. "Philip Melanchthon on Time and History in the Reformation." *Consensus: A Canadian Journal of Public Theology* 30 (2005): 9–33.

Wengert, Timothy J. *Philip Melanchthon's Annotationes in Johannem in Relation to Its Predecessors and Contemporaries.* Geneva: Droz, 1987.

Wengert, Timothy J. "The Rhetorical Paul: Philip Melanchthon's Interpretation of the Pauline Epistles." In *A Companion to Paul in the Reformation*. Edited by R. Ward Holder, 129–64. Leiden: Brill, 2009.

Wilcox, Peter. "Calvin as Commentator on the Prophets." In *Calvin and the Bible*. Edited by Donald K. McKim, 107–30. Cambridge, UK: Cambridge University Press, 2006.

Wilcox, Peter. "The Lectures of John Calvin and the Nature of His Audience, 1555–1564." *Archiv für Reformationsgeschichte* 87 (1996): 136–48.

Wilcox, Peter. "'The Progress of the Kingdom of Christ' in Calvin's Exposition of the Prophets." In *Calvinus Sincerioris Religionis Vindex: Calvin as Protector of the Purer Religion*. Edited by Wilhelm H. Neuser and Brian G. Armstrong, 315–22. Kirksville, MO: Sixteenth Century Journal, 1997.

Wilcox, Peter. "The Restoration of the Church in Calvin's Commentaries in Isaiah the Prophet." *Archiv für Reformationsgeschichte* 85 (1994): 68–96.

Wiles, Maurice. *The Spiritual Gospel: The Interpretation of the Fourth Gospel in the Early Church*. Cambridge, UK: Cambridge University Press, 1960.

Willis, E. David. *Calvin's Catholic Christology: The Function of the So-called Extra Calvinisticum in Calvin's Theology*. Leiden: Brill, 1966.

Wilson-Kastner, Patricia. Review of *The King's Progress to Jerusalem: Some Interpretations of David during the Reformation Period and Their Patristic and Medieval Background*, by E. A. Gosselin. *Sixteenth Century Journal* 10, no. 1 (1979): 102.

Woudstra, Marten. "Calvin Interprets What 'Moses Reports': Observations on Calvin's Commentary on Exodus 1–19." *Calvin Theological Journal* 21, no. 2 (1986): 151–74.

Wright, David F. "Calvin's Pentateuchal Criticism: Equity, Hardness of Heart, and Divine Accommodation in the Mosaic Harmony Commentary." *Calvin Theological Journal* 21, no. 1 (1986): 33–50.

Würgler, Andreas. "Buchdruck und Reformation in Genf (1478–1600): Ein Überblick." *Zwinglinana* 45 (2018): 281–310.

Zachman, Randall C. *John Calvin as Teacher, Pastor, and Theologian: The Shape of His Writings and Thought*. Grand Rapids, MI: Baker, 2006.

Zier, Mark. "The Medieval Latin Interpretation of Daniel: Antecedents to Andrew of St. Victor." *Recherches de théologie ancienne et médiévale* 58 (1991): 43–78.

Zier, Mark. "Nicholas of Lyra on the Book of Daniel." In *Nicholas of Lyra: The Senses of Scripture*. Edited by Philip D. W. Krey and Lesley Smith, 173–93. Leiden: Brill, 2000.

Zillenbiller, Anette. *Die Einheit der katholischen Kirche: Calvins Cyprianrezeption in seinen ekklesiologischen Schriften*. Mainz: van Zabern, 1993.

Index